The Lebanon Uprising

The Lebanon Uprising of 2019

Voices from the Revolution

Edited by
Jeffrey G. Karam and Rima Majed

I.B. TAURIS
LONDON • NEW YORK • OXFORD • NEW DELHI • SYDNEY

I.B. TAURIS
Bloomsbury Publishing Plc
50 Bedford Square, London, WC1B 3DP, UK
1385 Broadway, New York, NY 10018, USA
29 Earlsfort Terrace, Dublin 2, Ireland

BLOOMSBURY, I.B. TAURIS and the I.B. Tauris logo are trademarks of
Bloomsbury Publishing Plc

First published in Great Britain 2023

ISBN: HB: 978-0-7556-4442-1
PB: 978-0-7556-4443-8
ePDF: 978-0-7556-4444-5
eBook: 978-0-7556-4445-2

Typeset by Deanta Global Publishing Services, Chennai, India
Printed and bound in Great Britain

To find out more about our authors and books visit www.bloomsbury.com
and sign up for our newsletters.

To all the revolutionaries who dared to challenge the status quo and imagine a different world.

Contents

Contents

Figures

Foreword

Reliving the Joy That Accompanies Liberation

Lara Bitar

It is no easy feat in this hour of despair to reflect on revolutionary moments, moments of euphoria, and moments of collective dreaming in public. But recalling the impossible—that was briefly imagined possible—is most urgent precisely in times of despair.

In late 2019, when Lebanon was on the precipice of what turned out to be an unprecedented economic and financial crisis, protesters began agitating against the government and its regressive taxation policies. Resolute, they were: "we won't pay the price [of their crisis]." At the time of writing, winter 2021–2, the cost of Lebanon's economic collapse has been transferred disproportionately onto the most dispossessed residents of the country, while financial institutions and their partners in office prey on the disaster they have manufactured.

To write this book's foreword amid compounded and relentless crises, a suffocating pandemic, and in the aftermath of the devastating August 4 explosion at the Port of Beirut, I had to transport myself back to October 17.

It was a time when the demand "for everything [back] with interest" sounded realistic. "Everything belongs to us," read the walls of the city, everything between Beirut and the sea, crossing through parliament. It was a time when feminists and queers also laid claim to the streets even, if not particularly, at night, a time when radical activists saw an opening to loudly reject the widespread racism and xenophobia toward refugees, chanting every chance they got: "Refugees in, [Free Patriotic Movement leader Gebran] Bassil out."

The realm of dreams belonged to the powerless who took vengeful pleasure from taunting the prime minister they had just deposed: "Saad, Saad, Saad, don't even dream of it [returning as PM] anymore." The tables had suddenly and briefly turned; it was the people determining the future and projecting themselves and their enemies onto it.

"Revolution," in Arabic, al-thawra, was not just the chosen appellation for this expression of dissent. It also became embodied, a presence with its own ebbs and flows: "the revolution came here and shut down all the exchange shops"; the revolution was also a place and space: "I am going to the revolution."

For all this, and more, I felt this need to return to October 17.

I kept searching for one image, one sound bite, or one video that could encapsulate the significance of this moment. I wanted to convey to the activists and organizers of future generations the power of that time—but without romanticizing it or falling into the trap of nostalgia so prevalent in the leftist tradition. I thought it was possible to do this moment justice only by being close to it again, or perhaps by experiencing it anew, since it risked becoming a distant and contested memory.

So I started watching a video I shot at around 10 p.m. on the first night of the uprising, when tens of thousands of us were marching from Hamra to downtown Beirut. "The people want the downfall of the regime," in almost synchronized unison, bounced off the walls of a tunnel we effortlessly took over. Anger was palpable in our voices, as was determination to topple a ruthless and violent regime that has been entrenched for decades.

In that tunnel, on that night and for weeks to come, people on the streets wore expressions of surprise, unable to believe that this long-awaited moment had finally arrived. There was rage too, and anguish, and sadness, and fear, and so much more. But, above all else, there was joy, not the individual happiness promised to the neoliberal subject but the collective joy that accompanies liberation.

During the Arab uprisings that started in Tunisia in late 2010, and with the exception of rallies against the sectarian political system in 2011, Lebanon was largely absent from the blaze of revolt against authoritarianism and oppressive economic conditions that swept across South West Asia and North Africa. Finally, in 2019, the people of Lebanon were ready to stake their place in the public resistance that has stretched regionally from Iraq and Sudan to Algeria and globally from Chile and Bolivia to Hong Kong.

I am able to recall the feeling of that moment and, digging through my archive, relive the sentiment that a mass of people shared in the first few weeks of October 17. It was the awe of this moment that compelled me to compulsively document it. I have engaged in and with grassroots movements locally and internationally for nearly two decades, both as an organizer and a movement journalist, so I have long understood documentation and archiving as acts of resistance. And today, amid defeats that seem permanent and during periods of seemingly insurmountable enclosures, our memories, records, and reflections can serve as a catalyst to reawaken our radical imagination that last came to life collectively on October 17.

Over two years after it was ignited, the nitpicking over whether this time frame should be understood as a revolution, a popular uprising, a mobilization, or a social movement seems irrelevant. To my mind, the essential question that we have a responsibility to tackle is this: in what ways was it, or was it not, a revolutionary and transformative moment? *The Lebanon Uprising of 2019: Voices from the Revolution* ponders this critical question. Its coeditors, Jeffrey G. Karam and Rima Majed, view this period not as a singular, clearly delineated event or a series of linear events but as a "revolutionary situation" that is still unfolding and ought to be examined. This book interrupts both the solemn mourning (by some) and the joyful celebration (by others) of October 17's perceived demise and rekindles our memory of what was once possible and, by extension, what could still become. Reactionary and counterrevolutionary forces are currently rewriting October 17's history to ensure that it is remembered as an inconsequential public nuisance propelled by nefarious or outside agitators. This book stands in their way, testifying against the state's long practice of obfuscation and erasure of histories of dissent. In tandem with other contributions, it can help prevent the relegation of yet another chapter of Lebanon's history to enforced amnesia.

Rather than presenting its readers with a single authoritative account of these events, *Voices from the Revolution* upholds the promise of its title. It abides by the structureless structure of this revolutionary situation. October 17, as many commentators have remarked, was potent because it was decentralized, leaderless, and organized horizontally. This book is composed in that same spirit, offering reflections from a multitude of perspectives, backgrounds, and experiences. Just as October 17 decentered Beirut, this book's contributors don't stop at the capital but journey through Tripoli, Baalbek-Hermel, Chouf, and Aley, before reaching the diaspora. As the 2019 nationwide wave of contestation attempted to place all issues at the forefront of this struggle, so this book does too, by incorporating a feminist, an anti-capitalist, and an ecological lens. Disability rights, labor organizing, environmental justice, and refugee rights are not secondary to the struggle against "sectarian neoliberalism" and the "rule of the banks"; they cut right through them.

After the war and with the onset of neoliberal governance in the 1990s, growing inequalities, experiences of near-daily injustices, humiliation, and shame gradually isolated people from each other and from their communities. As the demonstrations of October 17 started growing in number, scope, and reach, it felt like a collective realization swooped across previously sequestered geographies. The communion of crowds was intoxicating, and a new sense of belonging was materializing in front of our eyes. It was history in the making, history-in-motion.

Belonging took on a new meaning and new forms. For a brief moment, at least for the mass of people who engaged with October 17, it no longer meant blind allegiance to or affiliation with a political party or sect. It meant belonging to and for one another and expressing genuine solidarity among the oppressed. And crucially, it explicitly identified the enemy.

"All of them means all of them" quickly became the call to battle. All those directly responsible—or complicit in their silence—for the impoverishment and humiliation of this country's residents became a fair target of protest, without any exceptions.

And so, on Monday, October 21, a general strike was declared and sustained for at least two weeks through roadblocks, acts of vandalism, student walkouts, work stoppages, and a wide array of acts of refusal to continue to participate in, or even engage with, the established order. This diversity of tactics and its acceptance by a significant segment of the population marked a significant break from the mass mobilization of 2015, when liberal organizers shunned militant activists.

October 17 marked a departure from former mobilizations not just in its tactics but also in its antagonisms, encompassing in its anger not only the sectarian political system but also the oligarchy, a conceptual shift that recreated the lost path for class antagonism and a class-centered struggle. This deviation was made obvious when working-class men were not just welcomed with open arms at demonstrations, but their presence in the early days of the uprising brought comfort to many and a sense of protection in the face of state violence and repression.

And here lay lies the powerful potential of "*All* of us means all of us"—a less referenced and somewhat forgotten rallying cry, beautiful in its simplicity. It manifested as a quotidian demonstration of the power of solidarity and mutual aid and was deployed to rally jail support, call for "backup" at a bank withholding a comrade's savings, or an employer stealing wages.

This revolutionary struggle, whose fate was never determined by its ability to permanently occupy city squares or indefinitely hold roadblocks, continues whenever and wherever people come together in revolt.

Acknowledgments

This book project started to see the light during one of the most challenging periods in Lebanon's history. While the trigger for this volume originated in the streets at the peak of the October revolutionary uprising in 2019, the writing and editing process did not start until later in 2020. With the strengthening of the counterrevolution in early 2020, the arrival of the COVID-19 pandemic and our withdrawal from the streets, the deepening of the financial crisis that transformed our society, and the horrendous August 4 Beirut Port explosion, this book became a journey of recollection, reflection, and personal coping in the face of the great collapse of life as we knew it, or dreamt about it, during the heydays of October 2019.

Working on a book about an event that deeply shook our lives was both exciting and challenging. Long discussions went into the choice of authors to approach, the topics to include, the structure of the book, and the different editorial approaches. As editors, we wanted to make sure to cover as many important aspects and discussions as possible. As the subtitle underscores, we wanted to showcase multiple and different voices and perceptions of the revolution. Similarly, we had in mind a book that is addressed to a broad audience, academic or not, that is interested in knowing more about the historical events of 2019 in Lebanon through analytical pieces and testimonies from the ground. While some of the invited authors could not deliver their reflections due to several personal or professional obstacles, the chapters of this book are a strong and inclusive representation that explores the state of mind, ranging from confusion to clarity and euphoria to disenchantment. We thank all the authors for trusting us with their work and for making this book see the light in spite of everyday challenges at new sites of political contestation, economic and social crises, and the recurrent faces of violence that manifest through daily humiliation and human agony. While some of the authors relocated during the research and writing phases to other countries and some sought temporary escapes away from Lebanon, the below chapters are the product of continuous conversations over the phone and online platforms that became the new norm during the pandemic.

As editors, we wanted to curate and produce exactly the book that you carry in your hands. We wanted to include people who work across different fields and write in different languages (mainly Arabic and English). We wanted a balance between producing a typical academic text and one that pushes and complicates the boundaries of scholarly publications. Likewise, we wanted a book that tackles many aspects of the revolution that are usually forgotten. Together with all the contributors, we are proud to have produced a volume that shows the importance of bridging the artificial boundaries between the academy and the outside world. To this end, we warmly thank Sophie Rudland, Yasmin Garcha, the editorial board, and the staff at I.B. Tauris and Bloomsbury for believing in our approach and supporting us along the way. We also want to thank the three anonymous reviewers for reading the book proposal and draft of the manuscript and for collectively supporting the production and publication of this book with very minor reservations.

We extend our gratitude to many colleagues, friends, family members, and partners for supporting us at different stages of the project. Dozens of people supported this book and across different milieus and various countries. Rather than name each individual, we want to extend our sincere gratitude to everyone who has taken the time to read through rough drafts, discuss the book's contributions, and offer both much-needed support and constructive criticism. Researching, writing, and editing such a book would not have been possible without the support of several individuals and organizations. In particular, we would like to warmly thank the American Political Science Association, the Arab Political Science Network, the Forum Transregionale Studien, the Middle East Studies Association, Masahat, the University of Helsinki, the University of Oslo, and the Scuola Normale Superiore for hosting us either individually or together to present some of the book chapters. The feedback at these panels and events virtually and in Beirut, Berlin, Cambridge, Helsinki, Istanbul, Oslo, and elsewhere was instrumental to the quality of the contributions. Similarly, we would like to thank the Rosa Luxemburg Foundation, Beirut office and their staff for providing some financial support to complete this book. Specifically, this pertains to the translation of many chapters from Arabic to English, the design of the book cover, and the completion of other related tasks. To this end, the editors would like to thank Fatima Mortada for designing the beautiful book cover. We also want to warmly thank Farah Baba and Viviane Akiki for translating some of the chapters from Arabic to English. We hope that the Arabic version of this book will also see the light soon.

Finally, Karam would like to thank the program directors and staff at the Rosa Luxemburg Stiftung in Berlin, Germany, the Europe in the Middle East-the Middle East in Europe (EUME) program at the Forum Transregionale Studien, the Center for Middle Eastern and North African Politics at Freie Universität Berlin, and the Middle East Initiative at Harvard University for providing the intellectual space and support for wrapping up the book. Similarly, Majed would like to thank the program directors and staff of the Finnish Institute in the Middle East (FIME) and the Carnegie Corporation of New York for providing the support needed to work on this book. Last but not least, the editors would like to thank their respective academic departments at the Lebanese American University and the American University of Beirut for all the support and encouragement.

We dedicate this book to all the revolutionaries who took to the streets of Lebanon in 2019 and to those who have been paving the way since 2011 both in the Arab region and beyond.

Jeffrey G. Karam, Beirut, Lebanon, December 2021
Rima Majed, Beirut, Lebanon, December 2021

Notes on Text and Translation

Arabic titles and names are spelled according to a simplified version of the transliteration system used by the *International Journal of Middle East Studies*. Familiar spellings of names and cities, such as "Beirut," appear in their commonly used form. All translations from Arabic, French, and other languages are by the authors of the respective chapters unless otherwise indicated.

1

Framing the October Uprising in Lebanon

An Unfolding Revolutionary Situation

Jeffrey G. Karam and Rima Majed

On the eve of October 17, 2019, Lebanon's revolutionary uprising (*Thawra*)[1] erupted. Following a week of wildfires that ravaged parts of the countryside while the state stood inept, and in the context of a financial crisis that had started to clearly implode, the Lebanese government announced the introduction of new taxes, including a tax on the popular WhatsApp voice and messaging application. Hours following the governmental decision, hundreds of protesters took to the streets in Beirut and other cities, blocking roads and burning tires. The mobilization quickly grew and spread across the country in an unprecedented way. By the early hours of the evening, hundreds of thousands were in the streets, in every corner of the country, declaring what they called a *Thawra*.

Despite having a long history of protest and contestation, this was the first time in the modern history of Lebanon that protests erupted concomitantly across the country in a geographically decentralized way, mobilizing such vast numbers of protesters. For those in the streets on that evening, the events felt different compared to previous waves of mobilization. This was a popular uprising that initially mobilized the working classes across the country in a spontaneous and concerted way. Raising the same revolutionary demand that echoed in the streets in 2011, the protesters wanted the downfall of the regime. Repeating the 2015 slogan that arose during the #You_Stink movement, protesters chanted "Kellon Ya'ne Kellon" (or "All of them means of all them") to highlight the multiheaded nature of the Lebanese consociational system. However, what was eye-catching on that October evening was the spontaneous mobilization of masses across the country with a clear class-based discourse, linking the economic and the political, targeting the sectarian leaders and the "oligarchy" at once, bringing back the social question to the center of contestation, and speaking of a clear "us" versus "them" in class terms.

The other interesting aspect of the early days of this uprising was the heavy prevalence of curse words in chants to express anger against the ruling class, with a focus on Gebran Bassil, the son-in-law of the president of the Republic (Michel Aoun). This discursive break with norms and hierarchies, with curses, addressed at all politicians and bankers from Riad Salameh[2] to Hassan Nasrallah,[3] made the early days of the uprising a powerful and celebrated "insolent revolution." The events of October 17 quickly took the form of road blockades as a move to shut down the country from north to south in the absence of unions to declare a general strike. The need to put the country to a halt, disrupt "business as usual," and declare the start of a new phase was evident. The historic images of that night and the spontaneous coming together of a population against a ruling class reflected deeper social and structural transformations and signaled an "intensification of history."

Lebanon's *Thawra* can only be understood within a broader historical context of internal, regional, and global movements and uprisings. Since the first wave of Arab uprisings in 2011, social movements and revolutionaries around the globe have been affected by this major critical juncture[4] that spread from the squares of some Arab cities to shape movements and revolts in other parts of the world such as the Occupy movement in the United States and the United Kingdom, the Indignados movement in Spain and Greece,[5] or the Africa uprisings that had been long underway and intensified in 2011.[6] The reverberations of this first wave of Arab uprisings were also felt in other countries of the Arab region that did not directly witness an uprising. In Lebanon, the year 2011 had reshaped and transformed local struggles. Starting with the emergence of the movement for the "Downfall of the Sectarian Regime" in 2011,[7] passing through the renewed feminist movement,[8] the 2013 mobilization of the Union Coordination Committee,[9] and the 2015 "#You_Stink" movement that formed an important turning point in the history of activism in Lebanon, and reaching the 2019 mobilizations in the Palestinian refugee camps for the right to work, Lebanon's sociopolitical history since 2011 has been shaped by a broader regional context of heightened mobilization and countermobilization. This context has been significantly affected by the reverberations of the Syrian revolution, and its counterrevolution, in Lebanon.

Like 2011, the year 2019 formed another critical juncture in the history of protest in the region and globally. With the Algerian and Sudanese uprisings starting at the end of 2018 and the Iraqi uprising erupting just a few weeks before October 17, 2019, when the Lebanon uprisings started, a "second wave" of Arab uprisings was soon announced. This wave continued to develop in the region with the outbreak of the Palestinian uprising in 2021.[10] As with the previous wave of 2011, the year 2019 also witnessed increased mobilization and revolt across the globe, spreading from Chile to Hong Kong. While these historical moments of uprising form what political scientist Kathleen Thelen and sociologist Donatella della Porta called "critical junctures," this book conceptualizes uprisings as both critical *events*[11] and longer-term historical *processes*[12] that need to be studied and understood as they unfold in their *longue durée*. In that sense, this book zooms into a critical moment in the history of Lebanon—the eruption of the revolutionary uprising in October 2019 and the initial aftermath—to analyze and position it within a broader history of social change and political transformation.

Framing the October Uprising: A "Revolutionary Situation" and Counterrevolutionary Forces

This book's approach to understanding the October uprising in Lebanon is rooted in the political and academic debates that have developed over the past decades to define, analyze, and frame moments of mass popular upheaval that have shaken societies and polities alike and that have attempted to change political regimes and social orders. Therefore, this book centers Lebanon's October revolutionary uprising as part of the wider revolutionary movements that have taken new shapes and higher frequency since the start of the twenty-first century, and more precisely, since 2011.[13]

One of the most heated debates today revolves around the nature of the events that started to unfold in the Arab region since 2011. While some scholars and commentators consider these events to be revolutions or revolutionary uprisings and revolts within a broader process of revolutionary unfolding in the region,[14] others are more skeptical of the revolutionary nature of these historical events and see them mainly as an Arab "spring" followed by a "winter,"[15] failed uprisings,[16] "refolutions,"[17] or even "brief moment of mobilization."[18] Some consider how revolutions reshape international order and why such transformational moments of political change pose unpredictable threats and generate instability between and within states.[19]

At the core of the more skeptical accounts lies a definition of revolution centered on successful outcomes in terms of regime change and state transformation. This has drawn a large body of literature on the Arab uprisings that focuses on the difficult process of democratization, the resilience of authoritarianism, the resurgence of Islamism, and the persistence of monarchies.[20] While this understanding of revolution tied to outcome is widely based on Theda Skocpol's classical definition of revolution as "rapid, basic transformations of a society's state and class structures . . . in part carried through by class-based revolts from below,"[21] more recent debates are inviting us to rethink the definition of revolution in the twenty-first century beyond the focus on the binary of success and failure in outcomes.[22]

Moreover, these newer accounts are also encouraging us to move away from a definition of revolution that is fixated on "political revolution" that changes regimes to an understanding of "social revolution" that centers social and economic transformations—an aspect of Skocpol's definition that has been widely overlooked in the mainstream discussions on the Arab uprisings. These debates have also opened bigger theoretical discussions on whether the study of the Arab uprisings is still considered part of the fourth generation[23] of revolution theories that had moved beyond the structuralism of the third generation to focus more on agency and processes. Moreover, there are discussions of whether a "fifth generation of revolution theory"[24] has developed in the past years of study of the Arab uprisings with an approach to these revolutions as being essentially nonviolent and nonconfrontational. While these debates are still heated and lively, there seems to be a consensus that new approaches and theories are needed to understand revolutions today.

To this end, Asef Bayat posits that there is an analytical distinction that needs to be made between "revolution as movement" (or uprisings) and "revolution as change." He explains that what he had previously called "refolution" refers to those twenty-first-century revolutionary movements—such as the Arab uprisings—that do not attempt to seize power but rather emerge "to compel the incumbent regimes to reform themselves."[25] On another hand, Jamie Allinson explains that one area that still lags in our understanding of revolutions, and their ability to take over power or not, is the study of counterrevolutions.[26] This stream of argument in the emerging literature on the nature of the Arab uprisings calls for a more balanced understanding of these revolutionary events in their dialectical relation with counterrevolutions as major factors shaping the unfolding and the outcomes of these historical events and processes.[27]

This book builds on these theoretical debates and considers that the Lebanon uprising, like the rest of the Arab uprisings, is best described as what Charles Tilly called a "revolutionary situation."[28] As explained by Bennani-Chraïbi and Fillieule, Tilly's definition of a "revolutionary situation" stems from Trotsky's concept of "dual power," or moments in which state power is threatened by an oppositional coalition that cannot be easily crushed or dismissed.[29] In that sense, the Lebanon uprising of October 2019 created a historical moment in which a revolutionary situation arose when state power was seriously threatened and politics intensified in the oppositional streets that managed to shut down the country for weeks, forcing the prime minister to resign and creating an alternative way of doing politics, even if temporarily. What remains crucial in the story of the October Revolution in Lebanon is how the counterrevolution managed to limit the expansion of this "revolutionary situation" and repositioned power dynamics despite the immense difficulties caused by the emergence of a revolution in tandem with one of the worst man-made financial crises in the world,[30] a global pandemic that forced protesters out of the streets and changed life as we knew it,[31] and the August 4 Beirut Port explosion that formed yet another turning point for the uprising.[32]

Borrowing from Charles Kurzman's[33] critique of the literature that attempts to reconstruct causal claims to explain revolutionary events in retrospect, this book grounds its discussion in the social and political moment of October 17, 2019, to reconstruct and think through the historical events as they unfolded. While the analysis that comes in hindsight and that benefits from the temporal distance to the event is important and much needed today, the book attempts to offer such an examination while moving away from the normative judgments to a more generous and thorough understanding on how the revolutionary moment of October 17 unfolded to take this shape and form and how people on the ground experienced and lived this extraordinary moment.[34] Therefore, rather than lamenting the "failure" of the uprising, or accusing the actors of not being revolutionary enough, this book adopts a more historically grounded approach that considers people's mass mobilization as genuinely revolutionary and that then asks the questions of how and why did this revolutionary upheaval unfold the way it did. In doing so, the book pays tribute to the lived experiences of the hundreds of thousands who mobilized believing in the revolutionary potential of the October 17 moment and takes seriously the claims of the actors who described their mobilization in terms of *thawra*. It also pays particular attention to the local, regional, and global counterrevolutionary forces that have played a major role in determining the unfolding of this revolutionary process so far.

Therefore, this book focuses on the process of revolutionary struggles rather than provide a binary analysis that gauges the outcomes of such transformational moments. While there is a tendency among scholars and commentators to label revolutionary struggles as either successful or failed outcomes, the contributors to this volume adopt a much more nuanced framework that accounts for the complexity of revolutionary struggles and that pays attention to the dialectical relation between revolutionary and counterrevolutionary forces in such moments of collective action. A focus on dynamics and processes of revolutionary struggle, an analysis of social and political transformations, and reflections from the field as these struggles unfold and deepen can demonstrate the particularity of this transformational moment in Lebanon without falling into the trope of Lebanese exceptionalism. While it is true that Lebanon and Iraq provide an addition to the literature in terms of the nature of the political regime (consociational democracy rather than authoritarianism or monarchy) the uprisings have risen against, this is by no means a reason to believe that these revolutions are exceptional or cannot be understood within a broader theory of revolution in the twenty-first century.

If anything, the very fact that such revolutionary uprisings are occurring within a wide range of regime types reinforces the argument that an understanding of revolution cannot focus solely on the political aspect but needs to also account for the social roots of revolutionary transformations. What links the Lebanon uprising to the rest of the revolts of the past decades are the social conditions under neoliberalism that reinforce market tyranny, widen social inequalities and injustices, and block the possibility for actual democracy to emerge. In this sense, the revolutionary path of the Lebanon uprising is still unfolding, and it remains early to judge whether it will eventually come to a halt, reform the system in some ways, completely revamp the existing neoliberal and sectarian political system, or charter a completely new path. Nonetheless, this book serves as the first appreciation of the initial phase of this transformational moment and one that deserves attention.

Contesting Disciplinary Boundaries and Highlighting Lived Experiences

This book results from several conversations between different activists, including ones who wrote the below chapters and many others who participated in various discussions and meetings at different junctures from the beginning of the revolutionary uprising of 2019 to the moment of writing this introduction. For brevity, we will focus on three important conversations. The first materialized informally and specifically in the streets of Lebanon and across different squares that hosted public discussions between many of the contributors and others in Beirut, Tripoli, Nabatieh, Sour, Chouf, Jal el-Dib, and other areas. The second emerged from different editorial pieces in Arabic, English, and French, political talk shows on traditional television networks and newly formed alternative media outlets, and podcasts and initiatives that surfaced before the October uprising and later became new sources of information during and after this transformational moment. While these were equally informal conversations, they paved the way for producing and disseminating timely analyses and opinion pieces on various phases and faces of the uprising. The third stemmed from formal conversations between the coeditors and different contributors during the first COVID-19 state-imposed lockdown in mid-2020 and especially after the

August 4 blast in 2020 that devasted the lives of thousands of people living near the Port of Beirut. These conversations underscored the need to provide a preliminary reading of the initial forces that pushed people to the streets, a discussion of different moments of euphoria and disenchantment, and a focus on ways to move forward after many setbacks. In many ways, these below chapters reflect the duality of confusion and clarity that characterizes revolutionary situations. Furthermore, they also emphasize the importance of gauging the different cycles of revolutionary processes that waver between the continuity and durability of everyday praxes and the promise of change and jubilation that shape a revolutionary's mindset and momentum.

The book is not representative of all the diverse voices and actors who took to the streets of Lebanon. However, it centers on the foundational and varied experiences of diverse individuals in and across different milieus. While this book is an early and deep appreciation of this complex, transformational, and still unfolding moment in Lebanon, it is a multifaceted, interdisciplinary, and intersectional treatment of the revolutionary situation that erupted in 2019. To this end, we will highlight three important points on methodology and sources.

First, this book brings to the fore the voices of activists/militants, scholars, journalists, lawyers, researchers, artists, and students to analyze and reflect on one of the most important moments in the history of revolutionary struggles, mobilization, and protests in Lebanon. While underscoring the importance of inviting academics and scholars to write, analyze, and reflect on the October 17 revolutionary uprising, we are fully cognizant of the limits of such conversations within the academy. Hence, we sought to rectify the problems with promoting an intellectual and scholarly echo chamber by complicating the artificial boundaries between scholars and activists. While we acknowledge that these are neither monolithic nor mutually exclusive categories and in other words, some scholars are not activists and many activists are not scholars, we are further contesting the artificial boundaries that separate activism from the academy and vice versa. By amplifying the voices of activists/militants on the ground across the different chapters, this book discusses the uprising's initial eruption, tactics, and setbacks and highlights the importance of endeavors that reconstruct history from below.

Second, this book includes analytical reflections and personal testimonies from activists/militants and scholars. It constitutes a body of knowledge that includes primary documents, photographs, materials, and reflections from the ground that have not been featured collectively. Given that most of the contributors were active in protests before 2019 and almost all partook in different demonstrations and protests after the eruption of the October 17 uprising, the below chapters serve as a unique source on the uprising for audiences in Lebanon, the region, and well beyond. One of the book's strengths and many contributions is the fact that it is written by local scholars, activists, and researchers who lived through the uprising and participated in its unfolding. Thus, these chapters reflect on the fine line between analytical reflections and lived experiences of the revolutionary situation that erupted in October 2019. These lived experiences stem from different meetings and exchanges between the contributors and many others in forming alternative labor unions and syndicates, political coalitions, and new political platforms to challenge the status quo. While the book is published in English, many contributors wrote their chapters in Arabic and were later translated into English. Importantly, the coeditors and contributors are working diligently on translating the book into Arabic to reach a wider audience in Lebanon and the Arab world.

Third, this book is among the first in the broader literature on the Arab uprisings to exclusively bring together local activists/militants and academics to reflect on their experiences and present their analysis of their own uprising. This forms an important step in bringing to the fore knowledge production from the Global South and giving priority to local scholars and activists to tell their stories while making important academic contributions to the broader fields of international relations, social movements studies, revolutionary and counterrevolutionary theory, and Middle East studies. By centering the knowledge and experiences of local activists and scholars, this book is a crucial contribution to the scholarly debates and serves as an invitation to make more space for local knowledge production in wider academic and disciplinary publications. Importantly, the book highlights the value of inter and multidisciplinary approaches and methodologies. The contributors include economists, lawyers, political scientists, historians, sociologists, filmmakers, anthropologists, journalists, ecologists, philosophers, and visual artists. However, their educational background and choice of profession did not impede a cohesive and engaging conversation throughout the book that cuts across strict disciplinary silos. While the framing of the book engages with how political scientists, sociologists, political theorists, and historians conceptualize and examine revolutionary situations, the below chapters are not geared toward particular scholarly fields or meant to engage with strict methodological and disciplinary concerns. For instance, some chapters engage with deep theoretical debates to demonstrate how the uprising in Lebanon is in conversation with other revolutionary situations. Others focus on how their participation in different protests allowed them to comprehend the immensity and complexity of revolutionary cycles and the need to think through and devise novel counterstrategies to challenge the existing political order.

Outline of the Book

The book is divided into three main parts. Part One historicizes the uprising and situates it within the historical, political, economic, social, legal, and environmental foundations of the Lebanese polity. For instance, in the opening chapter, Sana Tannoury-Karam addresses the foundations of the state and pillars of the political system by reimagining "the history of Lebanon through the transformational phases of the Grand Theater" and argues for moving away from "the classical periodization of a history of Lebanon in the 20th and 21st centuries—mandate, independence, civil war, and post-civil war" (p. 18). Through a macroeconomic lens, Mohamad Zbeeb gives us an account of the social and economic foundations that led to the financial collapse of the Ponzi scheme in 2019 and the subsequent eruption of the October uprising. On a social level, Samer Frangie argues that the October uprising of 2019 reflects how uprisings and breakdowns are moments of wonder, especially that "what appears and what is" become skewed and stem from one's social experience and disposition to moments of crisis (p. 43). From a legal standpoint, Lama Karamé focuses on how the Lebanese state used legal discourse, especially existing laws, to prosecute protesters and undercut massive mobilization and argues that effective legal mobilization could *still* support some of the uprising's sociopolitical goals. Narrating Lebanon's long history of environmental crises, Roland Riachi explains that "ecological struggles were leveraged to a new citizen-based level" that has challenged the control of partisan and elitist classes over such disasters (p. 65).

Moreover, Part One considers how the October uprising coincided with other revolutionary situations in the region, especially Iraq, and discusses the connections between local, regional, and international factors in exploring revolutionary and counterrevolutionary strategies. In this context, Rima Majed introduces "sectarian neoliberalism" as a novel concept and frame to understand the internal contradictions of these revolutionary uprisings within the particularities of the consociational regimes in Iraq and Lebanon and argues for the need of a new theory of revolution under twenty-first-century neoliberal capitalism. On the manifold connections between local, regional, and global forces, Jeffrey G. Karam examines the role of the United States and Iran as two important actors that supported counterrevolutionary strategies and discourse during the October uprising of 2019 in Lebanon and argues for an inclusive, multilayered, and novel account of revolt and counterstrategies as part of the "lifecycles of revolutionary processes that waver between euphoria and disenchantment" (p. 89).

Part Two explores the multiple and diverse faces of the uprising by analyzing different tactics and strategies devised by revolutionaries, the waves of domestic repression and counterrevolution, and the emergence of alternative movements and transnational networks of solidarity. To this end, Mona Harb argues that urban spaces shape collective action by incorporating "material and symbolic characteristics that prompt protestors to exploit them" and creating a diverse "range of performative stages" for mobilization (pp. 109–10). By tracing the emergence of alternative media and digital platforms, Claudia Kozman argues that new platforms have a strong potential and role for protesters to communicate, discuss, and plan various initiatives "for political and social reform" that challenge existing traditional media networks (p. 125). In discussing the advent of new alternatives before and during the uprising, Nadim el Kak argues that there is a glimpse of hope when tracing "the emergence of the Lebanese Professionals' Association and the radical imaginaries and regional inspirations that shaped this new wave of [labor] organizing" and could eventually spark the growth of effective revolutionary alternatives (p. 131).

Furthermore, Part Two discusses the positionality of feminists and queer activists in the streets and their clashes with conservative factions and explores the broader context of women mobilization in mobilization and political life. For instance, Sara Mourad argues that the appearance of women during the uprising should not erase the longer history of women's political engagement across political, cultural, social, and economic spheres; yet, it is critical to consider how the October uprising underscored the visibility of women not as individuals but as groups with their varied genres of action and revolutionary poetics. In probing and writing the narratives of three women in different sociopolitical and economic milieus, Nay el Rahi explains how the October 17 revolutionary uprising is an opportune moment to understand how women and feminist activists in Lebanon have revealed "a more pronounced, concrete and visible intersectional feminist articulation and practice of resistance, and of 'potential as politics'" (p. 153).

Likewise, in Part Two, there is a focus on the role and perceptions of partisans and regime loyalists during the revolutionary situation. It then considers the limits of disruptive tactics and strategies, such as roadblocking, and the forces of domestic counterrevolution and violence. In this context, Mortada Al-Amine argues that a focus on individuals, including political party partisans and regime loyalists, "who seek to maintain the status quo" rather than revamp it allows for a nuanced and inclusive account of the revolutionary uprising (p. 163). In terms of revolutionary tactics, Nizar Hassan explains how roadblocking is in many ways a shortcut to calling for a general strike, and in spite of many limitations of such a disruptive tactic, it still empowers traditionally marginalized actors to coordinate their efforts and paves the way for intersectional strategic collaboration. In focusing on how the Lebanese coercive institutions and some political parties repressed the revolutionary uprising, Joseph Daher argues that the regime's counterrevolutionary strategy centered on preventing the creation of an alternative political movement by employing typical forces of coercion, including violence and repression, and upgraded tactics that restricted freedom of expression, controlled the media, and maintained patronage networks.

The last two chapters in Part Two provide a thorough discussion of the role of Palestinian refugees in Lebanon and the Lebanese diaspora in building local and transnational solidarity with revolutionaries and alternative movements. To this end, Moné Makkawi argues that any analysis of the revolutionary uprising "remains incomplete without addressing the actions and experiences of [Palestinian and other] refugees and migrants throughout" (p. 198). In focusing on the role of the Lebanese diaspora and their capacity to "of implementing a long-term reforming impact on 'home' politics" in Lebanon, Paul Tabar and Yara El-Zakka highlight the importance and sustainability of transnational solidarity between protesters in Lebanon and across the globe to demonstrate that the revolutionary uprising of 2019 did "sow the seeds of a revolutionary generation in Lebanon" and "resonated within a diaspora eager to participate in transforming" the Lebanese political system (p. 210).

Part Three, as the final section of the book, consists of shorter reflections and testimonies from the field that cover stories about specific events and struggles. Some include reflections on personal trauma, disability rights, student activism, and the role of grassroots collectives. The first reflection by Hani Adada explains why various groups within the broader opposition coalition fluctuated between heightened optimism and the need to continue mobilization and retreat and a sense of defeat. In addressing the important contributions of the disability movement in Lebanon, Grace Khawam argues that the disability movement in Lebanon "has withstood conflicts and multilayered crises across the years and has a long-standing history of protests and collective political action" that precedes and paves the way for the revolutionary uprising that erupted in October 2019 (p. 243). In tracing and underscoring the varied "women's contributions" to the revolutionary uprising in 2019, Myriam Sfeir explains why "an intersectional perspective generates more rights for marginalized groups" and allows for genuine sociopolitical, especially gender, reform (p. 250). On the importance of student activism in the longer history of protests and revolutionary waves in Lebanon, Samir Skayni explains student protests before and during the October uprising of 2019 are a way to prepare and encourage students to further mobilize against crises within the educational sector and other social problems that will materialize in a new upcoming wave of protests. On the importance of grassroots movements before and during the revolutionary uprising in 2019, Rawane Nassif explains that initiatives such as the Qantari collective were triggered by a sense of "revenge," especially that they coordinated with other groups that "blocked roads, targeted banks" and "organized tools of public dissent" (p. 265).

Other reflections in Part Three focus more closely on struggles at and from particular spaces of political contestation. For instance, Mohammad Bzeih provides a detailed account of the famous "Night of the Banks" on January 14, 2020, which began as protests against the Central Bank of Lebanon in Beirut and later morphed into attacking and smashing the front glass of several private banks that were part of the financial engineering schemes that impoverished over 80 percent of the Lebanese populace. At another site of political contestation, Roland Nassour explains how "Save the Bisri Valley Campaign (or *Save Bisri*) aimed to stop the World Bank-funded dam" became "a new form of environmental activism that is more confrontational and highly politicized" (p. 284).

Some chapters in Part Three reflect on the unfolding of the uprising in different towns and squares across Lebanon. For example, Tamim Abdo reflects on how the revolutionary uprising unfolded in Tripoli, especially by explaining how "by establishing a food stand to distribute the food I cook with people in the square . . . I was able to talk to people, especially those coming from the poorest parts of the city," and why this allows for building strong bottoms-up alternatives (p. 288). Writing and reflecting on Baalbeck-Hermel, Lamia Sahili explains how the Shia Duo [Hezbollah and the Amal Movement] were disappointed with and anxious about the participation of their supporters and partisans in protests against the political system and their (Hezbollah and Amal) members of Parliament. Moving on to the Chouf-Aley area, Alaa al-Sayegh argues that "socio-economic, environmental, and political" forces and the role of grassroots organizations and political movements, such as Lihaqqi (For My Right), were instrumental in coordinating actions across sectarian, ideological, and class lines (pp. 303–4).

The last two chapters in Part Three compare the revolutionary uprising in Lebanon and other experiences in the Arab world, especially Tunisia and Syria. In this context, Olfa Saadaoui reflects on the similarities and differences between the Tunisian Revolution in 2010 and the Lebanese Uprising of 2019 and argues that "even with a failure to dismantle a regime, revolutions still create remarkable social shifts" and, consequently, impact the "collective revolutionary experiences" of individuals and can "shape societies" irreversibly (p. 311). In reflecting on the beginning of the Syrian revolution in 2011 and the unfolding of the uprising in Lebanon in 2019, Saad Choeb explores how the duality of new hope and thinking of defeat as a common feature of many revolutionary situations in the Arab world could *still* trigger a "feeling that everything is new" even within repetitive cycles of joy and despair (pp. 319–20).

In lieu of a conclusion, Leyla Dakhli's Afterword discusses some of the overarching connections between the different chapters, explains how the book engages with scholarship on the first and second waves of uprisings in the Middle East and North Africa, and provides some future trajectories for some of the issues that deserve further attention.

Notes

1   Thawra is the Arabic word for revolt, revolution, or uprising. For a discussion of the origin of the word and its meanings, check the opening chapter in G. Achcar, *The People Want: A Radical Exploration of the Arab Uprisings* (Berkeley: University of California Press, 2013).
2   Riad Salameh is the governor of the Central Bank—Banque du Liban.
3   Hassan Nasrallah is the secretary general of Hezbollah.
4   D. Della Porta, "Protests as Critical Junctures: Some Reflections Towards a Momentous Approach to Social Movements," *Social Movement Studies* 19, no. 5–6 (2020): 556–75.
5   B. J. Brownlee and M. Ghiabi, "Passive, Silent and Revolutionary: The 'Arab Spring' Revisited," *Middle East Critique* 25, no. 3 (2016): 299–316.
6   A. Branch and Z. Mampilly, *Africa Uprising: Popular Protest and Political Change* (London: Zed Books Ltd, 2015).
7   M. N. AbiYaghi, M. Catusse, and M. Younes, "From isqat an-nizam at-ta'ifi to the Garbage Crisis Movement: Political Identities and Antisectarian Movements," in *Lebanon Facing The Arab Uprisings*, ed. Rosita Di Peri and Daniel Meier (London: Palgrave Pivot, 2017), 73–91.
8   https://www.activearabvoices.org/uploads/8/0/8/4/80849840/mobilization_and _advocacy_-_v.3.5_digital.pdf.
9   L. Bou Khater, "Public Sector Mobilisation Despite a Dormant Workers' Movement," *Confluences Méditerranée* 92 (2015): 125–42.
10   https://www.dohainstitute.org/en/PoliticalStudies/Pages/Understanding-the-2021 -Palestinian-Uprising-and-Resistance-Movement.aspx.
11   These "events" are understood in the sense of William Sewel's "eventful sociology" or Alain Badiou's revolutionary rupture that breaks with repetition. For more see W. H. Sewell, "Historical Events as Transformations of Structures: Inventing Revolution at the Bastille," *Theory and Society* 25, no. 6 (1996): 841–81; A. Badiou, *The Rebirth of History: Times of Riots and Uprisings* (London and New York: Verso Books, 2012).
12   For more on revolutions as processes, check Achcar, *The People Want*; Jeffrey G. Karam, ed., *The Middle East in 1958: Reimagining A Revolutionary Year* (London: I.B. Tauris and Bloomsbury, 2020).
13   J. Allinson, "On Generations of Revolutionary Theory: A Response," *Journal of Historical Sociology* 34, no. 1 (2021): 153.
14   See M. Bennani-Chraïbi and O. Fillieule, "Towards a Sociology of Revolutionary Situations. Reflections on the Arab Uprisings," *Revue française de science politique (English)* 62, no. 5 (2012): 1–29; Achcar, *The People Want*; J. Allinson, "A Fifth Generation of Revolution Theory?" *Journal of Historical Sociology*, 32, no. 1 (2019): 142–51.

15 See J. Brownlee, T. Masoud, and A. Reynolds, "Tracking the 'Arab Spring': Why
    the Modest Harvest?" *Journal of Democracy* 24, no. 4 (2013): 29–44; N. J. Brown,
    "Egypt's Failed Transition," *Journal of Democracy* 24, no. 4 (2013): 45–58; P. O. Amour,
    "The Arab Spring Movement: The Failed Revolution. Preliminary Theoretical and
    Empirical Deliberation," *The Middle East Reloaded: Revolutionary Changes, Power
    Dynamics, and Regional Rivalries since the Arab Spring* (2018): 199–224; H. J. Wiarda,
    "Arab Fall or Arab Winter?" *American Foreign Policy Interests* 34, no. 3 (2012): 134–7.

16 See Brown, "Egypt's Failed Transition"; H. Agha and R. Malley, "This Is Not a
    Revolution," *New York Review of Books* (2012); J. Brownlee, T. Masoud, and N.
    Reynolds, *The Arab Spring: Pathways of Repression and Reform* (Oxford: Oxford
    University Press, 2015).

17 A. Bayat, *Revolution without Revolutionaries* (Stanford: Stanford University Press,
    2020).

18 R. Springborg, "The Rewards of Failure: Persisting Military Rule in Egypt," *British
    Journal of Middle Eastern Studies* 44, no. 4 (2017): 483.

19 See G. Lawson, *Anatomies of Revolution* (Cambridge: Cambridge University
    Press, 2019); R. Jervis, "Socialization, Revolutionary States and Domestic Politics,"
    International Politics 52, no. 5 (2015): 609–16; A. Anievas, "Revolutions and
    International Relations: Rediscovering the Classical Bourgeois Revolutions," *European
    Journal of International Relations* 21, no. 4 (2015): 841–66; G. Lawson, "Revolutions
    and the International," *Theory and Society* 44, no. 4 (2015): 299–319; D. Ritter, *The
    Iron Cage of Liberalism: International Politics and Unarmed Revolutions in the Middle
    East* (Oxford: Oxford University Press, 2015); S. Walt, *Revolution and War* (Cornell:
    Cornell University Press, 1996).

20 See R. Brynen, P. W. Moore, B. F. Salloukh, and M. J. Zahar, *Beyond the Arab
    Spring: Authoritarianism & Democratization in the Arab World,* Vol. 4 (Boulder:
    Lynne Rienner Publishers, 2012); J. Haynes, "The 'Arab Uprising,' Islamists and
    Democratization," *Mediterranean Politics* 18, no. 2 (2013): 170–88; E. Bellin,
    "Reconsidering the Robustness of Authoritarianism in the Middle East: Lessons from
    the Arab Spring," *Comparative Politics* 44, no. 2 (2012): 127–49; R. S. Snyder, "The
    Arab Uprising and the Persistence of Monarchy," *International Affairs* 91, no. 5 (2015):
    1027–45.

21 T. Skocpol, *States and Social Revolutions: A Comparative Analysis of France, Russia,
    and China* (Cambridge: Cambridge University Press, 1979), 4.

22 M. El-Ghobashy, *Bread and Freedom: Egypt's Revolutionary Situation* (Stanford:
    Stanford University Press, 2021).

23 See F. John, "Theories of Revolution Revisited: Toward a Fourth Generation,"
    Sociological Theory 11, no. 1 (1993): 1–20; J. Paige, "Finding the Revolutionary in the
    Revolution: Social Science Concepts and the Future of Revolution," in *The Future
    of Revolutions: Rethinking Radical Change in the Age of Globalization*, ed. J. Foran
    (London: Zed Books, 2003), 19–29; J. A. Goldstone, "Understanding the Revolutions
    of 2011: Weakness and Resilience in Middle Eastern Autocracies," *Foreign Affairs*,
    2011, 8–16; G. Lawson, "Within and Beyond the 'fourth generation' of Revolutionary
    Theory," *Sociological Theory* 34, no. 2 (2016): 106–27; Allinson, "A Fifth Generation
    of Revolution Theory?"; A. Bayat, "The Arab Spring and Revolutionary Theory: An
    Intervention in a Debate," *Journal of Historical Sociology* 34, no. 2 (2021): 393–400.
    Allinson, "On Generations of Revolutionary Theory," 150–60.

24 Allinson, "A Fifth Generation of Revolution Theory?"

25 Bayat, "The Arab Spring and Revolutionary Theory," 397.

26 J. Allinson, "Counter-Revolution as International Phenomenon: The Case of Egypt," *Review of International Studies* 45, no. 2 (2019): 320–44. doi:10.1017/ S0260210518000529.

27 See B. Smet, "Revolution and Counter-Revolution in Egypt," *Science and Society* 78, no. 1 (2014): 11–13; Allinson, "A Fifth Generation of Revolution Theory?"; G. Achcar, Morbid Symptoms. In *Morbid Symptoms* (Stanford: Stanford University Press, 2020); B. De Smet, "Authoritarian Resilience'as Passive Revolution: A Gramscian Interpretation of Counter-Revolution in Egypt," *The Journal of North African Studies* 26, no. 6 (2021): 1077–98.

28 C. Tilly, "From Mobilization to Revolution," in *Collective Violence, Contentious Politics, and Social Change* (London: Routledge, 2017), 71–91.

29 Bennani-Chraïbi and Fillieule, "Towards a Sociology of Revolutionary Situations," 3.

30 https://www.worldbank.org/en/news/press-release/2021/05/01/lebanon-sinking-into -one-of-the-most-severe-global-crises-episodes.

31 https://www.dw.com/en/arab-uprisings-struggle-amid-coronavirus/a-53027193.

32 https://www.hrw.org/report/2021/08/03/they-killed-us-inside/investigation-august-4 -beirut-blast.

33 C. Kurzman, *The Unthinkable Revolution in Iran* (Cambridge, MA: Harvard University Press, 2005).

34 C. Kurzman, "The Arab Spring Uncoiled," *Mobilization: An International Quarterly* 17, no. 4 (2012): 377–90.

Part One

Setting the Stage

Situating the Uprising within the Foundations of the Lebanese Polity, Regional Considerations, and Global Consequences

2

Reckoning with the Past

Selected Scenes from the Modern History of Lebanon

Sana Tannoury-Karam

The October 2019 uprising was a formative moment for many who participated in it. However, there were particular incidents during the uprising that stood out, specific moments that enabled those of us in the streets to feel empowered, relevant, and forever changed. One of my most memorable moments was when I entered the Grand Theater (GT), a building located a few meters off Martyr's Square. As demonstrators stormed the metal gates of this abandoned establishment, I took the opportunity to explore this closed-off space that bore the marks of the civil war's destruction and had remained under perpetual reconstruction. In fact, this claim over the city was one of the main triumphs achieved during the October uprising.[1] However, while most spaces that demonstrators made accessible during the uprising were once public spaces, including beaches, parks, squares, and other localities, this particular place was different.

The Grand Théâtre des Milles et Une Nuits (the Grand Theater of a Thousand and One Nights), built in 1929, was part of the colonial planning of Beirut during the French Mandate period.[2] Designed by Yusuf Aftimos and constructed by Jacques Tabet, it functioned as a theater, a connected hotel, and street-level shops. Apart from its elegant arches and iron cast railings, the building boasted a moon roof that mechanically opened up to reveal a star-studded Beiruti sky. The theater oozed of luxury and indeed was built by and for a bourgeoning middle class that performed its modernity and status through attending concerts and plays in the heart of a culturally booming city. What the theater's history thus represents is the foundations of a capitalist monopolizing oligarchy that owned the entertainment and services sector in Lebanon. This oligarchy, a political ruling class with massive concentration of wealth that is continuously protected by their positions of power, was the birth child of colonial and local elite plans for the nascently created state of Lebanon.[3]

As I stood admiring the remnants of its stained-glass dome ceiling and the echoes of songs that haunted its walls, I was struck by the historical weight of the place. Was the uprising "re"-claiming a public space or claiming the abolition of the private for the sake of the public? With that claiming, and/or reclaiming, came a reckoning, first, with what the spaces, and in this case the GT itself, represented in terms of the history of Lebanon. Second, by claiming spaces in the city, demonstrators were demanding a place in the center of that city from which they had felt alienated, especially following the postwar neoliberal era. These demands, for public spaces, as well as for social justice, also had a history.

This chapter reimagines the history of Lebanon through the transformational phases of the GT instead of the classical periodization of a history of Lebanon in the twentieth and twenty-first centuries—mandate, independence, civil war, and post-civil war. This chapter is in no way a complete overview of the history of Lebanon, a task that can hardly be achieved in the length of a chapter. However, the chapter zooms in on selected scenes from this history that illuminate the roots of the factors that led to the 2019 crisis and revolutionary uprising in Lebanon. Particularly, I focus on the socioeconomic foundations of the state and society, and the pillars of the political system, along with its alternatives and attempts to change it.

Lights On, Let the Show Begin: The Political, Social, and Economic Foundations of Lebanon

The state of Lebanon was established on September 1, 1920, under French colonization following the fall of the Ottoman Empire. During the first few years of its rule, the French administration, through its High Commissioners, intensified foreign, and particularly French, capitalist penetration into the Lebanese markets, which had already begun in the nineteenth century. The trade deficit sustained during the First World War increased during the 1920s, while trade was encouraged at the expense of the development of the sectors of industry and agriculture. French policies also encouraged the development of the services sector, as French banks opened their doors in Beirut and major cities, and French enterprises gained monopolies over certain industries.[4] This gradual French takeover of the Lebanese market allowed for the foundation of a modern capitalist state that was economically dependent on foreign capital. While this system primarily benefited French nationals who invested in Lebanon, a small group of Lebanese bankers, lenders, and merchants managed to tie themselves with French interests resulting in the development of a new Lebanese urban bourgeoisie intimately tied in its interests to French capital and trade.[5] This local bourgeoisie, which crossed sectarian lines, was initially supportive of the Mandate and opposed unity with Syria, but it would eventually become strong enough to challenge French rule and achieve political prominence that would benefit from independence.[6]

Politically, the French administration established sectarian quotas through an Administrative Council to be appointed by the High Commissioner, vaguely modeled upon the Mutasarrifiyya system of Mount Lebanon during the Ottoman rule. The Administrative Council was replaced in 1922 by a partly elected Representative Council, also divided along sectarian quotas. The Lebanese constitution, drafted in 1926, institutionalized political sectarianism and represented the triumph of the myth of harmony only through sectarian difference; that in a religiously diverse society, the only viable form of politics was sectarian representation.[7] This myth would be challenged by class-based and secular nationalist politics during the mandate era, but unsuccessfully.[8]

Colonial violence and the politics of difference also manifested in the way development was planned and executed. For instance, the state funded private education at the expense of the public, leading not only to the persistence of high illiteracy rates but also to a widening educational gap along lines of class, sect, and sex.[9] Furthermore, that period saw the unequal development between center and periphery, with regional differences within the peripheries as well. The Mandate period saw the expansion of Beirut at the expense of the Mountain and the countryside in general.[10] Beirut's modernization, engineered to resemble a European colonial city and to cater to European tastes, furthered inequalities along class, sect, and gender lines.[11] The commercialization of the entertainment industry was one particular node in this urban planning of Beirut. Technological advancements that had already started changing the face of this city by the turn of the century also revolutionized the entertainment industry, with electricity and ease of mobility contributing to the flourishing of a night life.[12] Luxury hotels were managed by foreign companies such as the Société des Grands Hôtel du Levant (Society of Grand Hotels of the Levant), a subsidiary of the Banque de Syrie et du Grand Liban (Bank of Syria and Greater Lebanon).[13] Financed by French and Lebanese investors, the seaside district of Minat al-Hosn and the Zaytunah area neighboring the GT's central district boasted by the mid-1930s major hotels, bars, and beach clubs, including the prestigious Hotel Saint Georges and the Kit Kat Club, both which opened their doors for upscale clientele in 1934. The GT was built in the same wave and to cater to the same bourgeoning middle class. It was an exclusive luxurious site that represented colonial and local elite's cooperation in the creation of the state of Lebanon and its particular service-based economy. However, this colonial capitalist project did not go unchallenged.

The Audience Moves to Another Theater: Roots of Resistance against the Nascent State

In the late Ottoman period, the accelerated integration of the empire into the global capitalist system and the Ottoman state's increased efforts to centralize its control over its population facilitated the dissolution of quarter-based loyalties, the creation of new urban spaces that allowed for public gatherings, and the proliferation of newspapers, coffeehouses, and literary-turned-political salons and clubs.[14] With the end of the First World War and the end of Ottoman rule, the shift in the way structures of power were organized allowed for greater participation of the masses in institutional and street politics, as well as the introduction into the political sphere of traditionally nonpolitical, nonelite, actors.[15] Leftist, nationalist, and various reformist Islamist movements emerged to challenge the state and reshape society.[16] Most of these movements would unite under the banner of anti-colonialism. The fall of the Ottoman Empire and the League of Nation's imposition of the Mandate system on Lebanon placed the latter within the "last" wave of colonization that the world would witness, and ultimately within the interwar continuum of anti-colonial resistance that developed not only globally but also regionally in the Arab world—the Iraqi revolt against British rule in 1920, the Great Syrian Revolt between 1925 and 1927, and the Great Arab Revolt in Palestine between 1936 and 1939.[17]

Those who organized against colonialism and for national independence also realized the link between capitalism and imperialism, and the local elite's complicity in this project. Moreover, class-based labor organization became the most serious threat to the idea of a communally divided Lebanon and therefore to the sectarian model.[18] In its first couple of years as a state, Lebanon witnessed workers' strikes and demonstrations against low wages, new taxes, and for fair labor laws.[19] The first workers-only syndicate was the General Syndicate of Tobacco Workers (al-Naqaba al-'Amma li-'Ummal al-Dukhkhan fi Lubnan) organized by Fouad al-Shamali in the town of Bikfaya in 1924.[20] The Bikfaya syndicate established contacts with other labor groups—such as printing press workers, carpenters, cooks, drivers, and shoemakers— and in 1925 created the Supreme Committee of Syndicates (al-Lajna al-Naqabiyya al-'Ulya). Workers' organizations gathered for the first time to celebrate May Day publicly and to demand workers' rights in Beirut on May 1, 1925. Under the banner of the Lebanese People's Party—the precursor to the Communist Party—those gathered met in Martyr's Square Cinema Crystal, a few meters away from the GT.

The syndicates that emerged out of these labor groups in the 1920s would continue to represent some of the few political organizations in Lebanon that crossed sectarian lines. This particular characteristic of these class-based organizations is the reason why Lebanese sectarian leaders have worked to dismantle and, when not successful, to penetrate and weaken these unions from the early days of their inception.[21] However, it is also important to note that organizing the working class along sectarian lines will also take place under the leadership of right-wing Lebanese political parties that emerge during the Mandate period as well.[22] Postindependence Lebanon will witness an increase in this trend.

A Dress Rehearsal to Civil War: The Theater's "Golden Age"

The Second World War—in which France was heavily embroiled—and the ascendence to power of nationalist parties in Lebanon contributed to increased demands for national independence from France. In autumn of 1943, a newly elected parliament amended the constitution and removed the French Mandate over Lebanon. Following French arrests of major political figures as a reaction to the imposition of national independence, mass demonstrations erupted that forced the mandatory power to concede. However, the newly independent republic did not revise the tenets upon which Greater Lebanon was created, primarily a sectarian patriarchal political system and a liberal capitalist economy. Lebanese national independence stood upon two textual pillars: an amended constitution and the National Pact of 1943.[23] The National Pact worked to negotiate the shape of communal representation and to consecrate the "power-sharing" formula of Lebanon upon which consequent power-sharing reconfigurations have been built (1989 Taif Accord of 1989 and the 2008 Doha Accord). The amended constitution of

1943 did not abolish or address articles 9, 10, and 95 of the 1926 constitution, which guaranteed the persistence of sectarianism as a mode of operation for independent Lebanon. The constitution therefore established citizens while maintaining them as subjects within a nonunified personal status law in which they were unequal vis-à-vis each other as sectarian subjects.[24] Sect-based personal status laws would become the basis for a patriarchal system that discriminates against gendered citizens as well.

In 1952, after a long and arduous battle, Lebanese women took the right to vote and to run for office. Emily Fares Ibrahim became the first Arab woman to run for parliamentary elections in 1953, in the face of strong conservative and patriarchal opposition. The battle for women's emancipation had been raging since the late Ottoman period, with Arab and Lebanese women intensifying demands for political rights particularly during the Mandate period. However, their achievement in 1952 was rather co-opted by the Western-oriented regime of President Camille Sham'un that framed women's liberation and therefore universal suffrage as its own achievement and as a culmination of the liberal paradigm that it stood for.

The Sham'un administration (1952–8) bragged about implementing liberal Western values in Lebanese society, but what that in fact meant was, first, a complete dismissal and even persecution of dissenting voices representing a long ongoing debate about the identity of the Arab world and of Lebanon particularly; and second, the use of a liberal economic and political framework to overshadow the further growth and proliferation of a financial oligarchy that owned most of the banking, commerce, and tourism sectors of the Lebanese economy. This oligarchy, which was predominantly Christian Maronite, continued to have strong neocolonial ties with France as it also cultivated relations with other Western powers, including a growing American power, and Arabian Gulf regimes. Following the Palestinian Nakba of 1948[25] and the rise of Ba'athist regimes in Syria and Iraq, Arab capital became heavily concentrated in Lebanese banks.[26]

This period is often referred to as the "golden era" of Lebanon, a term that needs to be complicated given the massive inequalities that it silences. If it was "golden," it was only for those from privileged backgrounds. Therefore, it is no surprise that this "golden era" was forged and performed very much on stage, with the inauguration of the Baalbeck International Festival in 1955 and the proliferation of the entertainment scene. Wealthy Beirutis flocked into the GT to watch the latest plays and hear international music icons perform. All of this disguised, first, the prosperity of Lebanon specifically at the expense of Palestine following the Nakba and, second, the profiteering of an urban middle class at the expense of a poor countryside that continued to be neglected except for its tourist-attracting sites. While the voices of international jazz icons and the legendary Oum Kalthoum echoed in the temples of Baalbeck, the voices of peasants in the Beqaa and Palestinian camps were muted and marginalized. Furthermore, the unequal rural/urban development also led to increased migration from the South— particularly following the Nakba—the Beqaa, and north Lebanon to Beirut and its suburbs, forming a poverty belt around the capital. However, calls for political and social reform would soon start emerging and, mixed with the global context of the Cold War and regional pan-Arab nationalism, would lead to Lebanon's first civil war in 1958.[27]

Sham'un used communist baiting to request American military intervention in order to safeguard his regime and oppose Nasser's popular pan-Arab nationalism and rising leftist voices calling for the abolishment of sectarianism and a rethinking of the socioeconomic foundations of the country.[28] The first Lebanese civil war that erupted in 1958 and ended with US marines landing in Beirut inaugurated a new phase for Lebanon, where Christian right-wing parties would emerge as the protectors of the political and economic status quo, foreign intervention would become an option for resolving internal conflicts, and leftist and reformist forces seeking change would opt for armed conflict to achieve that change. A new phase awaited the GT as well.

The Show Must Go On: The War as Fiction and Reality

The 1960s witnessed unprecedented social and political movements across the globe. The GT itself also changed in the 1960s, transformed into a cinema in keeping up with changing technologies and tastes. Growing social inequalities and rural migration to the city from the underdeveloped peripheries further contributed to the transformation of the landscape, with the suburbs and the development of shantytowns acting as refuge for the country's poorer population. While inequalities prompted social movements and an increase in mass mobilization, including general workers' strikes and union organization, right-wing political parties launched campaigns of "othering" of the poor and refugees, creating scapegoats for an ever-increasing political and social crisis. This crisis was further strained on the regional level with the ascendance of the Ba'ath to power in Syria and Iraq, the 1967 Naksa, and the relocation of the Palestine Liberation Organization (PLO) to Beirut in 1970 after Black September. These factors, however, should not be read as teleologically leading to an inevitable war. The Lebanese civil war, a political and military decision, could have been avoided despite local and regional developments.

With the eruption of the civil war in April 1975 and the division of the city of Beirut between sectarian enclaves, the GT became a section of the green line itself, severing Beirut between East and West. But the show went on. At the epicenter of the fighting, fighters often risked their lives in a sniper-ridden road to the theater, some even losing their lives seeking the narrow road now leading to it. The cinema of the GT began solely showing pornographic movies for an audience who sought refuge from the obscenity of the violence unleashed in the streets of the city.[29] This violence manifested itself between two major factions: the Lebanese National Movement, an amalgamation of nationalist and progressive parties primarily led by the Progressive Socialist Party of Kamal Jumblat, and the Lebanese Front, consisting of the Phalange Party and its right-wing allies. The former, seeking "reform by arms" and upholding the mantel of the Palestinian revolution, was met with the latter's desire to maintain the status quo, mainly the division of power set out by the National Pact upheld by the ruling oligarchy.

The war, stretching inconsistently for fifteen years, put a hiatus to the services and tourism sector upon which the Lebanese economy was built; however, it created its own economy between and within the established sectarian enclaves. In his reading of the post-1982 period of the civil war, Traboulsi explains, "Lebanon between 1985 and 1990 lived under the domination of associated armed mafias that had renounced fighting each other, respected their mutual borders and entertained close ties between themselves for a better spoliation and control of everything Lebanese."[30] War profiteering and infighting within the sectarian enclaves created by the various parties of the war led to a further depreciation of the Lebanese lira and an increase in public debt.

The war ended with a new power-sharing agreement, an updated National Pact: the Taif Agreement of 1989. This agreement revised the initial sectarian balance of power, but there were no socioeconomic reforms. Ironically, when the guns fell silent, so did the GT.

When the Curtain Falls: Neoliberal Reconstruction Silences the Theater

The postwar Taif Agreement and the amnesty law at the end of the civil war were both incorporated as constitutional amendments that legitimized warlords' continued administration of Lebanese political and economic life. The Taif replaced the Christian-favoring 6/5 ratio of parliamentary seats with parity. It also reshuffled sectarian power dynamics by considerably diminishing the power of the Christian seat of President of the Republic and increasing the powers of the two Muslim seats (PM and Speaker of the House). This, in turn, reaffirmed the dilemma of institutional gridlock that could only be resolved by deals between the three presidents and the coalitions they represent, the building blocks of Lebanon's consociational democracy. The Taif amendments to the constitution "entrenched . . . a temporality of the temporary," as Maya Mikdashi argues—the temporary being political sectarianism.[31] Temporary because the proclaimed end goal of the Taif Agreement is making sectarian citizens into national citizens. However, embedded in the Taif is the lack of any process or mechanism to achieve that goal and internal contradictions about the abolition of sectarianism, and therefore, nonsectarianism is suspended continuously for the fear of the tyranny of the majority. This "logic of the Taif" mirrors that of independence, which was based on balancing sectarian demographics. The importance of maintaining sectarian balance in terms of numbers becomes the basis for the xenophobia and racism directed against refugees. It is also the excuse that politicians, who base their power on it, use to defer any calls for gender equality and a unified civil personal status law.

An unwritten stipulation of the Taif was the Syrian regime's mandate over Lebanon in the postwar era. A remnant of the civil war, the Assad regime's military presence in Lebanon was blessed by a postwar parliament that ratified the Brotherhood, Cooperation and Coordination Agreement signed between President Harawi and Hafez al-Asad in 1991. The Syrian regime's tutelage over Lebanon and its profiteering provided coverage and further contributed to sustaining the patronage system of governance of postwar Lebanon.

The Taif did not address prewar economic inequalities; rather, the postwar era witnessed a series of fierce neoliberal policies of reconstruction led by Prime Minister Rafiq Hariri that further exacerbated these inequalities.[32] Postwar reconstruction, orchestrated by the neoliberal policies of Hariri, was a conscious and deliberate attempt to induce collective amnesia of the past. To help with the amnesia, any traces of the war needed to be removed. Enter Solidere, a Lebanese private company founded in 1994, which through an elaborate financial scheme bought the majority of land in downtown Beirut and claimed the rights for its reconstruction. Solidere, representing the financial interests of the maverick Hariri, was the hallmark of a postwar economic neoliberal policy of increased public debt and further unequal development between the economy's various sectors and along urban/rural lines.

Through the project of reconstruction, the past was intentionally "emptied," and so was the GT. While it stood silently deteriorating and awaiting reconstruction that never happened, Solidere decided to only restore its façade to go alongside the posh stores and reopened banks in downtown Beirut. In fact, Solidere's plan for the GT remained not only unrealized but also unconfirmed, with few rumors suggesting it was to be reconstructed as a cultural space. In the late 1990s, Solidere allowed for some limited performances to take place at the theater; all were privately funded and very exclusive.[33]

The neoliberal financial policies of the postwar era did not end with the assassination of Hariri in 2005 even when that explosion led to new demarcation of political lines along March 8 and 14 alliances and eventually to the withdrawal of Syrian troops from Lebanon. Rather, the economic and political developments in the postwar decade had created a fairly updated oligarchic class. While this ruling class had remnants of the few families that controlled state and the economy since Lebanon's inception, it also featured abilities to adapt and include newcomers, particularly in the post-2005 era (the Free Patriotic Movement "returnees," Lebanese Forces, Hezbollah, etc.). This mélange of old and new elements within the ruling oligarchy clashed in 2008 before going to Doha to reconfigure the power-sharing formula yet again.[34]

The financial crisis preceding the 2019 uprising and still unfolding in Lebanon was orchestrated by this latest version of the ruling oligarchy. More specifically, financial decision making in the postwar era, and arguably further back historically, has been "split among the central bank, the political authority, and the [Association of Banks in Lebanon] ABL." As Safieddine argues, this tripartite authority has been further solidified and institutionalized in times of crises.[35]

The response to the crisis, the uprising in October 2019, was also an amalgamation of old and new movements. Alongside a long tradition of agitation against the sectarian and neoliberal state, the 2019 uprising drew upon the spirit of the Arab revolutions of the past decade that had created a new turning point on the regional and global scales.

Now Showing: The October 2019 Uprising

When the October 2019 uprising "reclaimed" the GT, it was not reclaiming an uncontentious space. Greeting protestors on the walls of the theater stood Rafik

Majzoub's paintings of women as an homage to the theater's pornographic movies period and a painting on the theater's center stage, the angel of history.[36] History could not be missed; it stared us in the face. The reckoning the uprising has to do is with a contentious past, one where borders and exclusions applied, whether class, sect, race, or gender-based. Two banners hung from the GT during the uprising in 2019: restoring public ownership (istirja' al-amlak al-'amma) and restoring power to the people (istirja' al-hukum li-l-nass). Yet the history of the particular place, tied to the history of property and the economy of Lebanon, tells us that this was never public ownership.

The theater represents a space in which one could be in or out, belong or separated from, present or absent, dead or alive. Oscillating between these different categories allows us to push against these binaries in narrating the past. By reckoning with this past, the uprising opens the opportunity to revise and rewrite modern Lebanese history. Perhaps to reclaim power to the people, we need to reclaim our history, the power to first narrate that history, to document it, and ultimately to come to terms with it. That history included a robust albeit diverse tradition of contestation against the state, starting from its inception in 1920. However, if the uprising has taught us anything, it is also to acknowledge the pitfalls of that heritage and, instead of rescuing it, to create our own tradition of contestation, one that is progressive, intersectional, liberationist, feminist, and just.

Notes

1   Please see Mona Harb's chapter in this volume for a detailed discussion of the urban planning of Beirut and the politics of space.

2   Omar Naim, *Grand Theater: A Tale of Beirut*. Documentary Film (Beirut, 1999).

3   For more on the oligarchy see Julia Choucair Visozo in "What is Oligarchy" (Parts 1 and 2) in *The Public Source* (https://thepublicsource.org/what-oligarchy).

4   For more on the foundations of the Lebanese banking system see Hicham Safieddine, *Banking on the State: The Financial Foundations of Lebanon* (Stanford: Stanford University Press, 2019).

5   Roger Owen, *Essays on the Crisis in Lebanon* (London: Ithaca Press, 1976).

6   Masoud Daher, *Tarikh Lubnan al-Ijtima'i, 1914–1926* (Beirut: Dar al-Farabi, 1974).

7   For more on the origins of sectarianism in Lebanon see Ussama Makdisi, *The Culture of Sectarianism: Community, History, and Violence in Nineteenth-century Ottoman Lebanon* (Berkeley: California University Press, 2000) and *The Age of Coexistence* (Berkeley: California University Press, 2019).

8   Sana Tannoury-Karam, "Founding the Lebanese Left: From Colonial Rule to Independence," *The Legal Agenda*, January 11, 2021, https://english.legal-agenda.com/founding-the-lebanese-left-from-colonial-rule-to-independence/.

9   By the late 1920s, 85 percent of the population of Lebanon and Syria remained illiterate. See Daher, *Tarikh Lubnan al-Ijtima'i*, 259.

10 Marwan Buheiry, "Beirut's Role in the Political Economy of the French Mandate, 1919–1939," in Papers on Lebanon, Center for Lebanese Studies (1986). For more on the transformations of Beirut at the turn of the century see Jens Hanssen, *Fin de*

Siècle Beirut: The Making of an Ottoman Provincial Capital (Oxford: Oxford University Press, 2005).

11 Samir Kassir, *Beirut* (Berkeley: California University Press, 2011).

12 Diana Abbani, "Sina'at al-Tarfih wa-l-Hadatha fi Beirut Zaman al-Intidab," *Bidayat* (Issue 28029, 2020) https://bidayatmag.com/node/1282.

13 Kassir, *Beirut*, 306–7.

14 The longer period of Ottoman rule was characterized by decentralization of power, which encouraged local and quarter-based politics particularly in urban settings. James Gelvin, *Divided Loyalties: Nationalism and Mass Politics in Syria at the Close of Empire* (Berkeley: California University Press, 1998).

15 The constitutional revolution in 1908 led to further changes in Ottoman politics, which had begun in the nineteenth century with vast political and economic reforms. See M. Şükrü Hanioğlu, *A Brief History of the Late Ottoman Empire* (Princeton: Princeton University Press, 2008).

16 See Ilham Khuri-Makdisi, *The Eastern Mediterranean and the Making of Global Radicalism, 1860–1914* (Berkeley: University of California Press, 2010).

17 For Arab anti-imperialism during the Mandate see Sana Tannoury-Karam, "Long Live the Revolutionary Alliance Against Imperialism: Interwar Anti-Imperialism and the Arab Levant," in *The League Against Imperialism: Lives and Afterlives*, ed. Michele Louro et al (Leiden: Leiden University Press, 2020), 107–33, 98.

18 For the history of labor organization in Lebanon see Abdallah Hanna, *al-Haraka al-'Ummaliyya fi Suriya wa-Lubnan, 1900–1945* (Damascus: Dar Dimashq, 1973).

19 Jacques Couland, *Le Mouvement Syndical au Liban, 1919–1946* (Paris: Éditions Sociales, 1970); Ilyas al-Buwari, *Tarikh al-Haraka al-'Ummaliyya wa-l-Naqabiyya fi Lubnan 1908–1946* (Beirut: Dar al-Farabi, 1980).

20 For more on workers in the tobacco industry in Lebanon, especially women tobacco workers, see Malik Abi Saab, *Militant Women of a Fragile Nation* (Syracuse: Syracuse University Press, 2010).

21 For more on the history of labor movements in Lebanon see Nadim el-Kak's chapter in this volume.

22 See Dylan Baun's *Winning Lebanon* (Cambridge: Cambridge University Press, 2021).

23 For a discussion of this see Fawwaz Traboulsi, *A History of Modern Lebanon* (London: Pluto, 2007).

24 For a gender reading of Mandate Lebanon see Elizabeth Thompson, *Colonial Citizens* (New York: Columbia University Press, 2000).

25 For more on the role of Palestinians in Lebanon after 1948, particularly financially, see Safieddine, *Banking on the State*, especially chapter 6 on Intra Bank. See also Moné Makkawi's chapter in the volume for more on Palestinian refugees in Lebanon.

26 See Safieddine, *Banking on the State*.

27 Traboulsi, *A History of Modern Lebanon*.

28 See Jeffrey Karam ed., *The Middle East in 1958: Reimagining A Revolutionary Year* (London: I.B. Tauris, 2020).

29 Naim, *Grand Theater*.

30 Traboulsi, *A History of Modern Lebanon*, 231.

31 Maya Mikdashi, "The Magic of Mutual Coexistence in Lebanon: The Taif Accord at Thirty," *Jadaliyya*, October 23, 2019, https://www.jadaliyya.com/Details/40134.

32 See Majed's chapter on the foundations of a neoliberal system in Lebanon.

33 Iyad Kayali, "City's Grand Theater Rises Like a Phoenix," *The Daily Star*, October 27, 1997, https://www.dailystar.com.lb/Culture/Art/1997/Oct-27/99888-citys-grand -theatre-rises-like-phoenix.ashx.

34 For more on the Doha Agreement see the UNSC S/2008/392, https://www.securit ycouncilreport.org/atf/cf/%7B65BFCF9B-6D27-4E9C-8CD3-CF6E4FF96FF9%7D/ Lebanon%20S2008392.pdf.

35 Hicham Safieddine, "The Lebanese Troika: A History of Instability and Unilateral Decision Making," *Legal Agenda,* May 22, 2020. https://english.legal-agenda.com/the -lebanese-banking-troika-a-history-of-instability-and-unilateral-decision-making/.

36 Rafik Majzoub's angel was, according to him, a recognition of the theater as an "old place full of ghosts"; see Kayali, "City's Grand Theater Rises Like a Phoenix."

3

Lebanon's Postwar Political Economy

From Reconstruction to Collapse

Mohamad Zbeeb

The crisis consists precisely in the fact that the old is dying but the new cannot be born; in this interregnum a great variety of morbid symptoms appear.
—Antonio Gramsci, 1929

The "Lebanese crisis" is violently reorganizing society. These socioeconomic mutations are exacerbated by a political and economic elite adamant on prolonging and worsening the crisis. Following three decades of postwar reconstruction and national unification, Lebanese residents finds themselves back in the same living conditions they knew during the war (1975–90), specifically its second half after the Israeli invasion (1982). Similarly, talk of "reconstruction" is at the forefront of discussions, just as it was after the Taif Agreement and Syrian mandate (1989). The binary choice is clear, either destruction, sectarian polarization, violence, chaos, and misery or a renewed mandate for the "oligarchic government" and rebuilding the structure of exploitation and domination on the same bases that led to its destruction several times throughout Lebanon's modern history.

"Similar conditions" do not necessarily imply that today's circumstances and factors in play are identical to those of the war, nor that the competing factions remain unchanged. Quite the contrary, internal and external conditions have changed drastically. New structural and circumstantial factors were superimposed on a long history of accumulations, coincidences, collapses, and disasters. Many geopolitical changes have arisen, particularly after the liberation of southern Lebanon from Israeli occupation (2000), the withdrawal of Syrian forces (2005), the outbreak of the Arab uprisings, and the war in Syria (2011). Despite these differences, however, certain similarities make the current situation just as politically unsustainable as it was during the war. A paralyzed political system, a society in shock, a disintegrating state, a stumbling economy, a currency in freefall, a bankrupt banking sector, meager surpluses, skyrocketing debt, fleeing capital, black markets, inflation waves on the loose, deteriorating living conditions, overwhelming multidimensional poverty, vast qualitative and quantitative demographic movements, huge material losses, etc.

The war and subsequent neoliberal choices for reconstruction have squandered almost an entire generation. Gross domestic product (GDP) per capita did not regain its 1974 value until 2002. It took twenty-eight years to return to the same prewar conditions that contributed to the outbreak of that war. The current crisis threatens to squander at least one more generation. GDP per capita in 2020 dropped back to its 1994 value, after the war and prior to reconstruction. That is twenty-six years of economic growth, lost. The World Bank (WB) predicts that GDP per capita will require thirteen to nineteen years to regain its 2018 value,[1] meaning a return to the same conditions that contributed to the implosion of the 2019 crisis. The WB classified Lebanon's crisis among the worst ten, perhaps three, globally since the mid-nineteenth century.[2]

These numbers paint the ongoing crisis as an obituary of the reconstruction process. This relates not only to the collapsed material and financial infrastructure but also to the political choices and their long-term alterations of the socioeconomic structure and internal and foreign relations. It has been widely admitted that the "Lebanese economy is in free fall,"[3] that "the political and economic system has completely fallen,"[4] and that "this state, in its current form, can no longer protect its citizens and provide them with a dignified life."[5] There is also a consensus that the current crisis far surpasses the domestic economy's ability to absorb and compensate for the losses on the short term, and that society is not strong enough to withstand its effects on the long run. This discrepancy between the long-term recovery and the short-term resilience of society makes the previous funding mechanisms of consumption, expenditure, and debt settlement impossible. It is the hour of truth. The endlessly sustainable "Lebanese miracle" turned out to be conditioned by factors that are no longer available. The bills that have been accumulated are now due. This is essentially the issue around which events have—and will continue to—unfold, making this crisis one of political economy.

The 2019 financial collapse inflicted qualitative and quantitative changes on income and its distribution. Most families were stripped of their purchasing power. By mid-2021, the Lebanese pound (LBP) had lost more than 90 percent of its value compared to the US Dollar (USD). The Consumption Price Index had risen by 287 percent compared to late 2018, under a relative freeze of nominal wages. In 2020, GDP contracted by over 25 percent, meaning that income (profits and salaries) suffered a great loss. The bulk of the hit targeted the middle class whose consumption had previously been the engine of economic growth. The collapse of the banking sector also caused quantitative and qualitative changes in wealth and its distribution. Many families were stripped of their private savings accumulated over thirty years.[6] By mid-2021, banks were still confiscating 220 trillion LBP (78 percent in foreign currencies) by withholding payment and using arbitrary and illegal restrictions on transfers, withdrawals, and payment systems the first time in the history of Lebanon. The collapse destroyed the bulk of personal accumulated wealth and disrupted the mechanism of attracting foreign capital and of financing trade and consumption. Thus, the Lebanese economic and social structure is being completely redefined. Just as the war has mutated society, so will this crisis. This transformed society will serve as the basis for the new "reconstruction."

The Nature of the Crisis

During a crisis, the "ruling class" loses the approval on which it had established its hegemony, thereby hindering its ability to "lead" without releasing its grasps on "control." The ruling class may even resort to "coercive force" in order to maintain its dominion and attempt to reproduce itself. In the case of Lebanon, sectarian polarization, threats of civil violence, and drawing on the power of foreign players have repressed political participation. Naomi Klein calls this process the "shock doctrine,"[7] where "the politically impossible becomes the politically inevitable" as per Milton Friedman.[8]

People in Lebanon have expressed their conviction that the institutional foundations of the state do not serve them but work against them. That the economy is internally monopolized by a few powerful families with privileges that overrule the interests of the majority. That inequalities are rampant at the levels of class, sects, regions, genders, and generations. People have also voiced their distrust of the "ruling class" and their desire to overthrow it, using the infamous slogan "All of Them Means All of Them" (Kellon Yaani Kellon) or by describing it as a "political class" that is authoritarian, corrupt, and subservient to foreign powers. They blame the "ruling coalition" of wartime political-economic elites for causing and mismanaging the crisis. They have also experienced its willingness to sacrifice them to perpetuate its dominance and legitimacy. However, these people (uniquely) relive the fear they have internalized throughout past attempts to build a society, to a paralyzing extent. "Going to hell"[9] therefore becomes the only imaginable alternative when control is lost. This "fear of violence" is ideological before being societal.

The political administration adopted deliberately contractionary policies. Inflation was let loose to absorb some of the losses in the financial sector and to arbitrarily reduce the balance of trade (BOT) by limiting consumption and imports. According to the Central Administration of Statistics,[10] three-quarters of families saw a decline in their monthly income from US$1,600 to less than US$133, and more than a third have an income below US$55,[11] meaning less than US$0.5 per individual per day (for a family of four). The WB estimates that "more than half the population is likely below the national poverty line."[12] The World Food Programme estimated that by the end of 2020, 41 percent of families "found difficulty in obtaining food and meeting other essential needs." The United Nations Children's Fund (UNICEF),[13] estimated that 60 percent of families had to borrow money to purchase food, 76 percent faced dangerous implications of increases in medication prices, 36 percent had a hard time accessing health care,[14] 30 percent of children were deprived of primary health care, the rate of routine vaccination dropped by 20 percent, and 15 percent of families had to withdraw their children from schools.[15]

The United Nations Economic and Social Commission for Western Asia (ESCWA)[16] estimates that multidimensional poverty rose from 42 percent in 2019 to 82 percent in 2021, meaning that the overwhelming majority of the population suffers deprivation on one or more levels of poverty (jobs, income, health, education, property, and public services). Consumption and imports contracted severely, by over 40 percent.[17] The severe shortage in medical supplies and fuel accelerated the collapse of infrastructure, public services, and telecommunications. Dollar shortages and fleeing capital worsened.

Small and medium depositors were forcibly subjugated to an undeclared "haircut" by over 75 percent of the value of their deposits. The losses of the banking sector were estimated at US$85 billion.[18] The credit system—without which no capitalist system would function—broke down. The government defaulted on its foreign currency debt[19] and delayed restructuring US$100 billion worth of debts, five times Lebanon's national income (GNI) in 2020. Small and medium businesses, employing almost half the workforce, defaulted. Unemployment increased from 28 percent before the COVID-19 pandemic to 40 percent in late 2020.[20] Profits and salaries dropped, and minimum wage regressed from 450 to less than US$45 monthly.[21] A WB survey of enterprises between October and November 2020 showed that "17 percent of enterprises permanently closed, 79 percent saw a decline in sales, and 61 percent reduced their full-time employees by an average of 43 percent."[22] GDP dropped from US$55 to 20 billion between 2018 and 2020, according to the International Monetary Fund (IMF).[23] The Lebanese economy circled back to its state on the eve of the Paris II Conference,[24] when a foreign bailout bought increasingly expensive time and postponed the collapse until the present day.

The Fatal Dutch Disease

The aforementioned facts demonstrate that the ongoing crisis severely crippled the financial mechanisms that had allowed the political and economic system to survive until now, despite the many negative socioeconomic indicators. Lebanon harbored an extreme case of what economists call "Dutch Disease," "inspired by the developments that hit the Netherlands in the sixties of the last century while exporting natural gas from Groningen. Big capital inflow resulting from exporting bulks of raw materials (among other causes) strangely lead to a certain and permanent decline of other sectors of the economy that produce tradable commodities."[25]

Lebanon's national accounts show yearly current account deficits, ranging between 20 and 30 percent of its GDP, since the end of the war. This is highly abnormal, as current accounts represent net economic relations between residents and nonresidents. A quarter of Lebanon's annual revenue was required to fund this deficit in foreign currencies. Half of this deficit originated from fiscal deficit (revenue minus expenditure), while the other half originated from the private sector (savings minus investments). This structural gap was financed by enticing the influx of foreign capital, loans, remittances from expatriates, and nonresident deposits. This scheme allowed the balance of payments to score surpluses until 2010, when it reversed into successive annual deficits.

According to the IMF's 2018 External Sector Report, Lebanon came in thirteenth among the fifteen countries with the highest current account deficits worldwide. Lebanon's size is not the only reason behind its exceptional situation. The country comes in first place globally for its current account deficit to GDP, amounting to −25 percent of its GDP, largely surpassing Oman in second place (−15.5 percent).

The current account of any economy includes the total flow of goods and services (BOT), primary income (particularly interest payments), and secondary income (particularly remittances) between residents and nonresidents. The balance of current accounts reflects the difference between total exports and income, on one hand, and total imports and payments due, on the other. A surplus is made when the first sum is larger than the second; the opposite scenario indicates a deficit. This balance also reflects the gap between savings and investments in a given economy. Beyond technical terms, a current account deficit reflects the volume of financing needed annually to settle trade and income accounts with nonresidents. In 2018, the IMF estimated that Lebanon required US$14 billion in annual funding. The Lebanese economy had to settle this amount of external liabilities in foreign currencies. This meant that funds had to be secured by taking on more external debt and draining foreign exchange reserves, at a time when foreign direct investments (FDIs) and remittances were in sharp decline.

The economic theory endorsed by the IMF states that surpluses and deficits in current accounts are not necessarily problematic; they might be "convenient and useful." They explain the issue simplistically:

> developing economies require investments to grow, and use (in most cases) external resources, by importing more commodities than they produce and by taking up loans to cover the resulting deficit. On the other hand, rich countries with aging populations require building up savings in preparation for the labor force's retirement; that is why they maintain surpluses that are credited to countries in deficit.

This is the dominant theory, despite ample evidence that the matter is neither so simple nor so naive. Perhaps the most notable evidence are the ongoing trade wars, the bloating of global debt (US$164 trillion or 225 percent of Gross World Product), and rising disparities. The IMF also admits that "current account balances may become excessive," meaning that "they may exceed what the bases of economics and appropriate economic policies can justify." This applies to the case of Lebanon. The current account deficit seems like a structural economic phenomenon that has been far too long-standing and extravagant, that it has obstructed and even replaced growth itself. The IMF adds, "economies that borrow excessively by accumulating large deficits in their current accounts, are at risk of a sudden arrest of capital inflow, which undermines stability and increases the likelihood of confusing changes in exchange rates and the prices of assets of indebted countries." This is exactly what Lebanon is facing today.

A BOT (commodities and services) deficit is considered the main source of current account deficit. Lebanon's trade deficit in 2018 was at 27 percent of GDP, worth US$15 billion. This deficit was previously financed by directing capital inflow (70 percent toward real estate), net remittances from expatriates (around US$4 billion), and external debt (including increasing deposits of nonresidents to over 25 percent of total deposits). This meant increasing the liabilities of local banks (especially deposits) and loaning them to households and the state, to fund private and public consumption, thereby increasing the current account deficit and raising the demand for financing, and so on.

For a moment, there was "faith" that this mechanism could indefinitely fund consumption, like an endless "miracle." But foreign debt dried out and became increasingly expensive. FDIs also declined, as the signs of a looming real estate crisis emerged. Risks mounted on the exchange rate and banks, and the economic conditions of countries that harbored expatriates deteriorated. In sum, this past period was based on an acquisition of the present at the expense of the future, by eroding the real economy and burdening society with external debts worth more than 200 percent of GDP.

The Ideological Basis for Structural Imbalances

The dominant ideology reduces Lebanese society to a blend of fearful sects, "a promised land for anxious minorities."[26] This was the foundational narrative of the Lebanese political economy ever since its creation a hundred years ago.[27] However, this narrative had less to do with sectarian anxieties and geography than with the way those who monopolized violence constantly cooperated with those who monopolized capital, in order to expropriate private and public property and to snatch privileges and an ever-increasing share of society's surplus. This story expands over a long history that predates the Lebanese civil war and subsequent reconstruction. Its origins go back the Ottoman era, when the nucleus of the local trade and banking bourgeoisie started taking form in its comprador features; and Beirut was morphing into a center of banking and trade mediation, servicing European colonial capital interests.

North et al. theorize[28] that "society contains violence through the manipulation of economic interests by the political system, by incentivizing rent that make the power centers of groups and individuals, realize that their interests in refraining from using violence far surpass those of employing it." Naturally, societies are far more complex than this reductionist theory insinuates. However, Lebanese history holds much evidence that the postwar political economy was built on the war system itself and on the division of land, labor, capital, and opportunities. According to this theory, horizontal organizations form a dominant coalition, while vertical organizations constitute political parties, sectarian groups, nepotist networks, and families of organized crime. This amalgam of organizations constitutes the "system," which relies on channels of distribution and institutions to favor cooperation over violence, while snatching exclusive privileges for the members of that coalition. This theory assumes that "attempts to get rid of institutions and policies enabling corruption and rent-creation do not lead to a competitive economy, but to instability, which deviates the system towards violence."[29] This is particularly true when one party considers itself greater than the others or when economic changes occur such as the decline of the net inflow of foreign funds, the contraction of GNI, and the decline of salaries, profits, and rent. This forces members of the ruling coalition to restructure society—while being pitted against each other—and to put the mechanisms by which they regulate their popular bases, with their conflicting interests, to the test.

This theory also assumes that violence is inherent in society by claiming it is essentially prevalent instead of it stemming from the economy, its distribution mechanisms, and structures of exploitation and dominance. Ample evidence throughout Lebanese history proves that violence is inherent in the model of capital and wealth accumulation, combining both means of coercion (control) and exploitation (capital). Debt, corruption, dispossession of public and private properties, public-private partnerships (PPPs), alternative services substituting the state, trade and industrial monopolies, and the rising political power of banks were all among the main mechanisms of accumulation and the concentration of the economy in the hands of a minority. According to the national census in 1960, 4 percent of Lebanon's richest were privy to 32 percent of the GNI, while the poorest 50 percent shared only 18 percent. Inequality was significantly exacerbated after the civil war, reconstruction, and debt accumulation. Lydia Assouad concludes, "the top 10 percent of the country's richest individuals earned between 49-54 percent of the GNI from 2005 to 2016, whereas the poorest 50 percent earned only 12-14 percent of the GNI. As a yearly average, the richest 10 percent pocketed more than 50 percent of all income earned in the country."[30]

Lebanon's political economy is considered instinctively "neoliberal." Since its independence in 1943, the Lebanese state adopted the two main pillars of the "neoliberal" agenda long before their inception in the 1970s of the last century:

Complete deregulation of capital flows and influx of commodities and individuals across borders (liberalization of capital accounts and free trade).

Restricting the state and its economic activity (austerity) and constraining its interventions to either freeing the market or creating new ones, by expropriating public and private property (Solidere, public maritime, fluvial, and municipal properties), privatization, contracting, and PPPs.

Lebanon's modern history holds signs of a special kind of "economic liberalism." The evolution of the political system does not reveal that it originated from an avant-garde and original "economic thought" or from the political project of a capitalist class, free of foreign subservience. Michel Chiha and others attempted to give suspenseful qualities to "Lebanon's unique situation" or "miracle." They ended up creating a headquarters for the anti-welfare state ideology and a "haven for the rich."

Historical Features of the Economic Structure

Contrary to Chiha's claims, the employment of society's capabilities, resources, and wealth for the sole purposes of meeting external needs and the dominance of banking and trade on the economic structure were not representative of a Lebanese miracle. They did, however, cause the decline of productive industrial and agricultural sectors, a chaotic expansion of Beirut, a rural exodus that created densely populated areas, and a centralization of economic activity and public services in the center of coastal Lebanon. This came with a continuous flow of emigration. These consequences only worsened during and after the war, further reducing available resources to waste.

The Lebanese economy benefited from the occupation of Palestine (1948) by relocating transit from the port of Haifa to that of Beirut and hosting some of the Palestinian bourgeoisie that integrated with the Lebanese bourgeoisie. It later benefited from nationalization and agricultural reforms in several Arab countries that led to the migration of Syrian, Egyptian, and Iraqi capital to Lebanon. Until the 1970s, the Lebanese service sector received a golden opportunity to expand its role as an intermediary between these countries and the global financial market. Banking and trade activities flourished. Services' share of the GDP rose from 62 percent in the 1950s (which was high, even then, compared to other countries) to 72 percent in the 1970s, reaching 75 percent in the present day. That is how Lebanon historically acquired its status as a service economy, increasingly servicing a regional economy shaped by oil rents, militarization, and war economies.

Despite this concentration in the service sector, services were not diversified. According to national accounts, real estate activities (construction, contracting, cement production, quarries, housing equipment, and services) accounted for over a quarter of GDP. Adding trade, transport, and financial services would increase the share to over half of GDP. The dilemma was no longer constrained to the reliance on a weak service economy directed abroad. It complexified due to the hyperspecialization in lowly productive real estate and trade activities that neither provide employment nor acceptable salaries but waste the production capacity of the Lebanese workforce.

Between 1950 and 1974, the Lebanese economy recorded an average yearly growth of 7 percent. This relatively high rate gave a false impression of abundance and prosperity. Personal consumption (by households) was driving this growth, contributing nearly 80 percent to the GDP. Despite this "high" growth, the GDP per capita grew only by 3 percent—lower than the average recorded in neighboring countries. This indicates that prewar economic growth, reductively called the "Lebanese miracle," was merely a facade concealing massive social and regional disparities that greatly increased over time.

Commodity and agricultural production was further reduced after the war. Consumption remained the main driver of growth. According to national accounts, public and private consumption surpassed GDP, reaching 108 percent in 2019, meaning that consumption costs were higher than the total income. Households accounted for the bulk of consumption, amounting to 88.4 percent of GDP between 2004 and 2016.[31] The WB estimates that the import bill amounted to US$317 billion since 1993, while exports amounted to US$55 billion, meaning that the external trade deficit reached US$261 billion. How was this enormous deficit financed?

Between 1993 and mid-2018, Lebanon saw a large influx of capital and remittances of over US$280 billion. This sum was not diverted to investments but was used to finance the trade deficit instead. It fed into real estate speculation (real estate sales were estimated to be over US$170 billion) and imposed a public and private debt worth four times the annual GDP. These figures reveal the origins of today's crisis and explain the perpetual need for more dollars and the addiction to remittances, deposit inflows, and money printing!

To understand what these figures indicate, the WB compared the volume of capital that entered Lebanon after the civil war to that of Western Europe after the Second

World War. The amount of aid under the Marshall Plan for reconstruction was nearly US$170 billion (at the prices of 2005), with Germany's share not exceeding US$10 billion. Experts at the WB asked the following question: does Lebanon's situation today compare to that of 1965 Germany?[32]

To simplify further, the mechanism of attracting foreign capital inflow—which relied on fixing the exchange rate of the LBP, increasing interest rates on deposits and government bonds, and subsidizing real estate profits—increased the costs of domestic production, which strengthened the dependency on imports to meet rising demands. Financing Lebanon's trade deficit consumed 93 percent of Lebanon's capital inflow during that period. A tremendous amount of capabilities and resources were wasted in that process. Lebanon did not accumulate the necessary productive capital, wealth, and assets to avoid contracting the "Dutch Disease." This mechanism had succeeded in funding consumption without investments up until 2010. As of 2011, capital inflows were no longer sufficient to finance the trade deficit. According to WB figures, the trade deficit accumulated between 2011 and 2018 amounted to US$126 billion whereas capital inflows were under US$118 billion. Lebanon hence suffered a sizeable shortage in dollars, worth US$8.5 billion. The Central Bank of Lebanon (BDL) then used financial engineering schemes—in other words, confiscation—to control and maintain the remaining liquidity, pushing the Lebanese economy into further recession and instability.

Rebuilding the War System and Its Economy

Several internal and external factors led to the outbreak of war in 1975. Most notably, wealth and income disparities, the heavily monopolized economy, the dominance of foreign capital, and the failure of the economic structure to absorb the rural exodus to the city, specifically Beirut. The war caused considerable destruction. Around 5 percent of the total population between 1975 and 1990 was either killed or disappeared—in addition to the thousands wounded and displaced. Material and productive losses exceeded US$30 billion. Economic growth was halved. The material infrastructure and a significant portion of capital assets accumulated before the war were destroyed. Most importantly, the state was broken down and control of its rentier assets was seized, specifically between 1982 and 1992. During that same period, the LBP collapsed from less than 5 LBP/USD in 1981 to over 2,850 LBP/USD in 1992, paving the way to entrench the postwar political-economic system.

The war exacerbated the structural crisis by worsening many deformities and weaknesses on all levels. Area demarcation and isolation worsened the already constant loss of skilled labor and capital to migration. Both caused sweeping demographic changes. This culminated in the formation of the so-called *war system* with its economy and counter-society. It was established through the oppression and domination of civil society by militias and the division and sharing of markets, lands, and rent revenues. The state was substituted with lesser organizations that include judicial courts, taxation, the confiscation of private and public property, the control of trade, and the distribution of electricity, water, fuel, medications, and food. The role of nongovernmental organizations grew until they (almost) monopolized social welfare, health care, and education.

The onset of war, internal and external changes, ended Lebanon's previous role as a trade and finance mediator. Foreign capital fled, the traditional bourgeoisie weakened, markets were compartmentalized, and institutions were stripped. What followed the Taif Agreement, under the aegis of "reconstruction," was a consolidation, not a disintegration, of the war system. The same structure that caused the war was rebuilt, except this time, it was accompanied by grueling public and private debt, a complete financial domination over both economy and state, more structural imbalances, and a bigger dependence on foreign capital inflow.

Naomi Klein observes that "disaster capitalists have no interest in repairing what once was. The process deceptively called 'reconstruction' began with finishing the job of the original disaster, by erasing what was left of the public sphere, all before the victims of war were able to regroup and stake their claims to what was theirs."[33] Solidere embodied this theory intelligibly. As people were experiencing the aftermath of the Israeli invasion and sectarian infighting, Rafic Hariri, representing the rising wartime oligarchy, was plotting to seize historic downtown Beirut.

In 1991, before Hariri became prime minister in 1992, parliament passed a legislation creating the real estate company for the reconstruction of downtown Beirut. Property ownership rights were replaced with shares in the new company through reverse privatization, by transferring private property to a private company, and privatizing public property. An additional shock was required to silence any opposition. Between February and September 1992, the price of the LBP was subjected to waves of speculation. BDL governor, Michel El Khoury, oddly announced that he would not intervene to quell the speculation, and news implicated banks in instigating the devaluation. Wages plummeted, pensions evaporated, and deposits in LBP lost their value. And so, the postwar society was subjugated. Solidere became the favored model of capital accumulation, an "accumulation by dispossession" as per David Harvey.[34] Reconstruction entailed dispossessing public and private property for a wealthy powerful few. This was accompanied by land speculations, evictions, depriving many of their right to the city, seizing public and private money, particularly through interests on debts, mortgages, contractor agreements, and PPPs, and the protection of concessions and monopolies.

It came as no surprise that this system would end by stripping people of their savings and bank deposits. Banks were the primary tool for the disproportionate accumulation of wealth and for taking over society's surplus from the postwar reconstruction, until the collapse in 2019. The influx of foreign capital inflated banks' liabilities. Deposits and bank capital were invested in public and private debts, amounting to more than US$200 billion. It is through debt that the current economic model enabled the accumulation of capital via dispossession.

"Between 1993 and 2019, over 27 years, budget accounts show an income of 156 billion USD, and an expenditure, apart from debt service, amounting to 129 billion USD. Public debt interests paid were 87 billion USD. At the end of 2019, public debt attained 92 billion USD."[35] This broad financial overview shows that interest payments drained over 55 percent of the state's revenue. Were it not for these payments, the budget would have scored surpluses instead of deficits. It also shows that government has paid almost as much in interests as its total debt.

Public debt (and other expenditures) was neither a coincidence nor a mistake. It was the golden ticket to securing profits in one of Lebanon's longest bubbles. This bubble inflated bank capital 150 times over and piled up US$177 billion in deposits, half of which are owned by less than 1 percent of depositors. It also skyrocketed land prices, boosting real estate wealth to nearly US$1,100 billion, five times the value of financial wealth in bank deposits and capital invested in banks and corporations, according to Mansour Bteish's calculations.[36]

Usually, after a devastating war, states use debt to finance investments in reconstruction, expanding monetary aggregates, subsidizing demand, and boosting production and job creation. Debt, in this case, may be necessary, according to common economic theories, when increasing taxes is neither possible nor useful. However, this was never the purpose of the Lebanese public debt. Simply put, debt was the mechanism that capital chose in order to dispossess people of a large portion of their labor surpluses by reducing the value of their labor. What has been happening since 1993 confirms it. The government annulled progressive taxation on income, radically decreased tax rates on corporate profits to 10 percent, decreased customs fees on imports, exempted banking interests and real estate profits from direct taxation, and decreased Social Security fees, all while freezing wages between 1996 and 2012. These decisions have deprived the public treasury of substantial revenues that were compensated for with debt. Interest rates were raised to attract more deposits, instead of resorting to production and labor revenues. The monetary system was built to absorb these deposits and channel them to fund consumption and real estate sales.

The exchange rate of the LBP is the population's ultimate concern. This resulted from gargantuan efforts put into convincing people that its stability is a "mandatory" condition for the stability of the whole economy. However, the near total dollarization, tied to a fixed exchange rate of the LBP, was employed to attract capital inflow by guaranteeing massive profits.

At the beginning of 1993, shortly after Rafic Hariri's first government was formed, the former Central Bank governor, Michel El Khoury, and his deputies tendered their resignations, three years before the end of their term. Riad Salameh was appointed governor in his stead, where he remains to this day. All former governors of the Central Bank came from a background in "law," except Salameh whose specialization is in financial speculation. Hariri chose his "portfolio manager" at Merrill Lynch for the new governor position, confident that Governor Salameh would do just as good a job as he did in preserving and accumulating Hariri's personal wealth at an astonishing speed.

During the early 1990s, two illusions dominated the Lebanese mind: peace with Israel and the creation of an Arab fund for the reconstruction of Lebanon. Along these lines were also ideas of "catching up," compensating for time lost at war, and of anticipating the "prosperity of peace" that would take the form of huge investments. Paradoxically, the fall of these illusions did not incite a change of course in the economic modus operandi, to this very day.

Between 1993 and 1994, public debt jumped from 6,500 billion to over 12,000 billion LBP. By 1998, the government's public debt had exceeded the GDP (107 percent) and kept rising. Today, the state's total debt (government and BDL debts, after clearing) is valued at more than US$140 billion, US$90 billion of which is in foreign currencies compared to only US$300 million in 1992.

Between 1993 and 2004, ten years after launching "the project," the government's public debt service had surpassed the total investment expenditure five times over. Its accumulated total value exceeded all current expenditures on all public sectors, including salaries and wages, pensions, compensation fund for the displaced, the council of the South, containing the militias, and all the unwarranted public spending, waste, and corruption that came along with them.

To justify the high costs of his monetary policy, Salameh insists: fixing the price of the LBP is a "political decision" that he has to execute. His justification implies that he is well aware of the outrageous costs of his policy and of the presence of less costly alternatives. But his hands are tied, since the problem is not of his own making but that of the politicians who are not doing their job. They leave him to single-handedly deal with the consequences of their recklessness and selfishness, using his monetary skills and ample experience as a "financial engineer." These same tools he acquired at his (only) previous job at Merrill Lynch.

Salameh's words would have rung true were it not for one small detail that was deliberately left out. The idea that dominated the "reconstruction project" and what followed entailed keeping BDL neutral and granting it broad independence and power above (constitutional) powers. It also entailed constraining its actions to the sole purpose of attracting foreign capital and guaranteeing high revenues for capital surpluses invested in debt, real estate speculation, construction, imports, and tourism. This was the fastest way to fund public expenditure and stimulate consumption and economic growth. The problem does not seem to be with politicians not doing their duties, as much as it is with politicians passing them on to BDL from the very beginning. BDL was left to build a monetary system more powerful than any politician's ability to control or influence it, leaving them all hostages to that very system. Society was forced to come up with US$12 billion annually (a quarter of its GNI) to fund interests in order to maintain, increase, and absorb bank deposits through public, household, and corporate debts.

Thomas Piketty[37] says that central bank independence is "the source of numerous misunderstandings," especially after central banks became capable of creating money indefinitely. To the point where "faith in the stabilizing role of central banking at times seems inversely proportional to faith in the social and fiscal policies" and "there is no need for a welfare state and a prying government, only a good central bank governor." Here lies the crux of Lebanon's current crisis, "central banks do not create wealth as such; they redistribute it," according to Piketty. "It would be astonishing if central banks could simply, by the stroke of a pen, increase the capital of their nation or the world. What happens next depends on how this monetary policy influences the real economy." What was the actual impact of Lebanon's monetary policy on the real economy? Only one out of six newcomers to the job market ends up finding a job, often a low productive job in the service sector. Emigration of skilled labor increased and the share of labor from the total income dropped below 25 percent. Entrepreneurs turned to rent activities. This happened under the backdrop of a worsening addiction to foreign capital inflows and remittances from expatriates, in order to sustain an unsustainable situation.

The End of an Unsustainable Economic Model

The causes and consequences of the current crisis are being reduced to the collapse of the price of the LBP, as if the exchange rate is the end goal of any policy, not a tool to implement said policy. The Lebanese economy has only grown by an average of 1.8 percent between 2011 and 2017 and contracted by −11.3 percent between 2018 and 2020. Net job creation remained weak over twenty-five years and dropped to negative values in the past years—as the jobs lost have surpassed the jobs created. A very high percentage (55 percent) of the total workforce works in informal sectors, where wages are low and social and legal protection are absent. Entertainment services catering to rich Gulf tourists are dead. Real estate speculation is now teetering on the brink of collapse. FDIs are absent, and remittances will likely drop due to the declining economic conditions of host countries, oil-rich countries in particular. The balance of payments has been deficient since 2011 without serious indicators that surpluses can be made again without external support. Banks are bankrupt and the credit system is broken.

The current crisis has put an end to a stillborn economic system. We must now look to the future: who will benefit from our reconstructed economy? Will it serve society and achieve a better distribution of wealth and income? Or will it serve to accumulate and concentrate more capital in the hands of a happy minority at the expense of a miserable majority?

Notes

1 World Bank, Lebanon Economic Monitor, Spring 2021.
2 World Bank, Lebanon Economic Monitor: Lebanon Sinking (to the top 3), Spring 2021.
3 The Lebanese Government's Financial Recovery Plan, April 2020.
4 Lebanese parliament speaker Nabih Berri stated on August 31, 2020, that "the most dangerous revelation of the Beirut Port disaster, besides the failed factors in the state, is the fall of the political and economic structure completely."
5 Former prime minister Hassan Diab's speech at a meeting with honorary consuls in Lebanon, March 2, 2020.
6 Statistics of the balance of payments show that net deficits made between 2011 and 2020 surpass all net surplus made between 1991 and 2010.
7 N. Klein, *The Shock Doctrine: The Rise of Disaster Capitalism* (New York: Metropolitan Books, 2007).

8 Milton Friedman was an American economist and the recipient of the 1976 Nobel Memorial Prize in Economic Sciences. He is considered one of the leading intellectuals of the Chicago School of Economics and of economic liberalism.

9 President of the Republic Michel Aoun answering with "we are going to hell" when asked where the country was headed.

10 Central Administration of Statistics, Labour Force and Household Living Conditions Survey in Lebanon, 2018/2019.

11 Estimates of household income were converted from LBP to USD at the 15,000 LBP rate in June 2021.

12 World Bank, Lebanon Economic Monitor: Lebanon Sinking (to the top 3), Spring 2021.

13 United Nations Children's Fund (UNICEF), "Lebanon: Children's Future on the Line," June 2021.

14 World Food Programme (WFP), phone survey conducted at the end of 2020.

15 UNICEF, Ibid.

16 United Nations Economic and Social Commission for Western Asia (ESCWA), "Multidimensional poverty in Lebanon (2019–2021): Painful reality and uncertain prospects."

17 Customs Statistics, 2020.

18 The Lebanese Government's Financial Recovery Plan, April 2020.

19 The Lebanese Government decided to default on paying Eurobonds in March 2020.

20 WFP, Ibid.

21 At the change rate of 15,000 LBP in June 2021.

22 World Bank, rapid firm-level survey, August 2021.

23 International Monetary Fund (IMF), database of member countries.

24 The Paris II conference was held in 2002 with the participation of twenty-seven countries as well as regional and international financial institutions to give Lebanon an aid worth US$4.4 billion and support the Lebanese government in preventing a financial crisis that was imminent at the time.

25 Charbel Nahas, "An Economic and Social Program for Lebanon" (Barnamaj Iqtisadi Ijtima'i Min Ajl Loubnan), *Lebanese Center for Policy Studies*, 2005.

26 Michel Chiha, "Face and Presence of Lebanon" (Visage et présence du Liban), *Cénacle Libanais*, 1962.

27 In 1920, Greater Lebanon was announced through redrawing borders under the French and British mandates after adding areas in the South, Bekaa, and the North to the Mount Lebanon Mutasarrifate under the Ottoman rule.

28 D. C. North, J. J. Wallis, S. B. Webb and B. R. Weingast, *In the Shadow of Violence: A New Perspective on Development (2015)*. Available at https://ssrn.com/abstract =2653254 or http://dx.doi.org/10.2139/ssrn.2653254.

29 Ibid.

30 Lydia Assouad, "Lebanon's Political Economy: From Predatory to Self-Devouring," *Carnegie Middle East Center*, 2021.

31 World Bank, Lebanon Economic Monitor, 2018.

32 World Bank, Presentation to the Ministry of Labor under the Miles program, 2010.

33 Naomi Klein, "The Shock Doctrine: The Rise of Disaster Capitalism."

34 D. Harvey, *A Companion to Marx's Capital: The Complete Edition* (London and New York: Verso Books, 2018).

35 Charbel Nahas, An Economy and a State for Lebanon (Iqtisad Wa Dawla Li Loubnan), *Riad El-Rayyes Books*.

36 Mansour Bteish, "Public Budget: Lebanese State's Revenues (Reality and Aspirations)"
    (Al Maliyya Al Aamma: Iradat Al Dawla Al Loubnaniyya [Waqeh Wa Tatalloua'at]),
    Dar Saer Al Mashrek.
37 T. Piketty, *Capital in the Twenty-First Century* (Cambridge, MA and London: The
    Belknap Press of Harvard University Press, 2014).

4

Wondering about the Social

Samer Frangie

Boredom, Wonder, and Politics

It was a hot, humid, and sluggish summer in expectation, like summers have been in Lebanon for years. But this particular one, the summer of 2015, had a distinct taste to it, that of boredom.

A few years had passed since the excitement of the Arab uprisings. They were now a faint memory, buried under the violent counterrevolutionary restorations that closed the possibilities opened up for a brief moment in 2011. In their wake, the hopes of that moment were disciplined, forced into the binaries of success/defeat, and relegated to the margins of Arab politics. After some years of political turbulence, boredom settled also in Lebanon, with the ruling elites reasserting a precarious status quo whose sole purpose was to reproduce their hold over the dwindling resources of the country. Things seem to have returned to their "normal" state, normal being defined as closed political systems, with no possibilities of change.

Boredom is not simply an emotion or a sentiment that stems from encountering an uninteresting fact or from having nothing to do. It is a disciplinary tool: the imposition of the viscous sense that things are as they appear, as they have always been and will be, heavy in their repetitions, constrained in their potentialities, corrosive in their self-assurance. It is what Rancière's police intervention asserts every time it reminds individuals of the "obviousness of what there is, or rather, of what there isn't."[1] Boredom is the affect that accompanies the successful imposition or reimposition of a social order. There is nothing interesting in it, there is nothing to see there, move along.

Boredom found in the humid and sticky summer of 2015 its climate.

Boredom is not the topic of this chapter. Wonder is, the sense that things are not as they seem, the disposition that emerges from meeting the world *as if* for the first time.

This chapter is interested in thinking the uprising of October 2019 in Lebanon and the subsequent unraveling of the political and economic system from the perspective of that emotion, wonder. It approaches phenomenologically uprisings and breakdowns as moments of wonder, moments in which what *is* and what *appears* do not seem to be aligned anymore. In trying to recapture this disposition inherent to these moments of crises, the chapter draws our attention to the various ways wonder is disciplined, constrained, restricted, and evacuated from our social experience.

The present line of investigation begins from a personal sense of wonder, at the unfolding of the events on that fateful night of October 17. It was a personal sense of wonder but one that was echoed in different ways by most of those who were in the streets during this month: a sentiment of disbelief, of joyful incomprehension, of rediscovering the familiar, of frustration at those who wanted to make sense of it too quickly. It was a realization that spurred so many late-night discussions, but that was quickly brushed aside as nonpolitical, as a "feeling" that had no political implications or, worse, as a disposition that needed to be quickly disciplined to allow for politics, as the more serious activities, to emerge.

It is against this sense of "seriousness" that the chapter wants to push politics, not in order to deny its gravity but, on the contrary, to relocate it partly as a moment of wonder.

Trash

Back to the summer of 2015. Boredom was settling in, in anticipation of the recurrence of the same.

But then something happened. We did not at first notice anything out of the ordinary. A few trash bags accumulated here and there, explained away as localized incidents. After all, Lebanon was notorious for its inefficient social services. But this was not the usual temporary breakdown in the public infrastructure, like the summer electricity cuts or the routine shortage of water supplies. Silently, inexorably, relentlessly, the garbage kept piling up, closing whole streets transformed into makeshift dumps, erupting in mountains of fuming and fermenting waste. Suddenly, we were shaken out of our torpid boredom, forced to face, see, smell, feel, with a renewed sense of wonder, the decrepitude of our social existence. The "common-sense obviousness of the 'proper' position of things in space," in that case trash, was disturbed forcing us to examine anew the "naturalness" (in the two senses of the term) of our social existence.[2] This was not a simple institutional failure, resulting from the corruption of some political elites. It was a transgression, an eruption of unwanted matter in our social spaces, that brought to the fore the whole infrastructure of corruption and rent-seeking that sustained the postwar political economy. It was an eruption of historicity that drew unforeseen connections, or unmasked existing ones, ties that brought together makeshift landfills, the consumption habits of the population, the incidence of cancer rate, and the institutional decay of the postwar era.

Before a sense of outrage or injustice, it was this dissonance that shook everyone out of the boredom. There must be a question first, before we can start having answers to it. There was something to see after all, contrary to what the police was saying. And what was there to see was the slow and imperceptible erosion of the postwar political system, the imbrication of the political and the natural, and the inescapable disaster the country was heading into.[3] What might have been known at some analytical level was now felt viscerally, disturbing all senses of familiarity and propriety.

From the rift between how things appeared and how they were supposed to be erupted a long summer of demonstrations, itself an event that was deemed unthinkable previously. The cognitive dissonance freed the underlying sentiment of outrage and injustice from the shackles imposed by the boredom of the previous status quo. Things are not what they seem, do not have to be what they seem, a realization that provides outrage with the opening it needs to become a political emotion.

Wonder

Wonder is the disposition that results from encountering the world without the guarantees of social norms, familiarities, and expectations, *as if* we were meeting it for the first time. It captures the hesitation, fear, excitement, apprehension, aversion, surprise, and anxiety we face when taken by an object by surprise, when our sense of familiarity is ruptured, forcing us to face the world anew, or as if anew, without the guarantees of past understanding. It captures not only the hesitation but also the trepidation and curiosity that erupts at the sight of an opening that allows for a possible *new* to emerge, for an unexpected beginning to erupt. As a sentiment or disposition, wonder has often been considered as the "first passion of all" in the history of philosophy, the emotion we face when startled by the world, that sets in motion philosophy itself.

Wonder can start from trash.

Wonder is not, or does not have to be, a puritan emotion, a return to an unadulterated vision of the social world, prior to any historical sedimentation. In her discussion of wonder, the feminist theorist Sara Ahmed proposes an understanding of wonder that does not oppose it to historicity but rather sees it as a moment of reckoning with the historical nature of the social world:

> I would suggest that wonder allows us to see the surfaces of the world *as made*, and as such wonder opens up rather than suspends historicity. Historicity is what is concealed by the transformation of the world into "the ordinary," into something that is already familiar, or recognizable.[4]

The new is not opposed to historicity but on the contrary stems from it, from the encounter with the contingent manners we have been made who we are. The new does not emerge from a rejection of historical determinations but rather from the contingent interstices of that historicity. Ahmed writes:

> To see the world as if for the first time is to notice that which is there, is made, has arrived, or is extraordinary. Wonder is about learning to see the world as something that does not have to be, and as something that came to be, over time, and with work.[5]

To wonder is not to see a thing for the first time; it is to experience it *as if* for the first time, to experience it differently, in an unfamiliar way or an unexpected manner. It is to see it in new settings or behaving differently than it has for the foreseeable past. It is about discovering a different interconnectedness, one that coexists uneasily with the previous discourses that organized social life, so that they stand in a hesitant and tense relation to our established manners of making sense of them. It is to come face to face with the unavowed materiality of social existence and the various ways in which it is domesticated in "normal" times. It is to experience the world without the boundaries of a fully formed self, with the arbitrary reaching deep into our most intimate thoughts.

Historicity and Crises

It is when things break down that we start wondering about them.

The regime survived the trash crisis of 2015. But the systemic crisis it symptomatized was already well underway. Starting in 2016, the economic and financial indicators became uncontroversial in their conclusions, only questioned by the irrational hopes of economists welded to the system. Rumors started abounding about the upper classes sending their money abroad, interest rates skyrocketed to try to convince them otherwise, and the public infrastructure of the country continued its downward spiral.[6] In the summer of 2019, fires raged in Lebanon, made worse by the inability of the fire brigades to control them due to endemic corruption.[7] Following the proposal to introduce a tax on WhatsApp, a proposal that was as unjust as it displayed the incompetence of the ruling elites, anger erupted in spontaneous demonstrations all over the country, unleashing what will become the most significant protest movement in the contemporary history of Lebanon.

It was not simply anger that moved people, or a sense of outrage, but the realization that things were not anymore as they appeared.[8] The "regime" being opposed was a regime being discovered in the act of opposing it, its contours discovered at the rhythm of the growing street protests. The breakdown of the regime, the act of opposing it, and the discovery of its underlying logics all collapsed as different facets of the same movement. From opposing the endemic corruption, to resisting policy brutality, to questioning the financial and economic policies of the postwar regime, to militating for women's rights, the uprising, almost by *tâtonnement*, was an occasion to feel differently the regime, to look at the ways it has been made in its moment of unmaking.

The uprising was folded in an epistemological crisis, a breakdown of what Alasdair MacIntyre calls the "accustomed ways for relating *seems* and *is*."[9] And nothing captures better the distance between how things appear and what they are than a financial crisis, a crisis in the mode of representation of value, or even of value itself.

At the rhythm of the falling exchange rate, the mystification necessary for capitalist accumulation was corroded. Money lost its function, whether as a store of value or an instrument of exchange, destroying social conventions, economic lives, and collective temporalities. In this general state of corrosion, the financial structure that sustained the political economy of rent extraction that dominated the country's postwar settlement was laid bare for all to see. A hidden interconnectedness started appearing, linking various aspects of our social existence to that mystical figure of the exchange rate, itself now linked to governmental policies, economic entities, and global institutions such as the *International Monetary Fund*. It was not a cognitive appearance but an affective one. The "abstract" economic and financial crises reached deep into people's livelihood, destroying them, reshuffling them, transforming them in ways that were felt viscerally. The banks, previously sites of respectability, became sites of contestations, with daily scenes of protests at what was justly felt as theft and extortion.[10] And around these feelings of outrage and dispossession, common interests were discovered, leading to their own organized form of protests around particular grievances, such as the *Association of Depositors* or the *Lebanese Association for Parents of Students in Foreign Universities*.

Wonder does not have to be an encounter with the sublime; it could stem from the realization of the historicity of the manners we have been governed. The breakdown of the postwar system and the ensuing uprising were the occasion to discover, or even wonder, at the various ways we had been made as political subjects, as governed subjects: a realization of the ways we have been made into what we are, in the moment of our undoing.

Reflexive Crises

Wonder is contagious. Its suspicion, that things as they seem are not as they are, quickly turns to doubt the wondering gaze itself.

The "we" itself was engulfed by the crisis, the revolutionary "we" that was supposed to be the subject of the uprising. What seemed first as a homogenous popular uprising lost its self-certainty to appear as a more complex, hesitant, even contradictory event, fraught with lines of frictions and tensions. With the passing of months, the uprising was unpacked into the various dynamics that made it, the regional, gender, class, generational, or even sectarian dynamics that coalesced into a popular uprising before fragmenting again. There was no "we" at the end of these months, whether resisting, wondering, or discovering. It was not the world only that was experienced as something that does not have to be anymore; we were experienced as subjects that does not have to be, even though we were not sure what we could be.

To talk about failure or success with respect to revolutionary acts has become one of the taboos of committed scholarship, in its rejection of binaries and simplification. If such statements cannot capture the complexities of historical episodes such as uprisings and should be resisted, especially when they are the prelude to the reassertions of essentialist visions of the social world, their experiential weight cannot be denied that easily, nor should it. To feel or experience an event as having failed without being engulfed by that sentiment might be the dissonance needed to keep it alive by reexamining its conditions of existence. In his essay on the relationship between experience and method in historiography, Reinhart Koselleck writes about the epistemological potential of the experience of being vanquished. For the vanquished of history,

Their first primary experience is that everything happened differently from how it was planned or hoped. If they reflect methodologically at all, they face a greater burden of proof to explain why something happened in this and not the anticipated way. From this, a search for middle- or long-range reasons might be initiated to frame and perhaps explain the chance event of the unique surprise. It is thus an attractive hypothesis that precisely from the unique gains in experience imposed upon them spring insights of lasting duration and, consequently, of greater explanatory power. If history is made in the short run by the victors, historical gains in knowledge stem in the long run from the vanquished.[11]

Defeat, or the sentiment of failure, is not the end of the uprising. It is rather the occasion to move beyond its immediate political result to capture it as part of a broader questioning. It is what generalizes an uprising from an unexpected answer into a question, a question that can sustain the state of wonder against all the claims of defeat or failure.

Beginnings and the Viscosity of the Social

To experience the world as if for the first time is to experience beginnings.

What started as an uprising against a corrupt government, well delimited by the dominant discourses of civil society activism, quickly trespassed its respectable boundaries. The succession of crises in a short span of time culminated in a broader crisis of legitimacy of the regime, one that could not be contained anymore in the preexisting modes of vision and division of the social world. It was not *simply* a political or an economic crisis, but rather it was *felt* as a broader unraveling, one that trespassed the preexisting conceptions of disciplinary propriety and social divisions. What transpires from these long months of crises and uprising were a series of questioning as to how (and why) we have become these particular economic subjects, gendered subjects, national subjects and the particular institutional, discursive, and cultural mechanisms that contributed to these processes of construction.

It is in times of crisis that we start wondering about the social in these terms, as Latour writes:

> The question of the social emerges when the ties in which one is entangled begin to unravel; the social is further detected through the surprising movements from one association to the next; those movements can either be suspended or resumed; when they are prematurely suspended, the social as normally constructed is bound together with already accepted participants called "social actors" who are members of a "society"; . . .[12]

We can think of the question of the social, rather than the social question, as a concept of/in crisis. It is a reflexive form of knowledge, one that turns its gaze inward to question its own condition of conceptual possibilities. The question of the social is the state of generalized wonder, the name of the overarching questioning of society that happens in moments of crisis. It is this wondering that took to the streets, to the banks, to the port, to the intimate confines of the society, in a process of discovery and self-discovery, a process that could not end with the repression of the demonstrations.

To think of the question of the social as the questioning brought forth by an uprising is to approach it an almost antithetical way than Arendt has famously done.

Arendt opposed the notion of revolution to that of the "social," based on her radically different readings of the American and French Revolutions, the latter having devoured its own children because it succumbed to the diktats of the "social question." Arendt's deeply controversial opposition hinged on her definition of both terms, the revolution and the social. A revolution is neither a change in institutions, however violent nor a widespread popular uprising but has to do with what Arendt calls in *The Human Condition*, action, or the human capacity to begin anew, to do the unexpected in a condition characterized by plurality and publicness.[13] "Only where this pathos of novelty is present and where novelty is connected with the idea of freedom," Arendt writes, "are we entitled to speak of revolution."[14] What threatens this capacity to institute freedom is the social question, by which Arendt means in *On Revolution* the existence of poverty, which puts men under the control of a biological necessity with its ensuing emotions of rage and pity.

> When [the multitude of the poor] appeared on the scene of politics, necessity appeared with them, and the result was that the power of the old regime became impotent and the new republic was stillborn; freedom had to be surrendered to necessity, to the urgency of the life process itself.[15]

Arendt has been justly criticized for her reading that reduces the revolution to an act of freedom by an elite, freed from the hold of social considerations. As Hanna Fenichel Pitkin noted, Arendt's conception of the "social" takes on different meanings across her work, united by their opposition to the political. Whether it referred to the sphere of mutual dependence for the sake of life, the generalization of the household form, the conformism of society, the alienation of the modern mass, or the roots of totalitarianism, the social appears as an irresistible and inevitable outgrowth that threatens the possibility even of political action. And beyond its reduction to poverty, as it happens with *On Revolution*, the social according to Pitkin means "a collectivity of people who—for whatever reason—conduct themselves in such a way that they cannot control or even intentionally influence the large-scale consequences of their activities."[16] The social, in other words, is the realm of alienation, false appearance, deception, and falsehood, which stands in opposition to the political or the public and plural sphere of human action: "The social kind of 'unitedness of many into one is basically antipolitical; it is the very opposite of the togetherness' characterizing political membership."[17]

Closing Off Wonder

One does not have to accept Arendt's stark opposition between the political and the social, or her definition of either terms. But what remains from her analysis are questions that are still pertinent regarding today's revolution: How do we remain truthful to the moment of beginning and the sentiment of wonder that accompanies it? And can we maintain it or revolutions are by definition momentary moments, condemned to be "normalized," leaving those attached to wonder constantly looking to relive these initial moments? Or to put it differently, does wonder have any political value that requires us to protect it from the various ways in which it is disciplined and closed off, Arendt's conception of the social being one of them? Is there something in the aesthetics of beginnings that can provide some grounding for an ethics of justice?

Wonder is not only disciplined by the "regime" and its various claims that what appears is what is, irremediably and irrevocably. Wonder can also be disciplined or normalized by a tradition of social criticism, for whom the social has been not only an answer but also a space of promise and emancipation. Understood in this spatial way, the social was condemned to marginality, squeezed between subterranean sectarian logics on one hand and the mesh of geopolitical interests on the other, in a tragic play of never-ending betrayal, defeat, and heroic exile. And it was this space that was respectively inhabited by the Marxian critique of the prewar and then its liberal inheritor of the postwar, a space that has refused to wonder, preferring the certitudes of the margins to the questions of beginning.

Ironically, it is maybe the regime that has taken stock of the deep changes coming, adapting itself to what might be a new social structure emerging. Surveying the country after the collapse of its economy, the only certitude we have is that social life has changed and will change irrevocably. We are at the cusp of a major social transformation, one whose contours are still undetermined. Witnessing our social conditions of existence being violently transformed cannot but question our most basic social certainties. Wonder does not have to be a pleasant affect; it could also be triggered by a sense of collapse or catastrophe, spurred by the urgency of making sense of the senseless, just in order to survive. To wonder might be all we have, an acknowledgment that who we thought we were is now a distant past.

Notes

1　Jacques Rancière, "Ten Theses on Politics," *Theory & Event* 5, no. 3 (2001): 9.
2　Tim Edensor, "Waste Matter: The Debris of Industrial Ruins and the Disordering of the Material World," *Journal of Material Culture* 10, no. 3 (2005): 312.
3　Ziad Abu-Rish, "Garbage Politics," *Middle East Research and Information Project* 45, no. 277 (Winter 2015), https://merip.org/2016/03/garbage-politics/; Reinoud Leenders, *Spoils of Truce: Corruption and State Building in Postwar Lebanon* (Ithaca: Cornell University Press, 2012), Toufic Gaspard, *A Political Economy of Lebanon, 1948–2002: The Limits of Laissez-Faire* (Leiden: Brill, 2003), Roland Riachi, "Filthy Flows of Power: A Political Ecology of Disasters in Lebanon," in *The Lebanon Uprising of 2019: Voices from the Revolution*, ed. Jeffrey G. Karam and Rima Majed (London: I.B. Tauris and Bloomsbury, 2022).
4　Sara Ahmed, *The Cultural Politics of Emotion* (Edinburgh: Edinburgh University Press, 2014), 179–80.
5　Ibid.

6 Mohamad Zbeeb, "Lebanon's Post-War Political Economy: From Reconstruction to Collapse," in *The Lebanon Uprising of 2019: Voices from the Revolution*, ed. Jeffrey G. Karam and Rima Majed (London: I.B. Tauris and Bloomsbury, 2022).

7 Riachi, "Filthy Flows of Power."

8 Sara Mourad, "Appearing as Women," in *The Lebanon Uprising of 2019: Voices from the Revolution*, ed. Jeffrey G. Karam and Rima Majed (London: I.B. Tauris and Bloomsbury, 2022).

9 Alasdair MacIntyre, "Epistemological Crises, Dramatic Narrative, and the Philosophy of Science," *The Monist* 60, no. 4 (1977): 453–72, 459.

10 Mohammad Bzeih, "Night of the Banks: Uprising Against the Rule of Banks," in *The Lebanon Uprising of 2019: Voices from the Revolution*, ed. Jeffrey G. Karam and Rima Majed (London: I.B. Tauris and Bloomsbury, 2022).

11 Reinhart Koselleck, *The Practice of Conceptual History: Timing History, Spacing Concepts* (Stanford: Stanford University Press, 2002), 76.

12 Bruno Latour, *Reassembling the Social: An Introduction to Actor-Network Theory* (Oxford: Oxford University Press, 2005), 247.

13 Hannah Arendt, *The Human Condition* (Chicago: The University of Chicago Press, 1998).

14 Hannah Arendt, *On Revolution* (London: Penguin, 2006), 34.

15 Ibid., 60.

16 Hanna Fenichel Pitkin, *The Attack of the Blob: Hannah Arendt's Concept of the Social* (Chicago: The University of Chicago Press, 1998), 16.

17 Ibid., 194.

5

Law in Times of Revolution

A Double-Edged Sword of Repression and Resistance

Lama Karamé

The October 17 uprising brought up a difficult question for legal advocates: how can we serve the uprising's goals while employing law, the establishment's sharpest weapon? This paradox follows an appeal to law that is entrenched in our daily acts of mobilization. "Beneath the shattered streets and shallow graves almost ubiquitous in states tortured by civil war and political violence, the law is present and articulated as a form of salvation," Mark Fathi Massoud rightly notes in his ethnography of legal politics in postwar Sudan.[1]

Departing from the "normative position-taking on the instrumental value of legal tactics,"[2] this chapter offers an empirical examination of the multiple usages of law within the October 17 uprising. For that purpose, I focus on the impact of legal discourse on the collective mobilization of protesters and discuss the recourse to law by the Lebanese state for the coercion and persecution of protesters and by lawyers to leverage repression. The entanglement of law with political mobilization (and countermobilization)[3] will reveal to be at the service of both control and resistance. The chapter culminates with a reflection on the value of legal politics within a context of structural inequalities and the circumstances that may foster a space where legal mobilization can be at the service of the broader sociopolitical goals of the uprising.

I have drawn on data available in the public domain—namely, statements and documentation by the Lawyers Committee for the Defense of the Protesters (LCDP) and its collaborators, the Lebanese Association of Judges, protester groups, and media reports. Personal observations have undoubtedly shaped this analysis. I have limited the discussion to the events that unfolded between October 17, 2019, and March 15, 2020, the eve of the COVID-19 lockdown. This does not translate into an adherence to a short-term temporality of the uprising, as key events that occurred outside that time frame—the fatal August 4 blast, followed by a series of legal repressions and the trial of several protesters in April 2021—were incorporated into the analysis.

Law in the Streets: A Political Tool of Contention

Despite being a complex and diverse movement, a common thread could be observed in the October uprising: the reliance of protesters on legal discourse as part of a repertoire of contention.

A few weeks after the protests began, the regime attempted to stifle popular calls for change by enacting a series of "reformist" laws, the most prominent of which was a blanket amnesty law. Activists were quick to dissect the bill, revealing that it provided amnesty to public officials accused of serious misconduct, including embezzlement, corruption, torture, and forced disappearances.[4] On November 11, 2019, the Legal Agenda, the Lebanese Professionals Association,[5] and several legal experts held a press conference where they exposed the dangers of this bill, among other bills figuring on the parliament's agenda, and called for a general strike to halt the upcoming legislative session.[6] The Lebanese Judges Association issued a statement condemning the bill for prioritizing amnesty over accountability and slammed it as a blow to judicial independence.[7] Human rights organizations joined in the denunciation,[8] and the media picked up on the legal discourse, fueling calls for a general strike.[9] As a result, Speaker of the Parliament announced postponing the session scheduled for November 12 to the 19th of the month due to "security reasons."[10] On November 19, protesters took to the streets and blocked all six entrances to the parliament building, preventing lawmakers from reaching parliament and enacting a hollow piece of reform. The session was canceled again, this time due to a lack of quorum.[11]

Mobilization around the amnesty law became a milestone in the history of the uprising and provided an exemplary case study on how legal framing, or the inclusion of legality in collective action frames,[12] fuels political mobilization. While the regime attempted to use a series of legal reforms to gain public support, legal mobilization facilitated the deconstruction of the regime's rhetoric by mainstreaming legal knowledge and removing it from the grip of experts and technocrats.[13]

The space accorded to law during the uprising was both physical[14]—town squares across the country overflowed with demonstrators attending daily discussion sessions on legal issues ranging from constitutional reform and anti-corruption legislation to personal status laws—and symbolic, in the sense that legal discourse created a shared narrative among protesters to "name and challenge existing wrongs."[15] Political mobilization was nurtured with references to law, legal symbols, and discourses, thus resulting in the reliance on legal discourse in the course of "agenda setting."[16] For instance, a draft bill on the independence of the judiciary formerly presented to parliament in 2018, attracting little public attention then, gained considerable momentum with the uprising, and its enactment figured among the protesters' top demands.[17] Specifically, the unprecedented interest in the role of the judiciary was reflected in the slogans of the uprising, sit-ins in front of and inside courthouses,[18] and the mobilization of public opinion in support of internal judicial battles, such as the appointment of judges.[19]

The legal framing of contention was also made possible through the unprecedented involvement of legal professions—long considered pillars of the establishment—in the uprising.[20] In several ways, lawyers became the "backbone" of the uprising. In addition to the LCDP, the proliferation of legal counseling groups was remarkable: the Depositors Union,[21] the Union of Parents' Committees for the parents of students in private schools,[22] and the Lebanese Observatory for the Rights of Workers and Employees[23] are only a few examples. The involvement of lawyers extended beyond their traditional professional responsibilities, sometimes even playing active political roles. For example, they were frequently approached to give talks and interviews and write op-eds and articles explaining the law and offering their views on the uprising.[24]

The political commitment of lawyers created tensions in their relationship with their own bar associations. In its first statement, Houkoukiyoun, a newly formed group of lawyers, called on the Beirut Bar Association (BBA) to follow the lead of the North Bar and support the uprising, hinting at the BBA's lukewarm position.[25] The statement urging lawyers to wear their professional robes and head to a sit-in in Martyrs' Square was widely shared and adopted by rights groups. André Chidiac, the then president of the BBA, issued a text message on October 26, 2019, the same day of the sit-in, alerting lawyers of the illegality of wearing robes outside of official events.[26] Despite the many threats, lawyers attended the sit-in, defiantly attired in their professional robes, making their collective body strikingly visible among the protesters.[27] The lawyers' support was crystallized on the one-month anniversary of the uprising with the election of Melhem Khalaf as the new president of the BBA on November 17, 2019.[28] This was the first professional association election to take place since the uprising began, represented as a confrontation between the regime—a coalition of different political parties—and Khalaf,[29] a lawyer renowned for his civic engagement, who had volunteered in 2015 to defend protesters.[30] The announcement of the results was welcomed with the emblematic "Hela Ho"[31] echoing loud throughout the Beirut courthouse as Khalaf was celebrated as the "candidate of the uprising" and his election as its first victory.[32]

The breakthrough within the "legal complex"[33] was also noticeable in the judiciary, with a vocal Judges Association issuing over twenty statements in support of protesters' demands between October 2019 and mid-March 2020.[34] The association escalated its opposition after the August 4 blast, reiterating its demand for the resignation of public officials—yet, this time extending the invitation to the Supreme Judicial Council (SJC).[35] The political significance of these statements stems from the complex context leading to the establishment of the association in 2018, after a decade of discussions between judges and in overt defiance of the SJC and the regime.[36] It is worth noting the unprecedented involvement of legal professors in popular protests: the Faculty of Law and Political Science at the Saint Joseph University, the oldest law school in Lebanon, set a tent in the Azariyeh square, hosting several talks held by eminent professors of the elite school.[37]

Law against the Street? Policing Protests or the Penalization of Dissent

Between October 17, 2019, and March 15, 2020, there were 967 persons arrested,[38] whereas 230 were summoned for interrogation and questioning before the judicial police or public prosecutors.[39] Another 732 were injured, 109 of whom suffered permanent or temporary damages.[40] While 86.7 percent of the injuries resulted from attacks by various security forces, 11 percent resulted from assaults by civilian supporters of political parties keen on protecting the regime,[41] allegedly the Amal movement and Hezbollah.[42] Protesters were met with a plethora of rights violations, leading the regime to employ a legal discourse to justify the extreme violence.[43]

In Lebanese law, the decision to detain or release a suspect initially falls under the prosecutor's powers. The judge decides on the time of release, whether to prosecute the suspect, and if so, on what charges. It is at these three stages—detention, prosecution, and charging—that the judicial tendency to penalize protests emerged. Prosecutors resorted to "retaliatory detention" whereby they would delay the release of protesters, even after they had concluded their interrogations, thus transforming pretrial detention into a pretrial penalty.[44] The prosecution adopted a repressive interpretation of existing law, manipulating it to create new parameters of crimes to charge protesters with. In certain key demonstrations, protesters were charged with serious felonies, some of which carried the death penalty, such as inciting civil war, attempting to murder military personnel, kidnapping, and inciting sectarianism.[45] The prosecution also preempted protesters' accusations of torture by charging them with "violence against security personnel."[46] More ominously, on February 22, 2021, the military prosecutor charged thirty protesters with terrorism, following the events leading to the burning of the Municipality of Tripoli.[47]

This manipulation not only was dangerous in that it provided harsher penalties for protesters but also because it created a rhetoric of the "good and civilized" protester versus the "bad and dangerous" insurgent.[48] In deploying the narrative of the "civilized" protester, the regime provided grounds for security forces to continue the attacks and arrests and attempted to discredit the movement. This rhetoric transcended the regime's narrative and was ultimately echoed in the street, promoting ideological schisms between protesters calling for "nonviolent" and "civilized" protests[49] and others justifying more direct action.[50] The state's resort to law was an attempt to deter individuals from participating in the uprising, but it can also be read as an effort to transform a political issue into a question of law and order, a common tactic in policing protests.[51] Through arrests and detentions, the regime attempted to shift the issue from the sphere of political contention to that of (il)legality, thus depoliticizing the act of dissent and detaching it from its context.[52] When the August 4 port explosion stirred the protests, the regime renewed its legal tactics, this time announcing a state of emergency in the destroyed city, granting exceptional powers to the military,[53] and legitimizing the excessive use of force against mourning protesters.[54]

Undoubtedly, the selective use of law is neither exceptional nor limited to the cases of protesters, but rather a symptom of the lack of judicial independence and the ties of allegiances between public prosecutors and the regime.[55] Furthermore, it reflects the indeterminacy of law itself[56] and the extent to which the understanding and interpretation of law is informed by the personal and political considerations of criminal justice actors.[57] The malleability of law helps state power sustain itself,[58] and it is through this prism that legal activism should be understood.

Out of the Streets and into the Courtrooms

It only took a few hours into the night of October 17, 2019, for the emblematic image of a hand overlaid with the LCDP hotline's phone number to be widely shared.[59] The picture, first circulated in 2015, urged protesters to write the hotline's number on their hands in case of arrest.[60] Founded during the YouStink movement—a series of protests against the garbage crisis in 2015—the LCDP is a "group of Lebanese lawyers and legal professionals, volunteering to defend protesters and demonstrators."[61] Members follow up arrest outcomes, provide legal counsel, and represent those charged in court. While the involvement of lawyers in political movements is often associated with litigation rather than grassroots mobilization and effective political organizing, the LCDP's activism has revealed a merger of legalist lawyering with grassroots and political lawyering.[62] The intertwining of their dual roles as activists and professionals was enshrined in their slogan "In the Squares, Our Voice Is With You; In Police Stations, We Are Your Voice."[63]

Initially adopting a reactive strategy of "self-preservation" to defend protesters and fight for their release, state repression drove the LCDP to shift toward a proactive strategy of political and legal mobilization. Security forces attempted to thwart detainees' access to legal assistance by refusing lawyers' entry to police stations or allowing it only after the investigation had ended.[64] In doing so, they relied on a misinterpretation of article 47 of the Code of Criminal Procedure, which guarantees the right of detainees to meet with a lawyer, claiming such right was restricted to the appointment of legal counsel.[65] Lawyers who had formerly defied this practice through informal channels[66] gained considerable support with Khalaf's election. "No place shall be closed off to a lawyer!," Khalaf announced in front of the Helou police station after meeting with lawyers and detainees.[67] He would later intervene to allow lawyers access to detention centers, including the Information Branch and the Intelligence Directorate of the Ministry of Defense, two previously inaccessible security bodies.[68] This battle resulted in the amendment of article 47 in September 2020, which now unambiguously guarantees the presence of a lawyer during preliminary investigations.[69]

When protesters arrested by Military Intelligence were refused the right to call their families and authorities refused to disclose their whereabouts, the LCDP, making use of Law 105 on Missing and Forcibly Disappeared Persons—which until then had remained untouched—filed reports on the forced disappearance of twenty-eight of them.[70] Although the prosecution dismissed the reports and made no efforts to investigate the allegations of forced disappearance, lawyers succeeded in using the law to leverage and pressure authorities to disclose their place of arrest.[71] The LCDP also filed fifteen torture complaints on behalf of seventeen protesters who had been subjected to psychological and physical torture by security forces.[72] Unlike previous practices, the cassation public prosecutor transferred the complaints to the military court prosecutor, who assumed his jurisdiction over complaints against security personnel. When victims of torture refused to give their testimony before the forces that tortured them, the military prosecutor decided to close the case.[73]

Faced with the reluctance of the prosecution to investigate the cases of forced disappearances and torture, the LCDP escalated its offensive strategy. In a press conference at the BBA on February 6, 2020, lawyers publicly accused the prosecution of being the "protector of the regime."[74] With a poster of a beaten protester behind them, lawyers expressed their disenchantment with the role of the judiciary and the security forces, openly accusing the latter of torture. They insisted on the role of "institutions," calling on judges to assume responsibility for protecting protesters, risking the appearance of "popular courts" and the "mounting of gallows."[75] The LCDP's statements were no less critical of the orchestrated attacks by political parties or the organized robbery instigated by the financial banking system.[76]

A year later in April 2021, as court sessions were scheduled for prosecuted protesters, the LCDP brought its political discourse to the courtrooms, opting for a combination of traditional legal defense and political pleadings. In addition to proving the lack of evidence to prosecute the defendants, the LCDP's oral pleadings constituted a political indictment of the public prosecution, as lawyers argued that the arbitrary prosecution of protesters without evidence constitutes a form of preemptive and immediate penalty. In fact, lawyers further denounced the expansion of military court jurisdiction,[77] an issue the LCDP had been fighting against since the prosecutions of 2015. Calling on the court to issue a reasoned decision—that is, containing a detailed analysis of the rationale—lawyers culminated their pleadings with demands for the exoneration of the accused on the grounds of discharge (i.e., considering the grounds of prosecution as unsubstantiated) rather than acquittal. While, in practice, both decisions would have guaranteed the defendants' release, the LCDP's request was motivated by their strategy of attacking the prosecution's arbitrary charges.[78]

By April 2021, the LCDP had represented fifty-one protesters, forty-nine of whom were found innocent.[79] Although the military court dismissed the demand for discharge, the final verdict bears little significance compared with the legal and the public forum the trial offers.[80] Through their oral pleadings, lawyers brought their political discourse to the courtroom.

Conclusion: Beyond Liberal Rights, Speaking Law to Power?

The chapter demonstrated that law was employed by protesters to create a narrative of contention, by the state to police protests and by lawyers to politicize and resist state repression. A broader question remains unanswered: to what extent did (can?) law serve the goals of the uprising? Conscious of the vexing challenge in posing this complex question as a conclusion, a piece on law and revolution would be incomplete if it did not address it, albeit briefly.

The uprising occurred in a context of financial and economic collapse resulting from a postwar consociational power-sharing arrangement that consolidated a dysfunctional regime built on a rentier economic model and on neoliberal policies along sectarian and clientelist lines. In this context, there are expectations to what legal mobilization can offer to challenge the interests of the neoliberal regime and ensure a fair redistribution of losses. However, litigation and lawmaking relating to the economic question revealed limited potential.

Facing the inertia of dealing with the freefalling economy and the illegal seizure of bank accounts, the Depositors Union has assisted depositors in filing more than 300 lawsuits against banks between November 2019 and April 2021, the majority of which were related to the transfer of funds abroad, debt settlements, or the reopening of bank accounts.[81] Conventional wisdom has it that litigation can be understood as a "pragmatic" tactic of resistance or simply a lack of political opportunity.[82] However, and regardless of the judicial outcomes that may unfold later, what interests us here is that the Depositors Union's demand for an "equitable redistribution of losses and wealth" ultimately translated into individual legal battles for saving personal wealth.[83] I provide this example not to fault litigant depositors or allege that they are "duped by legal hegemony"[84] but rather to maintain how recourse to law in questions entailing structural inequalities has culminated in reformulating political claims to fit the legal mold, transforming structural, political, and social inequalities into disputes between competing rights.

It could be argued that this limitation applies only to litigation and not to lawmaking. However, this is not entirely accurate. After months of protesting, families of students studying abroad succeeded in pushing parliament to enact the "student dollar" law, which allowed banks to disburse up to ten thousand dollars for transfer abroad at the official exchange rate.[85] Yet the law remained mere ink on paper; banks refused to implement it, and legislators claimed to have fulfilled their obligations. Lawmaking inevitably foregrounds social and economic choices: Which social categories and interests are to benefit from the "remaining dollars" in the face of shrinking foreign currency reserves? What is the social interest justifying the exception of students? Accordingly, and if not inscribed within a comprehensive socioeconomic project that provides equitable answers to these questions, legal reforms are likely to be subverted by power relations or, at best, constitute symbolic reforms devoid of social significance.

Lessons from neighboring countries, such as Tunisia and Egypt, should be taken seriously. In his seminal work on law and revolution in the Arab uprising, Sultany has shown how legal reforms in postrevolutionary Egypt have reproduced the preexisting authoritarian framework.[86] Moustafa, in his analysis of legal mobilization under the authoritarian Egyptian regime, concluded that "the legal complex is best able to advance individual rights by leaving core regime interests uncontested."[87] Examining political lawyering during the Tunisian revolution, Gobe and Salaymeh argued that lawyers continued to "protect the very economic inequality that contributed to the revolution because they accept neoliberal economics,"[88] demonstrating the disconnect in Tunisia's political lawyering between political liberalism—entailing a modern state, an independent judiciary, and basic freedoms—and economic reform.[89] The statements of the "prorevolutionary" BBA in regard to depositors' rights are quite revealing of this affinity between legal actors and liberalism,[90] for they demonstrate a defense of "free market economy" as the "forfeited feature" of the Lebanese system[91] and a dissatisfaction with the use of "bank deposits to fund the public sector."[92]

Socio-legal scholarship offers a complex assessment of the legacies of legal mobilization,[93] and various examples have alerted us to the inherent risks of law in fractionalizing political action,[94] fragmenting interconnected struggles into isolated grievances,[95] narrowing the causes, legitimizing the status quo, and diverting attention from more radical alternatives.[96] However, ample evidence is also available to argue that this outcome is not inevitable. Reflecting a dialectic relationship to law, the uprising provided an exemplary depiction of the emancipatory potential of legal mobilization in the protection of basic freedoms. Does that mean that law was most conducive to protecting liberal norms rather than facilitating the redistribution of wealth? The answer to this question is still premature and complex to be captured in binary outcomes.

In sum, the uprising allowed the deconstruction of the myth of lawmaking as an objective expertise-driven activity and decisively ruptured the normative representation of law as an apolitical tool. The extent to which legal mobilization can dismantle the structures that contributed to the uprising and challenge the core interests of the regime is thus contingent on inscribing legal mobilization within a transformative political project and a broader narrative of political contention. In other words, unless we use law as a means to serve an end goal, legal reform risks being counterproductive or, at best, insignificant. Legal mobilization cannot and should not be a substitute for political action.

Notes

1 Mark Fathi Massoud, *Law's Fragile State: Colonial, Authoritarian, and Humanitarian Legacies in Sudan* (Cambridge: Cambridge University Press, 2013), 221.
2 Michael McCann, "Law and Social Movements: Contemporary Perspectives," *Annual Review of Law and Social Science* 2 (2006): 17–38.
3 See Joseph Daher's chapter in this volume.
4 Nizar Saghieh, "Awal al-Iṣlahat Qanun 'Afu 'Am? Mashrou' Shira' al-Thimam wa-l-Taṭyif wa-l-'Afu al-Thati Ghayr al-Mu'lan," *The Legal Agenda*, October 28, 2019.
5 The Legal Agenda is a Beirut-based nonprofit research and advocacy organization; see: www.legal-agenda.com.
    The Lebanese Professionals Association is a group formed during the first days of the uprising, including professionals from different sectors and aiming at supporting the goals of the uprising; see: https://www.facebook.com/LebProAssociation.
6 The Legal Agenda, "al-Mawqef min al-Jalsa al-Tashri'yya al-Muqarara Yawm al-Thulatha' wa-Jadwal A'maliha," video, 7:57, November 12, 2019, https://www.facebook.com/LegalAgenda/videos/2808154195869425/.
7 Lebanese Judges Association, "La li-Qanun 'Afu Yulghi al-Muhasaba," November 10, 2019, https://www.facebook.com/permalink.php?story_fbid=415875859351106&id=152231329048895.
8 Aya Majzoub, "Problematic Bills on Lebanon Parliament's Agenda: The Two Bills Should Be Amended or Withdrawn," *Human Rights Watch*, November 19, 2019, https://www.hrw.org/news/2019/11/19/problematic-bills-lebanon-parliaments-agenda.
    See also, "Proposed Amnesty Law in Lebanon Would Weaken Accountability and Reduce State Revenues," *Transparency International*, November 11, 2019, https://www.transparency.org/en/press/proposed-amnesty-law-in-lebanon-would-weaken-accountability-and-reduce-stat.

9 Interview Nizar Saghieh, *Vision 2030*. LBC, November 11, 2019, https://www.lbcgroup
   .tv/news/d/lebanon/482509/%D9%86%D8%B2%D8%A7%D8%B1-%D8%B5%D8
   %A7%D8%BA%D9%8A%D8%A9-%D8%A7%D9%84%D8%AB%D9%88%D8%B1
   %D8%A9-%D9%87%D9%8A-%D8%A8%D8%AA%D8%BA%D9%8A%D9%8A%D8
   %B1-%D8%A7%D9%84%D9%85%D8%AC%D8%AA%D9%85%D8%B9-%D9%84
   %D8%A7%D8%B1%D8%A7-%D8%B3%D8%B9%D8%A7%D8%AF%D8%A9-%D8
   %A7%D9%84%D9%87/ar?fbclid=IwAR2AHA-LQ8RF4ooP-S2oIvykAsFVhxP-mr7
   xeqkwmgxgujdcjOrGfqCdfK4.
10 "Tuesday's Legislative Session Postponed for Security Reasons," *Annahar*, November
   11, 2019.
11 "The Street Brings Down the Council," *YouTube video*, 1:25, posted by Megaphone,
   November 19, 2019, https://www.youtube.com/watch?v=3jJM8wHhtjg.
12 Emilio Lehoucq and Whitney K. Taylor, "Conceptualizing Legal Mobilization: How
   Should We Understand the Deployment of Legal Strategies?," *Law & Social Inquiry* 45,
   no. 1 (2020): 166–93.
13 The Legal Agenda, "Jalsa Tashri'yya bi ta'm al-istihtar," video, 2:48, November 10,
   2019, https://www.facebook.com/LegalAgenda/posts/3484097024941374.
14 See Mona Harb's chapter in this volume.
15 McCann, "Law and Social Movements," 25.
16 Ibid.
17 "Judiciary Independence: Does the Street Impose the Law?" *YouTube video*, 3:17, posted
   by Megaphone, November 29, 2019, https://www.youtube.com/watch?v=h9PvuY9SxVk.
18 Maher El Khechen, "Min Amam Qasr 'Adl Beirut," *The Legal Agenda*, November 7,
   2019.
      Majmou'at Shabab al-Masref, video, 0:17, March 10, 2020, https://www.facebook
   .com/msmasref/posts/191891365581494.
19 "al-Tashkylat al-Qada'iya ma baa'd al-Thawra," *YouTube video*, 3:24, posted by The
   Legal Agenda, May 8, 2020, https://www.youtube.com/watch?v=BHBBVOP84lo.
20 Austin Sarat and Stuart Scheingold, "What Cause Lawyers Do *For*, And *To*, Social
   Movements: An Introduction," in *Cause Lawyers and Social Movements*, ed. Austin
   Sarat and Stuart S. Scheingold (Stanford: Stanford University Press, 2006).
21 https://www.depositorsunion.com/.
22 https://www.facebook.com/na3am.liawladina.
23 https://lebaneselw.com/.
24 Interview with lawyer Nayla Geagea, *Vision 2030*, LBC, November 4, 2019.
      https://www.facebook.com/watch/?v=2275465372743497.
      Talk with lawyers Karim Daher and Nizar Saghieh, Azarieh Square, November 11,
   2019, https://www.facebook.com/BeirutMadinati/videos/2508824722570317.
25 Houkoukiyoun, October 25, 2019, https://www.facebook.com/houkoukiyoun/posts
   /101269857980581.
26 Laure Ayoub, "al-Naqabat al-Mihaniyya fi Tarablos . . .," *The Legal Agenda*, October
   27, 2019.
27 Legal Agenda, "I am a Lawyer and the Bar Forbid me from Wearing My Robe,"
   Photograph, October 30, 2019. https://www.facebook.com/LegalAgenda/photos/a
   .3448473981837012/3448482358502841/.
28 "Fawz Melhem Khalaf," *YouTube video*, 14:03, posted by Al Jadeed News, November
   17, 2019 https://www.youtube.com/watch?v=b6_MybMRt9Y.
29 The Legal Agenda, video, 2:20, November 16, 2019, https://www.facebook.com/
   LegalAgenda/posts/3505224622828614.

30 Ghida Frangieh, "Lebanese Uprising Enshrines Defense Rights for Detainees," *The Legal Agenda*, November 30, 2020, https://english.legal-agenda.com/lebanese-uprising -enshrines-defense-rights-for-detainees/.

31 Typically used to defy norms, the "Hela ho" chant was used in this instance to celebrate a victory.

    See: "Hela ho Transformations," *YouTube video*, 1:31, posted by Megaphone, November 19, 2019, https://www.youtube.com/watch?v=El_azb_TLQg.

32 Lynn Abi Raad, "A War on Two Fronts," *Diwan* (blog), Carnegie Endowment for International Peace's Middle East Program–Malcolm H. Kerr Carnegie Middle East Center, December 10, 2019, https://carnegie-mec.org/diwan/80540.

33 Lucien Karpik and Terence C. Halliday, "The Legal Complex," *Annual Review of Law and Social Science* 7 (2011): 217–36.

34 Lebanese Judges Association, *Facebook*. https://www.facebook.com/%D9%86%D8 %A7%D8%AF%D9%8A-%D9%82%D8%B6%D8%A7%D8%A9-%D9%84%D8%A8 %D9%86%D8%A7%D9%86-Lebanese-Judges-Association-152231329048895.

35 Lebanese Judges Association, "Kalimat Nady al-Qudat," *Facebook,* August 10, 2020, https://www.facebook.com/permalink.php?story_fbid=616960032576020&id =152231329048895.

36 "Silencing Lebanon's Judges," *The Legal Agenda*, January 15, 2019, https://english.legal -agenda.com/silencing-lebanons-judges/.

37 Université Saint-Joseph de Beyrouth, *Facebook*, October 26, 2019, https://www .facebook.com/usj.edu.lb/posts/1445956075572677/.

38 Ghida Frangieh, Nour Haidar, and Sarah Wansa, "Kayfa Istakhdamat al-Sulta Silah al-Tawqifat li-Qame' Horiyat al-Tazahur wa-l-I'tirad," *The Legal Agenda*, October 16, 2020.

39 Ghida Frangieh, "Muhawala li-Ta'dib al-Muntafidin wa Rad'uhum," *The Legal Agenda*, October 16, 2020.

40 Nour Haidar, "A Popular Uprising Met With Violence and Torture: Crimes Against Protesters During Lebanon's Uprising," *The Legal Agenda*, February 18, 2020, https:// english.legal-agenda.com/a-popular-uprising-met-with-violence-and-torture-crimes -against-protesters-during-lebanons-uprising/.

41 See Mortada Al-Amine's chapter in this volume.

42 LCDP, Statement, *Facebook,* October 29, 2019, https://www.facebook.com/ lawyersprotestleb/posts/2320181168294463.

43 Frangieh et al., "Kayfa Istakhdamat al-Sulta."

44 The extension of detention times was also driven by the need to conceal signs of violence and abuse in police stations.

45 For example, protesters accused of throwing Molotov cocktails toward the Free Patriotic Movement's office in Jounieh on December 6, 2019, and setting an ATM machine on fire in Zouk on January 5, 2020, were charged with arson, incitement to civil war, and sectarian conflict.

    LCDP, February 2, 2020, *Facebook*, https://www.facebook.com/lawyersprotestleb/ posts/2411519762493936.

46 Frangieh, "Lebanese Uprising Enshrines Defense Rights for Detainees."

47 Laure Ayoub, "Edi'a bi-l-Irhab Dod Moutazahiri Tarablos: Silah Jadid fi Wajeh al-Mou'arada," *The Legal Agenda,* February 23, 2021.

48 Lebanese Internal Security Forces, *Facebook*, January 19, 2020, https://www.facebook .com/lebisf/posts/2615602561994796.

    "Fabricating the lie of 'street vs. street,'" *YouTube video*, 2:15, posted by Megaphone, December 16, 2019, https://www.youtube.com/watch?v=MOk3bwS0FwE.

Saad Hariri (@SaadHariri), *Twitter*, June 13, 2020. https://twitter.com/saadhariri/status/1271726861761085440?s=20.

49 Khatt Ahmar, Poster, *Facebook*, January 14, 2020, https://www.facebook.com/KhatAhmarlb/photos/149701923121090.

50 Nayla Geagea, video, 0:47, January 19, 2020. https://www.facebook.com/watch/?v=479440672738332; Majmou'at Shabab al-masref, "Bayan Tawdihi," *Twitter,* January 15, 2020, https://twitter.com/msmasref/status/1217218007459647495?s=20.

51 Ignacio González-Sánchez and Manuel Maroto-Calatayud, "The Penalization of Protest under Neoliberalism: Managing Resistance through Punishment," *Crime, Law and Social Change* 70, no. 4 (2018): 443–60.

52 Ibid.

53 "Legal Agenda Statement: Four Objections to the Declaration of a State of Emergency," *The Legal Agenda*, August 21, 2020, https://english.legal-agenda.com/legal-agenda-statement-four-objections-to-the-declaration-of-a-state-of-emergency/.

54 Saada Allaw, "al-Sulta Tastashres fi-l-Difa' 'an al-Nizam Mutasabiba bi-Issabat Mi'at al-Mutazahirin," *The Legal Agenda*, August 11, 2020.

55 "Waraqa Bahthiyya 'an Islah al-Qada' fi Lubnan Raqm 17: Tanzim al-Niyaba al-'Amma," *The Legal Agenda*, August 1, 2018.

56 Duncan Kennedy, "The Critique of Rights in Critical Legal Studies," in *Left Legalism/Left Critique*, ed. Wendy Brown and Janet Halley (Durham: Duke University Press, 2002), 216–27.

57 Steven Barkan, "Criminal Prosecution and The Legal Control of Protest," *Mobilization: An International Quarterly* 11, no. 2 (2006): 181–94, at 184, doi:10.17813/maiq.11.2.a8671t532kww2722.

58 Massoud, *Law's Fragile State*, 228.

59 LCDP, Photograph, *Facebook,* August 28, 2015. https://www.facebook.com/lawyersprotestleb/photos/a.1492403887738866/1493127267666528.

60 Lama Karamé and Elham Barjas, "Tajribat Muhami Harak Sayf 2015," in *A'mal al-Marsad al-Madani li-Istiqlal al-Qada' 2014–2015*, ed. Nizar Saghieh (Beirut: The Legal Agenda, 2016), 156–98.

61 Ibid.

62 Thomas Hilbink, "The Profession, The Grassroots and The Elite: Cause Lawyering for Civil Rights and Freedom in the Direct Action Era," in Austin and Scheingold, *Cause Lawyers and Social Movements*.

63 Fawra, "Arrests & Summons," video, 1:47, January 13, 2020, https://www.facebook.com/112496093516689/videos/480040052696958.

64 Frangieh, "Lebanese Uprising Enshrines Defense Rights for Detainees."

65 Ibid.

66 Nour Haidar, "Radical Lawyering in Times of Revolution: Dispatches from Lebanon," *Socialist Lawyer*, no. 84 (2020): 30–4, https://www.jstor.org/stable/10.13169/socialistlawyer.84.0030.

67 "Arrests Are Still Taking Place," *YouTube video*, 2:09, posted by Megaphone, November 22, 2019, https://www.youtube.com/watch?v=wgAIRVASQzg.

68 Frangieh, "Lebanese Uprising Enshrines Defense Rights for Detainees."

69 Ibid.

70 Ibid.

71 Ibid.

72 Ibid.

73 Nizar Saghieh, "Buqaʾ al-Taʾdhib al-lati la Taraha al-Niyabat al-ʾAmma," *The Legal Agenda*, October 20, 2020.

74 The Legal Agenda, "Kalimat al-Muhamiyya Ghida Frangieh fi-l-muʾtamar al-Sahafi," video, 14:42, February 8, 2020, https://www.facebook.com/278035695547539/videos /122873252405681.

75 The Legal Agenda, "Kalimat al-Muhami Mazen Hoteit fi-l-muʾtamar al-Sahafi," video, 14:08, February 8, 2020, https://www.facebook.com/LegalAgenda/videos /1063242860676592.

76 Ibid.

77 The military court has broad jurisdiction over civilians and is often criticized for lacking fair trial guarantees.
    See: Myriam Mehanna, "Specialized Courts for Crimes of Terrorism in Lebanon: Unfulfilled Promises," *The Legal Agenda*, April 9, 2016, https://english.legal-agenda .com/specialized-courts-for-crimes-of-terrorism-in-lebanon-unfulfilled-promises/.

78 Laure Ayoub, "Usbuʾ Muhakamat 30 Mutaẓaher amam al-Mahkama al-ʾAskariah," *The Legal Agenda*, April 15, 2021.

79 Laure Ayoub, "al-mutazahiroun fi wajh al-niyaba al-ʾAmma al-ʾAskariya: idiʾaat siyasiyya li-qameʾ al-muʾarada," *The Legal Agenda*, April 22, 2021.

80 Otto Kirchheimer, *Political Justice: The Use of Legal Procedure for Political Ends* (Princeton: Princeton University Press, 1961).

81 "Taqrir Faransi sadim ʿan masarif Lubnan: sariqat al-qaren," *Al Modon*, April 5, 2021.

82 Chris Hilson, "New Social Movements: The Role of Legal Opportunity," *Journal of European Public Policy* 9, no. 2 (2002): 238–55, at 239.

83 Hicham Safieddine, "Houqouq al-mouwdiʾin: horriyya Iqtisadiyya aw aʿadala ijtimaʿiyya?," *The Legal Agenda*, April 27, 2020.

84 Lynette J. Chua, "Legal Mobilization and Authoritarianism," *Annual Review of Law and Social Science* 15, no. 1 (2019): 355–76, at 368.

85 Maher El Khechen, "al-Masarif la tutabeq taʿmim al-dollar al-tullabi wa la al-qararat al-qadaʾiyah," *The Legal Agenda*, December 18, 2020.

86 Nimer Sultany, *Law and Revolution: Legitimacy and Constitutionalism after the Arab Spring* (Oxford: Oxford University Press, 2017).

87 Tamir Moustafa, "Mobilising the Law in an Authoritarian State: The Legal Complex in Contemporary Egypt," in *Fighting for Political Freedom: Comparative Studies of the Legal Complex and Political Liberalism, Oxford and Portland Oregon*, ed. Terence C. Halliday, Lucien Karpik, and Malcom M. Feeley (Oxford: Hart Publishing, 2007), 215.

88 Eric Gobe and Lena Salaymeh, "Tunisia's 'Revolutionary' Lawyers: From Professional Autonomy to Political Mobilization," *Law & Social Inquiry* 41, no. 2 (2016): 311–45, at 340.

89 Ibid., 339.

90 Terence C. Halliday, *Beyond Monopoly: Lawyers, State Crises, and Professional Empowerment* (Chicago: University of Chicago Press, 1987), 369.

91 Beirut Bar Association, *Facebook,* January 3, 2020, https://www.facebook.com/ bbalebanon/posts/1342295325942426.

92 Beirut Bar Association, *Facebook,* April 1, 2021, https://www.facebook.com/ bbalebanon/posts/1767636863408268.

93 Gerald N. Rosenberg, *The Hollow Hope: Can Courts Bring About Social Change?* (Chicago: University of Chicago Press, 2008).

94   Stuart Scheingold, *The Politics of Rights: Lawyers, Public Policy, and Political Change*, 3rd ed. (Ann Arbor: University of Michigan Press, 2010), 214.

95   Orly Lobel, "The Paradox of Extralegal Activism: Critical Legal Consciousness and Transformative Politics," *Harvard Law Review* 120, no. 4 (2006): 937–88, at 951.

96   Ibid., 939.

6

Filthy Flows of Power

A Political Ecology of Disasters in Lebanon

Roland Riachi

On the eve of Sunday, October 13, 2019, massive forest fires erupted at different spots in the country, in the Chouf, Aley, and Metn areas, and extended to reach the limits of Beirut. A man was killed while volunteering to help understaffed and underequipped firefighters.[1] Fires were finally under control on the morning of October 17, thanks to the rain. In addition to the infamous WhatsApp tax, forest fires were another reason behind the Lebanese uprising according to early commentators.[2] One can argue that since 2015 trash crisis, ecological struggles were leveraged to a new citizen-based level, breaking previous molds of environmentalism long qualified as partisan and elitist.[3] The chapter seeks to emphasize the contemporary socioecological roots that culminated into the 2019 uprising.

During the war, tons of toxic waste were carried by ship *Radhost* in 1987 and smuggled by the Italian mafia in cooperation with Lebanese Forces militiamen.[4] Chemicals were sold as manufacturing products or dumped in Mount Lebanon's forests, highlands, quarries, and landfills. This ecological tragedy coincidentally resonates with the recent ship *Rhosus* that carried large quantities of ammonium nitrate causing the dramatic explosion of Beirut Port on August 4, 2020.[5] The cargo was found to be trafficked by Syrian businessmen, with the complicity of Lebanese and foreign allies, who usually supply the Ba'th regime with chemicals.[6] Ammonium nitrate, a fertilizer at high levels of concentration, is used as an explosive used for mining and military purposes.

Ecological catastrophes, so as man-made disasters, are never solely local issues. The main objective of the chapter is to analyze the power relations that are behind such "glocalized"—a combination of global and local scales—disasters in Lebanon that are (re)produced, maintained, and magnified by contemporary neoliberal policies. Disasters are central in the making of Lebanon since its inception following the Great Famine of 1915–18 amid the First World War—a dramatic event with one of the largest estimated fatalities of the war with one- to two-third of Beirut and Mount Lebanon population who died from starvation.[7] The case of Lebanon is also an important terrain to study contemporary post-disaster responses, from the endless reconstruction phase following the Lebanese war that lasted from 1975 to 1990, to the reconstruction phase that followed the 2006 Israeli war on Lebanon, up to the recent port explosion.[8]

Biopolitics and Neoliberal Disasters

In an interview on January 4, 2021, Health Minister Hamad Hassan said: "We can say that the explosion [at the port] and those killed is [a matter of] fate and destiny whereas those dying of the coronavirus or those being infected are in my opinion responsible, whether they wanted to or not."[9] This statement blends two interwoven signifiers that the chapter seeks to debunk: determinism in disasters and self-disciplining and self-resiliency biopolitics.

Disasters are not single events occurring in an ahistorical and apolitical vacuum; such crises unfold structural social unequal vulnerabilities. The word "disaster," from Latin words "bad" and "aster," refers to "acts of God," uncontrolled natural hazards. Hazard, from Arabic *zaher*, means dice for chance.

From a political ecological perspective, the natural and the social are not entities to be analyzed separately, so must be disasters. Disasters are not "accidental," as it takes more than an extreme natural event to produce a disaster.[10] What differentiate natural, biological (such as pandemics), or man-made technology-triggered catastrophes, such as infrastructural or military, is that depending on the origin of such events, survivors have different needs.

In contrast to divine interventions in disasters, Foucault's concept of "biopolitics" is defined as the politics of "making live and letting die," set by neoliberal governmentality during the last decades.[11] Since the mid-2000s, the concept of "resilience" emerged in neoliberal discourses, setting a regime of subjectification—a regime that is realized by producing resilient subjects that can adapt to the neoliberal modes of production and accumulation, exploitation and dispossession, crises, and disasters.[12] Neoliberalism has proven to be historically advanced in exploiting crises and proceeding in accumulation by dispossession of citizens' basic entitled rights.[13]

From a neo-Gramscian perspective, hegemony is deployed on three scales of activities constituting a historical structure: social relations of production, forms of state, and world orders.[14] Within those activities three elements are central: material, namely capital; discursive, creating a dominant discourse; and institutional, setting hierarchical relations. Co-opting is a durable form of power, a soft hegemony without coercion. For ideological reproduction, hegemon soft strategy tames civil society, academia, and media, and the NGOization of social and ecological struggles, as well as disaster responses by depoliticizing them.[15] The hegemony in development aid is paramount in international political economy since most large infrastructure projects in Global South countries are funded by international financial institutions. Lebanon makes another striking example.

Externally backed by foreign patrons providing funding and legitimacy, confessionalism in Lebanon forms the perfect neo-Gramscian structure of hegemony. This process is rooted in Lebanon's *longue durée* integration of its rentier economy, ruled by compradors, to global capitalism, deploying modes of accumulation that require human and ecological exhaustion.[16] The following sections respectively discuss those power relations and their impact on land, water, and air.

Land and Garbage Capitalism

The solution of solid waste was marked by early neoliberal aspirations to privatize public services. Granted with political connections, the initial Sukleen contract was expected to operate for six years only and use the Naameh landfill, from 1997 until 2003.[17] The contract was gradually postponed until the date of its closure was set on July 17, 2015. On that date, protesters from the neighboring of the landfill organized a sit-in on the main gate to stop trash trucks from entering.[18] Garbage piled up in the streets marking the beginning of a several months' waste crisis. Protesters massed in the capital asking for a basic cleaning service hijacked by the power-profit-sharing *muhasasa* system.[19]

After the refusal of Srar in Aakar and Masnaa in West Beqaa landfills by local protesters, the solution of the government was the creation of two sea landfills in Bourj Hammoud and Jdeideh. To make it simple, the new landfills are two adjacent U-shaped breakwaters that trash trucks progressively fill. Both already reached saturation, and the actual proposed solution is to join the landfills and make it one large rectangle. Promoted to be a land reclamation project, the area is later intended for real estate development and the construction of a wastewater treatment plant.[20]

The ultimate long-term strategy of the government has been centered on the construction of large incinerators, promoted as clean waste-to-energy technologies.[21] In parallel, more than fifteen sorting facilities were constructed with European Union funds covering the entire country over the last decade; none has operated.[22] The only sorting service in the country is informally provided by poor Lebanese, Palestinian, and Syrian children, working in extreme precarity, manipulating life-threatening dangerous waste.[23]

There are other coastal landfills in Lebanon, commonly called *jabal zbeleh* or "garbage mountain," in Saida, Tripoli, and the recent Costa Brava annexed to Beirut's airport runway.[24] Created during the 2015 crisis, the latter was marketed to become an extension of the airport, but it finally led to aviation security threats as it attracted seagulls on airport's runway. On the January 12, 2017, the Council of Development and Reconstruction (CDR) hired hunters to shoot the birds and resumed the filling of the dumpsite.[25]

Land reclamation using accumulated garbage for real estate purposes is not new; it is at the heart of the neoliberal-caused crisis hitting Lebanon today.[26] On the confluence of waste disposal and land reclamation stands the infamous case of Solidere, with its Waterfront city project standing on wartime Normady landfill.

According to numbers of the Ministry of Public Works and Transport in 2012, there were around 1,100 cases of illegal coastal occupation; only one-fifth of the shore is accessible to the public.[27] Backed by politicians' interests, the occupation is not perceived as hindering accessibility but as a missed opportunity to increase tax revenues. The privatization of beach access and other ecological-cultural destruction are numerous and erupted many civil discontents in recent years such as the coast of Adloun, which is one of the few remaining public beaches in Lebanon containing rich archaeological landmarks, destroyed to build the "Nabih Berri Fishermen's Port," Dalieh and the Eden Bay project privatizing the only remaining beach in Beirut, as well as movements in Kfaraabida, Anfeh, and Tyre.[28]

During the reconstruction, large quarries proliferated in Mount Lebanon and remote areas. Supplying the frenetic real estate speculation, politicians had a direct or indirect stake in quarries and cement industries by owning the business or controlling it through close relatives, such as the Hariri, Joumblat, Eddeh, and Fattouche brothers, to name few.[29] Sand mafia has also spawned of illegal sand extraction from beaches, under politicians' cover, in Tyre in the south or Heri in the north.[30]

Understanding the root causes of the imbalanced regional development in Lebanon requires delving into the prevalent agricultural history of the country, with the rise of local *zuama* landowners and a bourgeoisie nurtured from silk and European capital.[31] Agricultural land inequality is flagrant: 1 percent of landowners possess the quarter of total cultivated area, the largest 10 percent of landowners own around two-third of it, while the bottom half of farms represents less than 10 percent of the agricultural surface.[32] Large agricultural holdings in Lebanon can be traced to prominent politicians, agri-food businesses with political affiliations, and monasteries.

Irrigated surface tripled since 1960s. This profit-seeking specialization in water-intensive fruit and vegetable is essentially export-led satisfying markets of Gulf oil-rich countries, at the expense of exploited refugee children and women seasonal workers. An intensive agriculture putting high pressure on water resources, leading to a sharp decline in the country's water tables. Lebanon produces up to two and threefold its needs in many fruits and vegetables to supply this external market, which represents almost a third of the country's yearly freshwater use.[33]

Both cereal import dependency, perfectly symbolized by the blown silos in the August 4 port explosion, and fruit and vegetable export dependency have been a common trend in many agricultural countries in the region under neoliberalism.[34] Since 2011, land transit of products was completely disrupted due to the war in Syria, collapsing the export market and farmers' livelihoods on its way. The imminent fuel crisis in summer 2021 will have huge repercussions on the cost of running water pumps, which will hinder the availability of locally produced food. Those rapid changes in agricultural land use mirror the continuous rural deprivation and ecological disaster, namely water resources, in the country.[35]

Water and Sewage: A Century-old Bonanza

Large-scale water projects were introduced during colonial period in Lebanon as part of their "civilization and modernization" process. After independence, the modernization process was carried by the Point Four and the US Bureau of Reclamation as part of the containment foreign policies.[36] After the Qaraoun dam on the Litani river, the bureau engaged in a reconnaissance mission of other potential dams' sites. Those sites are the same proposed in recent strategies; the decennial plan (2000–9), then the National Water Sector Strategy in 2012. In April 2021, spectacular quantities of fish washed up on the shores of the Qaraoun artificial lake, a recurrent problem due to eutrophication.[37] Dams imposed politicians' territorial power and politically tied businesses, namely through connected construction companies and cement factories.[38]

Dam projects are closely linked to political ideologies and are almost always regarded as national symbols representing the technological progress and economic power of a nation. Gebran Bassil already announced that Lebanon will provide water to Cyprus and Jordan with its dams.[39] Harnessing a river with dam construction has long been a techno-political credo of regimes across the world as a proof of power, modernism, and independence.[40] Early during national construction, dams were presented by the "Cénacle libanais" and Arab nationalists intellectuals as a pillar of modernization and national sovereignty, preventing Zionism from coveting national waters.[41] After the civil war, the old narrative of unharnessed abundance will be replaced by one of water crisis and scarcity.[42]

With only two dams completed, Qaraoun in 1960 and Chabrouh in 2007, construction resumed at a rapid pace in the last decade; Brisa, Yammouneh, Qaysamani, Mseilha, and Bekaata were constructed, and others are under construction, Balaa and Janna.[43] Most of the recent dams had linkages to Aoun and Bassil's Free Patriotic Movement, in charge of the sector during the last decade.[44] All those projects knew local opposition with the support of the Lebanon Eco Movement, but only one was successfully stopped for the moment. Seven decades old Bisri Dam funding was canceled on September 5, 2020, for some missing documents and for not clearing the area from protesters to resume work as argued by the World Bank.[45] In addition to fierce opposition by activists, perhaps another reason behind the cancellation of the funding is Lebanon's first default on foreign debt in March the same year.[46]

Large water projects made a large part of donors' funds during the reconstruction phase, after roads. One-third of the latest French-backed CEDRE conference (Economic Conference for Development through Reforms with the Private sector) is dedicated to the water sector, around US$3.5 billion.[47] It is almost the same amount that was already disbursed in the water sector since 1990, and there has been no perceivable improvement of the network; on the contrary, it got worse.[48] If water is elemental in neoliberal biopolitics, in Lebanon this is best described by the increased reliance on bottled water as the primary source of drinking water for households in the last few years, increasing from 5.1 percent in 1995, 31.8 percent in 2004, up to 69.1 percent in 2018–19.[49]

In addition to the commodification of drinking water, another threat for universal water provisioning continuously looming is the desire to privatize the sector/resource. Law 221/2000 recentralized the sector by merging twenty-two historically decentralized water authorities into four Water Establishments.[50] The main objective behind the law was to enable financial and commercial autonomy of the establishments, preparing the grounds for the privatization of the sector. The privatization did not finally occur in Beirut and its suburbs as solicited by the World Bank in the 1990s but in Tripoli with the support of the Agence Française de Développement (AFD). French consortium Degremont-Ondeo-Suez was contracted the management of the service in the northern city between 2002 and 2007. As in many cases of "tied-aid" worldwide, the contract unlocked other projects funded by French loans and constructed with French expertise, such as Tripoli's wastewater treatment plant. The station was ready in 2008 and has never operated.[51]

Dozens of other wastewater treatment plants were built in the last decade with different donors and remain nonoperational.[52] Costing more than US$1 billion of public debt and high interest rates, those "white elephants" are a blatant example of the interest-driven of development aid and shortsightedness of donors.[53] Even though none is treated, the presence of sewage system shows large differences among regions. If Beirut and other cities are covered by a public sewage network, in remote areas households mostly rely on septic tanks. With the addition to dependence on private wells, those regions are much prone to water-borne diseases.

The absence of wastewater treatment has resulted in extremely high levels of pollution of rivers, aquifers, and coastal waters. There are more than fifty untreated sewage sea spills, making on average one spill every 4 kilometers on the Lebanese coast.[54] In addition to the flaws in sewage management, all strategies and reforms completely neglected groundwater management. Wells are still governed by Ottoman and mandate outdated laws, offering landowner usufruct rights on the resource in the name of property.[55] Lebanon has no less than ten wells every squared kilometer on average.[56] Out of fifty aquifers, only one is protected, Jabal Kneisseh, exploited by Nestlé water company.[57]

A new chapter was recently opened in water privatization reforms in Lebanon with the adoption of the Water Code Law 77/2018. Initiated under pressures from the AFD, the law is an adapted version of the French public-private partnership model. This public management model of water utilities has already proven to be a fiasco in its country of origin.[58] Although ready since 2005, the document was quickly adopted by the government a week from the Paris IV Conference, since the AFD director openly threatened to stop funding if the code is not approved.[59] With increasing electricity cutoffs, water provisioning in Lebanon, which was already not continuous, is witnessing even higher levels of rationing, reaching one day per week in summer 2021.

Cartels, Exhausts, and Air Pollution

The main sources causing the increase of air pollution in Lebanon are traffic, power plants, private generators, and industries.[60] One-third of the annual import bill goes to purchase fuel and diesel, representing the highest burden on the balance of payment.[61] According to relaying national energy and environmental strategies, an objective was set back in 2010 to reach 12 percent of renewable energy in 2020. Of course, this was not realized; instead, it was replaced by another more ambitious 30 percent commitment of renewable energy production by 2030.[62]

The electricity in Lebanon became under state monopoly in 1964, part of the Chehab's public utilities nationalization wave during his mandate from 1958 to 1964. This came following citizens' mobilizations against unstable water provision, frequent power cuts, and a hike in public transport prices, all ran by French mandate-era concessions. The civil war caused heavy damages to the electricity production and distribution infrastructure. In 2002, the government adopted Law 462 for the regulation of the sector and to prepare it for privatization.[63] This has been heavily encouraged by international funding agencies and became a notable reform condition for aid promised at the conferences of Paris II, III, and IV. Privatizing electricity became a dominant narrative endorsed by not only the governments, experts, and donors but also some civil society organizations.[64]

The long-standing sector's shortcomings translate into the very unequal distribution of electricity as the shortages are not distributed evenly on a national scale, prioritizing mainly Beirut.[65] As such, the mismanagement of electricity exacerbates social inequalities based on the ability to afford alternative solutions. Due to frequent power cuts, 84 percent of households were subscribed to a private generator provider in 2018–19.[66] Since October 2021, country's main power plants were completely shut down due to diesel shortage, followed by skyrocketing generators bills and drastic supply rationing.

With a continued lack of electricity production, Karadeniz Powership was offered a contract in 2013 for emergency power supply from two floating power barges to provide 385 MW, representing one-fifth of the country's production capacity, which barely meets half the demand. In May 2021, the company decided to shut down its production because of eighteen months' payment arrears.[67] End of November, the two powerships left the country.

In addition to electricity, fuel shortage and hyperinflation had tremendous impact on mobility. Over months since summer 2021, residents had to face what they called "queues of humiliation" massing outside petrol stations, sometimes overnights, waiting for filling their gas tank—a situation from which proliferated a fuel black market, supplying at tenfold the official tariff. Government's solution was to completely lift fuel subsidies in October, aligning to parallel market price. An estimated majority of 70.2 percent of households own at least one vehicle.[68] Lack of a proper public transport network led to a vital role of owning a car. Continuously cherry-picking profits, in March 2018, the World Bank approves a US$295 million envelope for Lebanon's transport sector, called the Greater Beirut Public Transport Project, based on a fleet of buses with combustion engines, which will "unlock private finance to a vital infrastructure sector," according to Bank's words.[69]

Car importers, fuel cartels, and generators mafia cherry-pick massive profits out of the lack of public electricity supply and public transportation. Finally, despite its huge potential of damaging environmental impact, oil and gas offshore reserves are portrayed by the government narrative as the redemption from country's multiple crises.[70] There is no difference to expect between foreign aid and oil windfalls. Luckily, no reserves were yet found.

Conclusion

Evoking Polanyi's pendulum, the future challenge of Lebanon's October 17 movement is to confront the statist-donors hegemony that has deployed its material, coercive, and discursive apparatus to adjust the pendulum to private interests.[71] One major common hegemonic dominant discourse in the last decade has been the scapegoating of Syrian refugees as burdens to public services and natural resources.[72] Such a Malthusian and environmental racist narrative is to be expelled to keep the pendulum on social grounds.

The purge must also reach organizations that play a role in reproducing dominant neoliberal paradigms in different sectors, such as the Integrated Water Resources Management (IWRM) mediatized by the Blue Gold project in 2014[73] or more recently the Extractive Industries Transparency Initiative (EITI), a voluntary transparency regime providing smokescreen to corruption.[74]

Lack of law enforcement is not behind ecological problems in Lebanon, because laws themselves are flawed. For example, the Environmental Impact Assessment study of any large project must be provided by the designated company itself according to decree 8633/2012, not by an independent body, clearly opening room to conflict of interests in the study. For example, the cost of environmental degradation in the EIA of Bisri Dam was estimated to a ridiculous US$148,000.[75]

Perhaps the most representing biopolitics in Lebanon are described by the high reliance on plastic water bottles and truck cisterns, private generators, and car dependency. Dispossession, appropriation, privatization, and commodification of natural resources, public services, and profiting from disasters are not new in Lebanon; they are rooted in the *longue durée* global history of colonial, state, and neoliberal capitalism and the rule of local compradors, made of feudal, mercantile, militia, and military confessional *zuama*—patrons.

Notes

1 Timour Azhari, "Lebanon Wildfires: Hellish Scenes in Mountains South of Beirut," *Al Jazeera*, 2019.
2 Kareem Chehayeb, "Opinion|Lebanon's Protests and Wildfires Tell the Same Grim Story," *Washington Post*, October 18, 2019, https://www.washingtonpost.com/opinions /2019/10/18/lebanons-protests-wildfires-tell-same-grim-story/.
3 For an overview of the politics behind 2015 trash crisis, see Ziad Abu-Rish, "Garbage Politics," *MERIP*, March 15, 2016, https://merip.org/2016/03/garbage-politics/. On 2015 social movements in general. On pre and early postwar environmental movements, see Paul Kingston, "Patrons, Clients and Civil Society: A Case Study of Environmental Politics in Postwar Lebanon," *Arab Studies Quarterly* (2001): 55–72.
4 Kingston, "Patrons, Clients and Civil Society."
5 See *The Guardian*, "Businessmen with Ties to Assad Linked to Beirut Port Blast Cargo," *The Guardian, 2021-01-15*, 2021, http://www.theguardian.com/world/2021/ jan/15/businessmen-with-ties-to-assad-linked-to-beirut-port-blast-cargo.
6 Ibid.
7 Roland Riachi, "Political Economy of Food in Lebanon: Food Regimes, Ecology, and Neo-Timocracy" (IDRC and FHS-AUB, working paper, 2021).
8 The port was not spared by early calls for a full privatization after being operated under clumsy private concessions. USAID, "Port of Beirut Assessment" (USAID Middle East Economic Growth Best Practices (USAID/MEG, 2021).
9 The National, "Fury over Lebanon Health Minister's Comments on Covid and Port Explosion Victims," *The National*, January 4, 2021, https://www.thenationalnews.com

/world/mena/fury-over-lebanon-health-minister-s-comments-on-covid-and-port
-explosion-victims-1.1140453.

10 Ben Wisner et al., *At Risk: Natural Hazards, People's Vulnerability and Disasters* (
London: Routledge, 2004).

11 Michel Foucault, *The Birth of Biopolitics: Lectures at the Collège de France, 1978–1979*
(London: Palgrave Macmillan, , 2008).

12 David Chandler and Julian Reid, *The Neoliberal Subject: Resilience, Adaptation and
Vulnerability* (Unit A, Whitacre Mews, 26-34 Stannary Street, London SE11 4AB:
Rowman & Littlefield, 2016).

13 David Harvey, *The New Imperialism: Accumulation by Dispossession* (New York:
Oxford University Press, 2005).

14 Robert W. Cox, "Gramsci, Hegemony and International Relations: An Essay in
Method," *Cambridge Studies in International Relations* 26 (1993): 49.

15 NGOization is the process where nongovernmental and civil society organizations
depoliticize social and environmental struggles, through dominant discourse
reproduction and the bureaucratization of their work, to secure funding from the
state, private sector, or international donors. See Aziz Choudry and Dip Kapoor,
NGOization: Complicity, Contradictions and Prospects (Michigan: Michigan State
University Press, 2013).

16 A comprador is a person who is an agent of foreign interests engaged in investment,
trade, or economic or political exploitation (Oxford dictionary).

17 Rish, "Garbage Politics."

18 Ibid.

19 *Muhasasa* is defined as the divide of spoils from public positions and state resources
among sectarian elites. See Reinoud Leenders, *Spoils of Truce: Corruption and State-
Building in Postwar Lebanon* (Sage House, 512 East State Street, Ithaca, New York:
Cornell University Press, 2012).

20 CDR, "Greater Beirut Water Supply Augmentation Project : Environmental and Social
Impact Assessment" (World Bank, Council for Development and Reconstruction,
and Dar El Handasah, 2013). EJOLT, "Bourj Hammoud Garbage Mountain,
Lebanon|EJAtlas," *Environmental Justice Atlas*, 2016, https://ejatlas.org/conflict/bourj
-hammoud-garbage-mountain.

21 EJOLT, "Beirut Incinerators Expansion Plans and Wastepickers Struggle,
Lebanon|EJAtlas," Environmental Justice Atlas, 2019, https://ejatlas.org/conflict/as-the
-plans-for-incinerators-in-beirut-lebanon-expand-wastepickers-recycle-to-survive.

22 The Solid Waste Management Program (SWMP) is funded by the European
Commission and implemented by the Office of the Minister of State for
Administrative Reform (OMSAR) since 2001. http://swmp.omsar.gov.lb.

23 EJOLT, "Beirut Incinerators Expansion Plans and Wastepickers Struggle,
Lebanon|EJAtlas."

24 EJOLT, "Costa Brava Landfill, Lebanon|EJAtlas," *Environmental Justice Atlas*, 2017,
https://ejatlas.org/conflict/costa-brava-landfill-lebanon.

25 "Beirut Rubbish Dump Birds Shot by Hunters near Airport," *BBC News*, January 14,
2017, sec. Middle East, https://www.bbc.com/news/world-middle-east-38624234.

26 Éric Verdeil, "Des Déchets Aux Remblais: Imaginaire Aménageur, Corruption et
Dérèglements Métaboliques à Beyrouth," 2017.

27 Cynthia Bou Aoun, "Framing the Lebanese Seashore: Crowding Out Public Interest,"
Legal Agenda, April 15, 2018, http://english.legal-agenda.com/framing-the-lebanese
-seashore-crowding-out-public-interest/.

28 For an exhaustive compilation of ecological movements in Lebanon check EJOLT, "Lebanon|EJAtlas," *Environmental Justice Atlas*, https://ejatlas.org/country/lebanon.

29 Leenders, *Spoils of Truce*.

30 EJOLT, "Lebanon|EJAtlas."

31 Riachi, "Political Economy of Food in Lebanon."

32 Ibid.

33 Roland Riachi, "Institutions et Régulation d'une Ressource Naturelle Dans Une Société Fragmentée : Théorie et Applications à Une Gestion Durable de l'eau Au Liban." (PhD Thesis, Université de Grenoble, 2013).

34 Roland Riachi and Giuliano Martiniello, "Manufactured Regional Scarcity: The Middle East and North Africa under Global Food Regimes," *Journal of Agrarian Change*, forthcoming (2022).

35 Riachi, "Institutions et Régulation d'une Ressource Naturelle Dans Une Société Fragmentée"; Riachi, "Political Economy of Food in Lebanon."

36 Riachi, "Institutions et Régulation d'une Ressource Naturelle Dans Une Société Fragmentée."

37 Reuters, "Tonnes of Dead Fish Wash up on Shore of Polluted Lebanese Lake|Reuters," April 30, 2021, https://www.reuters.com/business/environment/tonnes-dead-fish-wash-up-shore-polluted-lebanese-lake-2021-04-30/.

38 Roland Riachi, "Water Policies and Politics in Lebanon: Where Is Groundwater?" (France: International Water Management Institute, 2016, https://www.pseau.org/outils/biblio/resume.php?d=6812).

39 Naharnet, "Bassil Reveals Long-Term Water Plan for Lebanon," *Naharnet*, March 10, 2012, http://www.naharnet.com/stories/en/32891.

40 Timothy Mitchell, *Rule of Experts: Egypt, Techno-Politics, Modernity* (Berkeley and Los Angeles: University of California Press, 2002); Erik Swyngedouw, "Technonatural Revolutions: The Scalar Politics of Franco's Hydro-Social Dream for Spain, 1939–1975," *Transactions of the Institute of British Geographers* 32, no. 1 (2007): 9–28.

41 Riachi, "Institutions et Régulation d'une Ressource Naturelle Dans Une Société Fragmentée."

42 Ibid.

43 Riachi, "Water Policies and Politics in Lebanon."

44 Ibid.

45 See Nassour.

46 See Zbeeb.

47 Government of Lebanon, "Capital Investment Programme" (Economic Conference for Development through Reforms with the Private sector (CEDRE), 2018).

48 Riachi, "Water Policies and Politics in Lebanon."

49 UNDP and MoSA, *Mapping of Living Conditions in Lebanon between 1995 & 2004* (Lebanon: United Nations Development Programme and the Lebanese Ministry of Social Affairs, 2007); ILO and CAS, "Labour Force and Household Living Conditions Survey 2018–2019 Lebanon (LFHCLS)" (Beirut: International Labour Organisation and the Lebanese Central Administration of Statistics, 2020).

50 Riachi, "Institutions et Régulation d'une Ressource Naturelle Dans Une Société Fragmentée."

51 Ibid.

52 Riachi, "Water Policies and Politics in Lebanon."

53 Riachi, "Institutions et Régulation d'une Ressource Naturelle Dans Une Société Fragmentée."

54 Ibid.
55 Ibid.
56 Ibid.
57 Ibid.
58 Roland Riachi, "The Water Code Allows Private Interests to Prevail over the Common Good," *Commerce du Levant*, March 27, 2019.
59 Ibid.
60 Abdelkader Baayoun et al., "Emission Inventory of Key Sources of Air Pollution in Lebanon," *Atmospheric Environment* 215 (October 15, 2019): 116871, doi:10.1016/j.atmosenv.2019.116871.
61 See Mohammad Zbeeb's chapter in this volume.
62 Ministry of Energy and Water, "Renewable Energy Outlook: Lebanon" (IRENA in collaboration with Lebanon's Ministry of Energy and Water (MEW) and the Lebanese Centre for Energy Conservation (LCEC), 2020), https://www.irena.org/publications/2020/Jun/Renewable-Energy-Outlook-Lebanon.
63 Éric Verdeil, "Infrastructure Crises in Beirut and the Struggle to (Not) Reform the Lebanese State," *Arab Studies Journal* 16, no. 1 (2017): 84–112.
64 Government of Lebanon, "Capital Investment Programme."
65 Éric Verdeil, "Water and Electricity Networks between Stress and Reform: From Post-Civil War Reconstruction to the New Lebanese Wars," in *The Politics and Planning of Destruction and Reconstruction in Lebanon* (Oxford: 2008).
66 ILO and CAS, "LFHCLS."
67 "Lebanon: Karpowership Shuts down Electricity Supply," *BBC News*, May 14, 2021, sec. Middle East, https://www.bbc.com/news/world-middle-east-57112611.
68 ILO and CAS, "LFHCLS."
69 World Bank, "World Bank Supports Lebanon's Public Transport to Improve Mobility, Spur Growth," March 15, 2018, https://www.worldbank.org/en/news/press-release/2018/03/15/world-bank-supports-lebanons-public-transport-to-improve-mobility-spur-growth.
70 Timour Azhari, "Lebanon's First Offshore Gas Drill Is a Huge Disappointment," March 27, 2020, https://www.aljazeera.com/economy/2020/4/27/lebanons-first-offshore-gas-drill-is-a-huge-disappointment.
71 Karl Polanyi, *The Great Transformation* (Boston: Beacon Press, 1944).
72 Roland Riachi, "The Private Modes of Water Capture in Lebanon," Lebanon: Towards a Peace Economy (London: International Alert, 2015).
73 Promoted by the Civic Influence Hub.
74 Promoted by the Lebanese Oil and Gas Initiative-LOGI.
75 CDR, "Greater Beirut Water Supply Augmentation Project."

7

"Sectarian Neoliberalism" and the 2019 Uprisings in Lebanon and Iraq[1]

Rima Majed

Men Baghdad la Beirut, thawra wahde ma betmout *(From Baghdad to Beirut, one revolution that won't die)*
                    —chant that echoed in the streets of Beirut in October 2019

In October 2019, Iraq and Lebanon witnessed the eruption of revolutionary uprisings that brought millions to the streets in a wave of protest unprecedented in its scope, social composition, and magnitude. Quickly dubbed as *thawra* (or revolution), major historical events were in the making. From the initial moments, the scope, magnitude, and geographical breadth of the mobilizations made people realize that this was different—though not necessarily unrelated—to previous waves of mobilization that emerged in both countries since 2011.

Governed by a political and economic system that I describe as "sectarian neoliberalism," contemporary Lebanon and Iraq have suffered endemic social and political crises that were often met with street contestations and mass mobilizations. While not exceptional or unrelated to waves of uprising elsewhere, what makes the Iraqi and Lebanese cases particularly comparable is the political system that the protesters in these two countries are trying to topple. Revolutions in the Arab world since 2011 have all taken place in countries with authoritarian regimes or monarchies, with the exception of Lebanon and Iraq where uprisings erupted in a political system known as consociational democracy—an identity-based (sectarian and ethnic) power-sharing arrangement where the regime does not have one leader to be toppled. This—together with a fierce neoliberal economic system that heavily relies on rent, financial capitalism, and the deregulation of labor markets as well as sectarian clientelism and political patronage (known as *muhasasa*), foreign intervention and occupation, and a legacy of civil wars and violence—created what Fabio Armao would call "mafia-owned democracies."[2]

Interestingly, cycles of contention in both countries have frequently erupted concomitantly since 2011, despite the spontaneity of these protests and the absence of direct coordination between the two countries at the grassroots level. Prior to 2019, waves of protests that erupted almost in parallel in 2011, 2013, and 2015 have shaped the political trajectories in Lebanon and Iraq.[3] These trajectories have been particularly marked by the protest wave of 2015 that formed an important turning point with anti-regime mobilizations mainly focusing on socioeconomic and environmental demands beyond the overemphasized lens of identity politics.[4] This was also a pivotal moment since it resulted in the formation of "civil society" campaigns that organized and ran for municipal elections in 2016 in Lebanon[5] and parliamentary elections in 2018 in both Iraq and Lebanon.[6] Since 2015, protesters in both countries often stood in solidarity with each other in their banners and slogans (see Figure 1), acknowledging the similarities of their predicaments as countries trapped in sectarianized geopolitical dynamics between Iran on one hand[7] and the United States and its regional allies on the other.[8] However, while the streets of both countries have been boiling with popular mass movements for over a decade, it was only in October 2019 that Iraq and Lebanon came into the global spotlight as part of the second wave of uprisings that started in late 2018 with Algeria and Sudan.

The October 2019 uprisings started initially with mobilizations around socioeconomic and governance issues.[9] At the core of the demands in both Lebanon and Iraq were social questions of unemployment, unfair taxation, widespread corruption, lack of basic services such as water and electricity, financial collapse, sectarian politics, and bad governance. While this was not the first time such demands were voiced in the streets, the protests of October 2019 were clearly different in that they mobilized wide sections of society across both countries in a clear class-based discourse of "us versus them," demanding a radical change of regime rather than mere reforms.[10] This was also different in that the *thawra* in both countries mobilized, at some point, people who would have previously never mobilized or who had their political allegiance with sectarian ruling parties. The importance of these uprisings lies in the cracks they have created in the relations between many patrons/clients or leaders/followers within the Lebanese and Iraqi sectarianized clientelist polities.

The following discussion is divided into four parts. The first will briefly introduce the concept of "sectarian neoliberalism" and discuss how it has shaped the uprisings in Iraq and Lebanon. The second part will discuss whether these uprisings were "revolutions" or "revolutionary." The third part will focus on the internal contradictions of these revolutions, looking at the rhetoric of corruption, national unity, technocratic politics, and individualism. Finally, the last part will discuss the shift from the utopia and high hopes of late 2019 to the dystopia and pessimism of early 2020, with the arrival of COVID-19 and the deepening of the financial, social, and political crises in both Lebanon and Iraq.

"Sectarian Neoliberalism"

In analyzing the events that unfolded in Lebanon and Iraq since October 2019, I propose the concept of "sectarian neoliberalism," akin to "racial capitalism,"[11] to describe the particular—but not exceptional—type of regime structures these uprisings were trying to challenge. As in other parts of the world, the neoliberal capitalist system in Lebanon and Iraq depends heavily on social differentiation that takes the shape of gendered,[12] ethnicized, racialized,[13] regionalized, and sectarianized divisions.[14] In that sense, the story of sectarian neoliberalism in Lebanon and Iraq should be understood as part of a broader global story of neoliberal capitalism that strives on identity politics, social differentiation mechanisms, and right-wing populism.

However, an aspect of sectarian neoliberalism that distinguishes it from traditional understandings of "racial capitalism" is that its social divisions do not form "sticky" hierarchies but are rather fast-changing social orders that adapt identity saliencies to the often-changing economic and geopolitical dynamics.[15] In other words, while hierarchies of race and gender are relatively stable[16] within the pyramid of power relations, sectarian social saliencies are much more fluid and unstable, despite creating social hierarchies that can shape everyday practices and dynamics during given periods of time where moments of "stability" emerge. In that sense, rather than using the concept of "sectarian neoliberalism" as an analysis of identity politics at the individual level (such as discussions of "white male privileges" rather than racism as a structure[17]), this approach should help us understand how sectarianized social fields are built on legal differentiations, ideological apparatuses, security complexes, socioeconomic access and validation, and control over the state and its spoils. These dynamics shape social and political relations and intersect with class dynamics to create a structure that maintains sectarian oligarchic interests.

Moreover, "sectarian neoliberalism" differs from some understandings of "racial capitalism" in that it is not necessarily about the exploitation of the "lesser" race or sect for capital accumulation. Therefore, it is not a history of slavery[18] or the exploitation of one particular sect that led to the development of this particular type of capitalism. Sectarian neoliberalism is to be understood as a social order that can at once exploit and benefit the same group based on the individual's position within the grid of political allegiances, patronage networks, and gender and class privileges. In that sense, this system is not about capital accumulation solely from the labor exploitation of one group, but it is rather a form of "mafia rule"[19] governed by clientelist relationship between sectarian political leaders and their constituencies, based on exploitative labor relations that become perceived as privileges in the context of rampant unemployment, underemployment, informality, and precarity. In the absence of state welfare provisions and redistribution, and given the deregulation of labor relations under neoliberalism, these sectarian networks of patronage become the only alternative for wide sections of society to access security and livelihood.

Therefore, from the first moments of the uprisings in Lebanon and Iraq, people were clear in denouncing the two intertwined pillars of the regime: the sectarian structure and the neoliberal economic system, regardless of how they referred to it. In addition, a third important pillar of systemic differentiation was also highlighted in these movements: patriarchy.[20] Feminists in both countries played an important role in highlighting how, what I refer to as, "sectarian neoliberalism" is also heavily reliant on gender inequalities and oppression. From this perspective, many of the voices heard in the squares of Lebanon and Iraq highlighted the inability to dismantle one aspect of the regime (be it its neoliberalism, sectarianism, racism, or sexism) without tackling the others. This system of interlocking grids of oppression and exploitation needed to be radically transformed. Borrowing from Bhattacharyya's[21] discussion of "racial capitalism," the concept of "sectarian neoliberalism" therefore helps us understand "why we seem to be so divided and yet so intimately intertwined with each other."

Hence, I posit that "sectarian neoliberalism" is a useful framing that can help us grasp the complex intersections of an acute form of neoliberalism[22] and a disastrous social and political structure based on sectarianism in Lebanon and Iraq. In that sense, "sectarian neoliberalism" explores how sectarian differentiation can be useful for the development and maintenance of a neoliberal capitalist social order. This is not to say, as Bhattacharyya (2018) explains, that sectarianism is a neoliberal capitalist conspiracy, nor that neoliberalism in Lebanon and Iraq is a sectarian conspiracy. Beyond conspiracies, the system that governs both Lebanon and Iraq today is not a sectarian *and* neoliberal one but rather a "sectarian neoliberal" one—highlighting the intersectional rather than the additive nature of these structures. Therefore, (political) sectarianism and neoliberalism feed into each other to create social structures that strive on identity differentiation and class divisions—as is the case with the broader history of capital accumulation. Therefore, sectarianism and neoliberalism as systems that govern social and political relations have always gone hand in hand to shape the regimes of both Lebanon since independence in 1943 and Iraq since US-led invasion in 2003.

Revolution, Revolutionary, or Not? Rethinking our Conceptual Toolbox

The one-word chant *Thawra, thawra* (Revolution, revolution) filled the squares and the streets of most cities in Lebanon and Iraq in October 2019, when hundreds of thousands took to the streets to declare the start of what they saw as a revolution. The clarity of that liminal moment convinced people that what they were witnessing was revolutionary. However, pundits did not all agree with this description, with many adopting a more skeptical position.[23] The debate that erupted in 2011 around the accuracy of the term "revolution" in reference to the events then unfolding in the Arab region resurfaced once more in 2019. During the first wave of uprisings, some scholars and intellectuals warned us that these were not revolutions but merely revolts, upheavals, uprisings, or "refolution."[24] Others declared these events "revolutions without revolutionaries."[25] It might be true that these events do not fall under the traditional definition of "revolutions" found in social movement literature; however, it is important to think of them in terms of revolutionary *processes*,[26] rather than as *events* that either succeed or fail. It is also important to take into account the temporal aspect that governs the definition of revolutions.

Revolutions are often referred to as such only in retrospect, once they have overthrown a ruling class or regime. This process can take years, if not decades, and frequently fails. Even the most celebrated revolutions did not unfold without cycles of ebbs and flows and were decades in the making. For example, the widely celebrated French Revolution took around eight decades, and several rounds of conflict and counterrevolution, before the First Republic was established. Even the Russian Revolution of 1917 can be understood as a broader political process that started in 1905 and that had several episodes before the final blow was struck against the tsarist regime in 1917. Therefore, in thinking about the events of October 2019 in Lebanon and Iraq as revolutionary uprisings our theoretical and conceptual toolbox needs to be updated to make room for "finding the revolutionary in the revolution."[27]

Hence, it is important not to dismiss or downplay the role of these experiences as long-term processes shaping and transforming the political imaginaries of people in their everyday lives. This utopian and revolutionary potential of seeking and imagining an alternative—beyond sectarian, dictatorial, or capitalist realism—needs to be centered in our understanding of these historical moments. After all, sociologist Jeffrey Paige was right to say that "revolution has a future even if many theoretical definitions of revolution do not."[28] In that sense, we should not get bogged down in the highly normative, fixed, and sometimes misplaced debates about whether these are revolutions or not; and more importantly we should surely not shy away from adopting the term "revolutionary" in referring to the historical developments in Lebanon or Iraq since 2019. By using the words "revolution" and "revolutionary" we will, first, be honoring the experiences of millions who believed in the revolutionary potential of the moment in question, who themselves called the events a "revolution," and who considered themselves to be revolutionaries— even if it was just for a short moment. Moreover, we will also be pushing for a theoretical rethinking of the meaning and form of revolution under twenty-first-century neoliberal capitalism more broadly. This is therefore not a call to move away from theoretical debates about what revolutions constitute but rather to rethink our conceptual toolbox and adapt it to the realities of our era. This is particularly important in the case of Lebanon and Iraq, as it can help us understand how these revolutionary moments had considerable internal contradictions: rejecting the sectarian neoliberal system while at times also adopting its discursive and ideological pillars, as discussed below.

Fighting Sectarian Neoliberalism with Its Liberal Political Culture?

Revolutionary moments are often imbued with contradictory features and dynamics. Thus, it is possible for people to fight against sectarian neoliberalism while also adopting several of its liberal clichés and slogans, such as a focus on nationalism, a discourse of anti-corruption, an admiration for technocracy and leaderlessness, and an individualist approach that cannot grasp the radical collectivity of revolutionary moments beyond sectarian groupness. A closer look at the 2019 revolutions in Lebanon and Iraq reveals such contradictions.

Nationalism versus Sectarianism?

Waving the national flag and singing the national anthem were common, and sometimes predominant, in public squares across Lebanon and Iraq in 2019. This fixation on the

Lebanese or Iraqi national identity as a way to express a rejection of sectarian and ethnic divisions, and to highlight "coexistence" and "national unity," was not new or exceptional. The focus on a national identity and patriotism has been observed in many other countries (such as Algeria and Egypt) where the national question remains central in shaping the political imaginaries of revolutionaries. In other countries, such as Syria and Libya, protesters adopted the modified independence flag to mark a rupture with the dictatorial regimes (of the Ba'ath Party and of Muammar Gaddafi) and their associated flags. This play on the relationship between the flag, the national anthem, and the regime has unfolded in most squares and streets across the Arab region since 2011.

In Lebanon and Iraq, though, protesters have often adopted a nationalist approach not in order to express the legacy of a national struggle, pride in a strong nation, or a rejection of a certain flag associated with the regime but rather to illustrate their quest to establish a genuine nation, through their attempts to overcome sectarian divisions. However, is nationalism necessarily the opposite of sectarianism? Decades of literature on sectarianism and nationalism show that these two phenomena are often two sides of the same coin. In Lebanon and Iraq, nationalism has often been deployed with a sectarian connotation, in contrast to many national liberation struggles, in which nationalism represented a political ideology that was in opposition to colonization or occupation. The history of the region provides a nuanced account in this regard. To give two examples: Arab nationalism has historically been associated with Sunni overtones; and Lebanese nationalism has often entailed a Christian connotation. However, it remains common for ordinary members of society to use a nationalist discourse in order to signal their rejection of sectarianism. Seen in this light we can say that the uprisings in both Iraq and Lebanon have clearly attempted to address the question of sectarianism through the demand of an "imagined nation" as a remedy.

In Iraq's 2019 uprising, the main slogans in the squares were "The people want to overthrow the regime" (the famous chant of the 2011 protests across the Arab region) and *Nreed watan* (We want a homeland). This was coupled with chants and banners denouncing sectarianism and asserting the fraternity between Iraqi Sunnis and Shias. By demanding a "homeland"[29] and rejecting sectarianism, the protesters were signaling a desire for a modern state that would be able to serve its citizens and provide a sense of belonging beyond sectarian and ethnic fragmentation.

In Lebanon, a similar process of reimagining the "nation" beyond sectarian fragmentation was observed. Squares quickly filled with the national flag, and the Lebanese anthem was repeatedly heard on loudspeakers. While the main slogans also included the famous "The people want to overthrow the regime," a more custom-made slogan was added: *Kellon ya'ne kellon* (All of them means all of them), signaling a rejection of the sectarian power-sharing system and denouncing all leaders, regardless of their sectarian belonging. Like in Iraq, the rejection of political sectarianism was expressed through a desire to remove all sectarian leaders and build a "country," a "state," and a "nation" that will protect its citizens and treat them equally and justly.

However, sectarianism was not the only problem that needed to be tackled in the two countries: a dire economic situation also loomed over the scene. Therefore, the discourse of national unity and coexistence was coupled with slogans about the economic situation, often in the form of "anti-corruption" rhetoric.

Corruption or Structural Obstacles?

A trend that appeared in both revolutions, and that seemed to contradict the radical aspirations of the moment, was the predominance of a liberal discourse around "corruption." Of course, corruption is a major problem in Lebanon and Iraq. However, the alarmingly high rates of youth unemployment, the deregulation of labor markets, the expansion of the informal sector, the politics of austerity, the lack of development in productive economic sectors, the heavy reliance on imports for basic needs (such as food and electricity), the debt crisis, and the reliance on financial capital (the banking sector) or oil rent are hardly the result of corruption *only*. These are clearly indicators of a deeper crisis in the neoliberal capitalist system that has, in the case of Lebanon and Iraq, intersected with a sectarian political system and a heavy militarization of some political parties to create a sort of "mafia state," where ruling elites have acted to ensure the state and its spoils serve their economic interests and those of the business and banking cronies that sustain them.

The flourishing of such an oligarchy that controls the state and uses it for its own benefits, shielded from accountability or often protected by the law itself, has allowed for patronage networks and the politics of clientelism to strive and shape what has been called the "politics of non-state welfare."[30] In this context, revolutionaries in the streets of Lebanon and Iraq who were protesting unemployment or financial crisis were also—even if indirectly—protesting the structures of neoliberal capitalism and its local version of sectarian neoliberalism. However, the protesters' framing remained mainly fixated on anti-corruption and did not address the structure of the economic system. More and more, the crisis was reduced to the corruption of a few "bad leaders" who needed to be replaced by better and more ethical technocrats. Shaped by an NGO lingo of anti-corruption that fails to tackle neoliberal capitalism as a root cause, this trend obscured the more radical drive of the first few days of the protests, which called for the complete overhaul of the system, rather than merely the replacement of corrupt politicians.

Technocratic Politics and Leaderlessness

The popular demand for a technocratic government that emerged in the aftermath of the resignation of the prime ministers of Lebanon and Iraq in October 2019 became a life vest for the two regimes that later used it to form allegedly "independent" governments of technocrats to salvage themselves. How did the protesters that wanted to uproot the whole system end up demanding from the regimes to form technocratic governments?

This third contradiction in the 2019 uprisings in Lebanon and Iraq revealed itself in the schism between the radical demands of a complete overhaul on one side and the widespread celebrations of leaderlessness and technocratic political demands on the other side. Given the state of affairs in both countries, political organization and political leadership came to be equated by wide sections of society with corruption and criminality. A new generation had grown to perceive party politics as bad and to distance itself from political organization or leadership aspirations. For most people, being patriotic and honest meant staying away from politics. This "anti-politics" approach, although rooted in an aversion to conventional politics, translated in many cases into a rejection of all types of organizing or leadership. This resulted in a deep contradiction during the initial days of the uprisings, when the popular will to oust the regimes was at its highest, while the popular capacity to provide a political alternative was clearly weak. This crisis of political organization led the masses to raise demands that at times sounded anarchist (rejecting any rule or leadership) and at others liberal (the demand for the formation of a technocratic government).

Here again the demands fell short of addressing the radical and revolutionary potential of the moment. This situation needs to be understood as a consequence of the weakness of leftist political organization and the co-optation of unions and syndicates. The revolutionary fervor was thus guided by political trends that diluted the revolutionary political path, instead of strengthening it.

Given the weakness of unions in both countries, road blockades were a widely used tactic to indirectly bring the country to a halt, thus imposing a de facto general strike.[31] The imposed closure of businesses and institutions allowed for huge crowds to mobilize in the streets and created a revolutionary moment. Similarly, the student movements[32] played a crucial role in sustaining the uprisings in both Lebanon and Iraq, through their calls for strikes and mobilization. However, despite the huge collective efforts of hundreds of thousands who gave their best to ensure the success of this revolutionary moment, the lack of organization and leadership, and the decades of depoliticization and NGO-ization in Lebanon since the early 1990s, and in Iraq since 2003, created a political ceiling for the uprisings that was much lower than the popular aspirations that animated them.

My Revolution or Ours? In Search of a Collective "We"

The articulations and changing dynamics of the uprisings in Iraq and Lebanon remind us that neoliberalism is more than a question of financial structures: it is also an ideological manifestation. Hence, the contradiction between the collectiveness of the revolutionary moment and the individualism of the political framings that emerged from the collective action is emblematic of the neoliberal age. This was noticeable in how some of the major political initiatives during this period were largely framed by an individual subjective outlook. For example, a key electoral campaign that grew out of the 2015 mobilizations in Lebanon, and that was active in the 2019 uprising, was *Beirut Madinati* (Beirut, *my* city). Instead of emphasizing a collective "our" that rethinks the city as a shared space for all, the name emphasizes an individual relationship with the city. Similarly, in the aftermath of the financial collapse in 2019, activists in the Lebanese uprising sprayed graffiti on the windows of banks, saying, "Give *me* back *my* money"—not "Give *us* back *our* money." While the collective anger against the banks was clear, the political culture that shaped the activism of this period was still a product of the very system it was fighting against. Another example of this contradictory nature of neoliberal subjectivity is the emergence of a group called "Ana Khat Ahmar" (*I* am a Red Line), initiated by business owners mainly in the media and advertising field, mobilizing their employees and partners in an attempt to blur the lines between employee/employer relations, especially at a time when alternative labor movements were being created.[33] This group is not only an example of how such discourse is centered around the individual "*Ana*" or "I," but it also shows how such mobilization has served to hijack and co-opt the possibility of class-based organizations and alternative unions to emerge by using a nationalist/patriotic discourse that makes it appear as if the interest of the business owners and their employees are one, rather than conflictual.

Many campaigns also emphasized a legal and rights-based approach that seems to be detached from the realities of both Lebanon and Iraq. In both countries, the postwar sectarian neoliberal setting flourished in the context of a weakening of the legal and judicial systems. The language of "rights" therefore does not occupy a central space in the political imaginaries of people who have learned not to trust the legal pathway. However, several prominent political movements and campaigns have centered individual "rights" as the locus of their activism. Examples include the political campaign that ignited the uprising in Iraq under the slogan *Nazel akhod haqqi* (*I* am mobilizing to take *my right*) and the political group *Li haqqi* (For *my right*) that was very active in the Lebanese uprising.

This emphasis on individual rights in political organizations and campaigns speaks to the longing for an imagined state where the rule of law is respected. However, as suggested earlier, the pervasiveness of a neoliberal culture that enshrines individualism and individual rights seems to be at odds with the progressive politics of collectiveness embodied in the revolutions' squares—even if only for a short time.

From Utopia to Dystopia: Liminality, COVID-19, and Counterrevolution

"We did not want to sleep because the dream we were living while awake was much nicer." Interview conducted by author on May 11, 2021

This is how the experience of living the early days of the 2019 *thawra* was described by a young man from the Chouf-Aley region of Mount Lebanon. The liminal[34] experience of revolution as a dream-like feeling of "temporal limbo"[35] or a stark break from the previous "normal" led the protesters to believe that this was a moment full of possibilities. The rapid transformations in people's everyday lived experiences in Lebanon and Iraq, and the spontaneous emergence of a "communitas," where togetherness and comradeship reigned in the squares, were hard to miss in the early days of the revolution. Cooperation and camaraderie, meetings in tents, public political discussions, and a festive mood shaped life in the squares. However, this was disrupted by the heavy violence and repression of state apparatuses and their connected militias. While the repression backfired at first, leading more people to mobilize in outrage at the targeting of protesters, by the end of 2019 the revolution in both countries had started to enter a deadlock, with a lack of political alternatives, an inability to continue the strikes, and a repositioning of the regimes after the initial shock they had received in October 2019.

As 2020 started, a series of highly exceptional circumstances aligned to halt the revolutionary process in both countries: a global pandemic, a deep financial collapse, and, in Lebanon, the massive explosion at the Port of Beirut, which shattered both the city and its inhabitants. These external circumstances were added to the co-optation and counterrevolutionary wave that had deepened by the end of 2019. The formation of so-called technocratic governments became the ancien régime's way to continue governing, despite the difficulty of this task after October 2019 in both countries.

However, the arrival of the COVID-19 pandemic in the region came not only as a public health threat but also as a counterrevolutionary turn of events.[36] The squares were forcibly emptied and street mobilizations were halted. The state used the opportunity to crack down on dissent under the pretext of preserving public health. It became difficult to sustain the uprisings, despite the deepening of the political and economic crises. The sudden move from the intense communal experience of the revolution to the intense isolation of COVID-related lockdowns led to a general feeling of defeat.

The utopia of the early revolutionary days was quickly overshadowed by the dystopia of the pandemic and what followed. The downward spiral of both countries into economic misery made the possibilities of organizing more difficult. In Lebanon, the Beirut Port explosion of August 4, 2020, described as the third biggest nonnuclear explosion in history, devastated the city and led to a massive wave of migration out of the country.[37] Furthermore, a series of political assassinations in Iraq, and to a lesser extent in Lebanon, underlined that political opposition carried with it a real threat of death at any moment. However, now that the pandemic is starting to recede, and as the political deadlock and financial crises are deepening, the revolutionary processes that started in Lebanon and Iraq in October 2019 are bound to continue, albeit in new shapes and forms that will either take a more violent turn or reproduce more of the same until a revolutionary transition matures.

Conclusion

This chapter has argued that the revolutionary uprisings of October 2019 in Lebanon and Iraq can only be read as part of a broader revolutionary process that started to unfold in 2011, and that intensified in both countries in 2015, before reaching the eruption point of 2019 as part of the second wave of uprisings in the region. What distinguishes these revolutions from the rest of the region is their opposition to a particular system best described as "sectarian neoliberalism." While these uprisings might not fall under traditional definitions of revolutions—since they have not overthrown the regime as a whole—it is important to think of them as part of a revolutionary *process*. This is not only because we should avoid limiting revolutions to temporal *events* or qualifying them as political *dichotomies* (in which they either succeed or fail) but also because it is crucial to rethink the meaning and shapes of revolution under twenty-first-century neoliberal capitalism globally.

The chapter has discussed the internal contradictions that characterized the uprisings in Lebanon and Iraq in 2019, with the dominance of a liberal discourse of national coexistence, anti-corruption, individual rights, and technocratic politics that fell short of the radical potential of the initial moment of eruption. The analysis has suggested that one important consequence of the sectarian neoliberal system that governs both countries, and that therefore favors individual interlocutors, has been the weakness of political organizations or trade unions: in other words, the structures that could serve as a scaffold supporting the transition to a new political system. Such organizations are also needed to challenge the two-pole regimes in the two countries, where sectarianism and neoliberalism feed into each other to reproduce more of the same.

With the recent spread of COVID-19 in both countries, the emergence and organization of a lost "we" is a priority in order to defeat a system that is clearly unable to protect society, either from economic disasters or from health pandemics. New forms of organizing, whether in the workplace or at the neighborhood level, and organizations that bring together the unemployed, migrant workers, domestic workers, and informal workers, are all crucial in order to build a stronger movement that can move beyond sectarian neoliberalism as both an economic structure and an ideological apparatus that shapes our political imagination and delimits our political possibilities.

It is only by linking our struggles together, within our societies and across the colonial boundaries of the nation-state, that these revolutionary uprisings can prevail. Thus, it is by standing in solidarity with Palestine, supporting Amazon workers in the United States, and defending the rights of refugees and migrant workers or the ambitions of the feminist movement that the Lebanese and Iraqi uprisings will reach their full revolutionary potential, both ideologically and politically, beyond sectarian neoliberalism.

Notes

1   The author would like to particularly thank Miriyam Aouragh, Hamza Hamouchene, and Melanie Cammett for detailed comments of earlier drafts of this chapter. A previous formulation of this work has been published with the Transnational Institute in 2021.

2   F. Armao, "Mafia-Owned Democracies: Italy and Mexico as Patterns of Criminal Neoliberalism," *Tiempo devorado* 2, no. 1 (2015): 4–21.

3   See R. Majed, *Contemporary Social Movements in Iraq: Mapping the Labour Movement and the 2015 Mobilizations* (Berlin: Rosa Luxemburg Stiftung, 2020); and Maha Yehya, *The Summer of Our Discontent: Sects and Citizens in Lebanon and Iraq* (Beirut: Carnegie Middle East Center, 2017).

4   See Z. Ali, "From Recognition to Redistribution? Protest Movements in Iraq in the Age of 'New Civil Society,'" *Journal of Intervention and Statebuilding* 15, no. 4 (2021): 528–42.

5   A. K. Rønn, "The Development and Negotiation of Frames During Non-sectarian Mobilizations in Lebanon," *The Review of Faith & International Affairs* 18, no. 1 (2020): 87–96.

6   See N. El Kak, "A Path for Political Change in Lebanon? Lessons and Narratives from the 2018 Elections," *Arab Reform Initiative* (2019), https://www.arab-reform.net/publication/a -path-for-political-change-in-lebanon-lessons-and-narratives-from-the-2018-elections/; and T. Dodge, "Iraq: A Year of Living Dangerously," *Survival* 60, no. 5 (2018): 41–8.

7   See D. Postel, "The Other Regional Counter-Revolution: Iran's Role in the Shifting Political Landscape of the Middle East," *New Politics* (2021), https://newpol.org/the -other-regional-counter-revolution-irans-role-in-the-shifting-political-landscape-of -the-middle-east/.

8   See Karam's chapter in this volume.

9   See Bassel F. Salloukh, "Here's What the Protests in Lebanon and Iraq are Really About," *Monkey Cage (Washington Post)*, 2019.

10 N. Turkmani and Z. Alkinani, "From Iraq to Lebanon and Back: The People Want the Fall of the Regime," *OpenDemocracy* (2019), https://www.opendemocracy.net/en/ north-africa-west-asia/iraq-lebanon-and-back-people-want-fall-regime/.

11 For more on "racial capitalism" see J. Go, "Three Tensions in the Theory of Racial Capitalism," *Sociological Theory* 39, no. 1 (2021): 38–47; G. Bhattacharyya, *Rethinking Racial Capitalism: Questions of Reproduction and Survival* (London: Rowman & Littlefield, 2018); R. D. Kelley, "What Did Cedric Robinson Mean by Racial Capitalism?" *Boston Review* 12 (2017), https://bostonreview.net/articles/robin-d-g -kelley-introduction-race-capitalism-justice/.

12 See M. Mikdashi, "Sex and Sectarianism: The Legal Architecture of Lebanese Citizenship," *Comparative Studies of South Asia, Africa and the Middle East* 34, no. 2 (2014): 279–93.

13 See D. Dermitzaki and S. Riewendt, "The Kafāla System: Gender and Migration in Contemporary Lebanon," *Middle East-Topics & Arguments* 14 (2020): 89–102.

14 See B. F. Salloukh, R. Barakat, J. S. al-Habbal, L. W. Khattab and S. Mikaelian, *The Politics of Sectarianism in Postwar Lebanon* (London: Pluto Press, 2015).

15 See R. Majed, "In Defense of Intra-Sectarian Divide: Street Mobilization, Coalition Formation, and Rapid Realignments of Sectarian Boundaries in Lebanon," *Social Forces* 99, no. 4 (2021): 1772–98.

16 This does not mean that race or gender identity is fixed or unchanging but to highlight the structural hierarchies that racial and gendered systems create. Therefore, it is a comment about stratification and hierarchy rather than identity.

17 For more on this critique of identity politics see M. Aouragh, "'White privilege' and Shortcuts to Anti-Racism," *Race & Class* 61, no. 2 (2019): 3–26.

18 See W. Johnson, "To Remake the World: Slavery, Racial Capitalism, and Justice," *Boston Review* 20 (2018), https://bostonreview.net/forum/walter-johnson-to-remake -the-world/.

19 For more on this see Jason Sardell and Oleg V. Pavlov, and Khalid Saeed, "Economic Origins of the Mafia and Patronage System in Sicily (July 8, 2009)," in the *Proceedings of the 27th International Conference of the System Dynamics Society* (Albuquerque, New Mexico, July 26–29, 2009), Available at SSRN: https://ssrn.com/abstract =2983507; J. Walston, *The Mafia and Clientelism: Roads to Rome in Post-War Calabria* (London: Routledge, 2020); and T. Hilgers, "Clientelism and Conceptual Stretching: Differentiating among Concepts and among Analytical Levels," *Theory and Society* 40, no. 5 (2011): 567–88.

20 For more on this, see Z. Ali, *Women and Gender in Iraq: Between Nation-Building and Fragmentation* (Cambridge: Cambridge University Press, 2018); and Mikdashi, "Sex and Sectarianism."

21 Bhattacharyya, *Rethinking Racial Capitalism*, ix

22 One can argue that neoliberalism in Lebanon has started since its very inception as an independent state and especially with the political thought of some of its founding ideologues such as Michel Chiha. For more on this see: T. Gaspard, *A Political Economy of Lebanon, 1948–2002: The Limits of Laissez-Faire* (Leiden and Boston: Brill, 2004) or C. Farah, The Moral Limits of Michel Chiha's Economic Liberalism, 2021. In contrast, neoliberalism in Iraq started after the US-led invasion in 2003 and the shock doctrine that followed. For more see N. Klein, *The Shock Doctrine: The Rise of Disaster Capitalism* (New York: Macmillan, 2007).

23 For a discussion on the framing of 2011, see G. Achcar, "Introduction: Uprisings and Revolutions," in *The People Want: A Radical Exploration of the Arab Uprising* (Berkeley: University of California Press, 2013), 13–19.

24 A. Bayat, *Revolution without Revolutionaries: Making Sense of the Arab Spring* (Stanford: Stanford University Press, 2017).

25 Ibid.

26 See Achcar, *The People Want*.

27 J. Paige, "Finding the Revolutionary in the Revolution: Social Science Concepts and the Future of Revolution," in *The Future of Revolutions: Rethinking Radical Change in the Age of Globalization*, ed. J. Foran (London: Zed Books, 2003), 19–29.

28 Ibid., 19.

29 See Z. Ali, "Iraqis Demand a Country," *MERIP: Middle East Research and Information Project* 292, no. 3 (Fall/Winter 2019).

30 See Melani Cammett, *Compassionate Communalism: Welfare and Sectarianism in Lebanon* (Ithaca: Cornell University Press, 2014).

31 See Rawane Nassif in this volume.

32 See Samir Skayni in this volume.

33 See Nadim El Kak in this volume.

34 For more discussion on liminality in the context of Lebanon, see R. Majed, "Living Revolution, Financial Collapse and Pandemic in Beirut: Notes on Temporality, Spatiality, and 'double liminality,'" *Middle East Law and Governance* 12, no. 3 (2020): 305–15.

35 L. Ryzova, "The Battle of Muhammad Mahmoud Street in Cairo: The Politics and Poetics of Urban Violence in Revolutionary Time," *Past & Present* 247, no. 1 (2020): 278.

36 See Joseph Daher in this volume.

37 A. Ibrahim, "A New Exodus from Lebanon after Deadly Beirut Blast," *Al Jazeera*, 2020.

8

The Shadow Guardians of the Status Quo

The Lebanon Uprising of 2019 and the International Politics of Counterrevolution[1]

Jeffrey G. Karam

Many regional and global powers still guard the status quo in Lebanon against revolutionary movements and alternative groups that have tried to reform or overhaul the sectarian-based political system.[2] However, with the support of coercive institutions, especially the state's security apparatus and the alliances between public institutions and private corporations, the cross-sectarian class of political and business elite has so far been successful in undercutting calls for change and preventing any significant sociopolitical reforms, the latest being in what transpired after the eruption of the massive social uprising on October 17, 2019.[3] What explains the tenaciousness of the sectarian and neoliberal political system in Lebanon against revolutionary struggles and calls for reform?

This chapter explains the durability and persistence of the Lebanese political system by elucidating the causes of counterrevolutionary narratives and actions during revolutionary times, or what Charles Tilly labels as "revolutionary situations."[4] The chapter makes a threefold argument. First, it explains how foreign states perceive power vacuums and disruptions to established political orders and why they often bolster status quo regimes. Thus, I argue for considering the confluence between international, regional, and local forces. Second, it complicates the binary of revolutionary and counterrevolutionary situations by moving beyond common and temporal characterizations of either resistance or repression. Hence, I argue that an inclusive account of moments of revolt and counterstrategies is an important component of the lifecycles of revolutionary processes that waver between euphoria and disenchantment. Third, I argue for a new perspective on counterrevolution that underscores explicit and implicit forms of coercion. For instance, a foreign state could support protests against established orders and back different state institutions to safeguard the status quo.

The chapter draws on a selection of new primary records and secondary accounts to compare how Iran and the United States acted as the shadow guardians of the status quo from the initial phase of the uprising in October 2019 to February 2020.[5] This periodization is related to the fact that the Lebanese Parliament granted confidence to Hassan Diab's government on February 11, 2020.[6] Consequently, this juncture partly led to the loss in revolutionary momentum that characterized the period between October and February. Yet, it is important to note that many developments after February 2020, including the deepening of the economic crisis, the COVID-19 pandemic, and the August 4 catastrophe in Beirut, are likewise vital for analyzing revolutionary and counterrevolutionary trends.[7] Importantly, the focus on Iran and the United States pertains to two considerations. The first relates to the similarities between the United States and its allies in the Middle East on pursuing a dual strategy that supported the protesters in their movement and simultaneously provided aid to the government's coercive institutions. The second centers on the overlap between Iran and its allies that questioned the motives of different protesters and why they viewed that the intelligence services of some foreign states were funding and controlling the mass mobilization against the existing political order.[8] Both considerations reflect the fluidity of the different faces and phases of revolutions and counterrevolutions that are often discussed separately rather than jointly.

The chapter proceeds in the following manner. First, it briefly surveys existing explanations on counterrevolution and then focuses on these strategies in Lebanon. Second, it presents a novel explanation on the international and varied dimensions of counterrevolution. Third, it explores the role of Iran and the United States as two of the most important counterrevolutionary forces during the October uprising of 2019 and shortly afterward. Fourth, it recaps the various dimensions of Iran and the US counterrevolutionary strategies.

Existing Scholarship on Revolutions and Counterrevolutions

After the first wave of the Arab uprisings in 2011, many underscored the role of coercive institutions to maintain the status quo from disruptions.[9] Beyond the state's security apparatus, other pillars, including traditional media platforms, co-opted labor movements, established political parties, and regime loyalists, private corporations, banks, and civil society organizations interacted collectively to guard the status quo.[10]

Before briefly engaging with scholarship on counterrevolutions, it is important to define revolutions.[11] If one adopts Theda Skocpol's classic definition of a social revolution that centers on "rapid, basic transformations of a society's state and class structures" then, except Tunisia, much of the transformational developments that occurred between the first and second wave of uprisings in the Middle East are not "revolutionary."[12] An alternative definition moves from Skocpol's conceptualization and considers social protests as an integral part of a "revolutionary situation."[13] While many scholars still build on the Skocpolian definition and view that revolutions mark the building of a new sociopolitical order that results from mass mobilization, a few examine the different moments—failed, aborted, or defeated—of contestation during revolutionary situations.[14] Thus, many investigate "revolutionary processes" rather than focus on the binary of failed or successful revolutionary outcomes.[15]

A focus on "revolutionary processes" likewise allows for examining counterrevolutionary processes. While a classic definition of counterrevolution focuses on reversing revolutionary situations and restoring the status quo that existed *before* mass mobilization, a more inclusive account of counterrevolutionary processes centers on the variation in the institutional aspects status quo regimes could employ to repress revolutionaries.[16] As a result, counterrevolutionaries seek to drive a wedge between revolutionary actors by dismantling the "social embeddedness" that pushes people consciously and unconsciously to the street.[17] Hence, counterrevolutionary strategies employ implicit and explicit tactics to reestablish the status quo.[18] By focusing on the international dimensions of counterrevolution, the emphasis is on the interactions between local, regional, and global forces.[19]

The Conventional Wisdom and a New Explanation on Counterrevolution in Lebanon

The conventional wisdom on counterrevolutions in Lebanon focuses primarily on domestic factors, especially the sectarian foundations of the Lebanese polity and the formation of cross-sectarian alliances between the Christian and Muslim political elite that prevent fundamental changes to the existing political order.[20] Consequently, the power-sharing formula between Lebanon's political and business elite and flawed decision-making processes that thrive on communal consensus is a central pillar of counterrevolution. Others study the alliances between some Lebanese groups and regional powers, especially Saudi Arabia and Iran, and the recurrent gridlocks between various political movements.[21] These accounts suggest that regional and international powers support groups in Lebanon for power projection, strategic interests (political and economic), and bargaining leverage in the Middle East and globally.

Existing scholarship adopts a classic discussion of counterrevolution that analyzes how the state's security apparatus uses violence, reestablishes fear barriers that prevent continued mobilization, creates a wedge between revolutionaries, and provides limited concessions to decrease the momentum of protests. The emphasis is also on the role of legal institutions, traditional media platforms, regime loyalists, different lobby groups, including private business owners, and other organizations in supporting the regime's counterrevolution.[22]

My alternative explanation on counterrevolutions refutes the temporal and binary characterizations of resistance and repression and argues that moments of revolt and counterstrategies are critical junctures in the lifecycles of revolutionary processes that involve linkages between local, regional, and global forces.[23] For different policy considerations, foreign powers could bolster the status quo due to how they perceive political vacuums and the inability to find suitable alternatives to safeguard their interests. Moreover, foreign states could pursue policies that both bolster the existing ruling class and support revolutionary actors.[24] Foreign powers often bolster existing political actors that successfully prevent disruptions to the status quo.[25] For example, the United States propped up many authoritarian regimes in the Arabian Gulf to prevent price shocks to the oil market and preserve American energy security goals.[26]

The Regional and International Dimensions of Counterrevolution during the Uprising

On the eve of October 17, 2019, hundreds of protesters took to the streets of Beirut and other cities, blocked roads across the country, and smashed several shops and banks in Beirut.[27] The regime's initial crackdown began hours after people took to the streets on October 17.[28] A failed attempt by the political elite to promise quick economic reforms and massive pressure from the street forced Saad Hariri's government to resign on October 29, 2019.[29] This resignation partly undercut the popular momentum that characterized the first twelve days of the revolutionary situation and even led some protesters to vacate squares and halt roadblocking.[30]

In the initial months of the revolutionary situation, various foreign states opted for different counterrevolutionary tactics. An account of the various faces and phases of counterrevolution pursued by Iran and the United States suggests two observations. First, the Iranian government expressed its frustration with the protests in Lebanon and Iraq in 2019 and implicitly called on Hezbollah, its chief ally in Lebanon, to repress what it viewed as a Western-led conspiracy against the "Axis of Resistance."[31] Second, the US government wavered between expressing solidarity with the protesters and supporting the Lebanese Armed Forces (LAF)[32] that played a major role in repressing protests.

Focusing on the regional and international features of counterrevolution, and specifically, the role of Iran and the United States in Lebanon, is vital for two factors. It first explains why these two foreign states acted as counterrevolutionary actors during a transformational moment in Lebanon's modern history. Thus, it contributes to existing scholarship that explicates some of the factors that *still* lead foreign states to support unpopular and despotic regimes to maintain the status quo.[33] Second, it focuses on the Lebanon uprising as part of the ongoing intellectual conversation that addresses revolutionary struggles and counterrevolutionary actions during the first and second waves of Arab uprisings.[34] To this end, I explain how Iran and the United States *still* converged on guarding the status quo even though they were motivated by different factors and employed distinctive strategies.

It is important to avoid the trope of exceptionalizing this moment in Lebanon's modern history. In this context, I argue that Lebanon's revolutionary uprising is part of the wider regional and global context of mobilization and counterstrategies against established orders. Therefore, an analysis of revolutionary and counterrevolutionary action in Lebanon is part of the broader scholarly and activist dialogue of similar events in Algeria, Iran, Iraq, and Sudan in 2019.[35] It also frames these uprisings in the Middle East and North Africa in concert with mass protests in Colombia, Chile, Ecuador, France, Hong Kong, India, and elsewhere.[36] Much of these protests are *still* unfolding, partly due to economic grievances, the mishandling of the COVID-19 pandemic, and other intersectional considerations that cut across borders and regions in the Global North and South.

Maintaining the Status Quo: Iran's Counterrevolutionary Rhetoric and Actions

How did the Iranian regime that presents itself as "revolutionary" state play a major counterrevolutionary role in Lebanon in 2019?[37]

On October 19, 2019, Hassan Nasrallah, secretary general of Hezbollah, took to the screen to criticize the revolutionary situation.[38] Nasrallah wavered between calling the revolutionary uprising a foreign and mostly supported Western "*hirak* (movement)" and admitting that the protesters had legitimate socioeconomic grievances.[39] Nasrallah's target audience was Hezbollah partisans and broadly the Shiite milieu that were equally suffering from the dire economic situation. However, his immediate response that resurfaced regularly in speeches emphasized the role of Western intelligence agencies and embassies in funding and directing the protests against the "Axis of Resistance."

In parallel with Nasrallah's speeches, many regime loyalists unswervingly took to the streets to defy and intimidate protesters and used violence against different factions, especially in neighborhoods that included a majority of Shiite constituents.[40] The international dimensions of Hezbollah's counterrevolution are twofold. The first centers on Iran's perception of the Syrian uprising in 2011 and how the Assad regime repressed the opposition. The second relates to how the Iranian regime undercut protests in 2009 and 2017–18.

Learning from and Supporting the Assad's Regime Repression of the Syrian Uprising

Shortly after the outbreak of the revolutionary uprising against the Assad regime in March 2011, Iranian diplomats and military officers shuttled between Damascus and Tehran. The Iranian government dispatched special forces, provided riot equipment, and offered advice to security officials in the Assad regime to squash the opposition and maintain the status quo.[41] Iranian officials perceived the Syrian uprising as a foreign-led and mostly Western-inspired movement that would foster the rise of terrorist groups.[42] Iran's role as a counterrevolutionary actor from the Syrian uprising in 2011 to the present day served as an important lesson for suppressing the revolutionary situations in Lebanon and Iraq in 2019.[43]

Consequently, Hezbollah's military intervention in support of the Assad regime in mid-2012 was framed as part of a war against terrorist organizations growing between Iraq, Syria, and Lebanon. In 2013, Nasrallah openly declared Hezbollah's military involvement in and support of the Assad regime as part of the "resistance against Israel."[44] As a result, Hezbollah, with Iranian sponsorship, remains, as of this moment, one of the most important counterrevolutionary actors in Syria. Specifically, Hezbollah has steadfastly supported the Assad regime to maintain the status quo by deploying its military factions to quell the uprising.[45]

Accordingly, by supporting Hezbollah to bolster the Assad regime, Iranian officials were focused on maintaining their strategic interests and standing against Israel and the United States.[46] The Iranian regime perceived the revolutionary situations in Iraq and Lebanon in 2019 as a new source of threat that could destabilize the regional balance of power and possibly curb Iran's influence in both Arab states. Specifically, by reflecting on the revolutionary situation in Syria, Hezbollah and Iran concurrently warned of the dangers of changing the status quo and "any [political] vacuum" in Lebanon.[47] On October 25, 2019, Nasrallah even warned that "there might be someone preparing for a civil war similar to what they did in several countries and neighboring states."[48] By drawing on the example of a civil war in neighboring states and instilling the fear of a political vacuum, Iran, through Hezbollah, strongly voiced its support for quelling the revolutionary situation and guarding the status quo in Lebanon after the eruption of the October uprising.

Drawing on Iran's Playbook of Tactics

Against this background, one can understand Hezbollah's perception of the Lebanon uprising in 2019 and the overlap between Nasrallah and Ali Khamenei's, Iran's Supreme Leader, narratives on Western-led conspiracies. However, it is important to note that the violence unleashed by partisans close to Hezbollah and Amal was less intense than the coercion against protesters in Syria, Iraq, or Iran. Nonetheless, a few days after the beginning of the uprising in Lebanon, Khamenei confirmed the importance of drawing from Iran's experience in bolstering the status quo in Syria and Iraq.[49] Specifically, the Islamic Republic's Supreme Leader blamed the United States, Saudi Arabia, and their allies for "stoking unrest in Lebanon and Iraq."[50] Khamenei equally called on the protesters in Lebanon and Iraq to seek change in nonviolent and lawful measures and reiterated how Iran's "armed forces were present as well, and they helped to foil" a similar and Western-led plot that failed to spread turmoil in the Islamic Republic.[51] Mahmoud Vaezi, President Hassan Rouhani's chief of staff, equally called on different foreign states, especially the United States, Saudi Arabia, and Israel, to cease their interference in Lebanon and Iraq and halt financial support for forces seeking to disrupt the status quo.[52]

By summoning Iran's "success" with quelling the opposition in the period after the elections in 2009 and then again between late 2017 and 2018, Khamenei was bolstering Hezbollah's counterrevolution and providing a frame for labeling the revolutionary situation as a Western-led plot. Nasrallah's counterrevolutionary narrative of the Western-inspired plot in Lebanon has roots in Iran's role in propping up Hezbollah and "exporting the revolution" to the Middle East against US and Israeli interests.[53] Importantly, only a few weeks before the beginning of the revolutionary situation in Lebanon, Nasrallah praised Khamenei's support of Hezbollah in "the principles, goals, foundations, criteria, and guidelines that we [Hezbollah] had, [Khamenei] provided a solution to every issue."[54] The overlap in discourse between Khamenei and Nasrallah inspired Hezbollah's counterrevolution and inspired the Lebanese group to draw on Iran's playbook in suppressing the mobilization against the status quo.[55]

Iran's main objective as a counterrevolutionary actor in Lebanon, Iraq, and elsewhere is to maintain its strategic interests and political influence in the Middle East against the United States, Israel, and their allies in the region. This overt and covert support helps elucidate how and why Iran was one of the key counterrevolutionary actors during the Lebanon uprising of 2019 and clearly explains why Hezbollah and the Islamic Republic are one of the guardians of the sectarian status quo that is so far still intact.

Guarding the Political Order: The US Duality of Supporting Dissent and Coercion

A few weeks after the beginning of the uprising in 2019, various US officials voiced their support to protesters.[56] They also encouraged Lebanon's "corrupt political elite" to introduce reforms that would end corruption.[57] This duality is an integral component of US–Lebanon relations, which has allowed successive US presidents and their administrations to bolster the sectarian regime and its coercive institutions and extend support to some opposition movements that seek to revamp the existing order. In the initial months of the uprising and steadily thereafter, officials in the Donald J. Trump administration and others in the US government maintained the duality of supporting protests against the ruling regime and maintaining support for the political system, especially the state's coercive institutions, such as the armed forces, to prevent revolutionaries from challenging the status quo.

Only hours after people took to the streets of Lebanon on October 17, 2019, the US embassy in Beirut issued a "Security Alert," which would be the first of many to follow.[58] This dispatch noted that "anti-government protests are going on in downtown Beirut and other cities in Lebanon" and then mentioned that protesters are burning tires and "blocking major arteries, including roads to the airport."[59] On October 19, 2019, the US embassy dispatched a "Demonstration Alert" that mentioned "while protests remained largely peaceful, media are reporting sporadic clashes between protesters and security forces, isolated cases of looting and vandalism, some injuries, and two deaths in Tripoli and Beirut."[60] Much of these "demonstration" and "security" alerts constantly wavered between providing updates on different developments and qualifying the violent or nonviolent character of the protests and how the government's security organizations responded to people in the streets.

On October 29, 2019, almost twelve days after the beginning of the revolutionary uprising and following Hariri's resignation, Michael Pompeo, former US secretary of state, issued a statement on "the Political Situation in Lebanon."[61] This was the first official statement from Washington. Specifically, Pompeo's statement vibrantly captures how the US government pursued a dual policy with implicit counterrevolutionary features. Pompeo called on "Lebanon's political leaders to urgently facilitate the formation of a new government that can build a stable, prosperous, and secure

Lebanon that is responsive to the needs of its citizens."[62] Pompeo also highlighted the nonviolent and "peaceful demonstrations" and underscored the people's legitimate socioeconomic grievances.[63] Nonetheless, the US secretary of state mentioned that "any violence or provocative actions must stop [from some of the protesters in the streets]" and "call[ed] upon Lebanon's army and security services to continue to ensure the rights and safety of the protesters."[64] A close reading of this short statement captures the duality of supporting the protesters and calling on "Lebanon's army" to take the appropriate measures to end "provocative actions."

The duality that consisted of calling on state institutions to counterviolence and supporting the people's legitimate demands for economic reform and an end of corruption is motivated by several factors. For brevity, I will focus on two. The first centers on the US perception of a political vacuum in Lebanon and the need to bolster the LAF to guard the status quo. The second relates to supporting the "non-violent and peaceful protests" with the implicit strategy of containing Hezbollah's power and, by extension, curbing Iran's influence.

The Fear of Political Vacuum

From the Cold War in 1947 to the present day, successive US presidents and their administrations have supported the corrupt political class in Lebanon rather than engage with revolutionary forces. The fear of political vacuums and disruptions to established political orders remains an important driver of how the US government engages with Lebanon's ruling elite. For instance, in 1957, the Central Intelligence Agency and the US embassy in Lebanon provided the needed funds and support to rig the Lebanese parliamentary elections and ensure that Camille Chamoun's, Lebanon's pro-Western president, between 1952 and 1958, opponents were defeated.[65] In 1958 and after the successful military coup turned revolution in Iraq on July 14, 1958, removed the pro-British monarchy, the United States dispatched thousands of military troops to the shores of Beirut to protect the pro-Western political order.[66]

Likewise, before and during the Lebanese civil war (1975–90), successive US presidential administrations provided economic assistance and weapons to several right-wing political parties to maintain the pro-Western political order.[67] The Taef Accords that brokered a new power-sharing system between Lebanon's political elite involved deep US engagement that supported Syrian occupation until 2005.[68] US support for the March 14 coalition that the Future Movement led mainly against the March 8 camp spearheaded by Hezbollah was likewise tailored to maintain the existing pro-Western political order.[69] The period between 2005 and 2019, which included massive support, to the tune of over $2 billion in weapons, training, and equipment since 2005, for the LAF against terrorist movements in Lebanon, was framed as part of the global "war on terror" and so highlighted the role of the US government in bolstering the status quo.[70]

This historical snapshot of US–Lebanon relations suggests that from the beginning of the Cold War to the present day, US policymakers and government officials have converged on guarding the status quo. The fear of a political vacuum that could be filled by a local actor or a foreign one is captured vigorously by Jeffrey D. Feltman, US ambassador to Lebanon (2004–8), in his testimony before the House Subcommittee on the Middle East, North Africa, and International Terrorism on November 19, 2019.[71] While offering his analysis of the protests in Lebanon and how the rightful demands in the streets of Lebanon "coincide with U.S. interests," Feltman called on the US government to maintain its support of the LAF to ensure that the country remains "an Arab, Mediterranean country with relatively strong civil liberties, democratic traditions" that highlight the "success" of "multi-confessional co-existence."[72] The former ambassador equally noted that Lebanon has always been a "venue for global strategic competition" and if the United States "cede[s] ground," then other powers, especially China, Russia, and Iran, will "happily fill the [political and geostrategic] vacuum."[73]

Maintaining the Political Order and Curtailing Hezbollah's Influence

The multiple attacks by Hezbollah and their allies against US personnel and outposts in Lebanon and elsewhere in the 1980s are vital to understanding how successive US officials perceive this Lebanese party and Iran's continuous support for what the Islamic Republic conceives as a success of exporting the Iranian revolution to the Arab Middle East.[74] After the end of the Lebanese Civil War, consecutive administrations starting from the Bush administration to the current Biden administration have supported a political order that includes Hezbollah and maintained their standoff with this Lebanese movement. Even after the war between Israel and Lebanon in 2006, which involved the Bush administration's full backing of the Israeli onslaught, US officials and their allies realized that curtailing Hezbollah rather than defeating the group is a more practical strategy.[75] This strategy has triggered a massive campaign of support for the LAF with the fear that Hezbollah may benefit from the offered weapons and military training.[76]

The Trump administration likewise maintained support for the LAF and sanctioned several officials close to Hezbollah.[77] While the October uprising of 2019 erupted during the Trump administration's policy of "maximum pressure" on the Iranian regime in the form of financial sanctions and, by extension, on the regime's allies in the Middle East, the Biden administration has equally maintained a similar policy line that centers on bolstering the existing political class and maintaining pressure on Hezbollah and Iran.[78]

In this context, one can surmise that US officials were confused about whether Hezbollah loyalists were partaking in the protests. The confusion compelled US officials to maintain their dual policy of supporting the protesters and engaging with members of the political class. Even when some US funds for the LAF were suspended on October 31, 2019, because the Lebanese government did not introduce any reforms, US officials later reversed their decision on December 2, 2019.[79] The confusion about whether the United States was supporting a protest movement that included Hezbollah partisans or one that could be supported against this political party is apparent in Feltman's statements in 2019–20. For instance, Feltman wrote on November 1, 2019, that "Lebanon's protesters show that the once-unthinkable may now be plausible."[80] Specifically, the "unthinkable" relates to the "disintegration of the proxies of Syria and Iran in Lebanon," especially that "Shia protesters [are] on the street" and are defying Nasrallah's calls to leave the protests.[81] The ambassador writes that public support for the LAF "is soaring," while Hezbollah's "façade of invincibility is showing cracks."[82] In the same vein, Feltman argues that "the current demonstrations have the potential to shake the foundations of . . . the Iranian-Syrian solidary in Lebanon."[83]

In outlining the rationale for maintaining US support for the LAF to weaken Hezbollah's power and its "resistance narrative," Feltman called on the US government to support the protesters and maintain its support for the LAF. Specifically, he wrote that "we [the US government] should not want to make it easier for the pro-Syrian and pro-Iranian forces to overcome any differences and prevail in the end over the protesters."[84] While noting that the LAF's "reaction" was much more restrained than "Hezbollah and its junior partner Amal [that] sent thugs on motorcycles to beat up the demonstrators," Feltman justified the LAF's coercion by asking, "what would we Americans think if persistent protests prevented [road blocking] us from reaching our airports, hospital, schools or jobs?"[85] The ambassador strongly reasserted that the US government should maintain its support of the LAF in spite of the use of violence against protesters, especially due to the LAF's stellar performance in "counter-terrorism operations" against Fatah al-Islam in 2007 and others subsequently.

Less than two months after the eruption of the uprising, David Hale, undersecretary of state for political affairs, vowed to "encourage Lebanon's political leaders to commit the necessary reforms that can lead to a stable, prosperous, and secure country."[86] Hale also noted that "the unified, non-sectarian, and largely peaceful protests over the last 65 days [since 17 October] reflect the Lebanese people's longstanding and frankly legitimate demand for economic and institutional reform."[87] On January 22, 2020, Pompeo restated the US government's perception of the rightful demands of the Lebanese protesters and called on the newly formed cabinet, led by Diab, to respond to the protesters and "implement reforms and fight corruption."[88]

During February and March 2020, the US government designated over fifteen "Lebanon-based individuals" with links to Hezbollah's "financial support network" as "Specifically Designated Global Terrorists," reaffirmed its support for the Lebanese protests, and declared its support for the Diab government to devise "effective policies necessary to extricate Lebanon from its an unprecedented economic crisis."[89] Importantly, on May 1, 2020, the US government reaffirmed that "U.S. security assistance for the LAF is a key component of U.S. policy in Lebanon and aims to . . . build up the country's legitimate state institutions."[90] US officials praised the LAF's counterterrorism operations and how this coercive institution "historically served as a pillar of stability in a country facing extraordinary challenges, including the presence of the terrorist group Hi[e]zballah."[91] In brief, the US government, yet again, maintained the dual policy of bolstering the existing regime and continuing its assistance to the LAF while simultaneously acknowledging the rightful demands of protesters.

Conclusion

This chapter took the case of Lebanon in 2019 to show how Iran and the United States bolstered and guarded the status quo after the October 17 uprising. The United States and Iran had different security motives, ideological considerations, and political calculations for supporting the sectarian order. While Iran feared the curbing of its power in Lebanon through pressure on Hezbollah and the United States was concerned about whether a reliable partner from the "non-sectarian and largely peaceful protests" could be supported to contain Hezbollah's influence, the result was similar. Both Iran and the United States served as the shadow guardians of the status quo in Lebanon and limited the possibilities of change that inspired thousands of people to partake in a revolutionary situation that is *still* unfolding and will continue to challenge the existing political order.

The Lebanon revolutionary uprising of 2019 invites critical work on the stability of power-sharing and consociational systems in postwar states, especially when revolutionary situations will continue to develop against the false promise of neoliberal orders and upgraded authoritarian regimes that are mostly and *still* propped up by foreign states.[92]

Notes

1   The author would like to thank Lama Mourad, Jillian Schwedler, and Sana Tannoury-Karam for generous feedback on earlier drafts of this chapter.
2   By using status quo, the chapter refers to the existing sectarian-based political system that remains intact even when there are political gridlocks and stalemates, such as the inability to form a new government. Thus, the status quo refers to the state's sectarian structure.
3   See Daher, El-Kak, and Majed in this volume.
4   Ernesto Castañeda and Cathy Lisa Schneider, *Collective Violence, Contentious Politics, and Social Change: A Charles Tilly Reader* (London: Routledge, 2017); Charles Tilly, *European Revolutions 1492–1992* (London: Wiley, 1996).
5   While it is true that *other* regional and international powers, including Turkey, Russia, Saudi Arabia, and others, have similar interests, the chapter limits the analysis and comparison to Iran and the United States due to several considerations. The first lies in the fact that both states have bolstered the existing political order and the ruling class in different ways. The second relates to the fact that the study of these two foreign states are in many ways representative of the varied forms of implicit and explicit repression. For instance, similar to the United States, the United Kingdom and France support the ruling class by providing economic aid and military support to Lebanon's coercive institutions. Moreover, Russia's position is very similar to Iran and equally considered that the protests were driven and led by Western powers against "the Axis of Resistance." In brief, many foreign states acted concurrently as implicit counterrevolutionary forces and safeguarded the status quo.
6   Timour Azhari, "Lebanon Government Wins Parliament's Confidence Vote Despite Protests," *Al Jazeera*, February 11, 2020, https://bit.ly/3zAOj8d.

7   See Daher and Karame chapters in this volume.

8   Marianna Belenkaya, "How Russia sees Protests in Lebanon, Iraq," *Al Monitor,*
    November 7, 2019, https://bit.ly/36ZWVsD.

9   Mehmet Hecan and Fouad Farhaoui, "The Coercive Power and Democratic Transition
    in the Post-Uprising Middle East and North Africa," *Democratization*, 2021; Elizabeth
    R. Nugent, *After Repression: How Polarization Derails Democratic Transition*
    (Princeton: Princeton University Press, 2020); Eva Bellin, "Reconsidering the
    Robustness of Authoritarianism in the Middle East: Lessons from the Arab Spring,"
    Comparative Politics 44, no. 2 (2012): 127–49.

        Beyond the role of coercive institutions, scholars have focused extensively on
    a few cases, especially Egypt, Tunisia, and Syria during the first wave of uprisings
    in 2011. Their analyses have focused on why these authoritarian states did not
    become consolidated democracies. They focus primarily on domestic factors while
    not fully examining external factors. See Raymond Hinnebusch, ed., *After the
    Arab Uprisings: Between Democratization, Counter-Revolution, and State Failure*
    (New York: Routledge, 2018). Recent works that focus on the external aspects
    of counterrevolution have focused extensively on Egypt, such as Jamie Allinson,
    "Counter-Revolution as International Phenomenon: The Case of Egypt," *Review of
    International Studies* 45, no. 2 (2019): 320–44.

10 Jeffrey G. Karam, "Lebanon's Civil Society as an Anchor of Stability Crown Center for
    Middle East Studies," *Middle Brief* 117 (April 2018): 1–10, https://bit.ly/3j9gLrd; See
    Bzeih, Daher, el-Kak, Karame, Majed, Skayni, Tannoury-Karam, and others in the
    volume.

11 There is a vast body of works on revolutions that provide theoretical and empirical
    accounts. For example, see Amy Austin Holmes, *Coups and Revolutions: Mass
    Mobilization, the Egyptian Military, and the United States from Mubarak to
    Sisi* (Oxford: Oxford University Press, 2019); Asef Bayat, *Revolution Without
    Revolutionaries: Making Sense of the Arab Spring* (Stanford: Stanford University
    Press, 207); Sabah Alnasseri, ed., *Arab Revolutions and Beyond: The Middle East and
    Reverberations in the Americas* (New York: Palgrave Macmillan, 2016); Daniel P.
    Ritter, *The Iron Cage of Liberalism: International Politics and Unarmed Revolutions
    in the Middle East and North Africa* (Oxford: Oxford University Press, 2015); Marc
    Lynch, *The Arab Uprising: The Unfinished Revolutions of the New Middle East* (New
    York: PublicAffairs, 2013); Hannah Arendt and Jonathan Schell, *On Revolution* (New
    York: Penguin Classics, 2006).

12 Theda Skocpol, *States and Social Revolutions: A Comparative Analysis of France,
    Russia, and China* (Cambridge: Cambridge University Press, 1979), 4.

13 Castañeda and Schneider, *Collective Violence, Contentious Politics, and Social Change*;
    Tilly, *European Revolutions 1492–1992*.

14 For a discussion of the fourth and fifth generations of scholarship on revolutions
    see Jamie Allinson, "A Fifth Generation of Revolution Theory?" *Historical Sociology*
    32, no. 1 (2019):142–51; Jack Goldstone, "Understanding the Revolutions of 2011,"
    Foreign Affairs 90, no. 3 (2011): 8–16. ; George Lawson, "Within and beyond the
    'fourth generation' of Revolutionary Theory," *Sociological Theory* 34, no. 2 (2016):
    106–27.

15 For a discussion of revolutionary processes see Jeffrey G. Karam, ed., *The Middle East
    in 1958: Reimagining A Revolutionary Year* (London: I.B. Tauris, 2020); Neil Ketchley,
    Egypt in a Time of Revolution: Contentious Politics and the Arab Spring (Cambridge:
    Cambridge University Press, 2017); Brecht De Smet, *Gramsci on Tahrir* (London:

Pluto, 2016); Reem Abou-El-Fadl, ed., *Revolutionary Egypt: Connecting Domestic and International Struggles* (London: Routledge, 2015); Maha Abdelrahman, *Egypt's Long Revolution: Protest Movements and Uprisings* (London: Routledge, 2014); Brecht De Smet, "Revolution and Counter-Revolution in Egypt," *Science and Society* 78, no. 1 (2014): 11–40.

16 Mohammed Bamyeh, "Ma hiya khasa'is al-thawra al-mudd'ada? [What are the features of counter-revolution?]," *Jadaliyya*, June 21, 2014 (re-published on February 22, 2021). https://www.jadaliyya.com/Details/42408; Wendy Pearlman, "Emotions and the Microfoundations of Arab Uprisings," *Perspectives on Politics* 11, no. 2 (2013): 387–409.

17 Vivienne Matthies-Boon and Naomi Head, "Trauma as Counter-Revolutionary Colonisation: Narratives from (post)revolutionary Egypt," *Journal of International Political Theory* 18, no. 3 (2018): 258–79.

18 Dan Slater and Nicholas Rush Smith, "The Power of Counter-revolution: Elitist Origins of Political Order in Postcolonial Asia and Africa," *American Journal of Sociology* 121, no. 5 (2016): 1472–516.

19 Allinson, "Counter-revolution as International Phenomenon"; George Lawson, "A Global Historical Sociology of Revolution," in *Global Historical Sociology*, ed. Julian Go and George Lawson (Cambridge: Cambridge University Press, 2017).

20 Jeffrey G. Karam, "Beyond Sectarianism: Understanding Lebanese Politics Through a Cross-Sectarian Lens" Crown Center for Middle East Studies, *Middle Brief* 107, April 2017, 1–10, https://bit.ly/37dJrK5; Ibrahim Halawi, "Consociational Power-Sharing in the Arab World as Counter-Revolution," *Studies in Ethnicity and Nationalism* 20, no. 2 (2020): 128–36.

21 Aurélie Daher, "Regional Patronage and War-Fomenting Polarization: The Rivalry between Iran and Saudi Arabia in Lebanon," *Critique Internationale* 80, no. 3 (2018): 155–77.

22 See Daher, Karame, Majed, Bzeih, el-Kak, Tannoury-Karam, and others in the volume.

23 For a brief discussion of how international relations scholars discuss revolutionary and counterrevolutionary thought see Robert Jervis, "Socialization, Revolutionary States and Domestic Politics," *International Politics* 52, no. 5 (2015): 609–16; Nick Bisley, "Counter-Revolution, Order and International Politics," *Review of International Studies* 30 (2004): 49–69; Stephen M. Walt, *Revolution and War* (Ithaca: Cornell University Press, 1996).

24 It is important to note that several major powers, including the United States, could pursue "conservative" foreign policy lines that center on maintaining the status quo in friendly states from any disruptions. However, as the chapter demonstrates, during revolutionary times and "situations," actions by foreign powers that seek to bolster the existing political order become an integral part of counterrevolutionary processes and situations.

25 Christopher Phillips, *The Battle for Syria: International Rivalry in the New Middle East* (New Haven: Yale University Press, 2016); Mehran Kamrava, "Hierarchy and Instability in the Middle East Regional Order," *International Studies Journal* 14, no. 4 (2018): 1–35; Raymond Hinnebusch, "The Middle East in the World Hierarchy: Imperialism and Resistance," *Journal of International Relations and Development* 14 (2011): 213–46.

26 Robert Vitalis, *Oilcraft: The Myths of Scarcity and Security That Haunt U.S. Energy Policy* (Stanford: Stanford University Press, 2020; Doug Stokes and Sam Raphael,

Global Energy Security and American Hegemony (Baltimore: The John Hopkins University Press, 2010.

27 Jeffrey G. Karam and Sana Tannoury-Karam, "The Lebanese Intifada: Observations and Reflections on Revolutionary Times," *Jadaliyya,* November 10, 2019, https://www .jadaliyya.com/Details/40218.

28 "Violence Flares in Lebanon as Protesters Tell Their Leaders to Go," *The Guardian*, October 18, 2019, https://bit.ly/3iLn7wO.

29 Martin Chulov, "Lebanon's PM Saad Hariri Resigns as Protesters Come Under Attack," *The Guardian,* October 29, 2019, https://bit.ly/2WbMjoo.

30 For a brief overview of how some actors defined the uprising see Jeffrey G. Karam, "Misrepresentations of the Revolution Have Begun," *The Daily Star Lebanon,* November 4, 2019, https://bit.ly/3x7YaAJ.

31 "Khamenei says US Stoking 'chaos' amid Iraq, Lebanon Protests," *Al Jazeera,* October 30, 2019, https://bit.ly/3BImsVm.

32 "United States Designates Hizballah Affiliated Companies and Officials as Global Terrorists," U.S. Embassy Beirut, News and Events, February 26, 2020, https://bit.ly /3kQKzvc; "Treasury Designates Martyrs Foundation Companies and Officials as Global Terrorists," U.S. Embassy Beirut, News and Events, February 26, 2020, https:// bit.ly/3zx3dwf.

33 See, for example, Toby Matthiesen, *Sectarian Gulf: Bahrain, Saudi Arabia, and the Arab Spring That Wasn't* (Stanford: Stanford University Press, 2013); Allinson, "Counter-Revolution as International Phenomenon."

34 See for example De Smet, *Gramsci on Tahrir*; Abou-El-Fadl, *Revolutionary Egypt.*

35 Jillian Schwedler, "Thinking Critically About Regional Uprisings," *MERIP* 292, no. 3 (2019), https://bit.ly/3zxPLrS; Hashem Osseiran, "The Arab Spring Did Not Die': A Second Wave of Mideast Protests," *AFP,* November 30, 2020, https://yhoo.it /3zGyME1; See Majed in volume.

36 Erica Chenoweth, Sirianne Dahlum, Sooyeon Kang, Zoe Marks, Christopher Wiley Shay, and Tore Wig, "This May be the Largest Wave of Nonviolent Mass Movements in World History. What Comes Next?" *Monkey Cage, The Washington Post*, November 16, 2019, https://wapo.st/2TzGkc6.

37 Maximilian Terhalle, "Revolutionary Power and Socialization: Explaining the Persistence of Revolutionary Zeal in Iran's Foreign Policy," *Security Studies* 18, no. 3 (2009): 557–86; Danny Postel, "The Other Regional Counter-Revolution: Iran's Role in the Shifting Political Landscape of the Middle East." Center for Middle East Studies, *Occasional Paper Series*, University of Denver, Paper no.12, July 2021.

38 "Lebanon's Nasrallah Backs Government Amid Raging Protests," *Al Jazeera,* October 19, 2019, https://bit.ly/3eYtc82; Mersiha Gadzo, "'All of them': Lebanon Protesters Dig in after Nasrallah's Speech," *Al Jazeera,* October 25, 2019, https://bit.ly/3yaWGXK.

39 "Nasrallah's Full Speech on Imam Hussein [AS] Arbaeen Anniversary," *Alahed News*, October 19, 2019, https://bit.ly/3j7eexJ; "Nasrallah's Full Speech on Recent Developments Regarding Lebanon Protests," *Alahed News*, October 25, 2019, https:// bit.ly/3xgCe6q.

40 Nadia al-Faour, "Protests Continue in Nabatieh Despite Nasrallah's Support for Government," *Al Arabiya News*, October 25, 2019, https://bit.ly/3iMEz43; "Lebanese Protesters Clash with Supporters of Hezbollah, Amal in Beirut," *Reuters,* November 25, 2019, https://reut.rs/3y6Kmry.

To avoid exceptionalizing the violence used by Hezbollah and Amal partisans and supporters, it is important to highlight that *other* traditional political parties and regime loyalists, such as the Lebanese Forces, the Future Movement, the Free Patriotic Movement, and the Progressive Socialist Party, equally vacillated between taking to the streets to hijack the revolutionary situation and employing violence against protesters, especially when some chants denounced their party leaders. See "Lebanese Protests: Cross-Communal Rage," *Al Jazeera Centre for Studies*, October 30, 2019, https://studies.aljazeera.net/ar/node/257; Sahar Houri, "FPM Holds Demonstration in Support of Aoun, Bassil," *The Daily Star Lebanon*, November 3, 2019, https://bit.ly /3rB9mVx.

41 Phillips, *The Battle for Syria*.

42 Postel, "The Other Regional Counter-Revolution: Iran's Role in the Shifting Political Landscape of the Middle East."

43 Ibid.

44 Sarah Birke, "Hezbollah's Choice," Latitude (blog), *New York Times*, August 6, 2013, https://nyti.ms/3rImPe4.

45 Mohanad Hage Ali, "Power Points Defining the Syria-Hezbollah Relationship," *Carnegie Middle East Center*, March 2019, https://bit.ly/3BU5tzH.

46 Hassan Ahmadian and Payam Mohseni, "Iran's Syria Strategy: The Evolution of Deterrence," in *NL ARMS Netherlands Annual Review of Military Studies 2020: Deterrence in the 21st Century—Insights from Theory and Practice*, ed. Frans Osinga and Tim Sweijs (The Hague: T.M.C. Asser Press, 2021).

47 Khamenei's speech, "Insecurity in Iraq and Lebanon, the result of actions by the US, Israel, Reactionary Countries' Money," *Khamenei.IR*, October 30, 2019 https://bit .ly/3fczrVM; "Nasrallah's Full Speech on Recent Developments Regarding Lebanon Protests."

48 "Nasrallah's Full Speech on Recent Developments Regarding Lebanon Protests."

49 Khamenei speech, October 30, 2019.

50 "Pointing to Iraq, Lebanon, Khamenei Recalls How Iran put Down Unrest," *Reuters*, October 30, 2019, https://reut.rs/3zygy7u.

51 Ibid; Khamenei speech, October 30, 2019.

52 Ibid.

53 Aurélie Daher, *Hezbollah: Mobilization and Power* (Oxford: Oxford University Press, 2019).

54 "Nasrallah says Khamenei Heavily Involved in Establishment of Lebanon's Hezbollah," *Al Arabiya*, October 1, 2019, https://bit.ly/3ryEIMl.

55 "Iran Accuses Israel, US of Causing Protests in Lebanon, Iraq," October 30, 2019, https://bit.ly/3BQhYML.

56 "Political Situation in Lebanon," Statement by Secretary Michael Pompeo, U.S. Embassy Beirut, News and Events, October 29, 2019, https://bit.ly/3BIlV5O.

57 Ibid.

58 "Security Alert – U.S. Embassy Beirut Lebanon," U.S. Embassy Beirut, News and Events, October 17, 2019, https://bit.ly/3eVCPnW; "Demonstration Alert – U.S. Embassy Beirut Lebanon," U.S. Embassy Beirut, News and Events, October 18, 2019, https://bit.ly/3y9gdYs.

59 Ibid.

60 "Demonstration Alert – U.S. Embassy Beirut Lebanon," U.S. Embassy Beirut, News and Events, October 19, 2019, https://lb.usembassy.gov/demonstration-alert-u-s -embassy-beirut-lebanon-19-october-2019/.

61 "Political Situation in Lebanon," Pompeo.

62 Ibid.

63 Ibid.

64 Ibid.

65 Jeffrey G. Karam, "Cautious Revisionism and the Limits of Hegemony in 1958: A Revolutionary Year for the United States in the Middle East," in *The Middle East in 1958: Reimagining A Revolutionary Year*, ed. Jeffrey G. Karam (London: I.B. Tauris, 2020).

66 Jeffrey G. Karam, "Missing Revolution: The American Intelligence Failure in Iraq, 1958," *Intelligence and National Security* 32, no. 6 (2017): 693–709; Karam, "Cautious Revisionism and the Limits of Hegemony in 1958."

67 Jeffrey G. Karam, Review of James Stocker, *Spheres of Intervention: US Foreign Policy and the Collapse of Lebanon, 1967–1976* (Ithaca: Cornell University Press, 2016), *Arab Studies Journal* 25, no. 1 (2017): 175–8.

68 Hassan Krayem, "The Lebanese Civil War and the Taif Agreement," in *Conflict Resolution in the Arab World: Selected Essays*, ed. Paul Salem (Beirut: American University of Beirut Press, 1997).

69 Casey L. Addis, "U.S. Security Assistance to Lebanon," Congressional Research Service, CRS Report for Congress, May 20, 2009, https://bit.ly/2Vbg8Vw.

70 Nicholas Blanford, "The US Military Assistance Program to the Lebanese Armed Forces Must Endure," *The Atlantic Council*, April 30, 2020, https://bit.ly/3zL5xQe; Nicholas Blanford, "Weapons or Food? Lebanon's Armed Forces Risk Going Hungry," *The Atlantic Council*, March 23, 2021, https://bit.ly/3zGxV6h.

71 Jeffrey D. Feltman, "What's Next for Lebanon? Examining the Implications of Current Protests," Testimony before the House [U.S. House of Representatives] Subcommittee on the Middle East, North Africa, and International Terrorism, November 19, 2019, https://bit.ly/3y5zQR7; https://brook.gs/3rC4Sxz.

72 Ibid.

73 Ibid.

74 Jeffrey G. Karam, "Reflections on Beirut Rules: The Wider Consequences of US Foreign Policy and Security Policy in Lebanon in the 1980s," *Intelligence and National Security* 36, no. 3 (2021): 431–3.

75 Robin Wright and Thomas E. Ricks, "Bush Supports Israel's Move Against Hezbollah," *The Washington Post*, July 19, 2006, https://wapo.st/2Wgm1RX.

76 Blanford, "Weapons or Food?"

77 "United States Designates Hizballah Affiliated Companies and Officials as Global Terrorists"; "Treasury Designates Martyrs Foundation Companies and Officials as Global Terrorists."

78 "United States Central Command Commander Visits Lebanon," U.S. Embassy Beirut, News and Events, March 15, 2021, https://bit.ly/3eSndBu; David Schenker and Grant Rumley, "Preserving the LAF Amid State Decline," Policy Analysis|PolicyWatch 3497, *The Washington Institute for Near East Policy*, June 9, 2021, https://bit.ly/3zzkNQ1.

79 Patricia Zengerle and Mike Stone, "Exclusive: U.S. withholding $105 million in Security Aid for Lebanon – Sources," *Reuters*, October 31, https://reut.rs/31ZKnwF; Ellen Mitchell, "Trump Administration Releases $105M in Military Aid for Lebanon after Months-Long Delay," *The Hill*, December 2, 2019, https://bit.ly/3kWZOm8.

80 Jeffrey D. Feltman, "With Lebanon Making Fragile Progress, Now Is the Wrong Time to pull US Assistance," *Brookings*, November 1, 2019, https://brook.gs/2UGGpLS.

81 Ibid.

82 Ibid.

83 Ibid.

84 Ibid.
85 Feltman, "What's Next for Lebanon?"
86 "Visit of Under Secretary of State for Political Affairs David Hale," U.S. Embassy Beirut, News and Events, December 20, 2019, https://bit.ly/3eSnbJJ.
87 "Statement by U/S State for Political Affairs David Hale Developments in Lebanon," U.S. Embassy Beirut, News and Events, December 20, 2019, https://bit.ly/3rBHvo3.
88 "Government Formation in Lebanon," Press Statement, Michael Pompeo, Secretary of State, January 22, 2020, https://bit.ly/3iKQ6Rn.
89 "United States Designates Hizballah Affiliated Companies and Officials as Global Terrorists"; "Treasury Designates Martyrs Foundation Companies and Officials as Global Terrorists"; "Ambassador Richard Bids Farewell to Lebanon," U.S. Embassy Beirut, News and Events, February 26, 2020, https://bit.ly/3eYctlf; "Remarks of U.S. Ambassador to Lebanon Dorothy C. Shea," U.S. Embassy Beirut, News and Events, March 13, 2020, https://bit.ly/3y1vSZU.
90 "U.S. Security Cooperation with Lebanon," Fact Sheet, Bureau of Political-Military Affairs, U.S. Embassy Beirut, News and Events, May 4, 2020, https://bit.ly/3iNz70H.
91 Ibid.
92 Abbas Assi, *Democracy in Lebanon: Political Parties and the Struggle for Power since Syrian Withdrawal* (London: I.B. Tauris, 2016); Reinoud Leenders, *Spoils of Truce: Corruption and State Building in Postwar Lebanon* (Ithaca: Cornell University Press, 2012); Hinnebusch, *After the Arab Uprisings.*

Part Two

Faces of the Revolutionary Uprising

Tactics, Repression, and Alternative Voices and Movements

9

How Urban Space Shapes Collective Action

The Lebanon Uprising of 2019

Mona Harb

The revolution showed us . . . what it means to love, enjoy, and to be happy in our city. We saw the difference in the form and feeling of the city before 17 October and after. From the beginning of the revolution, people felt their power and ownership of the city; life, light and movement (and recycling!) returned to the city center, and street vendors selling corn returned to the [seaside] corniche, and art shows are taking place in front of Grand Theatre, art and graffiti are back on the walls and on the floor, fishermen are back to the Saint-George's bay, and I now like walking leisurely to downtown and spend time there, without consuming. I even love the holes in the asphalt caused by burned tires, even if I have allergies, but I feel am reclaiming the streets through them. The revolution gave us erased and forbidden parts of our memories, our movement, our feelings, and of our city. The revolution gave us back ourselves and our cities.

—Facebook post by a Lebanese protestor, November 20, 2019

The Lebanon uprising of 2019 is a textbook case illustrating the role of urban space in enabling collective action. Much has been written about the extraordinary spatial practices of the uprisings, celebrating self-organization, collective intelligence, subversive appropriations, creative placemaking, and transgressive urban transformations. Most contributions give little weight, however, to unpacking in what ways urban space matter and *shape* the uprisings. Building on the works of political sociologists, geographers, and urbanists who grappled with this issue,[1] this chapter is keen on providing intersections between critical urban studies' questions of spatial production and matters of collective action, activism, and social movements in order to explore how urban space matters to political mobilization and struggles for social justice.

Basing my analysis on my ongoing engagement with the urban activists' scene in Lebanon as an activist-scholar, I argue that urban space shapes collective action in two ways and matters substantively to the consolidation of political struggles.[2] First, urban space incorporates both material and symbolic characteristics that prompt protestors to exploit them, thus enabling collective action. I illustrate this component through three types of urban spaces that were extensively appropriated during the uprisings: public and open spaces, abandoned buildings, and infrastructure. Second, urban spaces produce a diverse range of performative stages, at various scales (street, neighborhood, city, region, nation), where collective action is rehearsed, nurtured, challenged, and, often, repressed and thwarted. Yet, these stages matter as they allow political imaginaries and "real utopias" to be deployed, albeit fleetingly, as Beirut's and Tripoli's rich panoply of stages demonstrates. In other words, as the Lebanon uprising reminds us so well, urban spaces are necessary for collective action because they provide vital ingredients for mobilizing and organizing—namely density, diversity, and strategic sites.[3] The chapter concludes with reflections on the uprisings in relation to Lefebvre's spatial triad and to the long journey of political struggle for social justice in Lebanon.

Urban Space as Material and Symbolic

Urban space incorporates both material and symbolic elements. The material elements of urban space make up its *built, physical* environment, in its various components, at multiple scales: buildings, streets, sidewalks, highways, bridges, roundabouts, infrastructure, parks, gardens, walls, fences, military and security devices, urban furniture, etc. All city dwellers recognize these material elements: they know what they are made for and how they should be used. The symbolic elements of urban space are less straightforward. They are *intangible* and not apprehended the same way by everyone. Symbolic elements include sites of historical significance for a large group— at the political, social, civic, or cultural level and can take the form of buildings, streets, and/or open spaces. They are not always systematically celebrated and landmarked as their historical significance may not be collectively shared and may be contested. In those cases, the symbolic elements of urban space remain latent. They may become activated, at certain contentious moments, when their proponents seek to claim them back and mark publicly their significance.

The material and symbolic elements of urban space are closely associated to collective action and to social movements, as they allow contention to take shape physically and to be amplified. Indeed, streets, highways, squares, roundabouts, gardens, open spaces, abandoned buildings, and others act as containers for large groups of people to gather, march, protest, sit in, and organize. They also make demands and claims widely and clearly visible to rulers and to the larger world. The choice to occupy particular spaces in times of collective action is often related to their symbolic significance, be it shared or contested, and may facilitate the expansion and decentralization of contention, beyond central geographies, to new sites, new neighborhoods, or even new cities and regions.

People in Beirut took to the streets spontaneously the night of October 17, 2019, angrily marching in groups of dozens, through roads, highways, bridges, and tunnels, toward the two emblematic historic squares of the city center: Martyrs' and Riad El Solh. Road blockades were set up and motorcycle convoys stared touring neighborhoods, honking and chanting loudly. Quickly, the protests spread to cities outside the capital, namely to Tripoli, Saida, Sour, and Nabatiyeh, extending to additional towns and regions: Tarchich, Chtaura, Baalbek, Aley, and Choueifat.[4] Over the next days and weeks, more and more people joined in. In Beirut, people marched across neighborhoods to reach the city center, where they grouped, organized, and occupied new sites, beyond the initial squares, connecting the city together in novel ways (e.g., the Egg and Grand Theatre buildings, the Azarieh parking, the Ring highway, Zaitouneh Bay, the Banks Association, the Central Bank, the ministries of Interior, Finance, and Labor). The uprising and its spatialities reached a national scale: people in streets and squares chanted and celebrated each city, connecting the territory in unforeseen ways that overwhelmed affect and emotions.[5] It was one of the highlights of the uprising, interpreted by many as the symbolic end of the civil war, a moment of collective communion and excessive patriotism.[6]

> So hard to explain the full-body jolt of how, after 15 years of civil war and then 30 years of silence about it, cities and towns across the entire length of the country, enemies of old, would chant and call out to one another in the squares, especially after any attack against protesters. "For you, Tripoli," chanted Beirut. "For you, Nabatiyeh," chanted Tripoli. "For you Akkar," chanted Nabatiyeh, "for you we remain in the streets"—and I remember being so choked up by this I could sometimes no longer chant along, only stand there and try to take it all in, letting other people's voices become your own.[7]

Protestors relied on different types of urban spaces in their mobilizing and organizing, which demonstrates well how urban spaces and contention are dialectically linked. Three types of spatial occupations particularly stand out: central squares and spaces, abandoned buildings, and infrastructure.

The occupation of central squares and open spaces is perhaps the most typical in collective action, although, in the context of the Arab region, squares are colonial impositions on the urban fabric as "system[s] of spatial control" that acquired civic meanings only in the early twentieth century, during the waves of nationalist movements when "these spaces were consecrated by the blood protesters who demonstrated for independence."[8] These spaces thus became sites where the material and symbolic ingredients combined in meaningful ways that made sense to the collective. We recall not only Tahrir square in Cairo, the Pearl square in Bahrain, and Istiqlal square in Istanbul but also central spaces of secondary cities in Tunisia, Egypt, Syria, Libya, and Algeria that became places for collective action and reclamation. During the 2019 uprising in Lebanon, people occupied open spaces in Beirut (Martyrs' Square, Azarieh, Riad El Solh) and Tripoli (al-Nur square). A system got set in motion: while some people arranged seating areas, tents, and even floorings, others secured electricity wiring for lights and plugs, and still others took care of food, water, and waste. Negotiations took place over which group will be allocated which sections. Funds were made available rapidly and also shared among members of groups—many received in-kind donations. In Beirut, the subdivision of space ended up in a distribution of functions that was celebrated by many as an example of the ingenious capacity of people to self-organize and appropriate space.[9] Antoine Atallah, a seasoned urban activist, drew this famous map that represents a snapshot of the ways urban space was demarcated by revolutionaries, protestors, volunteers, street vendors, peddlers, and daily visitors (see Figure 5 on p. 223).

In Tripoli, the square known as "Allah," because of the sign bearing God's name in it, was transformed into the site of rave parties nightly animated by a DJ, which images toured social and mainstream media, and the world. Ghanem analyzes the reconfigurations of the space around the square as attempts at desectarianizing its icon and spatially deactivating the dominant apparatus of power that ruled the city.[10] In Nabatiyeh, a city known for its strong allegiance to the two Shiʻa political parties that dominate much of Lebanon's politics, the occupation of the square was more about its symbolism rather than its materiality. Its footprint may not have been as visible and expansive as other cities' squares, but the mere presence of even few protestors in the den of Hizballah and Amal shattered their alleged legitimacy and sent revolutionary reverberations across every home in Lebanon, even if some people had to whisper about it. Squares were also reclaimed in Saida, Sour, and Baalbek. Thus, the occupation of open spaces and squares in various key Lebanese cities demonstrates how they act as a substantive ingredient for collective action to initiate, expand, and consolidate.

The second category of spatial occupation that enables collective action is that of abandoned buildings. In cities marred not only with wars and conflicts but also with real estate speculation and financialization, a main consequence on the built environment is the increase in the number of abandoned, dilapidated buildings.[11] When they are around and have the means, their owners await the right time for development and for maximizing returns on their capital. However, many such buildings become stuck assets, either because owners are multiple and become locked in the juridical labyrinths of inheritance laws or because owners do not have the means to develop them. Beirut and Tripoli include numerous such buildings. The Beirut City Centre (known as the "Egg") and the Grand Theatre in central Beirut and the Ghandour building in al-Nur square are among them.[12] All three were occupied by the protestors during the uprising and claimed as icons of the revolution. While the Grand Theatre was quickly closed off for security reasons as the building was unsafe, the Egg and the Ghandour buildings remained in use, although the "Eggupation" turned sour as it failed to produce "a collectively-formed platform for political change" due to what authors denounced as "purity competition and boundary work" of gatekeepers and civil society experts.[13] Yet, the ways the Egg's interiors and exteriors were used reveal how and why urban spaces matter for collective action. The Egg's interiors were repurposed, albeit for a short period of time, for teach-ins and public talks, bringing together protestors to converse and share. The Egg's exteriors were invaded by protestors who climbed onto the roof, poured colored paint upon the building's shell, and used it as a vista site observing and partaking in the protests from above. The exteriors also served as projection screens during the independence parade on November 22, 2019, transforming the structure into a postmodernist object. The Ghandour building in Tripoli, with its complex history symbolizing economic deprivation and urban decay, served as the site from which DJ Mahdi Karima played the rave music that animated al-Nur square for several nights; it also served as a canvas for a local architect who painted on it the Lebanese flag and three banners welcoming people to the city.[14] These complete alterations and appropriations of private buildings, re-*conceived* by the private real estate company that captured and commodified Beirut's cultural landmarks in the case of the Grand Theatre and the Egg, evoke the multiple possibilities of claiming back the city and of owning it as a shared, *lived* space—a notion I will return to at the end of this chapter.

Collective action is also spurred by a third category of spatial occupation, infrastructure: highways, roads, tunnels, bridges, spaces under the bridge, sidewalks, signposts, walls, fences, urban furniture, etc. These elements also helped protestors occupy space, make themselves visible, and have their voices heard. The most prominently appropriated infrastructures during the Lebanon uprising include the Ring and the Jal el-Dib highways, the Choueifat-Khalde crossing, as well as Palma in Tripoli and Taalbaya in the Bekaa. There, people not only disrupted traffic and protested loudly but also set up lounging areas. Protestors used to gather in these resting spots along the infrastructure and discuss their next course of action. In cities where vehicular infrastructure was prioritized over the human scale of walkable neighborhoods and inhabitable outdoor spaces, the sight of people lounging in the middle of roads and roundabouts and under bridges was clearly a claim for urban spaces that cater to people's needs for socializing and for organizing as a collective. Still, this direct action incurred much critique, violence, and repression, leading to serious injuries and the killing of a protester in Choueifat.

In addition to taking over large-scale infrastructure, people owned all other kinds of micro-infrastructure: they appropriated walls, fences, floors, signposts, and surfaces, which they plastered with graffiti and writings requesting justice and rights and denouncing corruption and theft. They also repurposed sidewalks, stairs, broken benches, and bus stops into food stalls or seating arrangements. When the police and thugs attacked them, they banged in unison on metal poles and edges to express rage.

Through this range of spatial occupations (of public and open spaces, of abandoned buildings, of infrastructure) that unfolded in various parts of multiple cities and towns, connecting a fragmented territory of strongholds, collective action got fortified and consolidated. The occupied and reclaimed spaces became inhabited and appropriated by protestors, visited by the curious and undecided, and transformed into semi-permanent protest sites, akin to "stages" where different kinds of contentious enactments were rhythmically deployed.

Urban Spaces as Performative Stages

As they got reowned, occupied urban spaces started producing diverse "stages" where collective action got organized, amid cooperation and antagonism. Beirut is a case in point as such "stages" were set up in various sections of the city center: parks became sites for teach-ins, while parking lots became headquarters for oppositional groups, gathered in adjacent tents, with spaces dedicated for communal kitchens, kids' spaces, and cleanups.

One could witness and experience, there, across the panoply of "stages," the two dimensions that *shape* urban social movements, identified by Nicholls and Uitermark. The first relates to how political groups *strategically* select and utilize urban spaces for their political action, organizing marches, sit-ins, or protests across or in certain sites, at certain times, depending on stakes. The second dimension relates to density and diversity, which are features substantively available in cities and urban neighborhoods, in ways that enable access to relational opportunities and to networks. I have shown elsewhere how urban activism was very much made possible by the concentration and multiplicity of organizations, collectives, and campaigns with innovative modalities of work that consolidated since the mid-2000s in Beirut.[15] Indeed, this density and diversity provided activists and political groups with networks and social capital that enabled access to resources. In Azarieh and in Martyrs' Square, these opportunities and networks were maximized: generations of activists, who had been organizing for decades, were discussing, organizing, planning, and strategizing; new groups were formed, large groups expanded, coalitions were created, others splintered. Additionally, the concentration of protestors and participants in a shared space endowed participants and organizers of collective action with "emotion-generating interactions" related to this sense of *togetherness* that fuels and shapes struggles and helps sustain mobilization.[16] These affective interactions supplied valuable sets of symbolic meanings to contention and allowed it to endure over time, against material constraints and other odds.

Accordingly, urban spaces serve as multiscalar performative stages where imaginaries of togetherness are rehearsed and experimented with. Within each type of urban space, the affective engagements that are essential for the expansion and consolidation of collective action and mobilization become nurtured and grow. Thus, urban spaces shape the *lived* experiences of protestors in ways that enable a preliminary, transient, envisioning of a shared future, and the imagining of *another kind of city*, one owned and shaped by its people.

Oppositional groups in Beirut and Lebanon have been organizing for long decades to change the hegemonic political sectarian system captured by sectarian political rulers and warlords who, with the support of banks and private firms, have hollowed out public institutions and extracted rents from most public and natural resources.[17] Among them, multiple urban activists have been challenging the growth-led global urbanism model and tinkering with modalities for a counter-dominant global urbanism.[18] It is beyond the scope of this chapter to present them but I will mention four initiatives that were successful in preventing projects threatening the public domain: the campaign to stop the Fouad Boutros highway from destroying the urban and green heritage of al-Hikmeh neighborhood; the campaign to protect the Dalieh seacoast from being developed into a touristic resort; the campaign of Nahnoo NGO to reopen the largest park of Beirut, al-Horch, for public use; and the campaign against the building of a World Bank-funded dam in the pristine Bisri Valley.[19]

Beyond their success in stopping extractive projects, these initiatives were also productive in advancing *other imaginaries of the public realm*:[20] imaginaries of vibrant, diverse, and inclusive built and natural environments. These imaginaries were envisioned and materialized in the narratives, representations, maps, and visualizations of the campaigns, perhaps most notably in the speculative visions of Dalieh's design ideas competition, which outlined scenic perspectives of a protected seacoast celebrating nature and culture, and in the rich Facebook page of the Save Bisri campaign. These imaginaries and their representations are necessary to rehearse other social lives, other political ecologies, even other types of economies, and an alternate urban life, grounded in solidarities and in the commons. They allow the envisioning of what Wright called "real utopias" (2010) and are thus prefigurative of a counter-dominant global urbanism, grounded in the political horizon of social and environmental justice, which urban activists advocate as their ultimate cause. For Wright, the

> vital belief in a utopian ideal may be necessary to motivate people to leave the journey of the status quo . . . [as] . . . "real utopias" [are] utopian ideals grounded in the real potentials of humanity, utopian destinations that have accessible waystations, utopian designs of institutions that can inform our practical tasks of navigating a world of imperfect conditions for social change.[21]

More concretely, Espiner conceptualizes an open-ended form of utopia grounded in feminist thought and combined with strands drawn from anarchism and radical environmentalism.[22] Like Wright, she underscores that the dominant discourse dismissing utopianism is misleading. For her, the real question is whose vision of utopia is dominant: currently, utopia is fueled by capitalist norms and discourses, by inequality, patriarchy, settler colonialism, and anthropocentricism. Espiner calls for an alternative utopianism, led by an ethics of feminism, inclusion, ecology, and equity. She reminds us that utopianism is already present in our everyday realities and "pertains to any feelings of hope and thinking of collectiveness and communalism." Utopias exist in and through micro-interventions and actions of progressive activists, feminists, anarchists, and radical environmentalists, in addition to the less visible tinkering of people within bureaucracies, state agencies, private enterprises, and homes. In other words, utopias are already out there, but they are often fleeting and imperfect and difficult to maintain. Further pleas for expanding the political imaginaries of another kind of city-making are aptly made by Kaika and Swyngedouw who call upon "extend[ing] the intellectual imaginary [toward] new politicized avenues for producing a new common urbanity."[23]

Concluding Remarks

Taking the Lebanon uprising as a laboratory, this chapter argued that urban space matters to collective action because of two of its interdependent components. On one hand, the material and symbolic characteristics of urban space are useful for protestors and organizers of collective action. Three types of urban space that were extensively appropriated in the Lebanon uprisings illustrate this well: public and open spaces, abandoned buildings, and infrastructure. On the other hand, urban space supports the production of multiple kinds of performative stages that enable the essential deployment of political imaginaries and "real utopias," materialized quite substantively not only in urban scenes across Lebanon but also particularly in Beirut where collective action was rehearsed by multiple groups quite intensely over the past decade.

Both components bring to the fore the spatial triad of Henri Lefebvre, which presents a cogent framework through which to further theorize urban space and revolutions.[24] Henri Lefebvre conceptualizes social space through a dialectical spatial triad, incorporating three intersecting dimensions: conceived space, practiced space, and lived space. *Conceived space* is the one produced by urbanists, professionals, and political decision makers who imagine and draw the space of the city. It is the space imagined, represented, and planned in maps, drawings, discourses, visions, and three-dimensional renderings—the one that forges the dominant political, economic, and moral orders. *Practiced space* is generated by dwellers who use space and navigate it variably, elaborating spatial practices related to home, work, and leisure. It is the space of mobility, of trajectories used on a daily level, and their associated perceived environment. *Lived space* relates to people's experiences of space and to the appropriations they make of space, in ways that subvert the dominant, conceived order. It is the space where people can live their desires, where they can own urban space, and, more importantly, where revolutionary politics are nested. It is also the space that hegemonic authorities and forces of capitalism want to control by all means, as it threatens their domination, and the space they will always seek to reproduce into conceived, planned space.

Applying the spatial triad framework to the Lebanon uprising of 2019 clearly shows how the power-sharing system in postwar Lebanon *conceived* cities, regions, and infrastructures that divided territories into fiefdoms where sectarian power and capitalist interests were nurtured. Dwellers *practiced* and navigated these territories in ways that often consolidated boundaries and demarcations, with limited opportunities to venture outside strongholds. Yet, throughout the political history of Lebanon, a wide range of opposition groups and individual practices regularly challenged this dominant political, moral, and spatial order. These contestations and collective action are attempts to wrangle the dominant power-sharing structure and its orders, disputing territories ruled by sectarianism and capitalism, albeit fleetingly—especially in the capital city. During the uprising of 2019, these attempts reached an unprecedented scale in their decentralized geographies, and in the nature of their collective spatial reclamations. As the chapter shows, people appropriated and inhabited multiple kinds of urban spaces in unique modalities that bonded them with the city in transformative ways, albeit full of contradictions and incongruities: still, they experienced *lived* space, as they collectively altered the way space was originally *conceived.* They made the city their own and recuperated it from the hegemonic powers that usurped land into property to be possessed or exchanged. The city became the shared space of the commons where people could start tinkering with how to dwell and enjoy life together. As the activist I quoted in the opening of this chapter fittingly expressed: "The revolution showed us . . . what it means to love, enjoy, and to be happy in our city. (. . .) The revolution gave us back ourselves and our cities."

Evidently, as Lefebvre teaches us, the hegemonic political, economic, and moral orders will not let the spaces it conceived to become appropriated and transformed without interfering. Its counterrevolutionary forces will fight back violently to reassert power and authority. Indeed, the first targets of the counterrevolution forces were not the protestors themselves but the spaces they appropriated, inhabited, and *lived*: their tents, their gears, their objects, and their belongings were destroyed and torched, more than once, in Beirut, Jal el-Dib, Choueifat, Saida, Nabatiyeh, and Tripoli. As if any material remnant, any physical trace that would remind people of how they collectively imagined another political and moral order, notwithstanding all its imperfections, had to be totally wiped.

The pandemic hit Lebanon in March 2020 and the virus came aptly to the rescue of the delegitimized sectarian political system. The government issued an emergency law, restored its powers, and consolidated its territorialities in record time.[25] The police dismantled tents in protests sites, using public health as an appropriate policy justification. Spaces were cleaned up, sealed off, and reorganized; security walls and fences were fortified; and graffiti were erased. Conceived, ordered, disciplined space was restored. Yet, people lived space, in extraordinary, meaningful ways that transformed them and that will critically determine their continued organizing for social justice. Despite the current times of compounded disasters and crises, where despair and helplessness have been trumping revolutions, we need to believe that new political horizons can still strike out, as they have done in other contexts, and continue experimenting and training for the next episode of struggle.[26]

Notes

1 See: S. Fregonese, "Elements of Contestation. Sectarianism as Extractive Violence and Lebanon's Revolution," in SEPAD, *Urban Spaces and Sectarian Contestation* (SEPAD, 2021); W. Nicholls and J. Uitermark, *Cities and Social Movements. Immigrant Rights Activism in the United States, France and the Netherlands* (London: Wiley Blackwell, 2016); D. Sharp and C. Panetta, "Introduction," in *Beyond the Square: Urbanism and the Arab Uprisings*, ed. D. Sharp and C. Panetta (New York: Terraform, 2016), 6–29; N. Rabbat, "The Arab Revolution Takes Back the Public Space," *Critical Inquiry* 39, no. 1 (2012): 198–208.

2 M. Harb, "A Counter-Dominant Global Urbanism? Experiments from Lebanon," in *Global Urbanism. Knowledge, Power and the City*, ed. M. Lancione and C. McFarlane (London: Routledge, 2021); M. Harb, "New Forms of Youth Activism in Contested Cities: The Case of Beirut," *International Spectator* 53, no. 2 (2018): 74–93.

3 Nicholls and Uitermark, *Cities and Social Movements*.

4 For more details on the rich history of both squares, see S. Khalaf, *Heart of Beirut: Reclaiming the Bourj* (London: Saqi, 2006). A great socio-spatial review of the architectural and urban history of Martyrs' Square has been produced by C. Aramouny, "Temporal/Reclamation: Martyrs Square," *Beirut Shifting Grounds*, Exhibition material for the Venice Biennale, 2021. Accessible on this link: https://beirutshiftinggrounds.com/Temporal.

5 R. Majed, "Living Revolution, Financial Collapse and Pandemic in Beirut: Notes on Temporality, Spatiality, and 'Double Liminality,'" *Middle East Law and Governance* 12 (2020): 305–15; L. Mounzer, "It Felt Like Love," *Newlines Magazine*, October 18, 2020.

6 Jeffrey G. Karam and Sana Tannoury-Karam, "The Lebanese Intifada: Observations and Reflections on Revolutionary Times," *Jadaliyya,* November 10, 2019, https://www.jadaliyya.com/Details/40218; M. Hammoud, "Reclaiming Public Space during the Revolution: How we are Reconnecting with Lebanese Cities," *Beirut Today*, November 20, 2019; M. Fawaz and I. Serhal, "Urban Revolutions: Lebanon's October 2019 Uprising," *IJURR Spotlight On: "Urban Revolts,"* 2020.

7 Mounzer, "It Felt Like Love."

8 Rabbat, "The Arab Revolution Takes Back the Public Space."

9 A. Atallah, "Reclaiming the City . . . Another Win for the Thawra," *L'Orient-le-Jour*, December 9, 2019; C. Bou Aoun, "Reclaiming Public Space and its Role in Producing the Revolution," *Legal Agenda*, January 9, 2020; W. Sinno, "How People Reclaimed Public Spaces in Beirut during the 2019 Lebanese Uprising," *The Journal of Public Space* 5, no. 1 (2020): 193–218; Hammoud, "Reclaiming Public Space during the Revolution"; Fawaz and Serhal, "Urban Revolutions."

10 H. Ghanem, "Spatial Profanation of Lebanese Sectarianism: al-Nur Square and the 17 October 2019 Protests," *Journal for Cultural Research*, March 23, 2021.

11 M. Fawaz, "Exception and the Actually Existing Practice of Planning: Beirut as a Case Study," *Urban Studies* 54, no. 8 (2017): 1938–55.

12 The Beirut City Center (the Egg) is an unfinished cinema building whose construction began in 1965 and was interrupted by the civil war. For a history of the Grand Théâtre of Beirut, see Sana Tannoury-Karam, "Reckoning with the Past: Selected Scenes from the Modern History of Beirut," in *The Lebanon Uprising of 2019: Voices from the Revolution*, ed. Jeffrey G. Karam and Rima Majed (London: I.B. Tauris and Bloomsbury, 2022). Both buildings are now managed by the private real estate company Solidere, which oversees the development of the downtown of Beirut. The Ghandour building is an abandoned, unfinished structure built in the 1960s that overlooks al-Nur square in Tripoli. As Ghanem explains ("Spatial Profanation of Lebanese Sectarianism," 6–7), it was supposed to be used for the refrigeration of agricultural products, but its construction was halted because of a building violation. Attempts to rebuild it failed, and it was ultimately occupied by the Syrian army for more than a decade, before being used as an informal shelter.

13 N. Kosmapotoulos, "Unhatching the Egg in Lebanon's 2019 Protests: Activism, Purity, and the Real-Estatization of Civil Society," *The South Atlantic Quarterly* 120, no. 2 (2021): 446–55.

14 Ghanem, "Spatial Profanation of Lebanese Sectarianism," 7–8.

15 Harb, "New Forms of Youth Activism in Contested Cities."

16 Nicholls and Uitermark, *Cities and Social Movements*, 11, 16.

17 See Rima Majed, "Sectarian Neoliberalism and the 2019 Uprisings in Lebanon and Iraq," in *The Lebanon Uprising of 2019: Voices from the Revolution*, ed. Jeffrey G. Karam and Rima Majed (London: I.B. Tauris and Bloomsbury, 2022).

18 Harb, "A Counter-Dominant Global Urbanism?"

19 More details about the history of urban activism are available in Harb, "New Forms of Youth Activism in Contested Cities." The campaign to stop the Fouad Boutros highway is documented on their website: https://stopthehighway.wordpress.com/. The campaign to protect the Dalieh seacoast has been analyzed by one of its lead activists, in A. Saksouk-Sasso, "Making Spaces for Communal Sovereignty: The Story of Beirut's Dalieh," *Arab Studies Journal* 22, no. 1 (2015): 296–319. The campaign of Bisri is discussed in this volume; see Roland Nassour, "The Struggle for the Bisri Valley,"

in *The Lebanon Uprising of 2019: Voices from the Revolution*, ed. Jeffrey G. Karam and Rima Majed (London: I.B. Tauris and Bloomsbury, 2022).

20 These ideas in the remaining part of this section are extracted from Harb, "A Counter-Dominant Global Urbanism?".

21 E. O. Wright, *Envisioning Real Utopias* (London: Verso, 2010), 4.

22 S. Espiner, "Daring Alternatives: Social Theory and Open-Ended Utopianisms," *New Zealand Sociology* 33, no. 1 (2018): 5–27.

23 M. Kaika and E. Swyngedouw, "Radical Urban Political-Ecological Imaginaries. Planetary Urbanization and Politicized Nature," *Eurozine*, March 14, 2014.

24 The unpacking of Lefebvre's spatial triad is largely inspired from A. Merrifield, "Place and Space: A Lefebvrian Reconciliation," *Transactions of the Institute of British Geographers* 18, no. 4 (1993): 516–31; H. Lefebvre, *The Production of Space* (London: Wiley, 1974, 1990).

25 M. Harb, A. Gharbieh, M. Fawaz, and L. Dayekh, "Mapping Covid-19 Governance in Lebanon: Territories of Sectarianism and Solidarity," *Middle East Law and Governance* 14, no. 1 (2021): 81–100. https://doi.org/10.1163/18763375-14011293.

26 D. Gould, "Political Despair," in *Politics and the Emotions: The Affective Turn in Contemporary Political Studies*, ed. P. Hogget and S. Thompson (London: Bloomsbury, 2012).

10

Alternative Media and Digital Platforms

Empowerment Tools for Civic Engagement

Claudia Kozman

For centuries, alternative media have forged close ties with activists, aiming to resist power and bring about social change in various parts of the world. Alternative media were once again at the center of activism in 2019, when Lebanon joined a host of Middle Eastern countries to demand political and social reform, staging countrywide protests that made use of various types of communication to facilitate the circulation of information and aid in the recruitment process. Although mainstream media have traditionally held a privileged position as the primary conduit of messages during social movements—thanks in part to their near monopoly over access to information as an institution deeply embedded in the existing power structures of society—technological advancements have given alternative media the tools to challenge this position by breaching the link between mainstream media and traditional sources of information. Alternative media, thus, took advantage of the rising to power of the protestors as the new sources of information, quickly establishing themselves as an alternate and, sometimes, central source of news about the uprisings. Drawing on personal experiences and research evidence from Lebanon and similar protests, this chapter examines the use of digital platforms and alternative media during the 2019 Lebanese uprising as a form of political participation that signals active civic engagement by the Lebanese public.

* * *

As the year 2019 drew to an end, so did the Lebanese public's reliance on mainstream media. The post-civil war Lebanese media scene has been as pluralistic and diverse as Lebanese society. Similar to most national media systems, the Lebanese media reflect the political and sociological setting of the country. For decades, this pluralism has allowed the media to enjoy relative freedom, providing the public with a range of different political opinions. Internally, however, Lebanese media are more or less unidirectional in their political and sectarian ideologies. Perhaps at no other time has this been as clear as the October 2019 uprisings that played out on the televisions screens as they did on the ground but with massive variations among the broadcasting outlets.

What has been documented in research on Lebanese media[1] became clearly evident to the Lebanese public. No scientific inquiry was needed to observe the glaring patterns in media coverage of the protests. Where one television station zoomed in on an empty corner of a rather packed street to undermine the protests, another took aerial shots of the thousands of protestors to show their magnitude, albeit in a dramatic fashion. What research did confirm, however, was high levels of selectivity on the part of the audience. Melki and Kozman's (2020) nationally representative survey of the Lebanese public during the protests revealed individuals exercised what media scholars call *selective exposure*, the act of selectively consuming media content that aligns with their beliefs. The study found attitude strength toward the protests predicted exposure to pro-protest TV channels *Al Jadeed*, *LBC*, and *MTV*. The same pattern emerged for opposers of the protests who were more likely to consume anti-protest channels *Al Manar*, *OTV*, and *NBN*.

In the midst of this activist and, at times, propagandist media behavior, the public did not feign indifference. Far from being passive observers, Lebanese people detached themselves to some degree from established media outlets, turning instead to alternative media and digital platforms. Among the most prominent ones were already existing platforms, such as *Akhbar Al Saha*, *Megaphone*, and *BlogBaladi*, in addition to the newly formed *Daleel Thawra* and *17 Teshreen*, alongside dozens of social media pages dedicated to the protests. Prior to delving into an analysis of this behavior, it is important to clarify the term *alternative media* and its subsequent usage in this chapter.

Alternative Media as Structures of Power Resistance

Scholars have long debated what constitutes alternative media. Whereas some highlighted the production line, others focused on the content or audience interpretation.[2] Notwithstanding the various postulates, many definitions seem to align themselves along the concept of alternative media to be media produced by activists,[3] for the purpose of critiquing and resisting power.[4] Given most conceptualizations of alternative media tie them to social movements and activism, it is expected to talk about them in the context of the 2019 Lebanese uprising. It is precisely the dissenting nature of alternative media that makes them a perfect fit for protests, which, in the Lebanese case, were further emboldened by the public's growing intolerance of the elites, among which are mainstream media and the political elites they support. This chapter does not scrutinize the theoretical definitions of alternative media; rather, it uses the simplified version of alternative media as nonmainstream and nontraditional media. Going by Atkinson's (2017)[5] advice that researchers themselves can draw the circle within which they define alternative media in their study, I will be using the term *alternative media* to refer to nonmainstream digital media platforms that served as alternative sources of information for the protestors and that produced content critical of the power structures in the country.

The mushrooming of alternative media is not confined to protests, to Lebanon, or to digital platforms. Long before the internet took shape, various types of anarchist media provided an alternative voice to mainstream media[6] that have traditionally favored organizational elites, such as authoritative institutional sources and political actors.[7] Centuries later, the birth of interactive web technologies in the form of digital platforms offered individuals the ability to create and disseminate information without the need of a license. The freedom to produce content away from the confines of traditional media practices additionally brought to light the latter's limitations, exacerbating discontent with these media. This growing ambivalence is partly due to the availability of options to mainstream media narratives that have long dominated the information ecosystem. And with these options came lack of trust toward mainstream media. Although variations exist among countries, people, in general, do not seem to trust traditional news media.[8] Interestingly, part of the distrust comes from alternative media. As they compete with traditional media in a high-choice media environment, some alternative sources attempt to undermine trust in the former,[9] reverting to criticism and accusations of bias, lack of impartiality,[10] and commerciality.[11] Others, however, do not necessarily oppose traditional media, breaking the misconception of a strictly binary existence. In the case of Lebanon, for instance, some alternative media served as complementary sources to traditional media, at times relying on them for information they cannot access on their own. The stance of alternative media vis-à-vis traditional media and the differences in the nature of the criticism reveal that "it is *the specific characteristics of mainstream media in national systems that drives the editorial agenda of alternative media*."[12] Thus, in order to assess people's use of alternative media during Lebanon's 2019 uprising, we need to first understand the media that serve them.

An Overview of Traditional Media

The Lebanese media system is set up along partisan lines where the media reflect the political divisions in the country, rendering political parallelism fairly high.[13] Specifically, the clientelism that exists between media and politics in Lebanon has resulted in the instrumentalization of the media that are reduced to being "a self-serving tool for the elite."[14] With such close links between the political powers and those reporting their activities, it is only natural to anticipate discontent and bitterness toward these media from a portion of the public, specifically those opposing the sectarianism of the ruling government and political parties. This resentment was further exacerbated by the oftentimes dubious behavior of some broadcast media reporters who appeared more personal than professional in their coverage of the protests. In such a case, adding alternative sources to their news diet seems to have been a logical option for individuals who still needed traditional media for information the alternative media could not deliver, such as talk shows with experts and public figures and access to governmental press conferences that are reserved for traditional media personnel. People's gravitation toward alternative media during the protests could have been additionally encouraged by the limitations imposed on traditional media, as well as those they themselves created.

As witnessed by anyone consuming a single day of television news during the protests, *Al Jadeed*, *LBC*, and *MTV* brazenly declared themselves pro-protests and devoted the majority of their programming for televised talk shows and live broadcasts of the protests, which included on-the-ground conversations with protestors. Survey data during the uprisings indicate this move was well received by the Lebanese people, 88 percent of whom consumed television news.[15] While some of the protestors broadened the reach of traditional media by disseminating their information on Facebook, Twitter, and other social media platforms, a portion of the protestors acted on their wariness and distrust of traditional media, comically including them in the most known slogan of the protests #all_means_all. With the exception of local broadcaster *Télé Liban*, Lebanese television stations are private entities that rely on donor and advertising money for their day-to-day operations. Broadcasting news about the protests would hardly fill advertising slots, forcing these stations to either continue with heavy protests coverage and risk losing money or partially sustain themselves through other means, such as paid programming. Whereas *LBC* and *MTV* resorted to the latter option, *Al Jadeed* remained steadfast in championing the cause, relying oftentimes on sensationalism and propaganda to attract viewers.

The doubtful stance of some of the public against these media was further provoked by the consistent failure of the reporting. On-site journalists were caught repeatedly asking protestors what they are doing there and what their demands are, even weeks into the protests. In other instances, news anchors were perceived as appearing too eager to be "part of the people," hence failing in their overzealousness. These perceptions were mostly evident in young people who seemed to have adopted a take-no-prisoners war approach, being quick to dismiss traditional media for their sectarian, partisan nature more than for their mediocre coverage. Beside the financial and professional components, certain political aspects weighed heavily against traditional media. For instance, political allegiances were purported to be behind cable distributors blocking pro-protest television station *Al Jadeed* in specific areas known to be pro-government Hezbollah strongholds. These problems combined put a toll on television stations to cover the protests fully, impartially, and professionally.

Alternative Media and Civic Engagement

Arguably, the most vocal group in the protests was the young Lebanese generation that was born after the Lebanese civil war ended, with the only memories of that war coming to them from their parents. Formed mostly from university—and sometimes high school—students, Lebanese youth organized sit-ins and publicly voiced their political demands, asking the government for accountability for its failures and responsibility to provide its people with their basic rights. Fearless, young Lebanese flocked to the streets and to digital platforms to make their voices heard. These digital and alternative media occupied significant spaces in the protests, primarily acting as channels the public used to share (mis)information about the protests, to ask for backup for unplanned protest gatherings, and to nullify the media blackout about which many protestors complained. From this perspective, Lebanese protestors weaponized digital platforms to serve their goals, reflecting high levels of civic engagement, both online and offline. They used social media platforms, particularly WhatsApp, Facebook, and Twitter, producing and consuming various types of information about the protests, in addition to more organized, and sometimes established, alternative media, such as *Legal Agenda, Daraj, Raseef 22, Akhbar Al Saha, Megaphone, BlogBaladi, Daleel Thawra*, and *17 Teshreen*, among others.

Experiencing the protests in the middle of the fall semester meant witnessing young activists in action, in and outside the classroom. During a class session in early November, my students told me they hadn't slept the previous night because they received a WhatsApp message asking them for support. As an academic, I understood support to take a virtual and moral form. Having heard of WhatsApp and Facebook groups that used these platforms to gather support for the protests but not knowing exactly what support meant, I asked, "What kind of support?" One of my students, Heba, laughed and said, "They asked for back-up at The Ring, as in *da3em*" (the Arabic word for backup). For Heba and others like her this was a simple message asking for simple help. But to scholars like me it was the manifestation of a change in mediated communication, a form of civic engagement that merges online with offline political participation. Although this uprising may not have been the first time Lebanese people reverted to digital tools to participate in political issues alongside protesting on the streets, the widespread uses of social media for all types of communication related to the protests arguably signaled a new and more consistent way Lebanese youth mobilized themselves using digital tools to complement their street participation.

Online Political Participation

What the civil war generation was shamed for—inaction against decades of the governments' violations to its rights—became the igniting fire of the new generation. Unlike their predecessors, the current youth cohort did not let its frustration go unnoticed. Perhaps it is the detachment from a war they never experienced or being part of a proactive, civically minded generation that is bold in its demands for its rights, young Lebanese people used their loud voices and digital skills to engage in political activism, online and offline. Using various digital platforms, at the forefront of which were Facebook, Instagram, Twitter, YouTube, and websites, activists reported on news, gave practical information about gatherings, transmitted public lectures and teach-ins, and covered street life in all its variations.[16] Not all alternative media, however, were new or created by protestors. Some were launched years earlier but were either reactivated in 2019 after years of inactivity, as in the case of *Akhbar Al Saha*, or dedicated themselves to the uprising the moment it started, such as *Megaphone, BlogBaladi, Daraj*, and *Raseef 22. The Public Source* is yet another platform that was conceptualized before the protests in anticipation of the financial crisis, with fundraising and planning activities starting March 2019, and was thus used as a reference source for many during the protests.

Others, the likes of *Daleel Thawra* and *17 Teshreen*, on the other hand, were created specifically for the protests. Joining them were more established entities, such as *Legal Agenda* that could also be considered alternative given its nature as an advocacy organization that focuses on the legal aspects of "political, civil, social, and economic rights."[17] During the uprising, *Legal Agenda* and others like it concentrated their efforts on uncovering legal violations to civic rights, acting as a go-to source of expert, legal advice for ordinary citizens. In addition to the above, dozens of websites and Facebook pages (e.g., @altmedia2019, @thawranews, @lebanrevolts, @lebrevoultion17october), some of which were decentralized (e.g., @tripolirevolution2019, @TyreRevolutionV, @Saida.tantafed), catered to the needs of the uprisings. The existence of these platforms outside the capital city Beirut further broke its centrality as a primary space for activism, highlighting the role other major cities played in the uprising. Another important mobilization role is attributed to individual activists, such as Gino Raidy (@ginoraidy), Oleksandra Zahran (@polleksandra), and Ghayd Chammas (@el_3ama), who rose to social media influencer status during the uprisings, due to their bold and more direct approach to issues. The protests also encouraged other initiatives such as the Alternative Media Syndicate that self-identified as a syndicate of journalists who are part of the people's uprising.

These alternative media ensured activist messages were abundant, shared through WhatsApp and Facebook, among others. They also guaranteed there was no shortage of information regarding where to go to protest or what time a specific march would start. However, to accurately assess the role of alternative media in the protests one must look beyond the social media pages and direct messaging services. In the following section, I delineate the nature of alternative media uses, their effects, and their potential impact beyond the protests.

Civic Engagement in a Competitive Media Environment

Today's high-choice media environment carries with it various types of competition not previously available. In Lebanon and elsewhere, more media platforms have been recently founded to serve the public, as an attempt to counter the traditional media hegemony. Undoubtedly, alternative media played a significant role in the 2019 uprising, prompting individuals to take part in online political discussions while also succeeding in mobilizing the people to take part in offline political behavior. While the online organically merged with the offline, and vice versa, evidence from the protests points to a spillover effect where online conversations were related to street participation, especially among supporters of the protests.[18]As such, alternative media became a valuable tool for the Lebanese public, specifically politically interested individuals who strongly supported the protests, to exercise its civic rights and call for political and social reform.

Beyond these cross-sectional statistical inferences, however, the longevity of these effects is unclear. Was the goal challenging mainstream media through any means possible or provide an alternate source of accurate and factual information? Was the goal mobilizing the masses riding on the momentum of the protests or establishing a system of political participation beyond the protests? Regardless of the answers, the realities on the ground indicate alternative media occupied a significant space in the communication landscape during the protests. To better understand their role, we must situate alternative media within the larger information-sharing environment that included various types of information sources that freely roamed the online world.

The internet, in general, is a double-edged sword. In the same manner marginalized communities found in the online world an avenue to express their voice, privileged elites used the same strategies to limit dissenting opinions. People in the Arab world witnessed this firsthand in the Arab uprisings in 2011, when national governments were as effective in limiting the reach/power of social media activism as the activists themselves in spreading their messages. Digital technologies, then, are not only restricted to alternative media but also include political and cultural elites, interest groups, and traditional media, among others, who use digital platforms to further their cause. Similar to other protests around the world, anti-protest groups in Lebanon, among which were political parties with elaborate digital strategies and media armies, swarmed the internet to push their agenda. Naturally, this digital counterrevolution—a notion Joseph Daher and Jeffrey G. Karam write about in more details in this book—presented a challenge for alternative media and their users, forcing them to compete in a high-choice media environment where information is abundant, but verification is not. As a result, digital platforms became a battleground for competing ideologies and, at times, a breeding ground for misinformation. Consequently, demands for media literacy education, with a focus on fake news, rose, prompting media faculty, interest groups, and nongovernmental organizations to raise awareness about the destructive effects of disseminating false news through public lectures and social media campaigns. Beyond these immediate challenges, digital platforms additionally fueled a much-feared consequence of online social groups: polarization and fragmentation.

Polarization and (In)effective Deliberation

Based on the tendency of the Lebanese public to selectively consume media that align with its beliefs,[19] the protestors found in both alternative and pro-protest traditional media a place to satiate their information-hungry appetites. Regardless of the source type, consumption of attitude-consistent media could create an isolated filter bubble around specific discussions. Hence, no conversation about online conversations can be labeled comprehensive without the mention of echo chambers and the related notion of polarization.

The nature of social groups, both real and virtual, entails belongingness. Group norms are generally enforced with a leaning toward perceived majority opinion, as the spiral of silence theory postulates.[20] More often than not, groups become fragmented, conversations narrow, and outgroup opinions not welcome. The nature of the internet and weak ties in online networks make online groups especially susceptible to this behavior, resulting in the formation of echo chambers that could exacerbate polarization as more people gravitate to the poles.[21] The propensity to select like-minded opinions becomes part of a vicious cycle where people view sources they perceive to be aligned with their attitudes as more credible than those who are attitude congruent.[22] Exposure to opinion-reinforcing content, which is most common in polarized groups, is harmful for political deliberation because it could limit the range of voices heard.[23] Opinion-challenging content, on the other hand, can significantly extend political discussion and lead to political participation.[24]

The prevalence of echo chambers in the online environment has been debated, with digital trace data pointing to the existence of echo chambers among the politically engaged, who do not represent the general population.[25] In the case of the Lebanese protests, however, the deep political and social divides that existed among the public, and between the public and the governing elites, suggest polarization is not a matter of contention here. Unlike normal situations, political turmoil challenges people's ability to peacefully engage in political discussions. With emotions running high, anger plays a role, decreasing exposure to anti-attitudinal news.[26] Survey results from the uprisings indeed revealed a polarized population with a tendency, especially among the protestors, to engage in selective avoidance on social media.[27] Our participants reported having either unfriended, blocked, or hid a user because they disagreed with them, providing further evidence for the existence of a fragmented public that coalesced into echo chambers, and by doing so, limited any opportunities to engage in conversations with others who might challenge their opinion.

Alternative Media: Challenges Ahead

This chapter sought to highlight the role alternative media played in the 2019 Lebanese uprising. It specifically examined the uses of digital and alternative platforms as a form of political participation that reflects the various degrees of civic engagement people in Lebanon, especially the youth, revealed at the height of the protests. Of particular importance to scholarship on political communication is the merging of the online world with the offline one, allowing individuals to voice their opinions not only on social media but also in the streets. Whether alternative media took the form of political tweets, WhatsApp groups calling for backup on the streets, or crowdsourced digital platforms announcing marches, they served an important role for protestors who used these platforms to call for political and social reform. Individuals' selective usage of media content, however, also points to the existence of polarized online communities that brought together like-minded people while cutting ties with those holding different opinions.

While alternative media served an important role for protestors, they nevertheless had to squeeze into the information ecosystem that has traditionally been dominated by legacy media and sometimes compete with the more established television stations. With limited funds, volunteer staff, and lack of professional means to assert themselves as media entities, a number of these alternative media themselves relied on mainstream media to carry out their duties.

Beyond the first few weeks of the uprisings, alternative media continued to perform their dissident, anti-establishment responsibilities well into 2020, in light of the spread of COVID-19 and traditional media's alleged partisan coverage of the pandemic. They rose to public attention once more after the Beirut Port explosion in August 2020, seeing the tragedy as an extension of governing elites' incompetence and their role as a crucial one in the people's fight against corruption. Finally, it is important to note while the existence of alternative media is a necessary tool for activism, these media face an uphill battle that could slow down their growth into a trusted go-to source of information. Lack of technical skills, expert personnel, and professional marketing tools are some of the areas with which alternative media in Lebanon struggle.[28] These challenges are further exacerbated by the economic collapse of the country and the toll of the pandemic on everyday life.

Notes

1 Sarah El-Richani, *The Lebanese Media: Anatomy of a System in Perpetual Crisis* (New York: Springer, 2016).
2 David Armstrong, *A Trumpet to Arms: Alternative Media in America* (Cambridge: South End Press, 1981).
3 Ibid.; Chris Atton, *Alternative Media* (London: Sage, 2002).
4 Joshua D. Atkinson, *Journey into Social Activism: Qualitative Approaches* (New York: Fordham University Press, 2017; John D. H. Downing, *Radical Media: The Political Experience of Alternative Communication* (South End Press, 1984).
5 Atkinson, *Journey into Social Activism.*
6 Armstrong, *A Trumpet to Arms.*
7 Michael Schudson, *The Sociology of News*, 2nd ed. (New York: W. W. Norton, 2011).
8 Jesper Strömbäck, Yariv Tsfati, Hajo Boomgaarden, Alyt Damstra, Elina Lindgren, Rens Vliegenthart, and Torun Lindholm, "News Media Trust and its Impact on Media Use: Toward a Framework for Future Research," *Annals of the International Communication Association* 44, no. 2 (2020): 139.
9 Ibid., 151.
10 Stephen Cushion, Declan McDowell-Naylor, and Richard Thomas, "Why National Media Systems Matter: A Longitudinal Analysis of How UK Left-Wing and Right-Wing Alternative Media Critique Mainstream Media (2015–2018)," *Journalism Studies* (2021), doi:10.1080/1461670X.2021.1893795.
11 Jennifer Rauch, *Resisting the News* (New York: Routledge, 2021).
12 Cushion et al., "Why National Media Systems Matter," 17, emphasis original.
13 El-Richani, *The Lebanese Media.*
14 Kjetil Selvik and Jacob Høigilt, "Journalism Under Instrumentalized Political Parallelism," *Journalism Studies* (2021), doi:10.1080/1461670X.2021.1897476, 13.
15 Jad Melki and Claudia Kozman, "Selective Exposure during Uprisings: Examining the Public's News Consumption and Sharing Tendencies during the 2019 Lebanon Protests," *International Journal of Press/Politics* 26, no. 4 (2021): 907, doi:10.1177/1940161220972892
16 Diala Lteif, "The Lebanon Revolution Takes on the Media: A Resource on Alternative News Outlets," *Jadaliyya*, December 23, 2020, https://www.jadaliyya.com/Details /40379 (accessed February 10, 2021).
17 Legal Agenda, "Who We Are," https://english.legal-agenda.com/about-us/ (accessed May 28, 2021).
18 Melki and Kozman, "Selective Exposure during Uprisings."

19 Ibid.

20 Elisabeth Noelle-Neumann, "The Spiral of Silence: A Theory of Public Opinion," *Journal of Communication* 24, no. 2 (1974): 43.

21 Cass R. Sunstein, "The Law of Group Polarization," *Journal of Political Philosophy* 10, no. 2 (2002): 175.

22 Craig T. Robertson, "Trust in Congruent Sources, Absolutely: The Moderating Effects of Ideological and Epistemological Beliefs on the Relationship between Perceived Source Congruency and News Credibility," *Journalism Studies* (2021), doi:10.1080/146 1670X.2021.1904273.

23 R. Kelly Garrett, "Politically Motivated Reinforcement Seeking: Reframing the Selective Exposure Debate," *Journal of Communication* 59, no. 4 (2009): 676.

24 Seong Jae Min and Donghee Yvonne Wohn, "All the News that You Don't Like: Cross-Cutting Exposure and Political Participation in the Age of Social Media," *Computers in Human Behavior* 83 (2018): 24.

25 Ludovic Terren and Rosa Borge, "Echo Chambers on Social Media: A Systematic Review of the Literature," *Review of Communication Research* 9 (2021).

26 Hyunjin Song, "Why Do People (Sometimes) become Selective about News? The Role of Emotions and Partisan Differences in Selective Approach and Avoidance," *Mass Communication and Society* 20, no. 1 (2017): 47.

27 Claudia Kozman and Jad Melki, "Selection Bias of News on Social Media: The Role of Selective Sharing and Avoidance during Uprisings," *International Journal of Communication* (under review), 2021.

28 Ghinwa Mikdashi, "A Study on the Alternative Media Platforms in Lebanon," Maharat Foundation, November 2020, http://www.maharatfoundation.org/media/1883/study -on-alternative-media-in-lebanon.pdf.

11

Lebanon's Alternative Labor Movement

In between Collapse and Revolutionary Imaginaries

Nadim El Kak

On June 17, 2021, Lebanon's General Labor Confederation (CGTL) called for a nationwide strike. Mounting fuel prices, resulting from the progressive lifting of subsidies, coupled with the dollar exchange rate surpassing 15,000 Lebanese Liras were some of the most recent outcomes in a protracted string of devastating socioeconomic developments. During the strike, the head of the confederation, Bishara Al Asmar, called for ruling parties to finally form a new government after extended delays.[1] Al Asmar's statement was quite paradoxical, as CGTL's leadership is controlled by ruling parties themselves, particularly the Amal movement headed by Parliament Speaker Nabih Berri. The Free Patriotic Movement and Future Movement also endorsed and joined the strike, in an attempt to deflect criticisms of their role in delaying government formation.

Due to these contradictions, the strike was met with ridicule by anti-establishment groups, alternative labor unions, and activists who refused to take part in what was termed the "regime's strike."[2] Their reaction was not meant to invalidate strikers' grievances but rather reflected their views of ruling parties and the General Labor Confederation, which used to be a true oppositionist actor until its co-optation in the late 1990s.[3]

Ultimately, the strike of June 17 exposed yet again the inability of formal labor organizations to represent working-class interests independently from ruling parties. This reality, and the broader need to rebuild labor networks for the success of the revolution and beyond, is what drove various actors in 2019 to mobilize across sectors and found alternative unions and professionals' associations.[4] These included nonregistered associations of university professors, teachers, doctors, engineers and architects, media workers, NGO employees, artists, and others. While some of these groups are no longer active or disbanded, others remain operational and effective. In fact, just ten days after the CGTL's strike, a coalition of revolutionary groups won 221 of 232 seats in the first-round syndical elections of the Order of Engineers and Architects—a much-needed tangible and moral victory in the midst of an exceptionally arduous year and a half.[5]

In many ways, political life in Lebanon has been marred by contradictions since the start of the revolution. On the one hand, the anti-establishment movement has grown and saw victories like that of the "Lebanon Revolts" list in the Order of Engineers and

Architects, or the election of independent Melhem Khalaf as the head of the Beirut Bar Association.[6] On the other hand, traditional parties have proven that, despite the challenges they face, they were able to maintain their hold on power and reproduce their clientelistic networks.[7] Lebanon is indeed stuck in a state of Gramscian liminality, where the old can no longer reproduce itself yet the new cannot be born.[8] The ruling but crumbling system has lost its hegemony and many of its tools, yet remains robust enough to resist being replaced by emerging alternatives struggling with their own sets of challenges.

Within that context, one of the key arenas where the struggle between old and new has been taking place is at the level of labor mobilization. In order to fully grasp the implications of the struggle, this chapter begins by revisiting the neoliberal regime's historical repression and co-optation of unions. It then looks at the emergence of the Lebanese Professionals' Association (LPA) and examines the radical imaginaries and regional inspirations that shaped this new wave of organizing. The chapter ends with a discussion of the potentialities as well as the challenges that the labor movement faces going forward. In line with the overarching framework of the book, this chapter does not view revolutions as static events but rather as long-term processes. It understands the anxious state of in-betweenness Lebanon finds itself in as a temporary one that will ultimately yield a new reality—one that has the potential of being conceived and led by a politicized, progressive, and well-organized revolutionary community—or not.

Neoliberal Consolidation: The Repressive Co-optation of Labor

Until the turn of the century, labor unions were one of the main vehicles through which opposition to Lebanon's regime was waged. In the prewar period, particularly the 1960s and early 1970s, industrial and agricultural workers were well organized and radicalized, engaging in multiple mobilizations against the political and business oligarchy.[9] After the civil war, the CGTL was the key player opposing exploitative and unsustainable neoliberal policies. In fact, the confederation played a key role in pressuring the Omar Karami government to resign in 1992 while also leading a series of strikes between 1994 and 1996 that mobilized more than 60,000 public sector workers.[10]

Consequently, the government of late prime minister Rafic Hariri cracked down on the CGTL and Elias Abu Rizq, the head of the confederation: In June 1993, Hariri imposed the first of various bans on street demonstrations.[11] In July 1995, the CGTL defied one of the bans after the petrol tax was raised by 38 percent in order to fund wage increases Hariri had conceded to the previous year. This resulted in clashes with the Internal Security Forces (ISF), as hundreds of demonstrators were arrested.[12] In February 1996, Hariri even mobilized the army against unions by declaring a semi-state of emergency.[13]

In the lead up to the 1997 CGTL leadership elections, it was clear that political elites had a concerted plan to get rid of Abu Rizq and co-opt the confederation for good.[14] During the election, the ISF was ordered to occupy the voting center in order to keep Abu

Rizq's supporters out. Results split the CGTL leadership, and Abu Rizq was subsequently arrested and released by security forces on several occasions. Soon after, anti-regime actors were entirely pushed out of the CGTL's leadership through what Baumann referred to as "new politically pliable trade union federations [created] out of thin air" to vote against Abu Rizq.[15] Indeed, Badran specifies that five new federations loyal to Parliament Speaker Berri were licensed by the government despite Abu Rizq's objection, and that the government intervened in the elections of at least three preexisting federations to make sure that their representatives would vote against Abu Rizq.[16] Badran and Zbeeb also documented that the number of federations went up from 22 in 1993 to 36 by 2004—14 of those had less than 500 members. Because each union was entitled to two delegates in the CGTL, these fourteen groups controlled nearly 40 percent of the executive council, despite representing only 6.9 percent of total members.[17]

With the co-optation of the confederation having been completed, the regime had contained the threat of the labor movement and a series of other political developments dominated the 2000s. In 2011–15, a teachers-led movement of public sector employees fought for a raise in salary scales and sought to reinvigorate the labor struggle.[18] The movement succeeded in pressuring parliament to approve the raise of salary scales in April 2014, but the project law was drastically amended by a parliamentary committee "in a way that mainly disadvantages civil servants."[19] Less than a year later, traditional parties allied against and defeated the list of independents and the Lebanese Communist Party in the elections of the board of the league of secondary public school teachers. The sectarian establishment had thus managed to repress and tame the workers' movement yet again.[20]

While the historical attacks waged by the neoliberal-sectarian establishment against unions are fundamental, they do not tell the whole story of the labor movement. The story of labor is also that of the Lebanese state—one that systemically opposed welfare mechanisms and working-class rights.

Following the political crisis and violent clashes of 1958, a Social Welfare Authority was founded by then president Fouad Chehab in order to address issues of poverty, in line with "the state's intention to interfere in social policy and to end its traditional neutrality."[21] Sectarian authorities—both political and religious—immediately resisted this push toward involving the state in social issues, in fear of losing the webs of clientelism that guaranteed their hegemony.[22] Whatever promises and hopes the 1960s brought in developing a dependable welfare state were quickly crushed by the advent of the civil war. Political parties, through their militias, controlled service distribution and expanded their patronage network during the postwar period by setting the stage for further neoliberalization.

Neoliberalism is often inaccurately thought of as the retreat of the state when, at its very core, it seeks to redeploy states and global institutions to protect markets and capitalist interests from demands for social justice and political change.[23] The Hariri-led policies of the 1990s and 2000s corroborate this, as they prioritized deregulation, financialization, privatization, wage repression, and other rent-creating mechanisms at the expense of the already struggling local productive sectors.[24]

The state's ensuing repression of unions and move toward an economy almost exclusively driven by the financial sector and service industry also undermined working-class identification.[25] Indeed, labor-based mobilization had primarily been driven, historically and globally, by workers in the agricultural and industrial sectors. As a result of neoliberal policies, people who were already reluctant to engage in politics because of their negative perception of parties due to the civil war were further dissuaded from engaging in any kind of organizing.

In sum, the foundations of Lebanon's regime are based around arrangements and events that not only serve to consolidate sectarian elites' hegemony but also aim to eliminate alternative political visions that threaten their rule.[26] While this model seemed to be robust and stable, the unsustainable policies that undergird it eventually evolved from chronic cracks to complete socioeconomic implosion. In the years prior to the financial collapse, many new groups had already begun challenging the neoliberal-sectarian status quo, proving that a new political imaginary was evidently needed. The October 17 revolution would provide the collective space, creative potential, and political enthusiasm needed for these alternatives to emerge—even if their organizational process is still unstable.

Alternative Imaginaries and the New Labor Movement

With that historical context in mind, the state of Lebanon's labor movement in the lead up to the October Revolution was rather discouraging. While new political groups had emerged during the municipal elections of 2016 and the 2018 parliamentary elections, alternative labor organizations were essentially absent and ruling parties continued to dominate most syndical elections.[27] The advent of Lebanon's revolution served as a reminder, though, that cracks within the global capitalist system are becoming increasingly visible, recurrent, and interconnected.[28] It also brought with it a powerful revolutionary fervor that created a new a wave of hope and energy. Indeed, what makes revolutions "revolutionary" is not their outcomes; it's the imaginaries that undergird them—this sudden ability to visualize and believe that a radically different reality is possible despite the odds.[29] This was the emotional driver that galvanized crowds of protesters and that led to the emergence of new political organizations, including the LPA. So how did the LPA precisely come about from the streets of the revolution?

On October 22, 2019, faculty from the Lebanese University (LU) and American University of Beirut (AUB) called for all university professors, students, and staff to participate in the protests of downtown Beirut the following day. Many responded to the call, which led some to gauge interest in forming an association of professionals for politically independent university professors.[30] By the end of the day, hundreds had joined a WhatsApp group in support of the initiative, and the Association of Independent University Professors (AIUP) was formed, although it was not officially registered.[31]

In the days that followed, many other similar initiatives emerged across sectors. These groups recognized their overlapping interests and decided to join forces under the umbrella of the LPA. They included professionals in the health sector (medicine, dentistry, and pharmacy), engineers and architects, lawyers, journalists, economists, teachers, writers, and artists, in addition to university professors. The LPA's first joint statement, which was published on October 28, expressed support for the revolution and opposition to the ruling establishment.[32] It also called for professionals to join the LPA and take part in protests, while urging all existing formal unions and associations to support the movement.

Beyond the need to reignite the labor struggle and fill the void left by the co-optation of formal unions, various members of the LPA noted that a main inspiration behind the formation of the association is the role played by the Sudanese Professionals' Association (SPA) and the Tunisian General Union of Labor in their respective revolutions.[33] Rima Majed—coeditor of this book—stated during an interview: "The only two revolutions [in the region] that were able to create some sort of transition were Tunisia and Sudan. It was clear that this was because of the presence of organized and independent unions."[34] While the leaderless character of the October Revolution was rightfully touted as a strength at the beginning of the movement, it became evidently clear in the period that followed that there was a dire need for organizations that can represent the interests of different subgroups within the ranks of protesters. By taking a closer look at the experiences of the SPA, one can notice some relevant and useful contextual and organizational overlaps with Lebanon's new labor movement.

The SPA initially emerged as a small underground organization in October 2012 but was formerly established four years later through an alliance between three of the largest professional unions at the time: the Central Committee of Sudanese Doctors, the Sudanese Journalists Network, and the Democratic Lawyers' Association.[35] By 2018, the association was comprised of seventeen groups and became a key player in mobilizations, as it amassed "broad appeal and demonstrated a know-how of protests, drawing from a fresh and dynamic repertoire."[36] Ousted dictator Omar al-Bashir, who was overthrown in April 2019 after months of collective actions, even labeled the group as the "ghost battalion" for its key role in the revolution's success.[37] Since August 2019, the SPA has been acting as a pressure group that oversees the thirty-nine-month democratic transition period and is represented in the Sovereignty Council—a collective body acting as head of state until general elections are held in November 2022.[38]

It is essential to note, though, that the SPA was not the sole grassroots-based organizational structure in the Sudanese revolution. It was part of a wider political coalition named the Forces of Freedom and Change, which included numerous women's rights groups, youth groups, and dozens of other civil society organizations, rebel groups, and political parties belonging to the opposition. Yet, the most important ally of the SPA were the resistance committees, also known as the neighborhood committees—an alliance of grassroots councils "born out of necessity for protestors to organize in their daily confrontations with the security apparatus during the peak of the protest movement in early 2019."[39] These groups distinguished themselves through their democratic structures that prioritized participatory decision making, allowing them to evolve into a "novel form of political authority challenging and often displacing the micro-organs of state power."[40] The resistance committees overtook Bashir's popular committees as the bodies representing the people at the local levels of government, which penetrated the everyday life of citizens. Just like the SPA, the resistance committees reaffirm the importance and power of class-based, decentralized, and participatory organizing.

In turn, the story of Sudan's alternative organizations had an important place in the collective imaginaries of labor activists in Lebanon. It was part of a broader imaginary that generated genuine belief in the ability of everyday people to reclaim a sense of political agency that had been stripped from us. Indeed, the fervor of the revolution generated intangible power, which translated into concrete collective action and organizing. Spontaneous acts of solidarity and resistance were widespread and decentralized, all contributing to the sustained momentum of the movement: People enforced nationwide strikes by blocking roads, protesters stormed and reclaimed government buildings, rioters broke into and set fire to private banks, and others sung chants that affirmed the intersectional and internationalist character of the revolution.[41] Along these same lines, LPA activists felt that organizing around their respective professions was their contribution to collective efforts, in the hopes that they would ultimately bring the movement one step closer to its penultimate goals of regime change and social justice.

It is important to note that while these new organizational structures and acts of resistance were emerging organically, they were all part of a broader collective imaginary that centered social justice and human emancipation. Despite the internal factions within these new organizations, this radical imaginary they developed was often a direct challenge to the neoliberal logics that pervade various aspects of daily social lives and that aim to reconfigure all aspects of human existence into individual economic relations. In *Undoing the Demos: Neoliberalism's Stealth Revolution*, Wendy Brown makes this precise point, arguing that neoliberalism has fostered widespread acceptance of the concept of "human capital." She contends that the economization of subjectivities undermines "democratic imaginaries"—or one's ability to conceive of humane and socially just alternatives of organizing the state, the economy, and society.

In other words, the soft power of neoliberalism seeks to eliminate all alternatives from our collective conscience. Besides undermining democratic imaginaries, it also looks to eliminate class consciousness. Brown argues that when human beings are conceived of in terms of capital, the human character of labor disappears as a category and so does "its collective form, class, [thus] taking with it the analytical basis for alienation, exploitation, and association among laborers."[42] In that sense, the radical imaginaries ignited by revolutions come as direct and foundational challenges to the hegemonic logics of capitalism. The emergence of alternative labor organizations is concrete manifestations of that emancipatory spirit, which not only recognizes the importance of class and labor as categories but is also aware of the threats they pose to the cultural and material foundations of the global system.

If we are to understand systemic and structural political change in their *longue durée*, then the clarity and rupture caused by revolutionary events are critical junctures within that process. Lebanon's revolution has already accomplished many things: The hegemony of ruling parties has been undermined, criticism of sectarian elites is no longer off-limits, a range of new anti-establishment groups have emerged, a previously depoliticized postwar generation is acquiring political maturity, and victories in syndical elections are a direct result of those efforts. However, Lebanon's revolution still has not accomplished its ultimate goals of regime change and socioeconomic justice. Many factors are behind this reality, including geopolitical ones,[43] yet there is no doubt that alternative labor organizations will have a key role to play in this revolutionary process. In light of the country's multilayered collapse, what are some of the main challenges and potentialities lying ahead for Lebanon's new labor movement?

Sustaining the Momentum: Organizing in Collapse

Transitioning from the revolutionary fervor of late 2019 to the present-day unease, grief, and anguish has had noticeable effects on mobilization efforts. In her auto-ethnography, Majed describes this experience as one of "double liminality" where she juxtaposes "the revolutionary moment of publicness, enthusiasm and clarity; [with] the pandemic moment of isolation, rumination and anxiety."[44] In the midst of this tension, most organizers have faced exhaustion, loss of hope, and socioeconomic insecurity. For these reasons, some of the alternative labor organizations that were founded during the revolution have become inactive or disbanded.

The LPA has also faced various internal structural challenges during that time. Due to the wide range of professions and sectors represented within the LPA, some have questioned the ability of "employees, self-employed, freelancers, and employers [to all] organize under one association."[45] Ultimately, an agreement was reached that the LPA would serve as a coordination platform rather than a leading organizational body. This meant that each alternative association within the LPA would operate separately and that formal coordination between them would be along pragmatic lines.

Another challenge that was raised within the LPA pertains to the association's relationship with nonprofessionalized workers and unions. Indeed, some have criticized the LPA for representing professionals who are largely middle class, hence excluding the poorest from their organizing efforts. There are no doubts that with mounting poverty rates, inclusive and intersectional organizational frameworks are necessary. However, it is worth noting that many of the members of alternative professionals' associations have been laid off or are working in different jobs. In many ways, the financial collapse has reshuffled certain class divisions and created various new challenges, such as the need to organize the unemployed. These are all important yet difficult questions that the LPA cannot address by itself. Ultimately, each revolutionary group aims to escalate its organizing efforts in order to become a foundational piece in a stronger oppositionist front of revolutionary actors, just like Sudan's Forces of Freedom and Change.

Conclusion

Organizational growth in a time of mounting poverty, anger, and pessimism is a difficult task. Late sociologist Erik Olin Wright spent a bulk of his career working on the "Real Utopias Project," which consists of a series of conferences, papers, and books dealing with the question of radical social change and emancipatory visions. The driving rationale behind this project is the idea that we live in an era of diminished expectations and imagination, an era where alternatives to the status quo are treated with cynicism. This skepticism, Wright argues, undermines possibilities for a more socially just and humane world. The project thus posits that what is needed is an optimism of the intellect: "an optimism grounded in our understanding of the real potentials for emancipatory alternatives which can inform our practical strategies for social transformation."[46] By embracing the tension between dreams and practice, Wright and his colleagues developed a range of scholarship, albeit Eurocentric, on a myriad of topics including associational democracy, market socialism, participatory governance, income redistribution, cooperative economies, and gender equality.

The power of utopic imaginaries lies in this ability to envision and map out emancipatory and disruptive alternatives. While the challenges brought about by an uncertain future are real and valid, I find it useful to combat pessimism and doubt by reflecting historically and remembering that alternatives are still alive and budding. The reemergent labor movement, through its organizational growth and recent syndical victories, is proving just that: Revolutions are processes that defy the impossible and ours, although still in its foundational stages, is now underway.

Notes

1 Political elites had not formed a government since former caretaker Prime Minister Hassan Diab's resignation on August 10, 2020—six days after the Beirut Port explosion. Many argue that this delay was deliberate, as it bought parties time by allowing the banking sector to impose a de facto haircut on small to medium depositors and hence improve its balance of payments.

2 G. Alsharif, "Lebanese Scorn Political Parties' Participation in General Strike," *L'Orient Today*, June 17, 2021, https://today.lorientlejour.com/article/1265545/lebanese-scorn -political-parties-banking-sectors-participation-in-general-strike.html.

3 S. Baroudi, "Economic Conflict in Postwar Lebanon: State - Labor Relations between 1992 and 1999," *Middle East Journal* 52, no. 4 (1998): 531–50.

4 A. Sewell, "Push for Independent Syndicates Emerges from Protest Movement," *The Daily Star*, November 14, 2019, https://www.dailystar.com.lb/News/Lebanon-News /2019/Nov-14/495538-push-for-independent-syndicates-emerges-from-protest -movement.ashx.

5 K. Chehayeb, "Anti-Government Engineers Hopeful after Lebanon Syndicate Victory," *Al Jazeera English*, July 1, 2021, https://www.aljazeera.com/news/2021/7/1/anti -government-lebanese-engineers-win-syndicate-elections.

6 Lama Karamé book chapter; "Independent Melhem Khalaf Voted Head of Beirut Bar Association," *The Daily Star*, November 17, 2019, https://www.dailystar.com.lb/ News/Lebanon-News/2019/Nov-17/495743-beirut-bar-association-elects-new-head -councilmembers.ashx.

7 "Jabs for Votes: Lebanon's Oligarchs Turn to Covid Bribery," *Agence France-Presse*, June 10, 2021, https://www.france24.com/en/live-news/20210611-jabs-for-votes -lebanon-s-oligarchs-turn-to-covid-bribery.

8 This expression is borrowed by Antonio Gramsci's famous line in his *Prison Notebooks* (1947): "The crisis consists precisely in the fact that the old is dying but the new cannot be born." Gramsci is referring here to the lacking political conditions for a

communist revolution in the aftermath of the Great Depression, when he saw Italy's fascist regime as an already dying order.

9 F. Traboulsi, *A History of Modern Lebanon* (London: Pluto Press, 2017), 244.

10 Baroudi, "Economic Conflict in Postwar Lebanon," 535.

11 H. Baumann, "Social Protest and the Political Economy of Sectarianism in Lebanon," *Global Discourse* 6, no. 4 (2016): 643.

12 Ibid., 644.

13 Ibid.

14 Baroudi, "Economic Conflict in Postwar Lebanon," 543.

15 Baumann, "Social Protest and the Political Economy of Sectarianism in Lebanon," 646.

16 Baroudi, "Economic Conflict in Postwar Lebanon," 543.

17 I. Badran and M. Zbeeb, الاتحاد العمالي العام: من يمثل من؟ (The General Labor Confederation: Who Represents Whom?) (Beirut: Friedrich Ebert, 2001). Foundation. Available online: http://www.ltutc.com/ArticleDetails.aspx?art_ID=2169.

18 L. Bou Khater, "Public Sector Mobilization Despite a Dormant Workers' Movement," *Confluences Méditerranée* 92 (2015): 125–42.

19 Some traditional political figures and their spokespeople even attributed the rise in salary scales as one of the reasons behind the country's current financial collapse. For more about how the salary scale law was amended, see p. 134 in: Bou Khater, "Public Sector Mobilization Despite a Dormant Workers' Movement," 125–42.

20 Bou Khater, "Public Sector Mobilization Despite a Dormant Workers' Movement," 138.

21 L. Karameh, "Manufacturing Poverty in Lebanon," *The Legal Agenda*, May 27, 2020, https://english.legal-agenda.com/manufacturing-poverty-in-lebanon/.

22 Ibid.

23 Q. Slobodian, *Globalists: The End of Empire and the Birth of Neoliberalism* (Cambridge: Harvard University Press, 2018).

24 H. Baumann, *Citizen Hariri: Lebanon's Neo-Liberal Reconstruction* (New York: Oxford University Press, 2016).

25 J. Krinsky, "Constructing Workers: Working-Class Formation under Neoliberalism," *Qualitative Sociology* 30 (2017): 343–60.

26 See Sana Tannoury-Karam's book chapter.

27 In 2017, independent candidate Jad Tabet from the "Naqabati" campaign was elected as the head of the Order of Engineers and Architects.

28 See Rima Majed's book chapter on neoliberal sectarianism and Iraq/Lebanon; B. Koenraad, "From the Haitian Revolution to the Spectre of Tahrir: Is a Global Revolution Possible?" *openDemocracy*, January 27, 2020, https://www.opendemocracy.net/en/north-africa-west-asia/haitian-revolution-spectre-tahrir-global-revolution-possible/.

29 J. Paige, "Finding the Revolutionary in the Revolution: Social Science Concepts and the Future of Revolution," in *The Future of Revolutions: Rethinking Radical Change in the Age of Globalization*, ed. J. Foran (London: Zed Books, 2003), 19–29.

30 "The Lebanese Professionals Association: Meeting with Rima Majed," *Arab Reform Initiative*, December 23, 2019, https://www.arab-reform.net/video/the-lebanese-professionals-association-meeting-with-rima-majed/.

31 More about the AIUP can be found on their Facebook page: https://www.facebook.com/IndependentProfessors.

32 The statement can be found on the LPA's Facebook page: www.facebook.com/LebProAssociation/photos/a.101690577941472/101894227921107/?type=3&theater.

33 F. Al Hajj, "تجمع مهنيات ومهنيين: المطالب الاجتماعية مدخلاً للتغيير السياسي" (The Lebanese Association of Professionals: Social Demands as a Gateway to Political Change), *Al-Akhbar*, November 18, 2019, https://al-akhbar.com/Politics/279585; N. Atallah, "Lebanese Protests: The Missing Trade Unions," *Le Commerce du Levant*, February 21, 2020, https://www.lecommercedulevant.com/article/29632-lebanese-protests-the-missing -trade-unions.

34 S. Akram-Boshar, "The Lebanese Uprising Continues," *Jacobin Magazine*, February 17, 2020, https://www.jacobinmag.com/2020/02/lebanon-uprising-protests-banks -sectarianism-hezbollah.

35 Official website of the SPA: https://www.sudaneseprofessionals.org/en/about-us/.

36 S. Majdoub, "Sudan Professional Association: The 'ghost battalion' at the Centre of the Revolution," *Europe Solidaire Sans Frontières*, August 12, 2019, http://www.europe -solidaire.org/spip.php?article50184.

37 Ibid.

38 A number of political developments and changes may have occurred in Sudan since this chapter was written.

39 M. El Gizouli, "Mobilization and Resistance in Sudan's Uprising: From Neighborhood Committees to Zanig Queens," *Rift Valley Institute*, January 2020, https://riftvalley.net/ publication/mobilization-and-resistance-sudans-uprising.

40 Ibid.

41 See Mohamad Bzeih chapter on banks, Zbeeb on political economy, Hassan on roadblocks, Harb on public spaces, and Tannoury-Karam on reclaiming government buildings.

42 Ibid., 38.

43 While Lebanon's oligarchy is responsible for the country's multilayered crises, their policies and hold on power have been reproduced and supported by foreign actors and a global capitalist system that has repeatedly prioritized the interests of political-financial elites over those of local populations.

44 R. Majed, "Living Revolution, Financial Collapse and Pandemic in Beirut: Notes on Temporality, Spatiality, and 'Double Liminality,'" *Middle East Law and Governance* 12, no. 3 (2020): 305–15.

45 L. Bou Khater, "Did Someone Say Workers? (Part 2/2)," *The Public Source*, May 8, 2020, https://thepublicsource.org/did-someone-say-workers-2.

46 This quote is from Erik Olin Wright's description of the "Real Utopias Project," available at the following link: https://www.ssc.wisc.edu/~wright/OVERVIEW.html.

12

Appearing as Women

Sara Mourad

The Extension of the Public

When Malak Alawiyye joined protests in downtown Beirut on the night of October 17, she did not predict that a video showing her kicking one of the armed bodyguards of a member of parliament would go viral. On that fateful night, thousands of people took to the streets in Beirut and across the country shortly after the announcement of a new tax on WhatsApp, the most widely used instant messaging application in Lebanon. With a national currency and economy on the verge of collapse, the announcement of a WhatsApp tax was the proverbial straw that broke the camel's back. When the armed bodyguards of MP Akram Chehayeb[1] started pushing through the converging crowds to make way for his car convoy, protests turned violent. It was then and there that Malak was captured on video kicking a Kalashnikov-wielding man in the gut. Overnight, "the kick" assumed iconic status.

In an interview with a local TV station, Malak explained that shortly after the confrontation, she ran in disbelief to her boyfriend. She was worried that he had not seen what happened, that no one did, and that her act had no witnesses to prove it. If no one saw it, was it even real? Within a day, Malak's still image—photoshopped in bright colors with a caption that reads "'Alehom" (which could be roughly translated into "attack" or "get them")—went viral on social media.[2]

In the visual archive of the uprising, Malak's image is one among many featuring women in direct confrontation with security forces.[3] Reaching the limelight in the first days of the uprising, the kick's virality set the tone for what was to come, foreshadowing the public's fascination with women in revolt. But it also demonstrated, early on, that in our hypermediated social existence, the revolution was bound to be televised and tweeted. By merely appearing when it did, in the street and on the screen, the kick seemed to signal that something had indeed changed in the place and role of women in public life.

The visible presence and participation of women in the months-long popular protests captivated the national and international imagination. With headlines like "In Lebanon, Women Drive the Fight for Change,"[4] "In Lebanon, the Revolution Is a Woman,"[5] and "Lebanese Women Kick Back,"[6] women's presence in large numbers was a widely recognized fact, seen by many as a promising indicator of the strides that women have made in their struggles for equality.[7] From feminist chants in the streets, to mothers' marches for civil peace, to the addition of "women" to a verse in the Lebanese national anthem,[8] the October revolt was marked by the feminization of the public sphere. By their mere presence in protests across the country, women laid claim to public space and to the male-dominated sphere of national politics from which they have been historically excluded and largely sidelined.[9] Nowhere is this feminization more clearly demonstrated than in the kitschy slogan *"Al-Thawra Untha"* (the revolution is female), sprayed on walls and floors and popularized as a hashtag on social media. As was the case in the popular uprisings that swept Arab societies since 2011, the culture produced in the ferment of the October uprising—its aesthetics and poetics—reflected and triggered a social reckoning with the status of women and their political agency.[10]

Beyond widespread popular discontent against the political and economic status quo, the uprising refracted a societal shift in gender roles and relations. This shift was most immediately perceptible in the streets and squares where thousands of men and women gathered for weeks on end to demonstrate against tyranny, injustice, and corruption. In photographs, TV reports, and online videos, the ocular fascination with women confirmed their appearance as political subjects on a national scale.[11] They owned the streets, carving within them a space for their long-standing and marginalized demands: for equal citizenship, for custody rights, for bodily autonomy, for sexual freedom. Women's engagement in street actions and mobilizations, across generations, regions, and socioeconomic classes, marked the revolutionary expansion of the public realm.

If it is to be properly understood, the ocular fascination with women, with their political appearance, must be situated within a broader context where the very boundaries of political life were being redrawn in the streets by those who have long been excluded from it. Ordinary people, people who never make the news, now appeared at the center of politics as its uncontested subjects. As political theorist Seyla Benhabib writes, "with the entry of every new group into the public space of politics, the scope of the public gets extended."[12] In the long moment of October 17, politics was no longer the work of male elites; paternalistic leaders were no longer its consecrated figures. Politics was now everyone's business. And in the streets, ordinary women laid their claims.

A Moment of Appearance

The uprising was an occasion for society to confront itself, to contemplate its image, and to face the cleavages, inequalities, and hierarchies that constitute the very fabric of its body politic. When I say that the uprising occasioned the appearance of women in the sphere of national politics, that is not to erase the history of women's activism and political engagement, nor to minimize their contributions to all spheres of social, political, economic, and cultural life.[13] Rather, it is to argue that the uprising, as a popular and highly mediated national event, was marked by the visibility of women not just as individuals but also as groups: ones with their own revolutionary poetics, repertoires of action, and enunciative positions.

On November 7, 2019, three weeks into the uprising, women organized a vigil march in response to police brutality and the violent repression of protestors in the city's center. Attended by hundreds of candle-holding, pot-banging, and sign-bearing women, the march was among the largest women's demonstrations that the country had witnessed over the last three decades.[14] In Beirut, feminist activists and collectives created and led anti-patriarchal and anti-racist chants that were picked up and repeated in other regions.[15] They organized a number of marches, including one against sexual harassment that ended at the Grand Serail, seat of government, with a flash mob performance inspired by feminist protestors in Chile. In protests in the Northern and Southern cities of Tripoli and Saida, women raised their long-standing demand for the right to pass their citizenship to their spouses and children.[16] The discourses through which women came to speak and act together were diverse. What unites them is not the expression of a common female identity, necessarily, but of a shared desire to politicize their social position as female subjects and to be visible as some sort of collective.

Visibility, to be sure, is a political question. It determines who gets to appear in public and under what conditions; it determines whose deeds and words are seen and heard by others and consequently whose political agency is recognizable as such. Visibility is at the core of Hannah Arendt's conceptualization of the public sphere as a "space of appearance," namely a space where people become visible to each other as acting and speaking subjects.[17] While Arendt has long been rightfully faulted by feminist critics for her rigid distinction between the private and public realms, her devaluation of the former, and her exclusion of women from the latter, I find her conceptual language, namely her use of appearance to describe the motion by which the public comes into being, useful to understand the political significance of the visibility of marginalized and disadvantaged social groups.

The mere fact of appearing, as media theorist John Thompson explains in his reading of Arendt, "endows words and actions with a kind of reality they did not have before, precisely because they are now seen and heard by others."[18] The public sphere is therefore, first and foremost, a space where one is heard and seen by others. For the nation's minoritarian and marginalized subjects, such as women, the desire for visibility attained through collective speech and action is a desire to be recognized as agential subjects in political movements and to be included in the narratives they engender. Through the expression of shared grievances and the articulation of common demands that are usually absent in male-dominated political discourse, women seized the moment of the uprising to appear, inserting their struggle for recognition into a nationwide popular movement.

Arendt's conceptualization of the public sphere is pertinent for thinking about the uprising as a *moment of appearance* whereby time, in addition to space, conditions political agency and gives it form. Revolutionary time, with its ebbs of popular euphoria and flows of state terror, with its uninterrupted news cycle and its synchronous protest waves, is disorienting. It unmoors us from the regular currents of everyday existence, suspends our daily routines, and disrupts the schedules of productivity that govern our weekly calendars.[19] It reorients us in space, upending the privatization of our individual and collective lives, their enclosure in the private sphere of domesticity and the ever-expanding spaces of consumption, and the containment of our political dissent within the virtual echo chambers of social media feeds. Revolutionary time is such because it propels us out into the world, toward those other beings whom we do not know but with whom we share the minutes, hours, days, and weeks on the streets and squares, or at home watching the live footage of those same streets and squares, now flickering on the screens of our mobile phones and television sets.

To consider the uprising as a temporal, not only spatial, frame of sustained collective action—of our being in common—entails a reckoning with revolutionary time's power to fuel and shape our desire and capacity for action. As a force that moves us by moving through us, the uprising is made not only of the spaces that come into being when we gather but also of the moments during which we act and therefore appear in public. In acting together, women were not only occupying space; they were also inhabiting this revolutionary temporality, which demanded quick and swift responses to events and incidents as they happened. Appearing in public in times of social and political upheaval becomes a matter of staking claims upon state and society when everybody is listening and watching. Here we can think of working-class youths flooding the high-end neighborhoods of downtown Beirut on their scooter convoys or setting rubber tires and garbage containers on fire in streets designed to exclude them.[20] We can detect in their flair for the spectacular a desire to appear, to be seen. As their photographs were captured by the cameras of journalists and photographers, their working-class masculinity turned into media spectacle.[21]

In revolutionary time, the acting and speaking together of marginalized and disadvantaged subjects brings to the fore of public life the affinities—class, age, or gender—around which they coalesce as a recognizable counterpublic. As a moment and space of appearance, of heightened media attention, the uprising revealed an oppositional public to itself. Not only were its members visible to each other, but they were also visible to society and the state.

The Spectacle of Female Leadership

In this regard, it is quite telling that in all their speeches, leaders of the ruling political parties addressed men and women in equal terms, and some even appropriated and incorporated women's demands into their reformist rhetoric. Women were visible as a political constituency, and this had an effect on official discourse. In a tweet on the occasion of International Women's Day in March 2020, Lebanese president Michel Aoun went as far as claiming that a civil personal status law is the only guarantee that would emancipate women from oppression.[22]

The spectacle of female power in the streets was thus countered by a spectacle of female leadership in the government of Hassan Diab, formed in the wake of Prime Minister Saad Hariri's resignation on October 29, 2019, under mounting street pressure. The appointment of six women at the helm of the Ministries of Labor, Defense, Justice, Information, Youth and Sports, and the Displaced was considered a historic milestone for Lebanon, with women occupying a third of cabinet seats,[23] more than any previous government since the country's establishment in 1920.

Many were quick to expose the tokenism behind this move,[24] dismissing women's representation in key ministerial positions as a merely cosmetic procedure, one that mystifies the traditional partisan nature of these appointments in a cabinet claiming independence from political parties. This was the regime's attempt to bank on the ocular fascination with women, putting them on display as tokens of progress and change. True as this may be, the media frenzy that followed the announcement of the cabinet focused much attention on its gender composition.[25] The female ministers were in the national and international limelight, with Zeina Akar hailed as the first female minister of defense in the Middle East.[26] Television reports, news articles, and social media posts triggered discussions on the role of women in Lebanese politics, their competency in holding public office, and the supposed difference they would make once they reach positions of leadership and authority.[27]

But the promised political boons of female leadership within the existing power-sharing system had already been tested and dispelled by the uprising. Nowhere was the myth of the benevolent and conscientious female leader more clearly busted than in the figure of Rayya al-Hassan, minister of interior in Hariri's cabinet and member of his political party, the Future Movement, who was notoriously tasked by the regime with the brutal and relentless repression of protests.[28] Her appointment in January 2019 as the first female minister of interior in an Arab country was much celebrated in local and international media,[29] sparking unwarranted optimism about her ability to reform and champion progressive changes in one of the most essential ministries.

But the uprising changed al-Hassan's public image overnight. As security forces carried out the government crackdown on protests, as they fulfilled orders of beating, arresting, torturing, teargassing, and shooting live and rubber ammunition at protestors, it became evidently clear that al-Hassan's womanhood did not translate into benevolent leadership.[30] Her inability or refusal to restrain the use of force by state security was compounded by her failure to protect protestors from the violence of party thugs who attacked them and destroyed their encampments in cities and towns across the country.

When women's inclusion in state politics is funneled through membership in paternalistic political parties, as al-Hassan's case demonstrates, their capacity to effect any significant and meaningful change is automatically compromised if not completely neutralized. As long as the political culture of these parties revolves around the cult of the male leader as savior and of his male offspring as legitimate heirs to his proverbial crown, the allegiance of female public servants to these parties normalizes paternalistic politics by giving it a feminine cover. By agreeing to toe the party line for a seat at the table, women like al-Hassan do not pose a real threat to the masculine and sectarian order. Few as they are in both the executive and legislative branches, they are unable to push for any systemic changes that may alter the status quo and that are needed to truly empower women politically: namely the redistribution of wealth, resources, rights, and privileges in a manner that does not discriminate on the basis of sex. Thus, the appearance of six women in Diab's cabinet was meant to convey a reformist and progressive face to the regime's puppet government in order to appease the masses and contain their anger.[31]

Women as a Group

In light of the above, we can surmise that "woman" alone does not constitute an emancipatory political identity, that female leadership is insufficient in guaranteeing the representation of women's interests, and that the conditional and selective inclusion of individual women in institutional politics does not automatically empower all women. First, an abstract notion of female identity that erases real differences and hierarchies among women in the name of representation offers no sturdy ground upon which to build a politics that leaves no woman behind. Second, an individualistic and top-down conception of empowerment, exemplified through female appointments by the ruling male elite, pays lip service to discourses of gender equality while throwing the vast majority of women and men under the bus.

In the remainder of this chapter, I want to unpack the affinities among women that materialized during the uprising and to explain the political significance of gender as a coalitional rather than identitarian category. I am inspired here by Iris Marion Young's conceptualization of gender as seriality, designating a set of relations or positions that women occupy in the social hierarchy. Intervening in feminist discussions on the difficulties and dangers of talking about women as a single group, Young argues that there are pragmatic political reasons for insisting on the possibility of thinking about women as a social collective.[32] While we may deconstruct and problematize gender to show its limits as an analytic category, Young explains, we still have to contend with the real affinities that bring women together and that we can observe in times of social and political upheaval.[33]

Beyond their appearance, how do we make sense of women's desire to insert themselves as a collective into the contentious universe of the uprising? By assembling in the context of a politically charged and highly mediatized moment, women acted as historical subjects, as if to declare in the present and for posterity: We are here; we were there. The uprising occasioned the appearance of this provisionally cohesive "we" and consequently the appearance of women as a distinct political body on a local, regional, and national scale.

The elusive notion that all female-bodied people share a common experience or a set of attributes that constitute them as a group produces gender as an essential identity, isolated from other social determinants that equally shape women's lives and sense of self and removed from other vectors of oppression that keep women down and out. In societies stratified by class, sect, nationality, and race, any attempt to speak of women as a cohesive social group must therefore proceed not from the negation of differences among individual women but through their affirmation as a condition of collectivity and coalitional politics. Whose reality are we invoking when we speak of "women"?

In her incisive critique of the Eurocentric optics of feminist theory, Chandra Talpade Mohanty explains that the very category "woman" as designating a single, coherent, and already constituted group leads feminists to regard all women as equally powerless and oppressed victims.[34] The idea that women can be oppressors, or that some may have privileges that are largely inaccessible to most men, is now a widely recognized fact. Since the 1970s, postcolonial, socialist, Black, and Third World feminists have produced an extensive body of knowledge that illuminates and critiques hierarchies that exist among women.[35] Through the fertile concept of intersectionality, they theorized power in relational rather than absolute terms, figuring it as a matrix of domination that includes but is not reducible to gender. As a spatial metaphor, intersectionality captured the multiplicity, interconnection, and simultaneity of systems of oppression, inspiring new ways of thinking about power. It demonstrated how patriarchy, a gender-based system of oppression and exploitation, was not enough to understand women's oppression, and that the struggle for women's emancipation cannot but also be the struggle for the emancipation of all people, from all systems of injustice.

There is no single female gender identity that defines the social experience of womanhood. And yet, in particular times and places, a certain provisional unity among women manifests itself. Even as we question the cohesiveness and universality of gender as an identity, even as we deconstruct it to show its limits and its normative effects, we still feel the pull of "women" as a label that we cannot afford to abandon. As Young explains, "Without conceptualizing women as a group, in some sense, it is not possible to conceptualize oppression as a systematic, structured, and institutional process."[36] Gender injustice may be experienced at an individual level, but it can only be remedied through collective struggles for redistribution and recognition. But were all the women who organized collectively during the uprising motivated by the pursuit of gender justice? And consequently, is feminism—as the paradigmatic discourse and movement for women's emancipation—the only framework through which we can understand women's coalitional politics?

The Power of Coalitional Politics

The straight answer is no. Women may and have assembled politically around issues that concern the common good, that are not gender specific, that are not about fighting for gender justice and equality or dismantling patriarchal structures. The mothers' march of Chiyyeh/Ain el-Remmaneh is a case in point.[37] On November 27, 2019, female residents of the neighborhood called for a mothers' march to protest against the sectarian tensions and skirmishes that had occurred the night before between the Christian supporters of the Lebanese Forces and the Shi'a supporters of Amal and Hezbollah. Women living on both sides of what used to be a demarcation line during the civil war jointly organized the march to condemn sectarian violence and call for civil peace, chanting "no return to civil war, this is a peaceful revolution, we don't want sectarianism" and "no to sectarianism, we want national unity, we want a civil state."[38] Hundreds of women and mothers walked the streets carrying Lebanese flags and exchanging white roses, in an event that was widely covered by the media.[39]

With news headlines like "Mothers' March from Ain el-Remmaneh to Chiyyah to Erase the Violence of Wars"[40] and "Mothers' March from Ain el-Remmaneh to Chiyyah: No to Violence, No to Sectarianism, No to Civil War,"[41] women attempted to counter the threat of sectarian violence used by the regime as a fearmongering tactic to disperse protests.[42] Footage of mothers affirming the cross-sectarian and anti-sectarian nature of the uprising went viral on social media, and the hashtags #Ain el-Remmaneh and #Chiyyah were trending with people tweeting in praise of mothers' engagement. By making motherhood a ground to denounce sectarianism, women also and indirectly challenged the dominant symbolic order where traits associated with masculinity are privileged and things coded feminine are pervasively devalued and disparaged.

By speaking as mothers, women made political claims in terms of kinship, momentarily subverting paternalistic authority through the performance of a kind of maternal resistance. In marching against sexual harassment, they framed the personal and intimate violence they are subjected to as female-bodied people as a symptom of the regime that must be toppled, declaring that sex too is a relation of power. In both cases, women politicized their social position—as mothers, as victims or potential victims of sexual violence—as a ground for collectivity. Different as they may be, the mothers' march and the anti-sexual harassment march both demonstrate that conscious bonds of solidarity among women need not rest on a common female identity. Rather, both illuminate gender as a coalitional category through which women—as disadvantaged subjects—can exercise collective power.

Conclusion

The coalitions of women who appeared in the October uprising may have been momentary. But long after the crowds have dispersed, what remains are embodied memories and photographic evidence of having been together, then and there; of feeling powerful. Overcoming androcentrism and sexism as systems that disadvantage and disempower women and that keep them out of the sphere of politics, Nancy Fraser writes, "requires changing the cultural valuations that privilege masculinity and deny equal respect to women. It requires decentering androcentric norms and revaluing a despised gender."[43] The appointment of women in key political positions is not enough to change value systems. In Lebanon and everywhere, overcoming systems that disempower women requires changes in the symbolic order in which women are imagined as "lesser than." The appearance of women as groups and collectives in the October uprising must therefore not be dismissed as "merely symbolic." Rather, it is precisely in the new symbolisms they offered that their collective actions were politically significant.

The importance of revolutionary moments such as October 17 is that they are rife with symbolic actions that call into question hierarchical cultural valuations, not just around gender but also around class and region. These symbolic actions constitute a space where people collectively and spontaneously question existing hierarchies and values, where they challenge privileges that were once believed to be untouchable. Women's symbolic actions are therefore part of this broader universe of discursive contestation. They are part of the ferment of human activity that constitutes the uprising as a moment of collective revision and redefinition of who we are as a society.

Even when they are not performed under the sign of feminism, such actions revalue "a despised gender" and assert the role of women in public life. As the mothers' march demonstrates, women were moved to act collectively not to denounce systems that disadvantage them specifically as women—they were marching against sectarianism, not against sexism or androcentrism. But in appearing together, they called into question their historical marginalization in the public sphere of politics; and in politicizing their experiences as women, they disrupted the masculinist norms of political discourse. Indeed, one of the political perplexities that women's collective actions in the uprising confront us with is the reconfiguration of the boundaries of the political: not just in terms of *what* counts as properly political but also *who* counts as a political subject.

Notes

1   Akram Chehayeb is a Lebanese politician who served as minister of education (2019–20) and is a member of the long-standing Progressive Socialist Party headed by Walid Jumblatt.
2   Image can be found here: https://www.instagram.com/p/B3v9mbopIBg/?utm_source =ig_web_copy_link (accessed June 25, 2021).
3   Photos can be found here: https://www.independent.co.uk/news/world/middle-east/ lebanon-protests-women-corruption-beirut-a9195166.html (accessed June 25, 2021).
4   "In Lebanon, Women Drive the Fight for Change," *Deutsche Welle*, September 19, 2020, https://www.dw.com/en/lebanon-beirut-women-reforms/a-54979011 (accessed May 3, 2021).
5   Sarah Boukhary, "In Lebanon, the Revolution Is a Woman," *Women's International League for Peace and Freedom*, December 7, 2019, https://www.wilpf.org/in-lebanon -the-revolution-is-a-woman/ (accessed May 3, 2021).
6   "Lebanese Women Kick Back," *BBC Monitoring*, November 22, 2019, https://www .youtube.com/watch?v=3UlSt66mDWE (accessed May 3, 2021).
7   For more on this, see chapters by Nay el Rahi and Myriam Sfeir in this book.
8   Lebanon's national anthem, adopted in 1927, pays tribute to men in the lyric "our mountain and our valley, they bring forth stalwart men." In an initiative to include women in the anthem, *Annahar* newspaper released a video on November 8, 2019, featuring Lebanese singer Carole Samaha singing revised lyrics, which now included "stalwart *women* and men." The video can be accessed here: https://www.youtube.com /watch?v=8dA_62tyd4U (accessed June 25, 2021).
9   Carol Sabbagh, "Lebanese Women and the Protests: Rebellious and Breaking Barriers," *Al Ain*, November 28, 2019, https://al-ain.com/article/lebanese-women -voice-revolution-corruption (accessed June 25, 2021).
10 For more on women in the Arab uprisings, see Andrea Khalil, ed., *Gender, Women and the Arab Spring* (London: Routledge, 2015); Frances Hasso and Zakia Salime, eds., *Freedom Without Permission: Bodies and Space in the Arab Revolutions* (Durham: Duke University Press, 2016); Rita Stephan and Mounira M. Charrad, eds., *Women Rising: In and Beyond the Arab Spring* (New York: New York University Press, 2020).
11 Vanessa Ghanem, "Role of Women in the October 17 Revolution," *Annahar*, February 18, 2020, https://www.annahar.com/english/article/1126207-naya-role-of-women-in

-the-october-17-revolution. See also "A Look at the Demands of the Young Feminists in Lebanon Leading the Soft Revolution," *she_in_politics*, November 4, 2019, https://www.instagram.com/p/B4cSDNpJkQr/ (accessed June 25, 2021).

12 Seyla Benhabib, "Feminist Theory and Hannah Arendt's Concept of Public Space," *History of the Human Sciences* 29, no. 2 (1993): 104.

13 For a brief narrative timeline of Lebanese women's activism and social and political struggles over the last century, see "Lebanese Women over 100 years," *Daraj and Khateera*, March 2020, https://daraj.com/40470/; Also see "Women's Movements in Lebanon," *Civil Society Centre*, https://civilsociety-centre.org/gen/women-movements -timeline/4938#event-_1920s-womens-union-established-in-lebanon-and-syria; and Rita Stephan, "Four Waves of Lebanese Feminism," *E-International News*, November 7, 2014, https://www.e-ir.info/2014/11/07/four-waves-of-lebanese-feminism/ (accessed June 25, 2021).

14 Ayeesha Starkey, "Day 21: Women Making Noise at The Lebanese Protests," *Beirut Today*, November 7, 2019, https://www.facebook.com/BEYtoday/videos /943441079362982 (accessed June 25, 2021).

15 It is worth noting here that the street chants of feminist activists and groups participating in protests in Beirut, containing as they did frequent references to the rights of migrant workers and refugees and articulating a broad vision of social justice, capture an intersectional understanding of power and injustice, which I discuss later in the chapter.

16 Sarah Khalil, "The Revolution is Female: Why Feminist Issues are Driving Lebanon's Protests," *The New Arab*, November 7, 2019, https://english.alaraby.co.uk/analysis/why -feminist-issues-are-driving-lebanons-protests (accessed June 25, 2021).

17 Hannah Arendt, *The Human Condition* (Chicago: Chicago University Press, 1958).

18 John B. Thompson, "Shifting Boundaries of Public and Private Life," *Theory, Culture & Society* 28, no. 4 (2011): 63.

19 For more on the question of revolutionary temporality, see Samer Frangie's chapter in this book.

20 For more on this, see chapters by Nizar Hassan and Rawane Nassif in this book.

21 Examples of these images, captured by photographers Myriam Boulos, Nabeel Yakzan, Marwan Tahtah, and Hussein Baydoun, can be found here:
> https://www.instagram.com/p/B5Hx19Dppv8/
> https://www.instagram.com/p/B6s6flMonZN/
> https://www.instagram.com/p/B_IQcKZJNZT/
> https://www.instagram.com/p/B30D1fvpQCq/
> https://www.instagram.com/p/B3zkX9sp40k/
> https://www.instagram.com/p/CBUTNBrJY0k/
> https://www.instagram.com/p/B3xfQylpQgb/
> https://www.instagram.com/p/B3xSwF3nLHF/
> https://www.instagram.com/p/B3wUlunHHgm/
> https://www.instagram.com/p/CQf3UUfn7zF/
> https://www.instagram.com/p/B7S3QLmJObf/

22 http://nna-leb.gov.lb/en/show-news/113264/Aoun-calls-for-39-unifying-personal -status-law-39 (accessed June 25, 2021).

23 Female appointments make up 30 percent of Prime Minister Diab's government, up from 13 percent in Lebanon's previous cabinet. The lineup includes Deputy Prime Minister and Defense Minister Zeina Akar Adra, Justice Minister Marie-Claude Najm Kobeh, Labor Minister Lamia Yammine Douaihy, Information Minister Manal Abdel

Samad, Sports and Youth Minister Varti Ohanian Kevorkian, and Minister for the Displaced Ghada Shreim Ata.

24 Mariam Saifeddine, "Women Ministering: A Patriarchal Propaganda Show," *Nida Al Watan*, https://bit.ly/3cHgdqc (accessed June 25, 2021).

25 For examples, see Anne-Marie El-Hage, "Four Female Ministers: A First . . . Yet Not Enough," *L'Orient Today*, February 4, 2020, https://today.lorientlejour.com/article /1155831/four-female-ministers-a-first-yet-not-enough.html; Zoe Dutton, "Record Number of Female Ministers to Serve in Govt," *The Daily Star*, January 23, 2020, https://www.dailystar.com.lb/News/Lebanon-News/2020/Jan-23/499787-record -number-of-female-ministers-to-serve-in-govt.ashx (accessed June 25, 2021).

26 "Lebanon Appoints First Female Defence Minister in Arab World," *Middle East Monitor*, January 22, 2020, https://www.middleeastmonitor.com/20200122-lebanon -appoints-first-female-defence-minister-in-arab-world/ (accessed June 25, 2021).

27 "The Appointment of 6 Female Ministers in the Lebanese Government Triggers Discussions about the Role of Arab Women in Politics," *CNN*, January 22, 2020, https://arabic.cnn.com/middle-east/article/2020/01/22/six-female-ministers-lebanon -discussion (accessed June 25, 2021).

    "Lebanon's New Female Ministers are the Talk of the Town," *BBC*, February 1, 2020, https://www.bbc.com/arabic/middleeast-47088734 (accessed June 25 2021).

28 "Lebanon: Police Violence Against Protesters," *Human Rights Watch*, January 17, 2020, https://www.hrw.org/news/2020/01/17/lebanon-police-violence-against-protesters (accessed June 25, 2021).

29 "Arab World's First Female Interior Minister Hails 'Point of Pride for Women,'" *The Guardian*, February 17, 2019, https://www.theguardian.com/world/2019/feb/17/arab -world-first-female-interior-minister-hails-point-of-pride-for-women-raya-al-hassan (accessed June 25, 2021).

30 Sunniva Rose, "Why Lebanon's Protesters Turned against Raya El Hassan," *The National News*, January 2020, https://www.thenationalnews.com/world/mena/why-lebanon-s -protesters-turned-against-raya-el-hassan-1.967295 (accessed June 25, 2021).

31 In his ministerial statement, Diab declared his government's commitment to achieve gender equality by eradicating all forms of discrimination against women and girls in Lebanese law and legislation. The full text of the ministerial statement can be found here: https://www.presidency.gov.lb/Arabic/Pages/MinisterialStatement.aspx.

32 Iris Marion Young, "Gender as Seriality: Thinking about Women as a Social Collective," *Signs* 19, no. 3 (1994): 713–14.

33 Ibid., 714.

34 Chandra Talpade Mohanty, "Under Western Eyes: Feminist Scholarship and Colonial Discourses," in *Third World Women and the Politics of Feminism*, ed. Chandra Talpade Mohanty, Ann Russo, and Lourdes Torres (Bloomington: Indiana University Press, 1991), 51–80.

35 Cherríe Moraga and Gloria Anzaldúa, eds., *This Bridge Called my Back: Writings by Radical Women of Color* (Watertown, MA: Persephone Press, 1981); bell hooks, *Ain't I a Woman? Black Women and Feminism* (Boston: South End Press, 1981); Audre Lorde, *Sister Outsider: Essays and Speeches* (Berkeley, CA: Crossing Press, 1984); Angela Davis, *Women, Race and Class* (New York: Vintage Books, 1983).

36 Young, "Gender as Seriality," 718.

37 "Lebanese Women Say Never Again to Risk of Civil War," *CNN*, November 28, 2019, https://edition.cnn.com/videos/world/2019/11/28/lebanon-protests-sectarian-faults -wedeman-pkg-intl-ldn-vpx.cnn (accessed June 25, 2021).

38 https://www.facebook.com/AliGharbieh/videos/10219509157416306 (accessed June 25, 2021).

39 Television footage of the march can be found here: https://www.youtube.com/watch?v =WNFCYdFDbmQ.

40 Mohamad Abi Samra, "Mothers' March from Ain el-Remmaneh to Chiyyah to Erase the Violence of Wars," *Almodon*, November 28, 2019, https://www.almodon.com/ politics/2019/11/28/%D9%85%D8%B3%D9%8A%D8%B1%D8%A9-%D8%A7%D9 %84%D8%A3%D9%85%D9%87%D8%A7%D8%AA-%D8%A8%D9%8A%D9%86- %D8%B9%D9%8A%D9%86-%D8%A7%D9%84%D8%B1%D9%85%D8%A7%D9 %86%D8%A9-%D8%A7%D9%84%D8%B4%D9%8A%D8%A7%D8%AD-%D9%84 %D9%85%D8%AD%D9%88-%D8%B9%D9%86%D9%81-%D8%A7%D9%84%D8 %AD%D8%B1%D9%88%D8%A8 (accessed May 3, 2021).

41 "Mothers' March from Ain el-Remmaneh to Chiyyah: No to Violence, No to Sectarianism, No to Civil War," *Annahar*, November 27, 2019, https://www.annahar .com/arabic/article/1075579-%D9%88%D9%82%D9%81%D8%A9-%D9%84%D8 %B3%D9%8A%D8%AF%D8%A7%D8%AA-%D8%B9%D9%8A%D9%86-%D8%A7 %D9%84%D8%B1%D9%85%D8%A7%D9%86%D8%A9-%D9%88%D8%A7%D9%84 %D8%B4%D9%8A%D8%A7%D8%AD-%D9%84%D8%B1%D9%81%D8%B6-%D8 %A7%D9%8A-%D8%A7%D9%82%D8%AA%D8%AA%D8%A7%D9%84 (accessed May 3, 2021).

42 "Hezbollah Warns of Chaos, Civil War in Lebanon," *Reuters*, October 25, 2019, https://www.voanews.com/middle-east/hezbollah-warns-chaos-civil-war-lebanon.

43 Nancy Fraser, "From Redistribution to Recognition? Dilemmas of Justice in a Post-Socialist Age," *New Left Review* 212 (1995): 79.

13

Clashing with the Patriarchy

The Promise of Potential as Politics

Nay el Rahi

Introduction

Think of it as a bus stop—and of the three characters in this chapter as travelers taking drastically different routes, lifelines that would never have converged. Think of it as the unlikely meeting of one traveler heading north, a second moving east, and a third going south; no bus stop would have accommodated this. This is an invitation to think of the October 17 revolutionary moment as this junction. How else can we tell the story of three women who had almost nothing in common had it not been for this moment?

The first is N. M., a single mother who did not choose what she calls "the militant life." Unsure whether to classify her life as "struggle"—*nidal*—or simply fate, as she describes it, N. is certain of one thing: that she would have preferred "a calm life" to having three children at nineteen out of a forced marriage, followed by eleven years of single-handedly supporting them and twelve years of remote motherhood.[1]

The second is G. K., who had spent a lifetime estranged from all the fragments of her identity. Her studenthood, gender, feminism, and political affiliation were scattered beyond repair, until what she calls the "magical moment" of October 17, when she "became a whole being"[2] and after which she decided to run for the student council at her university.

The third, we will call J. H. A leftist queer feminist and LGBT organizer for over a decade, she believes that the apolitical NGO-ized approach to political change vacated queer activism in Lebanon of its power.[3] "We tried to keep it political, but we failed," she says.

This is a call to frame the revolutionary moment of October 17 as a battlefield where women clashed with patriarchy—a moment that infused these clashes with potential to disrupt foundational tenets of the Lebanese system. By following the narratives of three women,[4] this chapter highlights the ways in which the October 17 revolutionary moment paved the way for an intersectional feminist political practice.

Feminists and women activists in Lebanon have come a long way from Asef Bayat's "life as politics" paradigm[5] and are practicing what I call potential as politics. While feminist movements in Lebanon have not yet amounted to a critical mass, and are not yet total, absolute, or complete, the October 17 moment that built on decades of feminist struggles revealed a more pronounced, concrete, and visible intersectional feminist articulation and practice of resistance, and of "potential as politics."

Context

The rage unleashed on October 17, 2019, in Beirut, was, for the first time since the end of the civil war in 1990, explicitly directed at both the sectarian political elites and the financial elites at once.[6] For decades, Lebanon had been ruled by a hybridity of neoliberalism and sectarianism[7]—maintained by an unaccountable oligarchy with undisputed powers that morphed citizen-state relationships into patron-client dynamics with basic rights and services dispensed in exchange of political loyalty.

The October 17 moment dented the Lebanese neoliberal-sectarian fort. For many, it felt like the long-awaited opportunity for the Lebanese to reinvent themselves and remodel their relationship with their country, and with politics, which had left the closed rooms and poured into the squares and streets. It seeped into first-time protesters' chants and slogans.[8] Exhausted but exalted, the Lebanese showed up, put their own bodies on the line as they voiced their discontent, and engaged in embodied practices of solidarity in their neighborhoods, communities, and streets. They dragged their weariness to the front lines, clashed with the police, and blocked streets and highways demanding long overdue structural, political, and institutional changes for over three months following October 17. Individuals who seldom participated in demonstrations experimented with diverse forms of protest and organizing—from neighborhood to workplace—with many creating and joining nascent political opposition parties. The Lebanese seemed to have broken their sect locks for a moment, demanding a new social contract, but in response, the ruling oligarchy escalated violence, deploying all its arms—military and paramilitary, judicial, financial, and media—to shut out dissent, disperse dissenters, and remain unaccountable while maintaining the established rule.

While perceived as enjoying a better status than their sisters in other Arab countries, women in Lebanon have all the reasons to be at the forefront of the uprising. They not only bear the brunt of care work in their families but also live under a complex patriarchal legislative, social, and political system that discriminates against them in personal status courts, access to services and protection, labor, citizenship, and political participation.[9] The various systems of inequality that shape women's intersectional realities in Lebanon were equally, simultaneously, and explicitly attacked during the October 17 protests. Feminist chants tied patriarchy to the multiple exploitative apparatuses, including sectarianism, clientelism, religious personal status courts, capitalism, and the banks.[10] Women from all backgrounds and age groups, particularly feminists, engaged in multiple practices of embodied political resistance, including carrying signs or flags for hours, chanting, organizing vigils, confronting the physical violence of police and parties' thugs, forming bodily chains to block roads and to separate protesters from police forces, burning tires, and banging pots and pans in protest. They protested along with men and held women-only demonstrations, such as the remarkable coming together of mothers from the neighborhoods of Chiyah and Ain El Remmene—the cradle of the Lebanese civil war and a historical sectarian demarcation line—to reaffirm solidarity, after a night of politically motivated tensions between old rivals on November 27, 2019.[11]

Potential as Politics

In the Lebanese system, sex and gender determine which practices of citizenship are available and which are foreclosed.[12] There are eighteen officially recognized religious sects and fifteen different personal status laws in Lebanon, governing marriage, divorce, inheritance, child custody, and alimony. Not only do these laws enshrine preferential treatment of men over women, they also differentiate among women of different sects, stripping them of their ability to make unified claims to authorities. Civil law, which applies to all citizens, also discriminates against women. Citizenship, for instance, is exclusively patrilineal and is not passed from a Lebanese woman to her spouse or children.[13]

Suad Joseph[14] theorized and discussed at length some of the notions constituting the Lebanese patriarchal matrix, such as patriarchal connectivity and political familism.[15] Patriarchal connectivity is rooted in connective selfhood. Connective selfhood describes the fluid construct of self among Arab families, where selves see intimate others as extensions of themselves. Although modeled in and by familial relationships, connectivity extends throughout significant relationships in the Lebanese society, so nonkin persons could evoke kin legitimacy and expectations in all spheres.[16] Coupled with patriarchy, connectivity organizes the selves with fluid boundaries in a gendered and aged hierarchy; so men and elders are authorized to enter the boundaries of the self of women and juniors to regulate, are entitled to direct the lives of women and juniors, and have legally recognized rights and responsibilities toward them. This reproduces patriarchal family structures, allows families to claim prior loyalty of their members, over and above the state's claims to loyalty,[17] and consolidates families as legitimate political actors and havens that the Lebanese turn to for protection and resources under an incapacitated state. Citizens' deployment of family practices and relationships to activate demands to the state, and state actors' governance based on a discourse privileging family—"political familism"[18]—is but one expression of the power of patriarchy in Lebanon.[19] Facing this insidious matrix of patriarchal structures, women in Lebanon and feminists in particular are left with a few avenues for action.

Assef Bayat[20] argues that by performing daily life practices of being and doing, women and other marginalized communities create micro-sites of resistance against the authoritarian repression of Middle Eastern political and social systems. Charting social movements, Bayat distinguishes between these daily actions he calls "non-movements," through which citizens passively resist the state, and the rapid, total, and violent political revolutions that have radically altered countries like France and Russia.[21]

He frames women's practices such as playing sports, removing veils, and exercising a power of presence by lamenting publicly, during the mobilizations of 1979 Iran and 1990 Iraq, as passive and fragmented forms of pushback on traditional roles. These practices he calls "quiet encroachments" upon power are the only route for the disenfranchised to change systems because of their marginal economic and political status.[22] While these quiet encroachments might resonate with some forms of resistance in parts of the region, feminists in Lebanon, particularly in the context of the October 17 revolutionary uprising, have marched far beyond the "life as politics" resistance paradigm and have practiced what I call potential as politics. While feminist mobilizations have not yet developed into a rapid, total, and violent revolution, I argue that the October moment has allowed for a more pronounced, visible, and concrete intersectional feminist articulation and practice of resistance, with potential to disrupt the status quo of the Lebanese sectarian system and challenge its foundational modes of operation. The following stories illustrate how.

The Chronicles of the Clashes

"The night of October 17th broke the cage I have been trapped in, defeated, for twelve long years."[23] This is how 58-year-old N. M. starts her story. On October 23, N. mustered the courage to stand in a protest in Nabatieh, South of Lebanon, with a banner demanding to see her children, after a decade of being denied their custody. N. M. is certainly not the first or only woman to suffer at the hands of Ja'fari courts in Lebanon, but she was among the first to publicly denounce them during the revolutionary uprising of October 17. Shiite mothers had been vocal about their battles for custody, individually and collectively, for years when the October 17 uprising erupted. The uprising, however, presented N. M. with the opportunity to talk about this "with a wider audience."[24]

Her bold move sparked a chain of similar actions. Several other women followed suit and shared their experience with the courts in protest squares, igniting the discussion on women's rights to custody as intrinsically embedded in the wider umbrella of political demands furthered by the uprising. Most importantly, this protest in Nabatieh Square allowed N. to finally meet her estranged son. Her banner and story went viral; protesters, prompted by her plea, rushed to help her find him. The two spoke for hours that day and had been in touch since then.

Born into a religiously and socially conservative family where girls' ambition and good grades mattered little, N. was forced to quit school to get married. She had three children in three years and was seventeen when she had her eldest. Meanwhile, discontent with her husband was increasingly growing, but divorce for Shiite women comes with the looming threat of losing their children. Jaafari laws allow women to have custody of the children until the age of two for boys and seven for girls; and Jaafari courts notoriously favor misogynistic traditions that serve men's interests. Luckily, N. managed to keep hers after her marriage ended.

Divorced at twenty-three, she was among the first single women to live alone with her children at this young age in Nabatieh. "I was bullied relentlessly; men I knew would persistently harass me with unwanted proposals of *mut'aa* contracts—temporary pleasure marriage, assuming all the patriarchal stereotypes attached to divorced women about me."[25] Years later, N. fell in love and remarried. Months into her second marriage, she discovered "all the ugly patriarchal values that our society can instill in people,"[26] in the man she married, so the marriage broke apart after she gave birth to two children. Expectedly, it wasn't long before he won custody over them. Although she had visitation rights, she was not allowed to see them. The children were too young for violently enforced visits at police stations, so she resigned to the powers that be. N. elaborates on the next twelve years of her life, watching her kids from afar, practicing her motherhood from a distance. "I would know that they were on a trip outside school, so I'd sneak into that location to secretly watch them."[27]

N. was among the first women to write and publish extensively, several years ago, about the horrors of custody battles that thousands of mothers live through. She wrote letters to her children on multiple platforms, attracting the attention of many in Lebanon and encouraging hundreds of mothers to do the same. "The 17 October uprising helped me reveal the crimes of the Jaafari courts against women beyond Lebanon, to the world; meet hundreds like me; and talk openly about the Shiite clerics' treatment," she explains. She stirred this conversation during the uprising because "all eyes were on Lebanon, and we needed the attention of the Arab media because people around the region are not aware of our situation."[28] She wanted to counter the rosy reductive image of Shiite women in Lebanon: "She is not only the mother, sister, and wife of the martyr. She is also the divorced, the disempowered, the forsaken woman stripped from her rights and dignity; the one buried alive to uphold the community's patriarchal glory."[29]

To N., the October 17 revolutionary moment collectivized the struggle and brought together many mothers who were strangers united by their denied rights; "our struggles were scattered; but in that moment, an invisible power convinced us that, together, we have the power to revolt."[30] Indeed, in the months following October 17, and since then, many mothers got court orders for custody and visitation "that we never dreamt we could get," she said. The outpouring of women's narratives, disseminated by the media,[31] intimidated the Jaafari court. This emboldened the mothers and "convinced us that only when we fight the political system as a whole, will we get our specific rights," she explains.

N. did not plan to be an activist; but being denied her children transformed her into "a soldier in an arduous long-term battle."[32] Her point of departure was her motherhood; and her activism became more politicized as she realized how enmeshed her private identity as a mother is in the wider political matrix. The history of women's movements reveals politicization processes that transform a private identity usually considered a basis for political exclusion into a lever for political participation.[33] Research on women's movements has explored the continuums between women's mobilizations based on gender roles and their mobilizations that contest these roles, rather than considering them as two mutually exclusive categories.[34] Struggles from Argentina's "Mothers of the Plaza de Mayo" and others from Chile and Mexico reveal how women's social positions as mothers could successfully spark and sustain their activism, as well as propel communities of feminists to support them.

Feminists in Lebanon—advocating for a unified civil personal status law—supported the Shiite mothers in their battles against Jaafari courts. Technically, the two demands are at odds. Calling for a civil personal status law conflicts, in fundamental ways, with reforming particular religious personal status courts.

Despite this, feminist support of the mothers, which started way before the October 17 moment, was overwhelming and became even more pronounced during the uprising protests, as feminists held the space for the mothers—mostly driven by their identity as mothers of a particular sect—and carried their demands, tying them to broader entanglements with the political system that all protesters shared.

Our second protagonist, 22-year-old G. K., had not planned to become an activist either. G. vividly remembers snapshots from her childhood. Political news was avoided like the plague at home. "Everywhere I went, even the grocery shops in my neighborhood had 'No Politics Please' signs up their walls, subliminally silencing any political engagement," she narrates. In the aftermath of late prime minister Rafik Hariri's assassination, 2005 Beirut was a minefield. "When people around me told me that my political opinion doesn't matter, I believed it; and supposed that politics is reserved for men so it shouldn't interest me," she starts. At fifteen, G. saw politics as "ambiguous and alienating."[35] Even at university, politics continued to demoralize her. During students' council elections, political parties only fielded women who "looked pretty and dressed nice."[36] Student councils in most universities have long been characterized by the divisive control of political parties, a guaranteed male representation, and a tokenistic approach to women who only "filled a gap," G. remarks. She felt that male representatives on the council do not know how to address women. "Sometimes at meetings, some representatives would refuse to even look at me, addressing my male colleague instead," she explains.

G. notes that before October 17, student demands were not tied to other vital demands in the country. Even though private universities' students communicated and liaised, the sense of a unifying cause was still lacking. "We were mostly fighting in siloes. Even off-campus activism was fragmented," she describes. "Then, October 17 happened," she exclaims, demarcating a new chapter of her story—a break from what seemed like an archaic way of doing life and politics. "October 17 signaled a clear message that all our demands are interlinked, because they're all the result of the same clan of incompetent men taking disastrous decisions affecting the entire population," she asserts.

Before the October moment, her issues as an architecture student never met her political positions; and these rarely intersected with her feminist politics. "Previously, when women's rights or sectarianism were discussed in class, I would spend the entire session processing my internal battles on whether I should have an opinion and say it, or avoid ridicule and stay silent," she says. Today, G. cannot separate the different fragments of her identity anymore. "It is impossible for me to be a student and leave my political identity aside, or my gender, or my feminist politics out of it. Even when I'm speaking in class about architecture, my politics come out. Everything is relevant," she explains. Not only does G. describe herself as "a whole being now,"[37] she also ran for the university's student council for the academic year 2020/2021 with the Secular Club, "empowered and emboldened by the revolutionary moment,"[38] and won.

As a politically active woman, she senses society growing worried when a woman does "what she has to do" or when she behaves "like an independent human being," G. states. She observes men receiving praise for taking on political responsibilities and women constantly "rushed out of politics," as if "they're waiting for us to move on to other things," she remarks. This "absolute rejection of women in politics convinced me that my daily battle is to be present and active as a feminist woman in political circles. In and of itself, this an achievement."[39]

Along with her peers from the Secular Club, G. is introducing a novel October 17-inspired work ethic to the council, driven by the momentum of the uprising. "Students' activism today, and the very way we do things have changed, becoming more feminist, intersectional, and political," she states.

While G. explicitly frames the October 17 moment as an enabling platform for feminist intersectional politics, queer LGBTIQ mobilizer J. H. views it as a missed opportunity for queer feminist activism to accentuate the intersectionality of politics in Lebanon. J. H., who spent over a decade as an organizer, describes the current frameworks of queer activism in Lebanon as plagued by "excessive identity politics" and absolute class- and capitalism-blindness. According to J. H., the LGBTIQ organizations "institutionalized activism," binding it to sources of funding and governmental apparatuses, restricting its mobilization and tools, and shaping its discourse in a way that does not disrupt the system that the October 17 tide set out to sweep away. It seemed like the interests of some LGBTIQ organizers intersected more with the clientelist political system than with the October 17 revolutionaries. "LGBTIQ organizations benefit from the Lebanese political capitalist system through relationships with institutions that have lost their legitimacy; but that organizations still need to implement their campaigns and activities, such as the banks and police," J. H. elaborates.

Indeed, the October 17 revolutionaries were calling out corruption everywhere when "LGBTIQ organizers were swiftly sweeping corruption allegations against individuals from the movement under the carpet."[40] The rift within the movement deepened as these allegations surfaced months after October 17 moment, polarizing the movement between those defending the accused and those calling for accountability. This created difficult dynamics and shrank the space for common values and visions to thrive within the movement.

This rift was not new to the movement, nor was it started by the allegations. LGBTIQ organizing in Lebanon had long been characterized by heated discussions on the class identity and politics of the movement and on how blind it was to the needs of underprivileged LGBTIQ communities in the country. In conversation with Nikhil Pal Singh, Amber Hollibaugh[41] argued that "new social movements, such as the queer and sexuality movements, have come to reflect more and more fundamentally the class of the people who dominate them; their politics determined by the economic position of those who own them."[42] Many LGBTIQ organizers, including J., find this to be true about the situation of the movement in Lebanon. The October 17 moment signaled that "not only is the system oppressing the queers is corrupt; but also that the tools used to fight it are equally oppressive, corrupt, and now obsolete," admits J. H. "We missed this chance to further our intersectional discourse," because "the movement did not reassess its tools and remained in denial about how invalid they've become."[43]

J. H. contends that "refusal to acknowledge the different social classes and positionalities, and the struggle between them,"[44] is partly responsible for this missed chance. Ironically, the more key LGBTIQ figures demonized class discussions, in favor of an "imagined conservative moralist class-blind scenario,"[45] the clearer the class rift became and the more disconnected its leaders appeared from the October 17 uprising mood.

Discussion

Sectarian control over personal status issues, and resultantly, over women's public and private lives, and male domination of political space are powerful tenets of the Lebanese patriarchal matrix and two of its most enduring features.

Custody rights under the Jaafari courts look like the exclusive battle of one group of women when it's crucially and intimately tied to the wider political matrix oppressing women in Lebanon. The religious personal status system is one of the foundational features of the Lebanese sectarian patriarchal regime. Religious personal status courts are the essence of this regime and exemplify the system's powerful grip over women's lives. So "changing those laws will inevitably destabilize the system," according to N. The Jaafari courts are under the political authority of the Shiite duo—Hezbollah and the Amal movement, a pillar of the Lebanese regime and its strongest arm. "These two fight about everything but unite against women. It is sectarianism and political domination, but it is also patriarchy and misogyny," she continues.

The October 17 moment was not the first platform where intersectional struggles unfolded; it however was a turning point—a moment of culmination, unprecedented in its scope, magnitude, and potential, that allowed for the articulation of these struggles as intersectional; an articulation that was neither as bold, pronounced, and visible nor as intimately tied to the broader political battle that feminists were fighting, before that moment. That moment was indeed destabilizing to a fundamental pillar holding this system together: sectarian personal status courts.

Like state outsourcing of personal status to religious courts, male-dominated political practice is another primary mode of operation within the Lebanese system challenged by the pronounced intersectional feminist articulation and practice of resistance that the October moment allowed. Not only do safe spaces for women, particularly feminists, to practice politics hardly exist in Lebanon despite feminist efforts, this reality has also been normalized and the women calling it out often silenced and gaslighted. This is exactly why the October 17 moment was "the precedent that we needed to prove that an undeniable, strong and capable female leadership exists."[46] G. saw examples of this leadership everywhere—in the streets, on campus, in the media—carrying causes that went beyond women's issues. Certainly, "women's duty is not only to fix women's problems, it is to have a say in how the system functions," she argues.[47] The October 17 uprising made it possible to "see ordinary people like me on the media and in the streets discussing political issues," she says. This moment set a benchmark for political practice and promoted safety for women to engage in politics.

"Now nobody can tell us women's rights have nothing to do with the right to electricity and clean water," she says.

The October 17 moment dented male domination of political space, though it remains to be seen how long it will be before the fort replenishes. When asked what intersectional feminist politics would look like in the Lebanese context, J. H. resounded G. K.'s words: "As a leftist woman, I'm proud of the legacy of the many feminists who significantly impacted leftist political groups, just by being present and disrupting the masculine prototype."[48] For J., the October 17 moment might not have impacted the queer movement as much as it should have; but this was due to the challenges within the movement. J. asserts that the October moment did accentuate feminist intersectional politics as a contending political practice in Lebanon. Feminism's most substantial input, J. argues, is "to impose itself as a political practice beyond women's legal rights." "The presence of feminists in political circles is an achievement in and of itself," she concludes, affirming what our second protagonist G. K. believes is the battle that she took upon herself after October 17.

Conclusion

Feminists and women activists in Lebanon have marched far beyond the "life as politics" resistance paradigm. The October 17 revolutionary uprising revealed that they practice what I call "potential as politics," through actions and clashes that disrupt the Lebanese patriarchal matrix and challenge two of its foundational modes of operation: male domination of politics and religious personal status legal system. By following the narratives of three women who have clashed with the Lebanese patriarchal matrix, this chapter attempted to prove that the October 17 moment, which followed decades of feminist struggles, exposed a pronounced, concrete, and visible intersectional feminist framing and practice of women's resistance in Lebanon. A generation apart, G. K. and J. H. are strangers who never met—not even at a protest, yet articulate their politics in an unusually analogous manner. The aspiration of one is the daily battle of the other.

Notes

1 M. N. Interview. By Nay El Rahi, March 3, 2021.
2 K. G. Interview. By Nay El Rahi, March 16, 2021.
3 H. J. Interview. By Nay El Rahi, April 29, 2021.
4 This chapter is based on interviews that the author conducted with the three women: N. M., G. K., and J. H. during the months of March and April 2021.
5 Assef Bayat, *Life as Politics: How Ordinary People Change the Middle East* (Amsterdam: Amsterdam University Press, 2010).
6 Rima Majed and Lana Salman, "Lebanon's Thawra," *MERIP*, Fall/Winter 2019.
7 See the chapter of Majed in this book for an elaborate conceptualization of the regime in Lebanon as "sectarian neoliberalism."

8 Some of the slogans seen in protests are: "I want to find a job in Lebanon," "I want bread and happiness," "I want my rights as a woman," "I want electricity, water and infrastructure," "I want to tweet without being arrested," "I want everything they stole from us," "Down with Our Fear," "I want to see my children," and "Freedom, Bread, and Theater."

9 This was discussed in several works—namely in Majed and Salman (2019) and Khatib (2008).

10 Some examples include: "(She is) Out to bring down the—patriarchal, sectarian, racist, capitalist – regime," "Our revolution is feminist," "Our struggles are many, our anger is one," and "Bring down the Kafala system."

11 See the chapters of Sara Mourad and Myriam Sfeir in this book for thorough discussions of this demonstration.

12 Maya Mikdashi, "Queering Citizenship: Queering Middle East Studies," *International Journal of Middle East Studies* 45, no. 2 (2013): 350–2.

13 Ibid.

14 Suad Joseph, "Political Familism in Lebanon," *The Annals of the American Academy of Political and Social Science* 636 (2011): 150–63.

15 For elaborate discussions on these notions, see Suad Joseph, "Gender and Relationality among Arab Families in Lebanon," *Feminist Studies* 19, no. 3 (1993): 465–82; and Joseph, "Political Familism in Lebanon."

16 Joseph, "Gender and Relationality among Arab Families in Lebanon," 3–4.

17 Joseph, "Political Familism in Lebanon," 159.

18 Ibid.

19 Suad Joseph, "Gender and Citizenship in the Arab World," *Al Raida* 129–130 (2010): 8–18.

20 Bayat, *Life as Politics*.

21 Ibid., 44.

22 Ibid., 46.

23 M. N. Interview. By Nay El Rahi, March 3, 2021.

24 Ibid.

25 Ibid.

26 Ibid.

27 Ibid.

28 Ibid.

29 Ibid.

30 Ibid.

31 Examples from PLW.

32 M. N. Interview. By Nay El Rahi, March 3, 2021.

33 For more on this, see Laure Bereni and Anne Revillard, "A Paradigmatic Social Movement? Women's Movements and the Definition of Contentious Politics," *Sociétés contemporaines* 1, no. 85 (2012): 17–41.

34 Ibid.

35 K. G. Interview. By Nay El Rahi, March 16, 2021.

36 Ibid.

37 Ibid.

38 Ibid.

39 Ibid.

40 H. J. Interview. By Nay El Rahi, April 29, 2021.

41 Amber Hollibaugh and Nikhil Pal Singh, "Sexuality, Labor, and the New Trade Unionism: A Conversation," in *Out At Work – Building a Gay-Labor Alliance,* ed. Kitty Krupat and Patrick McCreery (Minneapolis: University of Minnesota Press, 2001), 60–77.

42 Gabriel Hetland and Jeff Goodwin, "The Strange Disappearance of Capitalism from Social Movement Studies," in *Marxism and Social Movements*, ed. Colin Barker, Laurence Cox, John Krinsky, and Alf Gunvald Nilsen (Leiden: Brill Publishers, 2013), 82–102.

43 H. J. Interview. By Nay El Rahi, April 29, 2021.

44 H. J. Interview. By Nay El Rahi, April 29, 2021.

45 Ibid.

46 Ibid.

47 Ibid.

48 Ibid.

14

The Lebanese Uprising through the Eyes of Loyalists

Mortada Al-Amine

Most writings on the Lebanese uprising have left an important blind spot: the citizens who cling to some aspects of a regime even as they resent the system as a whole. Since the eruption of the uprising on October 17, 2019, supporters of Lebanon's ruling parties played a key role both in the massive protests and in the regime's ability to survive them. Partisan narratives alternated between supporting the uprising and protecting party interests within the regime but they all served more to justify the status quo than to articulate a vision for change.

When reflecting on the uprising, it is tempting to focus on the agents that seek change rather than those who seek to maintain the status quo. This bias, although necessary in driving the movement forward, leaves out a substantial segment of society: individuals who, for different reasons, perceive the uprising as a movement against their own interests. For some, this moment of political instability seemed to threaten their economic interests under the existent regime while others were motivated to protect identities that may be undermined with its overhaul. The current chapter aims to shed light on those who were driven by an interest in maintaining their own party's position within the regime. I argue that an understanding of the transformational moment Lebanon is going through remains limited unless it addresses the perspectives of those who have an interest in maintaining the status quo.

Overall, this chapter seeks to contribute to a well-rounded understanding of revolutionary struggles on the long run through discussing the voices of counterrevolutionary forces and status quo powers. Taken on its own, this chapter represents one of many lenses through which the Lebanese uprising can be understood, one that belongs to loyalists of the ruling parties. As such, in this chapter I will analyze the perspectives of those who supported the ruling political parties in Lebanon, focusing in particular on how they perceived both the political system and the uprising. In the rest of the chapter, the terms "partisan" and "loyalist" will be used interchangeably to refer to supporters of the ruling political parties in Lebanon.

First, this chapter draws on social-psychological theories of intergroup relations that deal with the question of what motivates individuals to identify with certain groups, justify political systems, and partake in revolutionary or counterrevolutionary collective action. Second, this chapter will offer an analysis of loyalists narratives toward the Lebanese uprising based on a series of interviews conducted between December 2019 and September 2020.[1] The aims of this chapter will be twofold: (1) present a theoretical framework that seeks to explain why individuals cling to aspects of the system and (2) offer a contextual analysis of the narrative of partisans during the first year of the Lebanese uprising. These include supporters and members of ruling political parties, specifically the Free Patriotic Movement, Lebanese Forces, Hezbollah, Amal Movement, Future Movement, and the Progressive Socialist Party. The analysis of partisan narratives will be particularly attentive to the role of clientelism—a salient political mechanism in Lebanon that plays a role in determining political support and loyalty to the party.[2]

Theoretical Framework

The social-psychological literature on intergroup relations and social change offers theoretical frameworks that enable us to view the uprising and the Lebanese political system from the perspective of partisans. The current chapter will present an overview of three types of motivations for why individuals cling to aspects of the political system. Although these motivations are intertwined, each paradigm presented here takes one of these motivations as its center. First, we will present system justification theory[3] that attempts to address situational and dispositional motivations for individuals to maintain the status quo even when it disadvantages them. Second, social identity theory[4] offers a paradigm for the role that group membership plays in individual motivations to defend or challenge the status quo. Finally, I build on the literature on selective incentives in collective action to elaborate on the role of material benefits in motivating individuals to defend or challenge the status quo while highlighting clientelism as a systemic embodiment of this process.

System Justification Theory

System justification theory proposes that individuals are motivated, to varying degrees depending on dispositional and situational factors, to defend aspects of the systems they live under, which sometimes occurs at the expense of their individual and collective interests.[5] System justification tendencies address fundamental needs and motives that all humans possess such as the desire for a predictable social order, a need to avoid threats and insecurities, and the need to maintain a sense of shared reality.[6] Even members of disadvantaged groups have the tendency to believe that the social order they live under is justified and legitimate. The theory provides an account of why individuals, especially those who belong to the lowest stratum in society, can be resistant to system-challenging movements and are hesitant to seek radical change. Indeed, studies have shown that system-justifying beliefs can be associated with lower tendencies to partake in system-challenging protests and are positively associated with counterrevolutionary actions or collective action that aims to support existent systems.[7,8] This has also been evident during the Lebanese uprising, where many of those disadvantaged by the system were either apathetic or opposed to the uprising, even going so far as to engage in counterrevolutionary movements that suppressed its growing momentum.

Social Identity Theory

Such system-justifying attitudes and actions are also largely motivated by individuals' social identity and group membership. Social identity theory posits that individuals, as members of social or political groups, strive to maintain a positive social identity. In order to develop a positive and secure self-concept, individuals strive to maintain a favorable image of their in-group and to defend and justify the behaviors of their fellow in-group members.[9] Even members of low-status groups develop strategies that enable them to maintain a positive social identity. Strategies of dealing with membership in a low-status group include leaving the group, downward comparison, and seeking social change to elevate the status of the group within the hierarchy. The decision to adopt any of these strategies depends on several factors, including the permeability of intergroup boundaries and the legitimacy and stability of status differences. In the Lebanese context, those who support the dominant political parties from within their sects might perceive the sectarian system as legitimate and stable and therefore might be willing to defend the parties they support in order to maintain a positive sectarian identity.

Selective Incentives and Clientelism

Social-psychological models of collective action have emphasized distinct pathways to collective action, as some models focused on cost-benefit calculations[10] while others stressed the role of identity processes, injustice, and efficacy.[11] The dual pathway model of collective action[12] integrates these two approaches and considers them two distinct pathways that exert independent influence on motivations for collective action participation. While the collective identification pathway seems to be concerned with intrinsic motivations to act in accordance with group-based standards and norms, such as the case with sectarian identification, cost-benefit pathway can be seen as motivated by extrinsic rewards, such as what would exist in clientelism. Hence, in addition to group-based motivations, material incentives play a key role in decisions to participate or oppose collective action.

Material incentives in return for political allegiance predominantly manifest in systems that harbor clientelist relations. Clientelism is defined through four different key elements: dyadic relationships, contingency, hierarchy, and iteration.[13] Early conceptualizations of clientelism emphasized face-to-face dyadic transactions and interactions between patrons and their clients. Contingency refers to the reciprocal nature of the exchange between the patron and the client. The provision of a service or good on behalf of one party comes as a direct response to a promise or delivery of a benefit by the other party. These benefits include a wide range of short-term material goods (e.g., money and food baskets) and long-term material benefits (e.g., jobs, access to social services, and protection). The relationship that characterizes clientelism is asymmetrical and hierarchical in a sense that the patron possesses resources, status, and influence that the clients lack. Finally, iteration is the element that differentiates the patron-client exchange from one-off interactions such as bribes. Clientelism is a repeated interaction that requires one of the parties to trust the other to deliver on their promises while anticipating future exchanges such as social services in return for political loyalty. Therefore, not only are identity theories of political action crucial for understanding counterrevolutionary action in relation to the Lebanese uprising but also theories that link material incentives to political action are powerful in outlining motivations for preserving the status quo.

Partisans and the Lebanese Status Quo

In this section, I present an analysis of loyalist narratives that attempt to illustrate how they situated themselves in relation to the Lebanese uprising in its earliest stages and to the events that transpired one year after. More specifically, the section will discuss the development of loyalist narratives as the uprising progressed while considering points of convergence and divergence and their centrality to the sustenance of the political system. This section will show how loyalists frequently voiced ambivalence regarding Lebanon's political future, only to then resolve their doubts through mechanisms that are surprisingly similar across the political spectrum. Then, I will elaborate on why loyalists are motivated in maintaining the status quo through a closer examination of clientelism in Lebanon. The analysis that follows is based upon interviews I conducted with individuals, who I will refer to in this analysis as "loyalists," who identified as supporters of at least one of the following ruling political parties in Lebanon: Free Patriotic Movement (FPM), Lebanese Forces (LF), Future Movement (FM), Hezbollah, and Amal Movement. The analysis also incorporates my own observations as both a researcher and a participant in the Lebanese uprisings.

Analysis of Loyalist Narratives during the Lebanese Uprising

Perhaps the most striking aspect of Lebanon's uprising was the extent to which it included large parts of a segmented and intensely polarized society. In the beginning, the protests did not just transcend boundaries of sect, class, generation, and geography; they also jumped the divide between those Lebanese who denounce the political class in its entirety and those who remain steadfastly committed to their own communal leaders.

Even the most stalwart partisans of Lebanon's diverse factions could unite behind slogans that decried poor national governance and growing economic hardship. "In the first few days, all my relatives were energetic and hopeful," said a student[14] whose family backs the Christian FPM, the party of Michel Aoun, president of the Republic.

"They joined some of the protests and shared their excitement over WhatsApp." A supporter of Hezbollah[15] similarly recalled: "I was really optimistic. I thought that we might finally get a decent country to live in."

A sense of unanimity between party loyalists and other protestors was reinforced through the all-encompassing, patriotic image that they projected together in the first few days of the October uprising. As people from different religious sects and political inclinations joined in public squares, protestors revived old clichés of communal coexistence, and the Lebanese flag spread ubiquitously. A consensus seemed to form around denouncing potentially divisive signs of affiliation, like party flags and chants. Indeed, in the first week of the uprising, many heralded the movement as an emphatic, nationwide rejection of the explicitly sectarian system that has governed the country for decades. "At the beginning, the protests were independent," said a student[16] who supports Hezbollah. "People were not voicing their traditional political views. I was super with it."

While some individuals loyal to parties in power (e.g., Hezbollah, FPM, and LF) participated in the uprising given that they share in the same sufferings and hopes as any other Lebanese, they feared its co-optation by rival groups almost from the outset. They warned against the movement's co-optation by their political rivals and resented any demand that would explicitly target their own faction.[17] Unity of purpose thus proved contingent on an abstract political agenda: the uprising's demands remained general, stopping short of anything more specific than "toppling the regime" or "recovering stolen wealth" siphoned off by a corrupt elite. Indeed, condemning the system as a whole is a well-established trope used by Lebanese— and Lebanese politicians—to vent widespread frustration. Nonetheless, the factions' initial bewilderment facilitated a genuine sense of unity, as partisan leaders remained momentarily silent.

Some of the earliest fault lines to emerge ran along divisions of class and religious piety. Although the protests were inclusive in some ways, their carnivalesque atmosphere soon alienated more conservative sections of society. Based on my own observations, some protestors, in Beirut's Martyrs' Square, played and danced to music. An abandoned cinema known as the Egg hosted both seminars and raves. Revolutionaries doing yoga on the centrally located, and hotly contested, ring road irritated those who viewed this as an expression of upper-class entitlement. Religiously minded participants pointed at groups openly smoking hashish or consuming alcohol to denounce the movement's rowdiness; some upper-class, elitist protestors did the same. A supporter of both Hezbollah and Amal later reflected:[18] "At that point it wasn't a revolution anymore. People were drinking and dancing—they even brought in a belly dancer!"

Above all, many loyalists struggled with what they saw as the uprising's anarchic agenda: not just removing a failed political system but everyone and anyone who ever held leadership within it. The movement's most iconic slogan—"all of them means all of them"—represented a frightening prospect for many loyalists, whose sense of security and communal identity is anchored to factional leaders. As a result, chants singling out politicians—running the sectarian gamut from Gebran Bassil and Nabih Berri to Saad Hariri, Walid Joumblatt, and Samir Geagea—brought out growing defensiveness within party ranks. When protestors sang "all of them means all of them—Nasrallah is one of them," some within the crowd would shout back: "Nasrallah is a red line."

Past the first few days of relative unanimity, growing numbers of loyalists rallied to their factions' official narratives. They nonetheless sought to strike a balance between endorsing the protest movement's demands for change and denouncing the supposed presence of corrupting elements within it—with each faction expounding its own understanding of who exactly these were.

As political identities crept back, society seemed to break down into three groups. Nonaligned citizens and many secular activists persisted with their original call for uprooting the system wholesale. Meanwhile, some factions attempted to recast themselves as "opposition" to the regime in which they were embedded (which is particularly evident in the position of the Kata'eb party that repositioned themselves as part of the uprising): the LF resigned in response to the uprising; Prime Minister Saad Hariri, head of the FM, stepped down soon after; and the Progressive Socialist Party walked out with him. This retreat left the government's majority coalition—namely the FPM, Hezbollah, and Amal—to embody, more than they would have liked, what was left of the regime. Implausibly, all sides claimed to defend the revolution's values.

This three-way split revived fault lines that have shaped Lebanese politics since the mid-2000s, between a pro-Western camp (known as March 14) and an alliance centered on Hezbollah (dubbed March 8), with unaffiliated Lebanese falling in between. As the initial bonds the uprising had created broke, old party politics took over once more: these loose coalitions mutually repelled and reinforced each other, shoring up the very system that protestors aspired to transform.

Loyalists often argue that the faction they endorse represents the best chance for any transformation amid Lebanon's confounding political gridlock. The uprising, as they see it, only echoed demands that their parties have long made. Indeed, several parties in power have issued their own calls to abolish sectarianism and transition to a civil state. They unanimously identify corruption as one of Lebanon's gravest afflictions and advocate for an independent judiciary. And all clamor for the need to repatriate "stolen assets," a catchphrase describing the corruption, capital flight, and tax evasion fueling the country's financial collapse. "The FPM will hold officials accountable," insisted a member of its youth division.[19] "We are the ones working to reform laws and institutions." Of course, such narratives systematically overlook—or at least downplay—the degree to which every party is complicit in and reliant upon the very problems they claim to redress.

Faced with such intractable obstacles, loyalists contend that the only solution to Lebanon's impasse lies in seeking more power for their own camp. While acknowledging the need for a transition, a journalist close to the FM[20] concluded that the way forward was to double down on the existing system: "The best thing that can happen to Lebanon is for each party to fully govern its own sect." A Hezbollah supporter painted his own ideal scenario: "This country should be ruled by a single person or party, whichever that is. Of course, my preference would be Hezbollah."

Indeed, across the political spectrum, the revolution has intensified factional affiliations rather than eroded them. "Our support for the FPM only increased since the uprising," said the member of its youth division. "We are convinced of our political project, now more than ever." This hardening of attitudes reverberates across party lines, as one faction's resolve reinvigorates the others'. Ironically, these mutually reinforcing dynamics only recreate the very stalemate that led to popular unrest in the first place. The absurdity of this cycle is not lost on party followers, who must resort to yet more powerful narrative devices to overcome it.

As loyalists seek to reconcile their earnest desire for change with deep-rooted factional loyalties, they fall back on a well-worn ability to reinterpret events in ways that suit their worldview. The ensuing narratives often take for granted the connection between faith and faction. One student drew a direct line from creed to partisanship: "As a religious Shia, my political views derive from my religious beliefs, and Hezbollah best represents this relationship."

This form of identity politics typically assumes the language of a greater cause, such as defending against Israel or otherwise upholding Lebanese sovereignty. But each faction is quick to translate such agendas into existential threats the community itself must fend off. For Hezbollah supporters, for example, a diffuse sense of danger will combine Israeli bombings, US sanctions, and Sunni radicalization. Sunni, Christian, and Druze loyalists all entertain their own feelings of insecurity, rooted in the assassination of their figureheads, armed clashes between partisans, and attempts to encroach on their political prerogatives or sectarian strongholds. For many loyalists, the overarching "cause" ultimately recedes into the background, overtaken by an ironclad belief in a given party's role in protecting its community.

The powerful association of religious identity and politics—and the defensive reflexes that underpin it—grants factions remarkable latitude. Rather than hold parties responsible for their shortcomings, loyalists shift responsibility toward rival groups and their foreign backers, whose designs are far more devious and dangerous than merely obstructing reform.

These narratives imply that rank-and-file loyalists can do little in the face of such high stakes: the magnitude, complexity, and opacity of the threats leave them to depend almost blindly on their leaders. "Hezbollah's leadership has always made wise decisions," said a party supporter. "I trust them whenever they say that it's not the right time for certain things—whether domestically or regionally, in the military or political spheres."

Consequently, loyalists have responded to each new phase of Lebanon's downward spiral by lowering their expectations, rather than asking more of their representatives. In the name of the cause, whether it is safeguarding the sect's rights or defending against an external threat, they take in stride the state's breakdown and its dire effects on their daily lives. When asked how he and his social network were dealing with the economic downturn, the Hezbollah and Amal supporter said: "We have a clear enemy that is working to undermine us; our only fight is with Israel. It's a challenge, but we need to be patient and strong. This is our doctrine, even if we starve."

Even as most loyalists decry the status quo, they nonetheless actively contribute to it through actively adopting their parties' narratives that resist system-challenging movements. This mechanism—which is almost identical across all factions—is precisely what makes the Lebanese regime so stubbornly coherent, despite all its dysfunction. It derives its strength not from any capacity to deliver services but from interlocking narratives that vindicate each other. Loyalists often recognize this vicious cycle, even as they remain hostage to it themselves. Speaking after the August 4 blast, a supporter of the LF[21] shared a bleak forecast:

> the uprising has lost most of its backing. Few still believe in its ability to bring about necessary change. Change could still happen through elections. But even then, I think that everything would stay the same: the Shia will vote for Amal and Hezbollah, the Druze for Joumblatt, and so on. Each sect will still vote for the same parties; even us, we will again vote for the Lebanese Forces. This is because sectarian identities are tied to these parties.

Clientelism and Political Mobilization in Lebanon

As Lebanon faces growing economic hardships, the Lebanese continue to pursue the basic means for survival. Lebanese politics has been characterized as "the epitome of patron client relations" in which political parties provide resources and services in exchange for political support and loyalty.[22] In that sense, loyalty becomes motivated by personal interests. In effect, the more loyalists internalize the perpetuity of the system of the factions, the more they hold on to their parties as their only hope for protection and accessing resources. Although the ability of the factions to provide for loyalists is shrinking, the lack of alternatives keeps loyalists in line.

The motivation to stay in line is reinforced by the clientelist relation that governs dynamics between political parties and their supporters in Lebanon. While such relations are evident under politically stable conditions, these dynamics appear to withstand pressure during times of dissent. More so, and in line with system justification theory, these relations appear to be exacerbated during times of unrest—particularly as unrest threatens epistemic and existential tendencies. In addition allegiance to the party manifests behaviorally in electoral and nonelectoral forms of support. During elections, clientelism takes the form of a one-shot transaction, which may include money and food baskets, whereas more valuable services are provided by political parties in exchange for long-term commitments to and activism with the party.[23]

Political parties are also invested in nonelectoral forms of political mobilization such as protests, riots, demonstrations, and, in some cases, formation of armed groups. Such forms of political mobilization require more valuable incentives and a long-term relationship of provision of services in order to secure committed members and increase their motivations to participate in more costly actions. These services can be part of an institutionalized form of clientelism, which includes service provision through schools, hospitals, community centers, and other social service institutions that are either run by or affiliated with political parties. Indeed, Cammett's study that analyzed nationally representative surveys and interviews with service providers and beneficiaries found that the likelihood of receiving social services from a political party was strongly associated with political activism with that party. More specifically, the results suggested that an individual that supports a political party and attends meetings and engages in protests is more likely to have access to financial assistance, scholarships, or medical care compared to a nonsupporter or a nonactive supporter.

This illustrates the extent to which clientelist networks are embedded in the Lebanese communities. Understanding the structure of the system that governs the relation between citizens and political parties and the power it holds is imperative for deconstructing the motivations of political party supporters for (dis)engaging in political action. Adherence to political parties in Lebanon is therefore not only driven by ideological and identity-related reasons, but it is also (in)directly incentivized through a complex web of clientelist relations.

Conclusion

This chapter aimed to emphasize a commonly neglected perspective in the discourse on social movements, the perspective of those who cling to aspects of the regime even as they resent the system as a whole. Through grounding our research in social-psychological paradigms and drawing on data collected from party loyalists following the Lebanese uprising, this text attempts to understand the motivations and structures that encourage loyalists to cling to aspects of the system. Additionally, this chapter presents an in-depth account of the narratives that allowed loyalists to rationalize their dynamic positionalities in relation to the uprising and the political regime. This transformational moment that Lebanon is witnessing is shaped in part by how partisans view it, foreseeing how this transformational moment transpires requires continuous assessment of their point of view.

This chapter explored the complexities behind why some individuals, despite being victims of the status quo in Lebanon, positioned themselves against the uprising that sought to uproot the very system that disadvantaged them. This research unveiled several pillars that protected the Lebanese ruling parties, particularly regarding maintaining their support base, during the time of upheaval. Drawing from their narratives, it was evident that regardless of positions from the uprising, loyalists conformed to their parties' rhetoric, which allowed them to resolve and rationalize their contradiction that emerged due to their despise toward the system as a whole and their active support of one of its protectors. Such reconciliation was possible due to a relationship between the party and its supporters composed of two main layers: one that provokes identities, sectarian tendencies, and exploits existential fears and psychological discomfort. The second layer pertains to material interests that fortify one's allegiance to their party.

Notes

1   The analysis of interview data presented under the section title "Analysis of loyalist narratives during the Lebanese uprising" has been previously published by the

author of this chapter for Synaps network: https://www.synaps.network/post/lebanon
-uprising-revolution-loyalists-parties.

2 E. Bray-Collins, "Sectarianism from Below: Youth Politics in Post-War Lebanon,"
(Doctoral Dissertation, 2016).

3 J. T. Jost and M. R. Banaji, "The Role of Stereotyping in System-Justification and the
Production of False Consciousness," *British Journal of Social Psychology* 33, no. 1
(1994): 1–27, https://doi.org/10.1111/j.2044-8309.1994.tb01008.x.

4 H. Tajfel and J. C. Turner, "An Integrative Theory of Intergroup Conflict," in *The
Social Psychology of Intergroup Relations*, ed. W. G. Austin and S. Worchel (Monterey:
Brooks/Cole, 1979), 33–47.

5 J. T. Jost, "A Quarter Century of System Justification Theory: Questions, Answers,
Criticisms, and Societal Applications," *British Journal of Social Psychology* 58, no. 2
(2019): 263–314. https://doi.org/10.1111/bjso.12297.

6 J. T. Jost, M. R. Banaji, and B. A. Nosek, "A Decade of System Justification Theory:
Accumulated Evidence of Conscious and Unconscious Bolstering of the Status Quo,"
Political Psychology 25, no. 6 (2004): 881–919. https://doi.org/10.1111/j.1467-9221
.2004.00402.x.

7 D. Osborne, J. T. Jost, J. C. Becker, V. Badaan, and C. G. Sibley, "Protesting to
Challenge or Defend the System? A System Justification Perspective on Collective
Action," *European Journal of Social Psychology* 49, no. 2 (2019): 244–69. https://doi.org
/10.1002/ejsp.2522.

8 J. T. Jost, V. Chaikalis-Petritsis, D. Abrams, J. Sidanius, J. Van Der Toorn, and C.
Bratt, "Why Men (and women) Do and Don't Rebel: Effects of System Justification
on Willingness to Protest," *Personality and Social Psychology Bulletin* 38, no. 2 (2012):
197–208. https://doi.org/10.1177/0146167211422544.

9 M. J. Hornsey, "Social Identity Theory and Self-Categorization Theory: A Historical
Review," *Social and Personality Psychology Compass* 2, no. 1 (2008): 204–22. https://doi
.org/10.1111/j.1751-9004.2007.00066.x.

10 B. Klandermans, "Mobilization and Participation: Social-Psychological Expansions
of Resource Mobilization Theory," *American Sociological Review* 49, no. 5 (1984):
583–600. doi:10.2307/2095417.

11 M. van Zomeren, T. Postmes, and R. Spears, "Toward an Integrative Social Identity
Model of Collective Action: A Quantitative Research Synthesis of Three Socio-
Psychological Perspectives," *Psychological Bulletin* 134, no. 4 (2008): 504–35. https://
doi.org/10.1037/0033-2909.134.4.504.

12 S. Sturmer and B. Simon, "Collective Action: Towards a Dual-Pathway Model,"
European Review of Social Psychology 15, no. 1 (2004): 59–99. https://doi.org/10.1080
/10463280340000117.

13 A. Hicken, "Clientelism," *Annual Review of Political Science* 14, no. 1 (2011): 289–310.
https://doi.org/10.1146/annurev.polisci.031908.220508.

14 Jana, twenty-five years, interview by author, December 16, 2019.

15 Mahmoud, twenty-six years, interview by author, January 21, 2020.

16 Abir, twenty-three years, interview by author, December 25, 2019.

17 Why Did the October 17 Revolution Witness a Regression in Numbers? (2020). *The
Lebanese Center for Policy Studies*.

18 Raed, thirty-one years, interview by author, January 2, 2020.

19 Shadi, twenty-four years, interview by author, December 29, 2019.

20 Mohammad, twenty-five years, interview by author, February 26, 2020.

21 Jo, twenty-five years, interview by author, September 8, 2020.

22 J. G. Karam, "Beyond Sectarianism: Understanding Lebanese Politics through a Cross-Sectarian Lens," *Middle East Brief*, 2017, 107.

23 M. C. Cammett, "Partisan Activism and Access to Welfare in Lebanon," *Studies in Comparative International Development* 46, no. 1 (2011): 70–97. https://doi.org/10 .1007/s12116-010-9081-9.

The Power and Limits of Blocking Roads

How the October Uprising Disrupted Lebanon

Nizar Hassan

Introduction

The October 17, 2019, uprising was not the first anti-establishment movement[1] that Lebanon witnessed in that decade. Many movements had opposed the post-civil war Lebanese social order, with a focus on sectarianism and cronyism, including the 2011 "campaign to overthrow the sectarian system" inspired by "Arab Spring" uprisings in the region and the 2015 protest movement triggered by the solid waste management crisis.[2] The 2015 Harak (movement) was more populous than its ancestor and expanded into a movement of thousands calling for the ousting of the ruling political class. However, October 2019 witnessed a social and political uprising rather than simply a protest movement. Along with the political and economic crisis fueling the popular action, the significance of the October uprising goes back to several key features of the movement itself, most importantly its spontaneity, its highly decentralized nature,[3] and its disruption of business as usual. This last aspect is the focus of this chapter, specifically the use of nationwide roadblocking as a primary disruptive protest tactic. While the uprising employed many other disruptive tactics, roadblocking was the most prominent and arguably the most impactful as it "paralyzed the country."[4] Despite the major role it had on the ground and in engendering protest dynamics and discourse, roadblocking as a disruptive tactic was not sufficiently addressed in the local circles of researchers and activists. Hence my decision to dedicate this chapter to try and fill this vacuum by examining the power and limitations of roadblocking.

The first section of this chapter attempts to explain why blocking roads is a remarkably strong disruptive tactic in the Lebanese political-economic context.[5] I argue that roadblocking, when performed on such a wide scale, is first and foremost a strong tool to physically disrupt the economy and public administration. Moreover, roadblocking offered a shortcut to achieving a general strike—one of the strongest disruptive tactics known to humans—to a population whose structural disruptive power had been curtailed by the postwar neoliberal transformation of the Lebanese economy.[6] And it did so without requiring any involvement of the typical organizers of strikes—labor organizations[7]—which in the Lebanese case have been either co-opted or sidelined by the political establishment.[8] The second part of the analysis will focus on the political impact and significance of roadblocking, specifically in terms of localizing the political conflict and decentralizing what I call the "strategic agency" among participants. The argument is that roadblocking empowered traditionally marginalized actors, especially working-class youths, and contributed to making the October uprising decentralized[9] and therefore more politically significant and sensitive. In turn, the third part analyzes the limitations of this protest tactic by examining the strategic and political factors that led organizers and protesters to stop blocking roads, including the government's resignation, protest exhaustion, repression, and counterrevolutionary propaganda.

The Power of Road Blockades

Shortcut to General Strike

When one talks about an uprising as opposed to more common movements or campaigns, the question of power becomes central. The October 17 uprising in Lebanon sought immediate, comprehensive change. It was not a campaign calling for a specific law or policy reform; the overwhelming demand, or more accurately the collective dream, was to overthrow the corrupt ruling class. In other words, the movement was closer to a civilian insurrection—similar in mobilization tools[10] to previous movements and uprisings in the region.[11] In such movements that aim for immediate systemic change, disruptive power is key because in the absence of a military coup, it is arguably only through disruption that ruling forces can be cornered into conceding authority or at least enacting reforms.

Understanding the disruptive power of roadblocks requires us first to define both power and disruption. Many scholars have written on disruptive tactics, social dynamics, and political impact. For instance, Francis Fox Piven defined power as the "rooted in the control of resources, especially in control of wealth and force, or in the institutional positions that yield control over wealth and force."[12] The strength of this definition is that it encompasses the sociopolitical, military, and material manifestations of power. Based on this notion, Piven looks at disruption as a "power strategy,"[13] specifically one defined by "the withdrawal of contributions to social cooperation by people at the lower end of the hierarchical social relations."[14] While this withdrawal can take numerous forms, the first tactic that comes to mind is a strike. When workers stop working, their company's process of profit accumulation is largely halted, giving workers leverage against their employers. When worker organizations coordinate a work stoppage on the national scale, we are then witnessing a general strike, which is arguably the highest degree of disruption that a population can achieve against its ruling elite.[15]

Here exactly lies the power of nationwide roadblocking such as that which defined at least the first two weeks of the October 2019 uprising in Lebanon and was resorted to more sporadically in later stages of the movement. By midnight on October 17, most vital highways and roads were blocked. In urban areas, even internal streets were blocked, usually by local working-class young men and women burning dumpsters and fire in the middle of streets. Blocking roads meant that most economic activity was halted, that is, disrupting "business as usual," and so was the movement of politicians themselves. In most parts of the country, especially in and around major towns and cities, people had a reason to be absent from work and participate in protest actions. In other words, workers had an excuse to strike due to the force majeure of blocked roads.[16] It was a de facto "general strike," a term that soon became on every tongue. One remembers here the marches in the streets of Beirut, where queer feminist protesters led crowds singing to the rhythm of a handheld drum: "tomorrow is a general strike, we will block the roads."

Piven theorizes that while dominant social relations, for example in capitalist democracies, allocate most of the power in the hands of the ruling elites, this does not leave people of lower classes without power. Blocking roads was a manifestation of this "power from below" and was as powerful, while it lasted, as the best organized labor strikes in human history. While this form of nationwide road blockades would be powerful in any current or past context, it was particularly powerful in Lebanon because it filled a power vacuum left by political-economic developments that stripped Lebanon's working classes of their disruptive power.

Filling the Organizational Vacuum

The extra importance of this forced general strike was that the typical tools to achieve such a strike were not viable. This is because labor movements in Lebanon have been suppressed, defeated, and co-opted by the postwar ruling class.[17] For example, around the mid-1990s, Lebanon's authorities were faced by strong union mobilization led by the General Labor Confederation (GLC) whose board had elected Elias Abu Rizq to lead it.[18] The mobilization peaked in a general strike in 1995 in light of Abu Rizq's disillusionment with the executive government's willingness to enact demanded reforms.[19] The government attempted to suppress the movement in various ways, including sending army troops and enacting a ban on demonstrations. Soon, the ruling class executed a smarter tactic to defeat the union movement, whereby they sought to win over the GLC through internal elections and control its leadership.[20] To do so, they had to not only unite in one ruling-class list against the supposed political differences but also manipulate the election by creating five pseudo-union federations to secure seats on the executive council, which in turn elects the board. Abu Rizq was removed indeed but soon returned to office when his opponent resigned.[21] It took ruling forces another two years to finally overthrow Abu Rizq and installing as replacement Ghassan Ghosn, known for his loyalty to Amal movement leader Nabih Berri, who has been parliament speaker since 1992.[22] Ghosn's terms were characterized by minimal confrontation with the ruling class, both in its political and economic factions, and he even went so far as to oppose policies that favor workers.[23] A similar story took place in 2014, when the ruling class united in union elections to defeat the active leadership of the Union Coordination Committee (UCC), which had been performing powerful strikes and demonstrations in favor of better wages and benefits. In summary, the ruling class has taken every opportunity to defeat and neutralize the union movement. Among Lebanon's workers who can be unionized, 93 percent remain unionized.[24] The war on organized labor left Lebanon's working class with little "associational" power as defined by Wright.[25] They did not have many organizations to fight for their rights or lead their mobilizations.

Rentierization and the Disruptive Power of the Working Class

In addition to associational or organizational power, Lebanon's working classes had also been stripped of a major portion of their disruptive power in the economic system through a variety of neoliberal policies that favored activities in rent-based sectors (such as banking and real estate) at the expense of productive sectors (such as agriculture and manufacturing).[26] In a rentier economy, the disruptive power of the working class is reduced, because the labor they provide is less central for the system of profit accumulation. While factories are relatively easy to disrupt for workers, it is very difficult to disrupt real estate trading or banking activities. This coincides with the fact that workers in the two latter sectors have also had their power neutralized; the bank employee's union is weak and co-opted by bank owners, and workers in construction are mostly poor migrants working informally, subjected both to workplace racism and classism, and a ban on their unionization by the labor law. Abdo et al. (2016) theorized that the rentierization of the economy "contributed to a new change in the nature of capitalist accumulation in Lebanon."[27]

> Workers and employees became excluded from this process [of capital accumulation], not only due to their own organizational issues and the fierce war waged by the regime against them in parallel, but also because of the transformation in the nature of added-value production in the Lebanese economy in the last two decades.[28]

In the context of a company, "structural power" is defined by Eric Olin Wright[29] as the leverage you have as workers in disrupting the process of production. This power is high on an assembly line where every worker's input is required for the successful production of an item or in a port where a worker strike can stop the maritime trade activity of companies and countries. If we think of the political-economic system as similar to a company, then we can discuss the extent to which people more generally possess structural power potential. In the context of the Lebanese political-economic order, people have been stripped of their structural power in the system as a whole. Road blockades came to fill that vacuum in an exceptional moment of public mobilization, whereby the leadership of unions and parties was no longer needed to achieve a nationwide general strike.

Class and Choice of Tactic

Despite it being highly efficient as a direct action and often resorted to by workers and farmers in Lebanon, road blockades as a protest tactic had been unpopular among many Beirut-based mobilizers, as it disrupts everyday life of fellow people and creates conflict between the protesters and masses that overshadows the original conflict with authorities. This discouraged middle-class activists in the previous decade seeking public support from resorting to roadblocking, except very briefly in moments of high momentum, such as the 2015 Harak.[30] On the other hand, when mobilizers in the October uprising employed this tactic nationwide and enforced a general strike, its perceived power eclipsed previous concerns—especially that people's movements were largely halted and therefore confrontations at blockades were less prominent. Supporters of the uprising soon started praising this tactic as the only thing that can force authorities to step down or act.[31] One would hear "we need to paralyze the country" in hundreds of voice messages shared on WhatsApp groups. After the power of blocking roads was showcased, disruption was seen as the only main leverage of the collective and became an explicit strategy for the revolting population.

> The power of road-blocking as a protest tool was in disrupting the arteries of internal communications in Lebanon. We didn't have a specific area or thing we were trying to disrupt; we wanted to disrupt everything. We wanted to stop everything, because all of it was not working and needed to stop. We wanted to set our own clock for reality.
>
> Rosa[32]

Political Significance and Strategic Impact

Roadblocking as a protest tactic was not only significant due to its disruptive power. Road blockades across the country created spaces for protest, discussion, and organizing. In most areas, soon after traffic was stopped, revolution tents were erected in roundabouts, and organizers immediately started conducting public discussions around the uprising's demands and the solutions for Lebanon.[33] These spaces, which will be addressed elsewhere in this book,[34] created a counterhegemonic political environment where previous political taboos were broken, including the criticism of sectarian political parties and leaders inside areas dominated by those.

Beyond the aspect of space occupation and reuse, road blockades had other strategic and political implications, mainly revolving around decentralizing the movement. When asked about what made the uprising different from other local social movements, most participants and organizers point at the aspect of decentralization.[35] While for example the protest movement of 2015 was primarily centered around demonstrations in downtown Beirut, the October uprising succeeded in becoming a national phenomenon because residents took to the streets in their districts, including major coastal cities such as Tripol and Tyre and rural areas such as Akkar, Chouf, and the Bekaa. As such, the political conflict between the revolting population and the dominant political forces was no longer diluted or mediated through generic slogans chanted from Beirut; it was a direct confrontation in the strongholds of these ruling elites, often including protesters sympathetic to the dominant political forces.

Moreover, roadblocks widely democratized strategic agency in the uprising. Rather than decision-making power being restricted in the hands of a central civil society elite that decides which day is a general strike, grassroots movements in many areas had the agency to make its choices. When it came to protests and demonstrations, call to action by political groups was more in line with local decisions and often came to confirm those decisions. Formal calls for protest were not important in the early days, because going to the streets for most was a self-evident activity.[36] "Calls were largely retrospective," says protester Rosa.[37] She recalls the sense of trust she felt toward supporting the decisions made by local groups. "I had full trust that the people who were blocking roads were aware of the strategic importance of blocking certain roads for disruption. When people of the north said block the roads with us tomorrow, it felt like a clear instruction. There was trust. As long as we do it together, at the same time, it's gonna work."

This decentralized blocking road tactic was also arguably a democratic process. A certain consensus among mobilizers in different areas was required over when to block roads, or otherwise the general strike attempt would fail.[38] Furthermore, inside each local environment, when blocking roads became the primary revolutionary act, actors that are traditionally marginalized suddenly had a leading role. Most blockades would be run by young people, including teenagers and working-class youth who were at the forefront. School students marched among their institutions to force a shutdown in solidarity with the general strike. Rosa recounts a debate between her younger sister, a sixteen-year-old enthusiastic about the uprising and determined to ensure her school is shut down, and her mother who was arguing that such action was no longer feasible or effective since momentum was decreasing.[39] This type of strategic conversations might occur on the grassroots level in many sorts of movements, but in this case, they are explained by the increased agency in the hands of "ordinary" participants. The question of "who is the rebel/activist" became obsolete, and as opposed to the 2015 protest movement, the direct-action manifestation of the uprising was not led by middle-class professional activists.[40] Arguably, this changed with the decreasing momentum and the end of the roadblocking episode after the resignation of Prime Minister Saad Hariri's government twelve days into the uprising.

Limitations of Roadblocking

The Cabinet's Resignation and Protest Exhaustion

Hariri's resignation, which topped the list of demands, was a turning point for the uprising and its tactics. "There were two phases in the uprising; the first was before Hariri's resignation, and the second after," says Hisham,[41] an organizer with the political group Lihaqqi. This moment had major implications for roadblocking as a protest tool. "As a protest tactic to overthrow the government, road blocking was very important, especially that the Lebanese ruling class had destroyed the union movement and with it the capacity to enforce a strike," Hisham continues, "After overthrowing Hariri, I believe the role of road-blocking became less significant."

Hisham argues that roadblocking works when it is performed temporarily to achieve a particular win, as opposed to a protest tool as part of a political agenda. "If the goal is not clear, well-articulated, and established in our mindsets, road-blocking loses its purpose," he says. This speaks to the transformation of the political environment following Hariri's resignation. At that point, the time of "bringing down" seemed to have ended, and it was now the time for advancing political agendas that represent the uprising. For instance, most organizers had advanced a discourse calling for the formation of a new independent government to enact immediate reforms and oversee the transitional period before a new general election.[42] Now that the government had resigned, all eyes were on what kind of government would be formed next, whether it would meet the uprising's demands, and what role forces from the uprising would have in it. The purpose of protest actions was aligned with this development, and most actions became related to what this transitional period should look like. Disruption in the purpose of negating the status quo was no longer enough; instead it was time for constructive mobilization. "You can't block the roads to demand the formation of a government. It doesn't make sense. Instead, you might mobilize for large demonstrations to showcase the wide support for your transitional political choice," Hisham argues.[43] This raises an important point on the usefulness of the roadblocking tactic in the context of civilian activism at different political moments. It could be one of the strongest protest tactics available to disrupt and overthrow, but that does not mean it necessarily has potential efficacy as part of a political agenda, except if the agenda entails armed insurrection—simply due to the ruling forces and state to repress those unarmed protests. Blockades can either be protected by public support or by weapons; and armed struggle was not on the general political compass of the uprising.

After Hariri's resignation, many organizers shared Hisham's belief that roadblocking was no longer the best protest tool, and large sections of the population seemed tired of daily protests and needed to go back to work. The choice of organizers was also influenced by the perceived lower public support for the tactic itself and the public's exhaustion. Scholars have demonstrated in other contexts[44] that the more broadly a claim or grievance resonates with the public, the higher tendency movements have to employ disruptive but nonviolent tactics. In the case of the October uprising, however, the popularity of the tactic itself and its general endorsement was the changing factor, as the claims and grievances were fairly general and shared across most members of the population.

However, there was a clear strategic and political problem with calling for an end to roadblocking. "People started calling us traitors, that we were only against Hariri and were satisfied when he resigned so we left the streets," recalls Bakhos,[45] a protest leader in the area of Barja, whose residents blocked the highway connecting Beirut to the South at the coastal town of Jiyyeh. Independent local organizers had raised the "killon ya'ni killon" (all of them means all of them) slogan to ensure they were not perceived as biased to the local population, many among whom were sympathetic toward Hariri. The accusation of being anti-Hariri was a serious one, as it could have damaged the credibility of the uprising locally. To further complicate the picture, there was also a discrepancy in the revolutionary momentum and therefore in the preferred course of action among different areas. Even in the same areas, there was a division on the rightfulness of this tactic between what Hisham calls "the thawra society" and other members of the population.

The link between momentum and the sustenance of road blockades was strikingly clear. What lied behind the decreasing momentum was a lower public morale and fewer expectations from the movement. There was clearly less hope in immediate system-level change, which made insurrection tactics such as blocking roads seem pointless. While Hariri's resignation could have fueled the momentum, it had the opposite effect because to many it felt like nothing more could be overthrown in the streets. The public rejection of road blockades had also increased as Hezbollah, arguably the most powerful political force in the country, took a firm stance opposing the uprising and its tactics, vowing to never allow the overthrow of its ally president Michel Aoun.[46] In turn, Parliament Speaker and Amal movement leader Nabih Berri, who is protected by state-employed security forces consisting of loyal partisans called the Parliament Police, made sure no one thought of approaching his position, either politically or physically.[47] Indeed, following the rain-induced flooding of streets in the first week of December, dozens of cars filled with protesters went around these ministers' residences in Beirut, throwing chants and bags of trash accusing the ministers of corruption and inaction.[48] When the convoy passed a few hundred meters away from Nabih Berri's residence, a group of his Parliament Police attacked protesters, dragged some of them out of their cars, destroyed their phones or cameras, and broke their windshields[49]. It was clear after weeks of protest that while disruptive tactics were powerful, they were not strong enough to overthrow the political class. After that, roadblocking became less self-evident as the primary revolutionary act. While the disruptive power of roadblocking had been able to temporarily disrupt "business as usual" and exert pressure on the cabinet into resignation, it was another task to overthrow the totality of the ruling political institutions.

Counterrevolutionary Propaganda and Repression

It was not only strategic concerns and protest exhaustion that forced protesters to abandon roadblocking. Before Hariri's resignation and after it, many ruling forces had maintained a propaganda war against road blockers. Free Patriotic Movement supporters adopted a discourse that portrays rebels as traitors, puppets, or degenerates.[50] Hezbollah and the Amal movement, the most powerful Muslim Shiite parties, took the campaign to the next level by using the sectarian card against road blockers like Bakhos in Jiyyeh.[51] They accused the protesters, many of whom happened to be Sunni Muslims, to be "cutting off" the South Lebanon, where the majority of people are Shiite Muslims. It took a tragedy for this discourse to gain its fullest momentum. In the night between November 24 and 25, a car crashed into the metallic barriers installed by the Lebanese army a few hundred meters away from the protest camp in Jiyyeh and subsequently caught fire. Two people died in the crash, and the Hezbollah-Amal duo jumped on the opportunity to accuse road blockers of killing the victims.[52] Hezbollah's official statement described the incident as a "crime," roadblocking as a "militia-like aggression," and the crash victims as "martyrs."[53] "The discourse of the victims' family changed dramatically after they went back to the south and were surrounded by partisans," Bakhos recounts. The army, which promised to issue a statement explaining what happened, never stood by their word, according to Bakhos, who headed with his comrades to nearby gas stations and purchased CCTV footage proving their claims.[54] Political parties succeeded not only in discrediting rebels but also in inciting sectarian anger that further distanced their Shiite supporters from the uprising. After the crash, the road had to be reopened immediately to avoid social tensions.

Besides strategy and popular and political backlash, a main incentive to abandon roadblocking came from the direct repression by police and army troops.[55] Beirut and Tripoli witnessed almost daily clashes between protesters and riot police and army brigades, and many of these clashes revolved around blockades. Security forces used excessive violence against protesters blocking roads as documented by Human Rights Watch[56] and shot rubber bullets and tear gas directly at crowds in protest squares. In the case of Jiyyeh, Bakhos says the army gave protesters an ultimatum of six hours to reopen the road on the day of Hariri's resignation.[57] To make evident the harsh reprisal protesters would face had they failed to comply with their orders, the army showcased around 300 troops with heavy vehicles. It was under this threat that the rebels of Jiyyeh decided to reopen roads for the first time since October 17.

From General Strike to Targeted Disruption

Following Hariri's resignation and the decrease in street momentum and state repression, one can observe that disruption was narrowed down in scope. Rather than disrupting movement in the whole country, protesters focused on shutting down specific institutions. While many areas witnessed protesters talking shop owners in shutting down their stores in solidarity, most of this narrower disruption was focused on government institutions and banks. Were these acts believed to have the same disruptive impact as nationwide road blockades? Not according to Bakhos. "At that point, honestly, we did not believe that shutting down the institutions was something that would influence the system. When youths went and shut down institutions, employees celebrated. They were happy that we were shutting down their institutions," he says.[58] But the class aspect comes back to play here. While working-class youths had a main role in the roadblocking episode, they were less involved in organizing after this episode. This goes back to their need to resume work for livelihood, as well as their lack of inclusion in political organizing. "We started coming up with new plans to start shutting down institutions in the Chouf district," Bakhos continues. "We were thinking of people who only realized themselves in physical direct action, and we asked them to use their power in shutting down banks, state institutions, and schools." These shutdowns brought up new strategic debates among protesters around the best protest tactics to use. For instance, some protesters walked into banks to disrupt their operation, and others destroyed ATM machines as a sign of rage against the banker elite and its role in the Lebanese ruling class.[59] Others disagreed with this tactic arguing that banks were the ones losing from people using ATM machines and visiting their branches, since virtually all operations revolved around account owners withdrawing their dollars before withdrawal limits were further reduced.

Conclusion

The story of the roadblocking episode and its end should inform our perspectives on both the power and limitations of such disruptive tactics when employed in the context of a civilian insurrection. On one hand, roadblocking provided a shortcut to general strike that effectively disrupted the totality of Lebanon for a number of days. It also had a remarkable effect on the dynamics of protest and the politics of the uprising. However, Lebanon's ruling class demonstrated its ability to withstand this pressure knowing that the momentum will eventually fade due in part to exhaustion and popular backlash, and that the hegemonic institutions and discourse will prevail. The tactic was a powerful disruptive tactic in forcing an already vulnerable government to resign but not to achieve further goals. Since October 2019, several factors have further caused the street momentum to shrink, including the COVID-19 pandemic,[60] disillusionment with street action, the financial crisis,[61] and arguably the Beirut Port explosion on August 4, 2020.[62,63]

By analyzing the power of roadblocking and its limitations and factors that led to its abandonment as the main protest tactic, this chapter aimed to contribute to activist and academic debates around social movement strategy and disruptive actions. Specifically, the findings indicate that political economy, public psychology, and the control of violent power are all factors that can boost or limit a disruptive protest tactic at a particular revolutionary moment. One strategic conclusion for organizers in Lebanon is that the physical disruption of movement by itself does not guarantee forcing imminent change, even when it is nationwide and effective. This is because while roadblocking could replace union organizations in achieving a general strike, a "mass political strike"[64] requires the presence of a clear political agenda beyond the demand for change in executive government, which the uprising lacked.

The strategic implications of this analysis might also extend to questioning the possibility of immediate systemic change through a civilian insurrection in Lebanon. Whether this change can occur depends on how vulnerable the ruling political-economic establishment is, how socially and politically entrenched the ideology and discourse it advances, and to what extent ruling powers are organized to exploit any fall in protest momentum. It also largely varies between political contexts, being arguably more difficult in the context of a power-sharing system like Lebanon's compared to one-party authoritarian states. The validity of nonviolent insurrection in the case of Lebanon has been the subject of many activist debates since the uprising and should likewise feature in future academic research.

Notes

1 I use the term "anti-establishment movement" to mean movements that erupt without a specific demand in mind, instead revolving around grievances over the political-economic system as a whole. Participation in them is primarily emotional rather than a calculated political choice, and the demands often revolve around overthrowing the ruling authorities. In Lebanon, the slogan that represented this

tendency in the 2015 protest wave and the 2019 uprising was: "All of them means all of them."

2 Triggered by a waste management crisis, the 2015 protest movement included sit-ins, demonstrations, and other direct actions across many areas. It has been documented by Carol Kerbage's 2017 working paper "Politics of Coincidence" published by the American University of Beirut's Issam Fares Institute for Public Policy and International Affairs. Also see my unpublished master's dissertation "Lebanon's 2015 protest movement: an analysis of class (and) power."

3 Mona Harb studies this decentralization aspect in Chapter 9 of this book.

4 This expression was common in the early days of the uprising.

5 This chapter benefits from the analysis in my dissertation, "Lebanon's 2015 protest movement: an analysis of class (and) power," on the 2015 protest movement's lack of disruptive power in relation to class dynamics and economic transformation.

6 Many social movement scholars have analyzed worker power and disruption in the neoliberal era, notably Beverly Silver in her chapter "Theorising the working class in twenty-first-century global capitalism" in the 2013 book *Workers and Labour in a Globalized Capitalism*, 46–69. This chapter's analytical framework endorses the notions of "structural" and "associational power" as presented by Eric Olin Wright in his article.

7 See Nada Atallah's article "Lebanese protests: the missing trade" on the October 17 uprising, published by Le Commerce du Levant on February 21, 2020.

8 For a historical account of the co-optation of the labor movement, see Nizar Hassan's dissertation or Lea Bou Khater's 2019 article, "Understanding State Incorporation of the Workers' Movement in Early Post-War Lebanon and Its Backlash on Civil Society," Civil Society Knowledge Centre, Lebanon Support. See Nadim el Kak's chapter in this volume.

9 The notion of movement decentralization in this context refers to the geographical distribution of protest actors and the diversity in leadership beyond traditional central protest actors. Decentralization has a particular importance in the case of Lebanon as it challenges the dominant sectarian hegemony and "localizes the conflict" as this chapter later argues.

10 The use of social media to mobilize demonstrators was the most prominent tool among most recent protest movements, as documented by Zeynep Tufekci's book *Twitter and Tear Gas* (Yale University Press, 2017).

11 For background on the "Arab Spring" uprisings and their socioeconomic roots, see Gilbert Achcar's book *The People Want* published by University of California Press in 2013 and Adam Hanieh's book *Lineages of Revolt* published by Haymarket Books in the same year.

12 See page 19 of Francis Fox Piven's book, *Challenging Authority: How Ordinary People Change America*, published by Rowman & Littlefield Publishers in 2006.

13 Ibid., 23.

14 Ibid., 20.

15 Rosa Luxemburg, in her 1906 text "The Mass Strike, the Political Party and the Trade Union," and others that followed have theorized the power of the general strike as a political tool for change in a capitalist system. While this tradition focuses on the centrality of labor unions in the process, the type of general strike witnessed in the October 2019 uprising was based on blocking roads, rather than industrial work stoppages, to disrupt economic activity.

16 This could be understood both as providing an opportunity for waged workers to skip work and enabling the participation in protest actions for many.

17 See Nizar Hassan's dissertation "Lebanon's 2015 protest movements: an analysis of class (and) power" and Lea Bou Khater's 2019 article, "Understanding State Incorporation of the Workers' Movement in Early Post-War Lebanon and Its Backlash on Civil Society," Civil Society Knowledge Centre, Lebanon Support.

18 See Sami Baroudi's article "Economic Conflict in Postwar Lebanon," *Middle East Journal* 52, no. 4 (1998): 531–50.

19 Ibid.

20 Ibid.

21 Ibid.

22 See page 74 of Bassel Salloukh et al., *Politics of Sectarianism in Postwar Lebanon*, published by Pluto Press in 2015.

23 Ibid.

24 Lea Bou Khater, "Public sector Mobilisation Despite a Dormant Workers' Movement," *Confluences Méditerranée* 92 (2015): 125–42.

25 See Eric Olin Wright's "Working-Class Power, Capitalist-Class Interests, and Class Compromise" published by the *American Journal of Sociology* 105, no. 4: 957–1002.

26 See N. Abdo, R. Fakhri, and F. Kubaisi, *'ummāl wa naqābāt . . . bilā ḥaraka!* [Trade Unions and Workers Without Movement]. (Issam Fares Institute for Public Policy and International Affairs, American University of Beirut, 2016.)

27 Ibid., 11.

28 Ibid.

29 See Wright, "Working-Class Power, Capitalist-Class Interests, and Class Compromise."

30 For instance, protesters in the Harak briefly blocked major highways leading to Beirut on March 14, 2016. Read *The Daily Star* newspaper's coverage in the article "Activists block vital roads leading to Beirut over trash crisis" published online on March 14, 2016.

31 This is supported both by the insights of activists interviewed for this chapter and my direct observations while participating as a protester and mobilizer in the movement. It is worth mentioning here that this chapter falls within the activist research category, as it is primarily motivated by and aims to inform the mobilizing strategies of revolutionary movements.

32 Interviewed in person for this chapter on March 28, 2021. Rosa is not the interviewee's real name.

33 Bakhos (interviewed by phone on March 20, 2021) recollects how he and other mobilizers immediately turned the road blockade in Jiyyeh to a space where every protester could give their opinion on a specific theme. He remembers an emphasis on "political education" especially given the wide youth presence in these protests. In addition, many initiatives and political groups toured the "revolution tents" in protest squares to advance policies and agendas.

34 See Mona Harb's chapter in this book *How Urban Space Shapes Collective Action*.

35 Insight based on conversations with fellow mobilizers during the uprising and personal observation on public discussions and media talking points.

36 This is not to deny that in some particular areas, traditional political groups that claimed to be part of the uprising influenced the effectiveness of roadblocking, such as the Christian party Lebanese Forces in the town of Jal el-Dib and the city of Jounieh.

37 Interviewed in person for this chapter on March 28, 2021. Rosa is not the interviewee's real name.

38 It is worth noting here that the decision to block roads was never technically a democratic process, and nonparticipant local residents were practically forced into accepting the reality of the disruption. Hence, the notion of democracy referred to is not about local decision-making processes; it is concerned with the grassroots mobilizational structure of the movement and the empowerment of typically marginalized local actors.

39 Interviewed in person for this chapter on March 28, 2021. Rosa is not the interviewee's real name.

40 On the other hand, the political and policy talking points that dominated the uprising could be associated with an educated middle class with more organizational experience.

41 Interviewed by phone for this chapter on April 2, 2021. The organizer's real name is not Hisham.

42 The extent elections were emphasized varied significantly among political groups, with many considering it a democratic necessity or an opportunity for institutional change and others dismissing it as a priority under the pretext of crisis-time priorities or cynicism toward electoral change.

43 Interviewed by phone for this chapter on April 2, 2021. The organizer's real name is not Hisham.

44 For example, Piazza and Wang came to this conclusion after studying twenty-three thousand protest actions in the United States between 1960 and 1995. See D. J. Wang and A. Piazza, "The Use of Disruptive Tactics in Protest as a Trade-Off: The Role of Social Movement Claims," *Social Forces* 94, no. 4 (2016): 1675–710.

45 Interviewed by phone for this chapter on March 20, 2021. The organizer's real name is not Bakhos.

46 This was made clear in the speeches delivered by Hezbollah's secretary general Hassan Nasrallah in speeches delivered following the start of the uprising.

47 The Parliament Police have been known for the violent suppression of protesters, especially those approaching speaker Nabih Berri's residence or attempting to enter the Nejmeh Square in Downtown Beirut where the parliament is located.

48 See Annahar's coverage "Security forces violently attack protesters near Berri's residence," published online on December 11, 2019.

49 I was one of the participants in the demonstration and saw the recounted details firsthand.

50 This FPM propaganda was mostly spread via social media platforms and the party's own television channel OTV.

51 As recounted by Bakhos (interviewed for this chapter on March 20, 2021) and witnessed in statements by partisans following the Jiyyeh traffic incident.

52 See *The Daily Star*'s coverage "Car crash claims two lives at Jiyyeh roadblock," published online on November 26, 2019. Some additional details were mentioned by Bakhos in his interview for this chapter om March 20, 2021.

53 See Hezbollah's statement published by Almanar and others on November 26, 2019.

54 Interviewed for this chapter on March 20, 2021. Bakhos is not the organizer's real name.

55 This is not to underestimate the attacks on protesters by partisans of many political groups, including Hezbollah, Amal, the Free Patriotic Movement, and the Progressive Socialist Party. For more insights on counterrevolutionary tactics, see Joseph Daher and Jeffrey Karam's chapters in this book.

56 "Lebanon: Protect Protesters from Attacks" was published by Human Rights watch on November 8, 2019.

57 Interviewed for this chapter on March 20, 2021. Bakhos is not the organizer's real name.

58 Ibid.

59 See Timour Azhari's coverage in the article "Banks targeted in Lebanon's 'night of the Molotov,'" published by Al-Jazeera on April 29, 2020; and Mohammad Bzeih's chapter "Night of the Banks" in this book (Chapter 24).

60 See the Lebanese Center for Policy Studies' extracts from interviews with organizers and intellectuals, published under the title "In What Ways Has the Pandemic Affected the Revolution?" on March 22, 2021.

61 See the Lebanese Center for Policy Studies' extracts from interviews with organizers and intellectuals, published under the title "Why Did the October 17 Revolution Witness a Regression in Numbers?" on October 31, 2020.

62 Human Rights watch's report "They Killed Us from the Inside: An Investigation into the August 4 Beirut Blast" published on August 4, 2021, summarizes key facts about the port explosion and allocates responsibility to state institutions that failed to prevent it.

63 Insights on how the port explosion might have affected revolutionary momentum can be found in the Lebanese Center for Policy Studies' extracts from interviews with organizers and intellectuals, published under the title "How Has the August 4 Explosion and Its Aftermath Affected the Revolution?" on April 1, 2021.

64 Using Rosa Luxemburg's words in her 1906 text "The Mass Strike, the Political Party and the Trade Union."

16

The Different Faces of Counterrevolution and Obstacles for Change in Lebanon

Joseph Daher

In October 2019, a protest movement erupted in Lebanon following the decision of the government to impose new taxes. The rebellion of large sectors of the Lebanese population, and especially its popular classes,[1] was however rooted in the destructive results of the country's political economy that had been pursued since the end of the Lebanese Civil War, with an emphasis on deeper integration into the global economy and private sector growth. These neoliberal policies strengthened the long-established characteristics of the Lebanese economy: a development model oriented to finance and services, in which social inequalities and regional disparities were very pronounced. The main Lebanese sectarian neoliberal parties and different fractions of the bourgeoisie have exploited privatization schemes and their domination of ministries to strengthen networks of patronage, nepotism, and corruption, while most Lebanon's population, both foreign and native-born, has suffered poverty and indignity.[2]

This protest movement of October 2019 differed from previous mobilizations by the fact that it challenged the whole neoliberal-sectarian system and explicitly denounced all parties combined as responsible for the deterioration of socioeconomic conditions. As one of the main slogans of the protest movement put it, "All Means All."

However more than a year later, and after the criminal tragedy of August 4, 2020, the ruling Lebanese sectarian neoliberal parties still dominate the country and its institutions amid a continual economic crisis, while the protest movement is very much weakened. The possibilities of change seem very far in comparison to October 2019 and the hundreds of thousands of Lebanese in the streets throughout the country.[3] So far, the protest movement remains very fragmented and has not been able to build a united front capable of channeling demands and organizing demonstrators across the country. How can we explain the resilience of the sectarian neoliberal system and its ruling parties?

This chapter will seek to understand the various tools, tactics, and strategies deployed by the ruling sectarian neoliberal parties to achieve their counterrevolutionary objectives by undermining and defeating the protest movement. It will also explain how these parties managed to maintain, and for some actors deepen, their domination on large sectors of society and prevent the building of an inclusive social political alternative.

This chapter relies mainly on newspaper and media articles published in Lebanon and reports by research centers and human rights agencies, as well as social media accounts of activist groups participating in the protest movement.

Strategies of Counterrevolutions to Maintain the Sectarian Neoliberal System

The tactics and strategies of counterrevolutions adopted by the ruling classes are rarely only through coercive means such as violence and repression but can also rely on modes of consent such as through the provision of job opportunities and delivery of social aids, to put an end to upsurge of dissent or protest movement, such as with the Lebanese October *Intifada* (Uprising). The Lebanese neoliberal-sectarian ruling classes have used various tools to maintain its hegemony.

Modes of Coercions—Intimidations, Repressions, and Violence

Since the beginning of the protest movement in October 2019, the ruling Lebanese sectarian parties have, on numerous occasions, accused the protesters of creating chaos in the country and of being manipulated by foreign forces. At the same time, foreign states have expressed different political positions since the outbreak of the uprising in October 2019,[4] but they have a similar objective: the preservation of the neoliberal-sectarian system and its elites.

State and Militias' Repression and Violence

Alongside the attempts to discredit the protest movement and their demands by the Lebanese state and its ruling sectarian parties, the repression against protesters increased at the end of 2019, including through the use of force such as live ammunition, rubber bullets, and tear gas. In one incident, at least 409 individuals were injured over two nights in January 2020 as a result of the state authorities' forces repression and violence, and, in another incident, 230 were injured in a single day as they protested few days after the terrible Beirut blast of August 4.[5]

The violence against the protesters was not only limited to the state's forces but also included sectarian parties. Specifically, members and supporters of political parties have used social networks and threats to attack journalists and activists critical of their parties in clear attempts to intimidate and silence them.[6] Moreover, the refusal of any forms of dissent has not stopped to social media networks but also took the form of physical assaults against activists and intellectuals opposed and critical of sectarian parties. The main objective through these shows of strength and intimidations was to quell the demonstrations and reoccupy in some cases public places in the regions dominated by the ruling sectarian parties.

Broadly, sections of the ruling sectarian neoliberal parties' popular base have been indeed acting as agents of repression for the protection of their leaders and to oppose any change of the system. Hezbollah was the most significant party to use forms of intimidations and violence, but this was not restricted to the party. Amal's members behaved in a similar manner in Shi'a majority-inhabited areas, while individuals affiliated with the Progressive Socialist Party (PSP) and Free Patriotic Movement (FPM), respectively, in the Chouf and the Metn also intimidated and even attacked protesters on various occasions.

The repression also took the form of assassinations of protesters and activists. A new level of violence was reached with the assassination, in February 2021, of writer and activist Lokman Slim,[7] a well-known critic of Hezbollah. Slim received several threats because of his political activity, including during the protest movement when leaflets accusing him of being a foreign agent and being instrumentalized by the United States were posted in front of his home in Haret Hreik.[8] While the identity of the killers remained unknown, this assassination was considered as a message to all forms of political dissidence of Hezbollah and Amal to silent them. Similarly, individuals involved in the investigation of the August 4 blast have also been assassinated. Joseph Bejjani, a photographer who participated in the tours in the port with some foreign investigators after the explosion, was gunned down outside his home in December 2020. His death was most probably connected to similar assassinations and mysterious deaths linked to the investigations of the Beirut Port blast, such as the deaths of Colonel Mounir Abou Rjeily and Colonel Joseph Skaf, both of whom worked at customs.[9]

Restricting Freedoms and Controlling Media

At the same time, Lebanese state authorities harassed journalists and activists through the use of defamation laws and unduly restricted people's rights to exercise their freedom of expression,[10] while sectarian parties also targeted them. According to Samir Kassir Eyes Center for Media and Cultural Freedom, nearly 200 media workers were assaulted by security forces and sectarian militias between October 2019 and March 2021 while covering protests and the economic crisis.[11]

Alongside these actions, sectarian ruling parties have attempted to restrict freedom of speech in the media outlets outside their control. In February 2021, Hezbollah through the voice of MP Hussein Hajj Hassan, who was occupying the position of chairman of the Parliamentary Information and Telecoms Committee, called to censor "defamatory" political content broadcast on Lebanese television channels, in an allusion in particular to the political program of the journalist Dima Sadek, who openly criticized Hezbollah following the assassination of intellectual Lokman Slim. The week before MP Hajj Hassan's statement, the television channel MTV, known for its editorial line critical of Hezbollah, was blocked in neighborhoods in the southern suburbs of Beirut, the Bekaa, and the south of the country, areas where Hezbollah and its supporters are the dominant actors.[12]

In addition to this, the Lebanese Press Editors' Union, controlled by the main ruling sectarian neoliberal parties such as Future Movement, FPM, Hezbollah, Amal, and PSP, held a meeting few days after these events titled "The reconsideration of the media profession in Lebanon and the need for a unifying law to regulate it."[13] The Union invited media officials from various Lebanese political parties and asked them to agree to a statement in support of the new draft law, without distributing it to them in advance for review. However, this did not prevent all political parties from approving the statement and to pressure parliament to pass the law.[14] The Lebanese Communist Party representative was the only one who disagreed and left the meeting, considering that this step is part of an agenda to restrict media and liberties.[15]

The deterioration of freedom of expression was reflected in the report of Reporters Sans Frontières (RSF) published in April 2021, which noted a rise in attacks on media personnel by protesters of sectarian neoliberal parties, police, and security forces. This was reflected in Lebanon's five-place loss in RSF's 2021 Index.[16]

Modes of Consents—Services and Job Opportunities

Violence and repressive tactics have considerably increased from the state and sectarian neoliberal ruling parties, but this was not the sole tool to maintain the domination of the ruling parties.

The patronage and clientelist networks were also useful to mobilize its own popular bases and maintain the passivity of large sectors of the society during the protests. For instance, recent research finds that public sector employees were largely underrepresented among protesters (1 percent) at the beginning of the protest movement.[17] In fact, the public sector employs today around 300,000 civil servants or 14 percent of total labor force—most of whom did not mobilize in October 2019 even though they likewise suffered from the economic crisis and the loss of their purchasing power.[18] This was mostly connected to the role of sectarian clientelism in public sector employment, but also the co-optation of the Union Coordination Committee (UCC) in 2015,[19] as further explained below. The control over a ministry has been key instruments by ruling sectarian parties to distribute resources (financial assistance, public investment in particular regions, or provision of a job) to its own popular base. These trends of nepotism and clientelism affect the entire public sector, going from schools to hospitals, passing through the judicial system.[20]

Similarly, large segments of the popular classes receiving particular services by the sectarian parties remain also largely passive. The deepening of the financial crisis and the subsequent COVID-19 pandemic provided opportunities for the ruling sectarian parties to provide services, such as campaigns to sanitize public spaces and distribute food to the needy in an attempt to rehabilitate their image. For instance, the Lebanese Forces provided bread and petrol vouchers to its partisans and supporters, alongside a health support system in various regions, such as Zahle and Bcharre, where they distributed medicines for free and/or sold other forms of drugs at a reduced price, while the PSP also distributed food boxes and aid in the Chouf, as well as fuel.[21] The distribution of anti-COVID vaccines was also used as a tool for political clientelism. The Qubayyat town council, in the northern region of Akkar, announced for instance in the end of March 2021 that it would be able to vaccinate some of its residents with Chinese vaccines purchased "thanks to a donation" from the family of the Saad Hariri.[22]

In this context, Hezbollah was one of the main actors benefiting from the financial crisis because of its massive networks of institutions and resources. In April 2021, Hezbollah started delivering to its popular basis a card called "al-Sajjad" to help people in need. This magnetic card can be used in the al-Nour cooperatives owned by the party, which are otherwise off-limits. The al-Sajjad cardholder enjoys a discount on food products available in the cooperative of up to 70 percent, up to a sum of 300,000 Lebanese pounds.[23] Hezbollah provided direct assistance to 50,000 impoverished families, stated Hezbollah MP Hassan Fadlallah in April 2021.[24] All these measures contributed to the continued policy of the party to establish and act as a state of its own within Lebanon.[25]

The dual use of coercion and consent allowed ruling sectarian neoliberal parties to maintain their hegemony on wide sectors of the population, especially in the absence of a political alternative.

Preventing the Building of a Popular, Social, and Democratic Alternative

The protest movement has lost momentum since October 2019 but never completely stopped despite the repression, the financial crisis, and the COVID-19 pandemic. The protest movement definitely recorded some victories initially in challenging the power of sectarian neoliberal parties after the withdrawal of the taxes that had triggered it, the resignation of Prime Minister Saad Hariri on October 29, 2019, and the electoral victory in some professional syndicates. Melhem Khalaf, an independent candidate from the civil movement, was elected head of the bar association, while the Bekaa League candidate Ali Yaghi, an independent supported by the protest movement, won the elections of the council of the order of dentists.[26] Moreover, in the end of 2020, university student elections witnessed significant victories in major private universities of independent democratic and secular lists opposed to all the ruling sectarian parties, which often decided not to run.[27] In addition to this, the coalition "the order revolts," featuring various political groups from the uprising and independents, won 15 out of 20 seats in four departments of the Order of Engineers and Architects, as well as 220 of 283 representative seats against the alliance of almost all ruling sectarian parties, which formed an united list despite being unable to form a government since August 2020.[28]

The protest movement, however, has faced many challenges, most notably the lack of mass organizations and alternative representations likely to counter the domination of sectarian neoliberal parties and ruling economic groups. There have been various and diverse organizational attempts by different social and political actors to structure the protest movement beyond sectarian and geographical differences, and channel the main demands, but unsuccessfully.

The protest movement has been and is still lacking the popular institutions to do so. Several political parties participated in the movement, notably leftist and democratic forces such as the Lebanese Communist Party, the *Mouwatinoun Wa Mouwatinat fi Dawla* (Citizens in a State) led by former minister Charbel Nahas, and civil society movements such as Beirut Madinati. Their representativeness at the street level nevertheless remains modest and sometimes criticized, especially at the level of their programs, by the more radical elements of the movement.[29] At the same time, smaller sectors of the left are very fragmented within the protest movement and have not been able so far to build a united front capable of channeling demands and organizing demonstrators across the country.

Furthermore, the weakness of trade union structures poses a recurring problem. Sectarian neoliberal parties have actively contributed to weakening independent trade union movements since the 1990s and then co-opting the main federation of trade unions, first the General Confederation of Lebanese Workers in 2000 and the UCC in 2015. The absence of autonomous and mass trade unions weakens the protest movement's ability to cohere itself into a social and political challenge to the sectarian parties and their system.

At the same time, some sectarian parties such as the Kataeb, and to a lesser extent the Lebanese Forces, tried to portray themselves as part of the protest movement and sought to ally with some liberal actors. This weakened the appeal of the protest movement for radical change and the main slogan "All Means All," while increasing tensions within the movement among different groups because many considered these parties to be major components of the sectarian system.[30] At the same time, these parties are seeking through these actions to reinforce their positions in the state's power structure and not to change the system.

The movement needs to develop mass organizations and progressive, inclusive, and nonsectarian parties rooted in the popular classes of Lebanon. The creation of forms of dual power is an urgent political necessity in order to challenge the state and the sectarian bourgeois political parties.

Preserving the Alliance with the Banks: A Pillar of the Sectarian Neoliberal System

The Lebanese sectarian ruling classes have similarly tried to secure the pillar of the Lebanese neoliberal system: the private banking sector. The rejection by the ruling sectarian parties of any serious challenges to the power of the banks is a mean to protect the political economy of the country, which they benefit from, and therefore the structures of power allowing their domination. There are many examples of close connections between the banks and ruling politicians, by acting as major shareholders such as well-known former prime minister Saad Hariri (major shareholder in BankMed) or as members of the banks' boards of directors.[31]

The strong collaboration between the Lebanese private banking sector and the Banque du Liban (BdL), on one side, and the ruling sectarian neoliberal parties has been consolidated after the end of the Lebanese Civil War. For instance, to fund a state plagued by corruption and patronage, the state took loans from local private banks at extremely high interest rates. In turn, private banks offered attractive rates to depositors, while achieving very comfortable margins. The mechanism paved the way for the artificially engineered USD-LBP peg in 1997 with the establishment of the parity of the Lebanese pound and the state's debt in dollars, which fueled the inflow of capital and kept afloat the ruling political elite system.[32] The banking sector particularly benefited from these policies. Between 1993 and 2019, the Lebanese state paid $87 billion in interest to the banks.[33] Over this period, public debt rose from $4.2 to $92 billion, an increase of more than 2,000 percent, while bank assets increased by more than 1,300 percent (reaching a total amount of $248.88 billion) and the GDP by only 370 percent.[34] The alliance between the ruling class and the banks was not ignored by large sectors of the protest movements. Specifically, groups of demonstrators targeted various banks and ransacked their respective head offices and branches in different regions of the country.[35] Protesters and activists targeted them because of their role in the country's current economic crisis and for allowing the big financiers to smuggle their money out of the country. Since the end of summer of 2019, depositors have been suffering unilateral and illegal banking restrictions on their withdrawals and transfers, in addition to the significant devaluation of the Lebanese Pound and the circulars adopted by the BdL authorizing the coexistence of several rates in the market. This has led many depositors to be forced accept large "haircuts" on the value of their deposits in order to collect portions of them. All this occurred with the total approval and collaboration of Lebanese state's authorities.[36]

After the country defaulted on its sovereign debt in March 2020, the Lebanese ruling sectarian neoliberal parties have sought to protect the Lebanese banking system. The country's banks and the BdL hold large portion of the debt denominated in Lebanese pounds.[37] The private banks and the BdL, supported by the ruling political class, do not want to bear responsibility for all of the losses attributed to them by the recovery plan of the former government of Prime Minister Diab. Discussions between Lebanon and the International Monetary Fund (IMF) started in mid-May 2020 to restructure its debt and negotiate a support program;[38] however, they have hardly progressed in spite of several meetings.

At the same time, the main ruling sectarian neoliberal parties have also prevented any real accountability on the actions of banks and politicians connected to them. At the end of May, a law lifting the banking secrecy was completely emptied of its substance. The text initially provided for the lifting of banking secrecy on accounts held in particular by ministers, deputies, civil servants, advisers, candidates (former and future) in legislative and municipal elections, and presidents of media boards, as well as by their spouses and children, in particular in cases of corruption and money laundering. The Speaker of Parliament, Nabih Berri, asked to remove the reference to "all judicial authorities in the framework of an investigation" among the parties authorized to lift bank secrecy.[39] This literally rendered the text inoperative in the absence of the establishment of a national commission against corruption.

In this context, major depositors, bankers, and the ruling elites were thus united in safeguarding a common interest capital, because if at the shareholder level the banks are more associated with the March 14 camp, the major depositors come from both camps. A similar scenario is occurring regarding the demand for a forensic audit of the BdL. A law eventually passed in the end of November 2020 after months of delays allowing for the lifting of the banking secrecy law for a period of one year on the accounts of the BdL and those of public institutions, namely those held at the BdL.[40] However, the new law does not include third parties, in other words private actors connected to the ruling class, which could hamper the action of auditors to trace the accounts of perpetrators/beneficiaries of acts of corruption and embezzlement in commercial banks.[41]

By opposing any measures challenging the power of banking sector and the BdL and demanding accountability for their actions, the sectarian ruling class is seeking to protect their modes of capital accumulation and the key pillar of the neoliberal system in Lebanon. This policy ran in complete opposition to the demands of large sectors of the protest movement for social justice and redistribution of wealth.

Conclusion

Despite their rivalries, the ruling sectarian neoliberal parties have indeed cooperated with one another at multiple points of crisis—as indicated by their similar attitudes toward labor and other social movements, their orientation toward neoliberal reform in Lebanon, and their cooperation in government following the departure of the Syrian army from Lebanon in 2005—and/or when the sectarian system is threatened by significant protest movements such as in October 2019 protest movement.

In this framework, they have used various counterrevolutionary tactics and strategies, through both coercive and consent means, in order to prevent the building of an inclusive social and political alternative and protect this economic and political system that serves their interests, while receiving the support of all their regional and imperialist state sponsors.

The demands of the protest movement of the October 2019 for social justice and economic redistribution cannot be separated from their opposition to the neoliberal-sectarian political system, which protects the privileges and wealth of the different fractions of the ruling classes.

The absolute necessity remains in Lebanon, and elsewhere, the building of mass political alternatives able to challenge the hegemony of ruling classes and their state.

Notes

1   The largest share of protesters were wage earners, informal workers, and students. According to a research conducted by Lea Bou Khater and Rima Majed, the average monthly income was relatively low, around US$998, while the majority of protesters are neither registered at the National Social Security Fund (NSSF) nor benefit from

private medical insurance, which underlines the precarity of social protection and safety nets.

2 See Chapter 7 of Rima Majed.

3 See Chapter 9 of Mona Harb.

4 Western countries led by the United States and Gulf monarchies called for an efficient and effective government, economic reform, and an end to endemic corruption. On its side, Hezbollah's sponsor, Iran's Supreme Leader Ayatollah Ali Khamenei blamed the United States and its allies (Israel and Saudi Arabia) for spreading "insecurity and turmoil" in Lebanon, as well as in Iraq, urging anti-government protesters in both countries to seek changes in a lawful way (see Chapter 8 of Jeffrey G. Karam).

5 Amnesty International, "Lebanon Must End Impunity for Human Rights Abuses Following UN Human Rights Council Review," 2021, http://bit.ly/3dFQXSf.

6 See Chapter 14 of Mortada Al-Amine.

7 Slim was the founder of UMAM Documentation and Research and Dar al-Jadid institutions. He transformed part of his home in Beirut's southern suburb of Haret Hreik into an exhibition and cultural center and has repeatedly expressed his criticism of Hezbollah policies.

8 After Slim was found killed, Hezbollah leader Hassan Nasrallah's son Jawad shared a tweet saying "Loss of some is in reality an unexpected gain and kindness for others" with the hashtag "no regret." He then deleted the tweet saying that it was personal and not intended in the way that some understood it as subtweet on the death of the activist.

9 The New Arab, "Lebanese Ex-Army Photographer Shot Dead Outside His Home," 2020, https://bit.ly/3xaKPrR.

10 Amnesty International, "Lebanon Must End Impunity for Human Rights Abuses Following UN Human Rights Council Review," 2021, http://bit.ly/3dFQXSf

11 Aya Mahzoub, "Freedom of speech in Lebanon Is Under Threat," *Middle East Institute*, 2021, https://bit.ly/3xjLPKl.

12 Anne Marie el-Hage, "Après une convocation par Hajj Hassan, des médias dénoncent une tentative de museler l'information," *Orient le Jour*, 2021, https://bit.ly /356ff2j.

13 Al Jadeed, "A Meeting of Media Officials in the Lebanese Parties in the Editors Syndicate and This Is What Was Agreed Upon," (in Arabic), 2021, https://bit.ly /3giDJL2.

14 Ibid.

15 Megaphone, "Political Parties Give their Blessings to Campaign Against Media," *Facebook*, 2021, http://bit.ly/2ZB0emy.

16 Reporters Sans Frontières, "RSF 2021 Index: Covid-19, Latest Ailment to Afflict Middle East's Moribund Media," April 2021, https://bit.ly/2RN592Y.

17 Lea Bou Khater and Rima Majed, "Lebanon's 2019 October Revolution: Who Mobilized and Why?" *Asfari Institute for Civil Society and Citizenship*, 2020, https://bit .ly/3aeEwuR,, 20.

18 The nature of state employment was, however, rather unequal in terms of distribution through the different institutions, as out of 300,000 Lebanese public employees in 2019, between 120,000 and 150,000 were active in the security forces and the Lebanese Armed Forces.

19 Lea Bou Khater, "Public Sector Mobilisation Despite a Dormant Workers' Movement," *Confluences Méditerranée* 92 (2015): 125–42.

20 Magali Abboud, Joseph Farchakh, Kenza Ouazzani, and Anthony Samrani, "In Lebanon, the Clientelist Octopus is in Need of Food," *L'Orient Today*, 2020, https://bit.ly/3geO3oE.

21 Hussein Tleiss, "Lebanon Returns to the Era of 'rations'. . . and the Parties Display Their 'primitive achievements' with High Technologies" (in Arabic), *al-Hurra*, 2021, https://arbne.ws/3cFjUfN.

22 Lorenzo Trombetta, "COVID Vaccines Used for Political Clientelism in Lebanon," *Ansa Med*, 2021, https://bit.ly/3vfZxMA.

23 Yassine Mohammad, "Ces militants chiites menacés pour avoir critiqué le Hezbollah," *Orient le Jour*, April 19, 2021, https://bit.ly/3vHuudv.

24 Orient Le Jour, "Le Hezbollah fournit une aide à 50.000 familles, selon le député Fadlallah," 2021, https://bit.ly/3gbl05f.

25 For more see Daher Joseph, *Hezbollah: The Political Economy of Lebanon's Party of God* (London: Pluto Press, 2016).

26 Walid Hussayn, "Dentists' Union: An Independent Candidate Elected with the Support of the Parties!" (in Arabic) *Al-Modon*, 2019, http://bit.ly/3cOC3GI.

27 Kareem Chehayeb, "Lebanon: Sectarian Parties Trounced in Unprecedented Student Elections," *Middle East Eye*, 2020, https://bit.ly/3zjR4eL.

28 Claude Assaf, "Raz-de-marée de la thaoura à l'ordre des ingénieurs," *Orient le Jour*, 2021, https://bit.ly/3w9bWCt.

29 Informal discussions with leftist activists in February 2020 in Beirut, Lebanon.

30 Jalk Jeanine, "Comment les Forces libanaises tentent de surfer sur la revolution," *Orient le Jour*, 2021, https://bit.ly/35irHMz.

31 Nada Maucourant Atallah and Omar Tamo, "Banquiers et Politiques, Une Grande Famille," *Commerce du Levant*, 2020, http://bit.ly/3sDUtln.

32 Salah al-Attar, "Toufic Gaspard: « Ceux qui ont provoqué la crise ne peuvent pas la résoudre," *Commerce du Levant*, 2020, https://bit.ly/3iHo1Me.

33 Nada Maucourant Atallah and Omar Tamo, "Banquiers et Politiques, Une Grande Famille," *Commerce du Levant*, 2020, http://bit.ly/3sDUtln.

34 Ibid.

35 See Chapter 24 of Mohamad Bzeih.

36 Orient Le Jour, "Contrôle des capitaux: le FMI critique poliment le réveil tardif des deputes," 2021, https://bit.ly/3cGWtmi.

37 In October 2020, Lebanese banks held 28 percent of the debt denominated in Lebanese Pound, with 60 percent held by the Central Bank (Reuters Staff, "Factbox: Lebanon's Spiralling Economic Crisis," 2020, https://reut.rs/2RHNfiq).

38 Reuters Staff, "IMF Urges Lebanese to Unite Around Government Financial Rescue Plan," 2020, https://reut.rs/35hbh6Z.

39 Orient le Jour, "Trois textes de loi sur 27 adoptés, l'amnistie fait sauter la séance," *Orient le Jour*, 2020, https://bit.ly/3pM79Wg.

40 Maggy Abboud and Phillipe Hage Boutros, "La Levée Temporaire et Ciblée du Secret Bancaire Pour Faciliter l'Audit de la BDL Pose Nombre de Questions," *Orient le Jour*, 2020, http://bit.ly/3d1kW70.

41 Ibid.

17

The Lebanese* Uprising

Revisions from Refugees and Migrants

Moné Makkawi

Palestinian refugees launched the Lebanese uprising. In July of 2019, months before millions of protestors flooded Lebanon's streets, inaugurating the start of Lebanon's revolutionary uprising, demonstrations erupted in the Palestinian refugee camps across Lebanon, protesting new Ministry of Labor (MoL) restrictions on refugee work opportunities.[1] Colloquially dubbed the Camp Revolts, Palestinians gathered, marched, and held general strikes to underscore the centrality of refugee labor and demand their right to dignified livelihoods.[2] Overlapping with and overshadowed by the start of the uprising three months later, refugees began attending Lebanese demonstrations while carrying out their own. The Camp Revolts were prophetic: the strikes' core demands and emphasis on class solidarity across sect, camp, and nation dovetailed—in practice and rhetoric—with Lebanon's countrywide protests.

The significance of noncitizens to Lebanon's political history, economic development, and social fabric is often underrepresented, and the case of Lebanon's revolutionary process has been no different. Despite speaking to and emerging out of many of the same issues that sparked the Lebanese uprising, the Camp Revolts have been largely absent from analyses concerning the lead up to Lebanon's revolutionary fervor. Missing too are critical reflections on the spectrum of refugee and migrant involvement throughout the uprising, as protestors, critics, role models, leaders, and scapegoats. These gaps are particularly glaring when considering that non-Lebanese communities make up (at least) one-third of Lebanon's population.[3] Complicating these dynamics are the ways in which migrants and refugees in Lebanon are unwilling participants in, yet most affected by, the racial capitalism, government corruption, and systematic inequity that engendered the uprising and web of compounding crises that emerged in its wake.

Against that discursive separation, this chapter reexamines Lebanon's shifting political landscape since 2019, suggesting that any analysis of the uprising remains incomplete without addressing the actions and experiences of refugees and migrants throughout. The chapter begins by extending the timeline of Lebanon's uprising to include the Camp Revolts. In the first section, the Camp Revolts serve as a launchpad for multiple goals: recontextualizing underlying causes of the uprising, supplementing understandings of uprising strengths, and outlining the stakes involved in including refugee and migrant narratives. The second section further integrates noncitizen perspectives to reconsider the uprising's shortcomings. Far from a complete account of their experiences, I suggest that in foregrounding refugees and migrants, we gain a richer understanding of Lebanon's uprising and a deeper capacity to articulate its revolutionary future.

New Timelines, New Solidarity

Months before proposed taxes on Voice over internet protocol calls—a move widely commemorated as sparking the uprising—government officials sought to counter mounting discontent with Lebanon's worsening economic crisis via crackdowns on noncitizen laborers. In early June of 2019, Minister of Labor Kamal Abusuleiman announced a one-month deadline for business owners to obtain work permits for foreign nationals, including those with refugee status.[4] Despite MoL claims to the contrary,[5] the renewed push to enforce regulations on foreign workers directly affected Palestinians, who are denied clear legal status and protection under Lebanese law.[6] After the deadline MoL officials issued citations, made arrests, shuttered noncompliant (refugee-owned) shops, and dismissed Palestinian workers from their jobs.[7] In response, demonstrations erupted in and around the camps, which soon after blossomed into a popular, decentralized, and coordinated movement across all twelve refugee camps.

The intensity of the Palestinian response to the MoL decision underscored how early on, refugee communities were hit hardest by and mobilizing against the matrix of dispossessive conditions that became rallying cries for the uprising. Compounded by years of sociopolitical oppression,[8] the chronic unemployment, (hyper)inflation, skyrocketing national debt, and political negligence that came to a crescendo in 2019 had already taken a major toll on Palestinian refugees: in 2015, 65 percent of Palestinians were reported as living below the poverty line and Palestinian unemployment had reached 56 percent.[9] The MoL decision effectively eliminated remaining labor markets accessible to Palestinians, rendering refugees particularly vulnerable as Lebanon's banking sector faced a dollar shortage and the economy stagnated. And while Camp Revolt demands grew to address the spectrum of issues Palestinians face in Lebanon, they also spoke to issues implicating communities across the country, namely the suffocating nature of Lebanon's neoliberal system.

By no coincidence then, the Camp Revolts and uprising converged, with Lebanese protestors echoing many of the same frustrations Palestinians had addressed over the summer. Equally significant were continuities in protestor tactics, demands, and motives, with questions of class, solidarity, and coalition-building bridging both movements. The Camp Revolts intervened against decades of economic, political, and socio-spatial marginalization, carving out public space for Palestinians demanding civil and workers' rights while underscoring refugee centrality to urban capital accumulation.[10] Likewise, the early uprising was characterized by cross-class mobilizations composed of varying socioeconomic groups, religious sects, genders, and ages. Across the country, protestors responded to regional, identitarian, and neoliberal fragmentation long reinforced by Lebanon's oligarchy.[11] Within cities, protestors painted anti-capitalist graffiti and smashed bank windows; between cities, protestors introduced new channels of communication to express solidarity.[12]

Strategies for challenging segregative geographies bled from one movement into the other. Across both, the co-option and manipulation of urban space served as ways to disrupt flows of capital, amplify demands, and craft new forms of claims-making. For example, public protests held during the Camp Revolts asserted Palestinian identity and joy in a Lebanese public sphere that socially rejects Palestinians yet remains indisputably dependent on their labor. Simultaneously, and underscored by general strikes across camps, Palestinian centrality loomed large through a discernable absence—of roadside vendors and agricultural workers, empty vegetable market stalls, and unpurchased produce left to rot.[13] In parallel, Lebanese protestors also fought urban battles, reclaiming privatized beachfronts, abandoned buildings, and green spaces, symbols of a ruling class that long privileged tourists, real estate speculation, and glitzy aesthetics over cultural heritage, local communities, and accessibility. Novel political collectivities flowed from the Camp Revolts into the uprising: during the Camp Revolts, Palestinians forged new trans-camp mutual aid networks for organizing in consensus and upholding their boycott of Lebanese goods.[14] From the uprising's start, sites like Beirut's downtown—a capitalist shrine of restaurants and malls—became spaces for teach-ins, film screenings, and community art.[15]

Here, reading the uprising through legacies of the Camp Revolts nuances a "disruptive potential" for emancipation.[16] Because the phenomenon of class is tied to processes of urbanization, where (re)producing capitalism requires both exploiting poor communities for surplus value and urban sites for absorbing that surplus, Lebanese and noncitizen attempts to reclaim urban environments reveal interconnected goals of recovering the social value of city spaces and demanding collective dignity.[17] Not only do these transformations signal possibilities for reimagining urban space through community ideals over nationality, sect, and region, they also demonstrate shared stakes involved in redefining social collaboration to defy securitarian governance and neoliberal market rule. Noncitizen participation demonstrates that this is best done by excavating visions of class coevality and anti-racism.

Though diverse in practice, noncitizen support that materialized during the uprising often embodied a commitment to ideals of revolution and class-based solidarity beyond strategic or rhetorical similarities.[18] In part, this was evidenced by the fact that a small, yet noteworthy number of refugees and migrants shaped how the uprising unfolded from the beginning, as vocal and active participants to the uprising's achievements and discursive development. Some helped charge an already electric atmosphere by joining protests, while others took the opportunity to voice their grievances and contribute to a growing list of protestor demands.[19] Many who did not attend protests voiced support online or remotely.[20] One video from October 20 was particularly inspiring, showing Palestinians in Ein al-Helwa camp (heart of the Camp Revolts) enthusiastically dancing, waving Lebanese flags, and chanting, "*min ein al-helwa tahiyeh le thawrat libnaniye*" (from Ein al-Helwa (camp) a salute to the Lebanese Revolution).[21]

For some noncitizens, the uprising signified a necessary continuation of self-determination movements. Some Syrians felt hopeful, the uprising indicating renewed sentiments of pan-Arab unity seen during the 2011 Arab Spring; many Palestinians saw the uprising as a natural extension of the Camp Revolts.[22] Several Syrians shared advice from experiences of revolt in Syria, aiming to help Lebanon's uprising avoid the fate of Syria's revolution.[23] Public declarations of solidarity and encouragement emerged from Syrians in the diaspora, Idlib, etc.[24] That non-Lebanese communities believed in the uprising's goals is evidenced too by how some refugees continued to show up to demonstrations despite mounting danger. Friends from camps in Tyre, for instance, attended even after Hezbollah and Harakat Amal members allegedly trashed protestor tents in downtown Tyre or the Lebanese army prohibited anyone with Palestinian identification from entering protest areas.[25]

Complementing matters of principle, some Palestinians and Syrians felt welcomed into and emotionally connected with the uprising, underscoring the growing impact and evolution of intersectional coalition-building in Lebanon. Remixes of famous Syrian songs and banners,[26] pro-refugee art, chants, and marches, the presence of Palestinian flags and keffiyehs, and teach-ins centering the rights of domestic migrant workers (DMWs) were interspersed throughout Lebanon's various landscapes of protest. These unprecedented displays of solidarity were especially significant because for some noncitizens they signaled novel moments, however brief, of feeling *seen* in Lebanon. For example, in response to a demonstration in solidarity with Gazans, a friend from Burj al-Shemali Camp posted pictures on Facebook and wrote that it was his "first time hearing the Palestinian national anthem on Tyre's streets."[27] Another friend mentioned feeling safe and free to express himself, something unimaginable during the Syrian revolution when regime forces would arrive and shoot at protestors within minutes.[28] Others revealed that, for the first time, they felt the Lebanese flag was not a symbol weaponized against them.[29]

These experiences were, in large part, a testament to the thoughtful and diligent organizing of feminist activists before and during the uprising, a number of whom were refugees or migrants themselves. Among the most radical in their demands, feminists centered LGBTQ+ issues, race, gender, labor, and noncitizens in their mobilizing, leading chants like the instantly iconic "*laja'een juwa juwa, Bassil bara bara*" ("refugees in, [Gibran] Bassil out").[30] These activists have always incorporated revolutionary visions of global scale into their organizing; unsurprisingly, many marched and coordinated protests in solidarity with Palestinians during the Camp Revolts.[31] And though a small percentage of protestors, feminist activists included noncitizens into uprising spaces, often risking personal safety.[32] That their chants gained traction with other protestors highlights growing attention to the interconnectivity of struggles beyond the scope of Lebanese politics, something missing from 2015's "You Stink" protests, for example.[33] Such shifts demonstrate how noncitizens consistently frontline the crafting of progressive discourse in Lebanon, literally and figuratively.

Increased collaborations between Lebanese and noncitizens, alongside the appearance of alternative coalitions, suggest flourishing opportunities to reclaim union(ized) spaces or organize along shared interests of socioeconomic status instead of fabricated identitarianism. As the Camp Revolts or progress in DMW union contract negotiations confirm, folding refugees and migrant workers into movement organizing is crucial to advance grassroots mobilizing in Lebanon.[34] These communities have always couched their demands within broader questions of class struggle and constitute(d) a substantial part of Lebanon's workforce, scaffolding construction, agriculture, and leisure industries, to name a few.[35] Noncitizens have already established efficient mutual aid networks, formed diverse coalitions, and withheld labor for strategic strikes.[36] Understanding and building on momentum seen during the uprising therefore necessitates including refugees and migrants if recent showings of solidarity are to become foundations for future solidarity.

Revolution's Impasse

Despite promising displays of solidarity, idealized accounts of inclusivity do not adequately capture noncitizen experiences of the uprising, where most felt hesitant or afraid of attending demonstrations, briefly participating, if at all. Importantly, these experiences highlight existent myopia in Lebanon's uprising.

The nationalist thread that was woven throughout the uprising threatens its legacy as both inclusive and revolutionary. Early demonstrations saw a range of emotions and communities represented; protestors were largely united by a shared disavowal of Lebanese sectarianism and neoliberalism. There was a widespread populism embodied by a sea of Lebanese flags, the Lebanese national anthem, and other nationalist songs like Julia Boutrous's *mawtini* flooding the streets. And while overcoming sectarian divisions marked an important step forward, such stunning displays of Lebanese nationalism did not pose effective, let alone progressive, counters to the institutionalized political sectarianism that protestors aimed to challenge.[37] In fact, what were for many Lebanese transcendent moments of national unity were for noncitizens reiterations of the same inflammatory rhetoric long used to justify Palestinian and Syrian subjugation, often propagated by the same oligarchy Lebanese claimed to be protesting.[38] As a result, many refugees and migrant workers were indifferent, torn, or apprehensive about joining protests, fearing that they would be interrogated about their intentions, that their presence would somehow undermine the validity of Lebanese demands, or that it was simply none of their business.[39]

But underlying this atmosphere of exclusivity were also (learned) anticipations and experiences of social and institutional violence. For some Syrians, omnipresent Lebanese flags (and even some Lebanese Armed Forces—LAF flags) as (allegedly neutral) alternatives to flags of political parties were stark reminders of their transience and forced exile, conditions inextricable from LAF policing of Syrians and LAF's connection to the Syrian regime.[40] Refugees feared that attending protests would lead to their being labeled as instigators or result in (misdirected, (un)intentional) violence from protestors and Lebanese soldiers, loss of vital residency permits, illegitimate detention, and deportation.[41] Tragically, some of these fears were realized, for example, when Palestinians were blamed for the burning down of Tyre's Resthouse[42] or when two Syrian workers died on the second day of the uprising.[43]

Lebanese citizens and protestors should not be absolved of their complicity in realizing and safeguarding politics of exclusion or oppression, especially as they purported to demand their own civil rights. Some Lebanese protestors maintained that the uprising was for Lebanese people first and foremost; for example, Palestinians in Lebanon and abroad were told to lower Palestinian flags they had brought to demonstrations, and discussions of the uprising on Twitter were littered with xenophobic and racist accusations levied at refugees.[44] Though these sentiments were not shared by every Lebanese protestor, it is important to note the presence of Lebanese prejudice during the uprising and how they materialized as violence enacted by ordinary people. For instance, as the uprising began, many DMWs, subject to the Kafala system's neo-slavery and barred from leaving the homes of their employers, could not imagine attending protests.[45] Disparities marking who the revolution was for only grew as shifting uprising dynamics coalesced with escalating crises. By early 2020 Lebanese employers capitalized on deteriorating economic conditions to further exploit DMWs. Employers withheld salaries, paid workers in lira (Lebanon's official currency, the Lebanese pound—LBP) without accounting for devaluation, and even forcibly detained workers.[46] Many dehumanizing acts were exacerbations of long-standing abuses, but new and expressly heinous was how some sponsors claimed they could no longer afford workers' salaries and abandoned migrants in front of their consulates and embassies, often without their passports or belongings.[47]

Discrepancies between Lebanese actions and demands throughout the uprising present a formidable obstacle for the evolution of Lebanon's revolutionary process because they mark a persistent refusal to confront sociopolitical interconnections between Lebanese and non-Lebanese communities. For example, during the uprising, while some protestors asserted that a post-sectarianism government should prioritize Lebanese, it follows that eradicating sectarianism for a more just form of governance would also subvert arguments used to legitimize refugee marginalization—namely, that refugees pose a demographic threat to the confessional balance.[48] More broadly, mobilizations of Lebanon's security apparatus could be better understood and contested if noncitizen experiences are considered. *Deuxieme Bureau*'s policing of Palestinian camps in the 1950s and 1960s, militarized checkpoints limiting refugee movement, or gendered sousveillance of DMW in Lebanese homes, all shaped and sharpened the repression, torture, and surveillance protestors faced during the uprising.[49]

Further, these short sights buoy and fortify counterrevolutionary movements.[50] Emboldened Lebanese nationalism and enhanced perceptions of noncitizens as "others" empower a ruling class that seeks to cultivate polarization between communities. Thinking back to the Camp Revolts, many refugees (and importantly, some Lebanese) emphasized that the MoL campaign was not random but, rather, emerged amid ongoing crackdowns on—and illegal deportations of—Syrians.[51] Activists branded the MoL move an obvious attempt to occlude their own culpability in Lebanon's politico-economic crises by pitting Lebanese people against vulnerable communities with xenophobic and racialized scapegoating. Lebanon's politicians have long orchestrated incendiary propaganda to frame "illegal" foreign labor as principal threat to the Lebanese working class[52]—as if ruling elites had not accumulated vast amounts of wealth by intentionally undercutting the local workforce with cheap migrant labor,[53] crushed union movements after the civil war,[54] or promoted neoliberal austerity measures that gutted the public sector and social safety nets during Rafiq Hariri's era as prime minister.[55]

Likewise, inflammatory rhetoric deployed by ruling elites during the uprising often invoked the civil war,[56] a dog whistle for Syrian occupation and postwar tropes that painted Palestinians as a fifth column undermining Lebanese sovereignty. These are not subtle hints or cryptic messages hidden in politician speeches but accusations levied at refugees from the highest reaches of the Lebanese government, amplified by national news and media outlets.[57] When these dynamics are replicated in domestic spheres and revolution squares, they unnecessarily heighten tensions with noncitizen communities, undercut possibilities for collaboration in the streets, and strengthen the very coercive apparatus protestors hope to abolish. Consequently, the ruling class has, so far, dodged accountability and weathered the uprising to emerge largely unscathed, even consolidating power and championing themselves as saviors to culminating crises in 2020.[58] For example, when sectarian political elites attempted to resuscitate their reputations and augment a botched COVID-19 response while also enacting discriminatory lockdowns on refugee communities, implying that refugees constitute a public health risk.[59] Importantly, these divide-and-conquer schemes reveal that socioeconomic crises Lebanese face today are not recent or incidental but systematic and by design—as extractive and exploitative machinations often are.

Although revolutionary movements are shaped by competing ideological streams,[60] confronting their dissonance is key. Attempts to challenge counterrevolutionary movements and solidify revolutionary organizing must include noncitizens, in great part because their lives, wellness, sovereignty, and aspirations are the most affected by political turbulence in Lebanon. Refugees and migrants can contribute histories of socialist and anti-colonial organizing,[61] desperately needed guidance for a movement that has yet to produce a unifying political vision beyond romanticized identitarianism. Further, noncitizens have already enacted clear alternatives to the prevailing status quo, supporting their own communities in the state's absence.[62] Blueprints exist, but enacting them requires, beyond moments of collectivity and encounter, a sacrifice of specific Lebanese lifeworlds that have not fully acknowledged entanglements of class, race, gender, and empire. Without doing so, the uprising's capacity for meaningful progress will remain stunted.

Conclusion: *Kilna Ya'ne Kilna* (All of Us Means All of Us)

The actions and experiences of noncitizens continue(d) to shape understandings of revolt in Lebanon, even after the initial surge of uprising demonstrations. As protests progressed intermittently throughout 2020 and 2021, noncitizens continued to bear the brunt of Lebanon's multilayered crises, the reverberations of which were amplified along the lines of class, race, and gender. The spread of COVID-19 saw increased surveillance, policing, and limitations of movement on DMWs and refugees.[63] Simultaneously, as the lira plummeted in value, many refugees and migrants had no choice but to work through the pandemic, delivering food so that Lebanese citizens could quarantine; shopping at supermarkets for their sponsors; and picking fruit and vegetables for distribution across Lebanon and abroad without pause.[64] Consequently, Palestinians and Syrians have died from COVID-19 three and four times more than the national average, respectively, and remain underrepresented in Lebanon's vaccine rollout.[65] After the Beirut Port explosion, protests again took on new urgency. On August 4, 2020, 2,750 tons of ammonium nitrate—improperly stored for 6 years—exploded, decimating the port and part of Beirut, killing 207 people, and rendering approximately 300,000 homeless. Again, refugees and migrants felt the ramifications most acutely, with much of the destroyed or damaged housing belonging to low-income migrant communities. Syrians also faced a wave of forced evictions, displaced by rubble and landlords alike.[66] Concurrently, as employer abuse worsened, DMW ramped up demands for repatriation, with many eventually leaving Lebanon.[67]

While writing this chapter, the lira hit a record high of 18,000 LBP to the USD, sparking another wave of protests with renewed intensity. The next stage that unfolds in Lebanon's revolutionary process will mark another test and opportunity to think more strategically. Lebanese protestors should take note of how noncitizens in Lebanon have long incorporated a broader architecture of oppression in their organizing—as Palestinians stressed during the Camp Revolts, they are not *foreign* but *forcibly displaced* workers.[68] Just as Palestinians linked labor issues to colonial dispossession, Lebanese must connect frustrations with corruption or sectarianism to wider political constellations and structural conditions. Embracing demands like optional citizenship for refugees and migrants, reparations for DMW, or Palestinian representation in Lebanon's government, among others, are not suggestions but prerequisites for Lebanese liberation. It is only when the interests of refugees and migrants are reflected and centered within Lebanese political organizing will Lebanon's revolutionary uprising become a revolution.

Notes

1 Julia Kassem, "Lebanon's Labor Minister Vows to Continue Crackdown Despite Wave of Protests," *Mondoweiss*, August 20, 2019, https://mondoweiss.net/2019/08/lebanons-minister-crackdown/.

2 See Moné Makkawi, "Your Decision and Ours: Palestinian Strikes in Lebanon and Contemporary Urban Rights," *Arab Urbanism Magazine*, 1, August 2020. https://www.araburbanism.com/magazine/your-decision-and-ours.

3 Human Rights Watch, "Lebanon: Refugees, Migrants Left Behind in Vaccine Rollout," April 6, 2021, https://www.hrw.org/news/2021/04/06/lebanon-refugees-migrants-left-behind-vaccine-rollout.

4 Amena ElAshkar, "Palestinian Refugees in Lebanon Denounce New 'Inhumane' Work Restrictions," *Middle East Eye*, July 23, 2019, https://www.middleeasteye.net/news/palestinian-refugees-lebanon-denounce-latest-work-restrictions.

5 Camille Abusleiman, (@camilleasleiman), "We Are Ready to Provide All Facilities for Palestinian Workers to Obtain Work Permits," *Twitter*, July 18, 2019, https://twitter.com/camilleasleiman/status/1151937432679587840.

6 Palestinians in Lebanon are subject to discriminatory anti-naturalization laws and murky legal framework categorizing them as either foreigner or refugee. Today,

Palestinians cannot own land, work in over thirty-nine syndicated professions, or move freely within Lebanon, among other restrictions.

7 Marie Kortam, "Lebanon: Anger in Palestinian Refugee Camps Gives Rise to a New Mobilization for Dignity," *Arab Reform Initiative*, August 14, 2019, https://www.arab -reform.net/publication/lebanon-anger-in-palestinian-refugee-camps-gives-rise-to-a -new-movement-for-dignity/.

8 See Sara Kaddoura, "The Camp Movement Was Killed, But it Revived Something in us," *Sawt al Niswa*, https://sawtalniswa.org/article/647, and Islam Khatib and Hana Sleiman, "حراك المخيّمات الفلسطينية في لبنان: محاولة جديدة للخروج من الهامش" August 9, 2019, https://www .7iber.com/politics-economics/حراك-المخيّمات-الفلسطينية-في-لبنان/.

9 Jad Chaaban, Nisreen Salti, Hala Ghattas, Alexandra Irani, Tala Ismail, and Lara Batlouni, "Survey on the Socioeconomic Status of Palestine Refugees in Lebanon," Report published by the American University of Beirut and the United Nations Relief and Works Agency, 2015.

10 International Labour Organization (ILO) and Committee for the Employment of Palestinian Refugees in Lebanon (CEP), *Palestinian Employment in Lebanon: Facts and Challenges. Labour Force Survey Among Palestinian Refugees Living in Camps and gatherings in Lebanon* (Beirut: ILO Regional Office for the Arab States and CEP, 2014), 54.

11 See Julia Vizoso, "What Is Oligarchy?" *The Public Source*, February 18, 2020, https:// thepublicsource.org/what-oligarchy.

12 See Mona Harb's chapter in this volume.

13 Borj News, حسبة صيدا, Facebook, July 16, 2019, https://www.facebook.com/borjNews/ posts/891979951159492.

14 Makkawi, "Your Decision and Ours."

15 Mona Fawaz and Isabela Serhan, "Urban Revolutions: Lebanon's October 2019 Uprising," *IJURR*, October 2020. https://www.ijurr.org/spotlight-on/urban-revolts/ urban-revolutions-lebanons-october-2019-uprising/.

16 Mona Fawaz, "Beirut Madinati and the Prospects of Urban Citizenship," *The Century Foundation*, April 16, 2019, https://tcf.org/content/report/beirut-madinati-prospects -urban-citizenship/?agreed=1&agreed=1.

17 David Harvey, *Rebel Cities: From the Right to the City to the Urban Revolution* (New York: Verso, 2019).

18 Mat Nashed, "Refugees Deserve a Place in Lebanon's Uprising," *Ozy*, November 4, 2019, https://www.ozy.com/news-and-politics/refugees-need-a-place-in-lebanons-uprising /228431/, Sara Kaddoura, "فلسطينيات-في-الشارع-دخلنا-ما-دخلنا," October 24, 2019, https:// suhmatiya.wordpress.com/2019/10/24/ فلسطينيات-في-الشارع-دخلنا-ما-دخلن/.

19 Nashed, "Refugees Deserve a Place in Lebanon's Uprising."

20 Taha Bali (@tahabito), "I'm Starting a Thread to Capture the Ways Syria & Syrian Revolution Are Being Featured in the ongoing, *beautiful* Lebanese protests," *Twitter*. October 20, 2019, https://twitter.com/tahabito/status/1185909363338338305, Irene Tuzi, "The Syrian Participation in Lebanon's Revolution," *ISPI*, March 13, 2020, https://www.ispionline.it/en/pubblicazione/syrian-participation-lebanons-revolution -25369.

21 Sara Kaddoura (@hakinasawi), "من عين الحلوة تحيّة للثورة اللبنانية." *Twitter*, October 20, 2019, https://twitter.com/hakinasawi/status/1185857830299021313.

22 Tuzi, "The Syrian Participation in Lebanon's Revolution," Muzna al-Masri, Zeina Abla, and Rana Hassan, "Envisioning and Contesting a New Lebanon?" *International Alert*, August 2020. PDF.

23　Yazan Al-Saadi, "From Hope to Dismay: How Crises Affect Syrians in Lebanon," *The Public Source*, May 8, 2020, https://thepublicsource.org/hope-dismay-how-crises-affect-syrians-lebanon.

24　Bali, "I'm Starting a Thread to Capture the Ways Syria."

25　Bahaa Joumaa, "قرار جديد بساحة العلم بصور," *Facebook*, November 27, 2019, https://www.facebook.com/bob.a7la.7ob.

26　Issa, "What Translationality."

27　Bahaa Joumaa, "النشيد الوطني الفلسطيني من ساحة الثورة," *Facebook*, November 14, 2019, https://www.facebook.com/bob.a7la.7ob.

28　WhatsApp message to author, April 3, 2021.

29　Kaddoura, "فلسطينيات-في-الشارع-دخلنا،-ما-دخلنا."

30　Amany Khalifa, (@Amanykhalefa), "هي الصبية عظيمة," *Twitter*, October 19, 2019, https://twitter.com/Amanykhalefa/status/1185578436632436736.

31　Sara Kaddoura, (@hakinasawi), "الاصدقاء اللبنانيات/ين," *Twitter*, July 27, 2019, https://twitter.com/hakinasawi/status/1155118014880239616, Sara Kaddoura (@hakinasawi), "اليوم فاتت مسيرة إلى مخيم شاتيلا," *Twitter*, August 9, 2019, https://twitter.com/hakinasawi/status/1159889313397649409.

32　Helen Patuck, "Refugees and the Lebanese Revolution," *MENA Solidarity Network*, April 18, 2020, https://menasolidaritynetwork.com/2020/04/18/refugees-and-the-lebanese-revolution/.

33　Sara Kaddoura (@hakinasawi), "من أكثر الأمور الفخورة فيها بهالثورة هو إنه الهتافات يلي طلعت فيها المجموعة النسوية صارت علسان الكل," *Twitter*, November 19, 2019, https://twitter.com/hakinasawi/status/1196787067189112832, Rima Majed, "The Lebanese Revolution Advances," *Redflag*, February 12, 2020, https://redflag.org.au/node/7016.

34　Human Rights Watch, "Lebanon: New Safeguards for Migrant Domestic Workers," September 18, 2020, https://www.hrw.org/news/2020/09/18/lebanon-new-safeguards-migrant-domestic-workers.

35　See Nadim el Kak's chapter in this volume.

36　Richard Hall, "The Secret Networks Saving Lebanon's Migrant Maids from Abuse," *The Guardian*, August 1, 2018, https://amp.theguardian.com/global-development/2018/aug/01/secret-networks-rescuing-lebanon-migrant-maids-from-abuse?__twitter_impression=true, Aya Majzoub, "RAMCO Strike a Key Moment for Labor Rights in Lebanon," *Human Rights Watch*, June 5, 2020, https://www.hrw.org/news/2020/06/05/ramco-strike-key-moment-labor-rights-lebanon.

37　Rima Majed, "Lebanon's 'October Revolution' Must Go on!" *Open Democracy*, October 20, 2019, https://www.opendemocracy.net/en/north-africa-west-asia/lebanons-october-revolution-must-go-on/.

38　Ibid.

39　WhatsApp messages to author, March 7, 2021.

40　Dara Foi'Elle and Joey Ayoub, "Syrian Melancholy in Lebanon's Revolution," *Aljumhuriya*, December 6, 2019, https://www.aljumhuriya.net/en/content/syrian-melancholy-lebanons-revolution.

41　Kaddoura, "فلسطينيات-في-الشارع-دخلنا،-ما-دخلنا."

42　Lebanon News, "Lebanese and Palestinians Arrested on Charges of Vandalizing Tyre's Resthouse," October 22, 2019, https://web.archive.org/web/20191103034939/https://www.lbcgroup.tv/news/d/lebanon-news/478090/lebanese-and-palestinians-arrested-on-charges-of-v/en.

43　Activists held a vigil for the Syrian workers, even including their names in chants and statements as martyrs of the uprising. Though well-intentioned, Ibrahim Younis and Ibrahim Hussein's deaths did not occupy prominent space in the uprising's narrative. Naming the two workers "martyrs" occurred without consent from the families, compensation was never paid for the deaths, and no accountability for those responsible followed. Al-Saadi, "From Hope to Dismay."

44 Patuck, "Refugees and the Lebanese Revolution."

45 Banchi Yimer, "The Lebanese Revolution: A New Chapter of Kafala Misery," *The Public Source*, February 18, 2020, https://thepublicsource.org/lebanese-revolution -kafala-misery.

46 Ibid.

47 Sara el-Deeb, "Lebanon's Migrant Workers' Plight Worsens as Crises Multiply," *AP*, May 26, 2020, https://apnews.com/article/ethiopia-embassies-financial-markets-ap -top-news-virus-outbreak-e4be0f5eeaeec1e1174d90bf17159e8f.

48 Nashed, "Refugees Deserve a Place in Lebanon's Uprising."

49 Rosemary Sayigh, *Palestinians: From Peasants to Revolutionaries* (London: Zed books, 1979), Andrew Arsan, *Lebanon: A Country in Fragments* (London: C. Hurst (Publishers) Limited, 2018).

50 See Joseph Daher's chapter in this volume.

51 Human Rights Watch, "Lebanon: Syrians Summarily Deported From Airport," May 24, 2019, https://www.hrw.org/news/2019/05/24/lebanon-syrians-summarily -deported-airport.

52 Elias Abou-Jaoude and Joey Ayoub, "Lebanon's Scapegoating of Refugees Did Not Start With Syrians, but With Palestinians," *The Wire*, February 4, 2018, https:// thewire.in/external-affairs/lebanons-scapegoating-refugees-not-start-syrians -palestinians, Kareem Chehayeb, "Lebanese above All: The Politics of Scapegoating Syrian Refugees," *The New Arab*, June 17, 2019, https://english.alaraby.co.uk/opinion/ scapegoating-syrian-refugees-lebanon.

53 Hani Adada, "Labor in Lebanon: Between Racism and Capitalist Exploitation," *The Public Source*, July 15, 2020, https://thepublicsource.org/labor-lebanon-racism -capitalist-exploitation#footnoteref3_rfqs4mu.

54 Lea Bou Khater, "Did Someone Say Workers?" *The Public Source*, January 29, 2020, https://thepublicsource.org/did-someone-say-workers.

55 Hannes Baumann, *Citizen Hariri: Lebanon's Neoliberal Reconstruction* (London: Hurst, 2016).

56 See Sayyed Hassan Nasrallah's speech on October 25, 2019.

57 Chehayeb, "Lebanese above All."

58 Majed, "The Lebanese Revolution Advances."

59 Dalal Yassine, "Clamping Down on Refugees Will Not Save Lebanon from the Pandemic," *Aljazeera*, April 11, 2020, https://www.aljazeera.com/opinions/2020 /4/11/clamping-down-on-refugees-will-not-save-lebanon-from-the-pandemic, Kareem Chehayeb, "'You have no one but us': Lebanon's Political Elite Resurrected Amid Coronavirus Crisis," *Middle East Eye*, March 31, 2020, https://www .middleeasteye.net/news/coronavirus-lebanon-health-hezbollah-maligned-political -elite-influence.

60 Majed, "The Lebanese Revolution Advances."

61 Patuck, "Refugees and the Lebanese Revolution."

62 AJ+ (@ajplus), "This All-Female Group of Domestic Workers Are on a Mission," *Twitter*, May 26, 2020, https://twitter.com/ajplus/status/1265215205153353728.

63 Yassine, "Clamping Down on Refugees Will Not Save Lebanon from the Pandemic."

64 Timour Azhari, "Palestinian Refugees in Lebanon Three Times More Likely to Die with covid-19," *Thomas Reuters Foundation*, February 16, 2021, https://news.trust.org/item/20210216153654-lwurk/.
65 HRW, "Refugees, Migrants Left Behind."
66 Alicia Medina, "The Beirut Blast Lays Bare a Shockwave of Evictions Hitting Syrians in Lebanon," *Syria Direct*, September 20, 2020, https://syriadirect.org/the-beirut-blast-lays-bare-a-shockwave-of-evictions-hitting-syrians-in-lebanon/#.X2eUnyKQfaI.twitter.
67 Kafa employee, interview by author, January 7, 2021.
68 Hajj Rifaat Shana'a, "We Are Not Foreign Workers, We Are Forcibly Displaced," *Al-Watan*, July 20, 2019. https://pulpit.alwatanvoice.com/articles/2019/07/20/497485.html.

18

Lebanese Diaspora, October 17 Uprising, and Political Transformation in Lebanon

Paul Tabar and Yara El Zakka

Given the vitality of their diasporic engagement in the development of the nation-state, this chapter will reveal how the Lebanese diaspora has a strong capacity of implementing a long-term reforming impact on "home" politics—as recently shown by the events occurring during the October 17 uprising and its unfolding process. This impact is best captured by using the concept of "political remittances"[1] that are shaped by both the sending and receiving countries, in measurable forms such as financial flows and in immeasurable forms including political identities, political activism, and diasporic solidarity. However, we argue that the dimensions of the diaspora's engagement have not yet reached their full potential and are strongly affected by certain limitations imposed from both diasporic and home actors. These included the influence of traditional political parties at home and abroad and the absence of unity among groups engaged in the uprising and a clear mechanism connecting these groups to reform the political system in Lebanon. To this end, the findings of our research suggest that the uprising succeeded to reverberate in major countries where Lebanese immigrants vigorously engaged with the uprising since its beginning. In other words, not only did the uprising sow the seeds of a revolutionary generation in Lebanon, but it also resonated within a diaspora eager to participate in transforming the power structure in Lebanon.

The repercussions of the uprising were illustrated by a strong abstention from supporting the ruling elite that arose from both diasporic and home actors, caught in a revolutionary moment whereby they publicly participated and engaged in multiple activities, directed against the sectarian regime that has been predominant in Lebanon for decades. These activities are illustrated by protests, marches, talks, and discussions, as well as petitions, letters, and different forms of fundraisers and financial remittances. The findings presented were derived from field observations, a thorough analysis of social media platforms, newspaper articles, online blogs, and interviews[2] conducted with activists in Lebanon and in major cities of the diaspora.

Transnational and Diasporic Relations

It is important to first distinguish between transnational and diasporic relations when studying the relationship between immigrants and their countries of origin in the realm of cross-nation relations. While diasporic relations are transnational and involve state and nonstate actors, transnational relations are not necessarily diasporic and, consequently, are not reducible to it.[3] Additionally, diasporic communities tend to have stronger sentimental and materialistic connections with their homelands driven by their ethnic national belonging.[4] More specifically, this common ethnic identity accentuates diaspora activities in "home" affairs and may serve as a boost to their political power directed at their homeland.[5]

In this context, James Clifford also argues that the term "diasporic" transcends being transnational to become highly significant to local political struggles leading to define the local as distinctive community in historical contexts of displacement.[6] This is highly evident in the case of the Lebanese diaspora that is actively attached to the political scene in Lebanon. This scene of both *traditional* and *emerging* forces is replicated abroad and reflected in the diaspora's engagements in Lebanon and receiving countries.[7] The findings of our research suggest that these diasporic engagements are however homogeneous neither in their influence nor in their implications, in that they fall within a political struggle of power and may serve opposing purposes: a deep-rooted diasporic power that is keen to maintain the current political scene in Lebanon and an emerging one that aims at reforming the sociopolitical status quo, mirroring the revolting scene in Lebanon. Therefore, these diasporic engagements fall in a cross-national border space best referred to as diasporic political field. Actors engaged in this field aim at imposing their political views in what they consider to be the best political interest of the Lebanese people in the homeland. This cross-border phenomenon takes the form of political remittances, which go through three main stages as follows: "(1) genesis or formation of political remittances and their embedding in groups and associations, (2) travelling back 'home' through specific conduits and (3) impacting on the political structures and power relations in the country to which they are remitted."[8] The following findings will be discussed with reference to these three phases to understand the progression of diasporic engagement. The role of the diaspora had been recently significant since October 2019 in response to a series of events: the fires that broke out over large areas of forests in Lebanon on October 13; the October 17 uprising; the economic crisis and the devaluation of the currency exacerbated by the COVID-19 pandemic and its impact on the economy in Lebanon; the August 4 Beirut blast causing material damage, human loss, injury, and displacement. While the political remittances of the Lebanese diaspora could be extensively explored during this scope, the discussion will be narrowed down to remittances flowing in the early stages of the October 17 uprising and after the August 4 Beirut blast.

First, it is important to note the role of the Lebanese diaspora in opposing the political system during the October 17 uprising, at a time when this system has long fed on the supporting political (social and economic) remittances of the diaspora. This new political development suggests that the Lebanese diaspora has the potential to play a crucial role in transforming the political system in Lebanon. In what follows, a general overview will be provided on the emerging political identity in the diaspora, the formation of diasporic organizations—part of which engages in activism on ground and another in advocacy—and the material aid provided by the diaspora during the uprising and after the Beirut blast.

Diasporic Solidarity with October 17 Uprising

The political position taken by the diaspora in the wake of October 17 uprising suggests a radical divergence from its historical political outlook, which had been mainly fragmented along sectarian and other subnational lines.[9] Contrary to Abdelhady's[10] expectations that many exclusionary identities emerge from the diasporic communities that attempt to reify ethnic boundaries and totalitarian traditions, we argue that the diaspora's involvement in "home" politics also allows them to challenge the constraints and traditions in their countries of origin. With the reformation of their identities, their participation in the home politics begins to insinuate change.

"Looking at the protests that happened in 2011 and 2015, the October 17 protests marked a huge shift in Lebanese political activism," "Salma," a Lebanese activist residing in Pennsylvania, says.[11] She adds, "the revolution was a steppingstone, especially that it wasn't centralized in one city, and that it encompassed different age groups, minority groups, and created a platform to voice out many ignored demands. It was different and the diaspora had a huge role to play." Undeniably, countless protests of solidarity with the uprising took place across the globe within days of its start.[12] The protesters in the diaspora were as diverse as those taking the streets in their homeland. However, they had a common vision of a strong unified Lebanon[13] against the sectarian regime and its political representatives.

The first diaspora network that emerged was *Meghterbin Mejtemiin* (Diaspora United), kicking off in Paris within 24 hours from the beginning of the uprising and currently active in 45 cities worldwide with over 250 active members and a countless number of volunteers.[14] "What started as a very organic system to try and be there for the revolution and mirror it is now not just [that], but rather a way to push it forward," says "Chloe," active member at *Meghterbin Mejtemiin*.[15] Their political activism was mainly prominent in the demonstrations and protests that were organized globally on a weekly basis. Major protests included expats flying back to Lebanon on November 22, 2019 (Lebanese Independence Day) and during December to join the protests in Martyr's Square, Beirut, and other cities and towns across Lebanon.[16] They also coordinated with groups in Lebanon to synchronize many of their protests worldwide with marches and demonstrations happening in Lebanon, which were broadcasted (live) on all of the revolution's social media platforms, such as Daleel Thawra, Meghaphone, Akhbar El Saha, Meghterbin Mejtemiin, Beirut Madinati, Lihaqqi, and others mainly on Facebook and/or Instagram.

Another network, Impact Lebanon, was formed in London, UK, to support change from abroad with over 150 active members working on several initiatives and collaborations with other groups in Lebanon and abroad.[17] Some of these initiatives were (1) launching an Instagram page, *Lebanese Corruption Facts*, which highlights statistics including reports and analyses by the International Monetary Fund (IMF), the International Development Association (IDA), the International Bank for Reconstruction and Development (IBRD), and others to expose corruption in Lebanon; (2) launching a website, *Thawra (Revolution) Chronicles*, that documents daily events in the revolution by reposting content from

Megaphone (the alternative media platform[18]), as well as documenting pictures, videos, art, and talks[19]; (3) launching a webinar series in collaboration with Coffee and Politics to encourage political conversations and discussions; as well as (4) launching a directory for the uprising, *Daleel Thawra (Revolution Directory)*, a collective project between home and diaspora members to organize all information and calls for protests taking place.[20]

Moreover, political activism in the diaspora has also been strongly present in the form of art across continents and media as it has the potential to "move, persuade, inspire, and activate."[21] "Joelle," Lebanese Canadian video artist, had showcased an installation in an exhibition in Montreal to raise awareness on the Lebanese revolution. "It is what I want to convey to the audience. To present the reality of things . . . My way is through art and it is very simple and interesting."[22] In addition to her work, she cohosts and participates in panels that encompass art and politics in an attempt to uplift the revolution through alternative forms.[23]

Advocacy in the Diaspora

Furthermore, Lebanese associations and groups forming prior to and in light of the October 17 uprising abroad had been lobbying for Lebanon in their host countries. Forming several alliances, these organizations and groups that include but are not limited to Beirut Madinati, Lihaqqi, Le Mouvement des Citoyens Libanais du Monde (Lebanese Citizens of the World Movement), *Meghterbin Mejtemiin (Diaspora United)*, the Lebanese Swiss Association, with the legal support of lawyer Nadine B. Moussa have been key actors in starting petitions and sending official requests addressed to the International Criminal Court, the United Nations, and the Federal Council of Switzerland in an effort to flag and combat corruption in Lebanon.[24] While the attempt for lobbying has not been entirely successful, its potential for reform may be expanded if more outreach is made, especially that the Lebanese diaspora had a key role to play throughout history in appealing before foreign governments and international organizations, to advocate for Lebanon's sovereignty.[25]

Financial Remittances

Apart from these hard-to-measure political remittances, the diaspora has shifted its financial flows, aside from private remittances, to monetary aid away from governmental institutions.[26] While their solidarity had been historically rampant through supporting political parties and governments, Lebanese immigrants have been recently allocating their donations to support individuals, NGOs, and INGOs based in Lebanon. This was especially prominent after the Beirut blast, where Impact Lebanon managed to raise more than 8.6 million USD that were transferred to NGOs submitting project proposals and selected based on specific criteria, of which was being apolitical and nonsectarian.[27]

Furthermore, several groups, such as *Meghterbin Mejtemiin*, have been continuously sending material aid and donation boxes to families affected by the economic crisis and the Beirut blast.[28] Therefore, as a significant fraction of the diaspora has been shifting its support to the civil society, it has demonstrated a potential capability of weakening the current political system that is reinforced historically by immigrants' financial support. Furthermore, the diaspora has been widely contributing in providing jobs for Lebanese residents to ensure the independence of seeking jobs from political patronage.[29] One example is Jobs for Lebanon, a platform initiated by a group of Lebanese expats to create online job opportunities for those residing in Lebanon through expatriate employers. This initiative was in response to the deteriorating conditions in Lebanon toward the end of 2019 and the increased unemployment rates. It also resonated with the uprising's demands in a secular state as the platform allowed Lebanese expats to hire based on competency rather than political belonging. "The diaspora is dispersed around the world and almost all of its members are not chained to the economic cycle of Lebanon—that is, they are not dependent on a political party or religious sect to provide them with a job." "Toufiq," member of Impact Lebanon, says.[30] He explains how this economic freedom enables them to push for initiatives that could support the nonsectarian generations in Lebanon. Moreover, "Chloe," who is also a menswear designer, is developing a sustainable and long-term project that will bring back jobs to Lebanon. "It's insane how much skills we have in the country that are not being put into work. The Lebanese are resilient in the way they work, so before they immigrate, why not try fixing what's there and create jobs for Lebanese in Lebanon?" she says.[31] Therefore, the diaspora is partaking a significant role in shifting the financial remittance dynamic to become more directed toward individuals and organizations that do not serve the ruling elite.

Engaging with the Diaspora

Reciprocally, initiatives from Lebanon to engage with the diaspora have been launched. Several emerging nonsectarian groups and political parties and movements based in Lebanon, such as *LiHaqqi*,[32] Beirut *Madinati*,[33] and others, are spreading their roots in the diaspora to promote a nonsectarian political culture among the diaspora and had a vital collaborative role to play in advocacy.[34] They have been also organizing political talks with the diaspora and engaging in others organized by groups in the diaspora, such as the Lebanese diaspora,[35] to explore areas of collaboration and organization and to reach potential solutions for reform. Moreover, Lebanese individuals residing in Lebanon have also reached out for the diaspora during the uprising and demonstrated a sense of commitment sprung from the solidarity felt with the diaspora. For example, "Dima," a Lebanese activist, says,

> When we first took the streets, we didn't feel like we needed external support, but later through the revolution we were exhausted seeing no tangible change. Realizing the immensity of the chain reaction created by the protests across the world, we felt a sense of solidarity on ground that kept us going, coupled with

a sense of responsibility towards ourselves as citizens in Lebanon and towards Lebanese abroad. We didn't want to let either of them down.[36]

While Lebanese in the homeland have realized the importance of engaging with the diaspora and have initiated several attempts to collaborate with Lebanese abroad, a more structured engagement mechanism is needed to define the role of each actor in this political diasporic field and maximize the collaboration between Lebanese in the diaspora and at home.

Reflections: In Lieu of a Conclusion

Examining immigrants' experiences through a diasporic lens is crucial to discern their engagement in the politics of their homeland and their impact on the political dynamics. This home-diaspora relationship is a two-way relationship in which home and diasporic actors are affected mutually with the possibility of either facilitating the process of change in the homeland or hindering it.

The findings of our research and interviews suggest that the engagement of the Lebanese diaspora in the political scene in Lebanon, specifically during the uprising, is met by a double limitation. Looking at this home-diaspora relationship from the perspective of the home actors, it seems that the groups involved in the uprising were not united with a common political platform including a strategy to maximize the benefits of engaging with the diaspora. On the other hand, Diaspora actors did not manage until now to fully succeed in their attempt to engage proactively in home politics that would drive the process of political and social change in Lebanon beyond the limits imposed by the local actors. This is illustrated by diasporic political activities mirroring mostly the activities occurring in the homeland. Paralleling the situation in Lebanon, various political groups in the diaspora fell short of achieving a united front too, despite the push by *Meghterbin Mejtemiin* to unite the diaspora in a structured framework.[37] In addition, the diaspora has not yet reached its full potential in lobbying the governments in the countries of their settlement in favor of their diasporic political outlook. Financial resources enjoyed by the diaspora and their potential voting power could better be mobilized to achieve this potential.

Against this background, the diaspora's actions are still dispersed—only resonating what is happening in Lebanon through initiatives that are fragmented and divisive, at a critical moment at which profound and independent diasporic initiatives are needed. While some initiatives did take place, they remain of a predominantly charitable character, deeply affected by the handout mentality the diaspora had historically displayed.[38] That said, the material (financial and in-kind) support to the uprising seems to be the most distinguished contribution made by the Lebanese diaspora across the world. This support seems to be transcending traditional channels bound by religion, sectarian, and familial ties—a step toward breaking the hegemony of the political system in Lebanon that feeds on these channels.

Having observed the Lebanese diasporic activities during the uprising and after the Beirut blast amid political antagonism between two main actors: supporters and opposers of the political regime, it is safe to conclude that the interaction of Lebanese abroad and at "home" falls within a diasporic field of fierce political struggle between individual and collective actors. This struggle is best described as an emerging force of diasporic actors who exert relentless efforts to defy the legitimacy of the dominant political capital "possessed" by the ruling elite in Lebanon.

In this context, diasporic actors wanting reform deploy massive efforts to replace the political vision of the ruling elite with their own opposing vision.[39] As Lebanon's economy and political system continue to deteriorate, diasporic political (plus financial and technical) support, if properly marshaled and collectively remitted, is capable of playing a vital role in reforming the economic and political scene in the country. Looking closer at how the alternative nonsectarian force that is emerging in the diaspora can be, together with activists in the homeland, a potential force for reforming the Lebanese political system and challenging the historically dominant political powers, the following conclusive remarks could be made.

First, as the emerging diaspora supporting the October uprising is capable to free itself from the constraints of the sectarianism and fragmentation that dominate the Lebanese political system, it then can reform not only its political identity but also that of its kins in the homeland. Second, this diaspora's political participation can build a politically unified structure that rises above communal interest, through positioning its well-established political capital in lobbying and advocating for Lebanon. Third, the diaspora's solidarity can be a vital means of channeling the voice of Lebanese citizens, showcasing the reality of the events occurring in Lebanon for others in their host countries to be aware of and transmitting back hope and power to their homeland. Fourth, the diaspora is capable of supporting those in the homeland economically through financial remittances to the civil society and creating job opportunities free from the interference of the political patrons in the homeland. Finally, the production of a "solid"[40] diaspora is best achieved by two types of practices: activities initiated in the diaspora and oriented toward the country of origin and initiatives originating from the homeland aiming to engage with the diaspora and benefit from its political and financial remittances.[41]

As "Dima," a "home" actor engaged with the diaspora, states: "Our relationship with the diaspora needs not be one-sided. Change can only happen if efforts are deployed on both ends: in Lebanon and in the diaspora."[42] In other words, not only does the diaspora need to form a structured agenda to remit politically, but an organizational effort also needs to be exerted in Lebanon to strategically maximize the potential carried by the diaspora to reform. "It is important to keep in mind that the October revolution was more of an awakening to start working towards the Lebanon that we want rather than an immediate shift in the political system,"[43] says "Toufiq."

Notes

1   See Paul Tabar, "'Political Remittances': The Case of Lebanese Expatriates Voting in National Elections," *Journal of Intercultural Studies* 35, no. 4 (2014): 442–60, and Paul

Tabar, "Transnational Is Not Diasporic: A Bourdieusian Approach to the Study of Modern Diaspora," *Journal of Sociology* 56, no. 3 (2020): 1–17.

2 All names used in the chapter are pseudonyms.

3 Tabar, "'Political Remittances,'" and Tabar, "Transnational Is Not Diasporic."

4 Wei-Jue Huang, William J. Haller, and Gregory P. Ramshaw, "Diaspora Tourism and Homeland Attachment: An Exploratory Analysis," *Tourism Analysis* (Cognizant Comm. Corp.) 18 (2013): 285–96.

5 Tabar, "Transnational Is Not Diasporic."

6 Waltraud Kokot, Khachig Tololyan, and Carolin Alfonso, *Diaspora, Identity and Religion: New Directions in Theory and Research* (London: Routledge, 2004).

7 Jennifer Skulte-Ouaiss and Paul Tabar, "Strong in Their Weakness or Weak in Their Strength? The Case of Lebanese Diaspora Engagement with Lebanon," *Immigrants & Minorities: Historical Studies in Ethnicity, Migration and Diaspora,* 2014, doi:10.1080/0 2619288.2013.877347.

8 Tabar, "'Political Remittances,'" 444.

9 Skulte-Ouaiss and Tabar, "Strong in Their Weakness or Weak in Their Strength?".

10 Dalia Abdelhady, *The Lebanese Diaspora: The Arab Immigrant Experience in Montreal, New York, and Paris* (New York: New York University, 2011).

11 Salma, interview by Yara El Zakka. (November 10, 2020).

12 See Victoria Yan, "Leave so We Can Come Back," Lebanese Diaspora Joins the Protest," *The National,* October 27 and Meghterbin Mejtemiin (@uniteddiasporalb), *Meghterbin Mejtemiin: Community Organization.* October, 2019, https://www .instagram.com/uniteddiasporalb/.

13 Yan, "Leave so We Can Come Back."

14 United Diaspora Lebanon, *Who Are We: United Diaspora Lebanon.* 2020, https:// uniteddiasporalb.com.

15 Chloe, interview by Yara El Zakka. (November 9, 2020).

16 See Meghterbin Mejtemiin (@uniteddiasporalb), "On the 26th of December," *Instagram.* December 19, 2019, https://www.instagram.com/p/B6P_QFxI721/ and Meghterbin Mejtemiin (@uniteddiasporalb), "We're Flying Back to Beirut for Independence Day!" *Instagram.* November 13, 2019, https://www.instagram.com/p/ B4zvcjmI09N/.

17 See Impact Lebanon (@impact.lebanon), "Impact Lebanon: Non-profit Organization," *Instagram,* 2019, https://www.instagram.com/impact.lebanon/, Impact Lebanon (@ ImpactLeb). 2019. "Impact Lebanon: Noon-profit Organization," *Facebook,* October 18, https://www.facebook.com/ImpactLeb and Impact Lebanon, "About Us: Impact Lebanon," *Impact Lebanon,* 2019, https://www.impactlebanon.org/about.

18 Claudia Kozman, "Digital Media and Alternative Platforms: Empowerment," in *The Lebanon Uprising of 2019: Voices from the Revolution,* ed. Jeffrey G. Karam and Rima Majed (London: I.B. Tauris and Bloomsbury Academic, 2021).

19 Tarek Ali Ahmad, "'By the people, for the people,' Lebanese Diaspora Launches Platform Documenting Lebanon's Revolution," *Arab News,* November 3, 2019.

20 Ayah Bdeir, "Lebanese Diaspora: It's Our Turn Now," *Medium,* January 29, 2020.

21 Abdelhady, *The Lebanese Diaspora,* 167.

22 Joelle, interview by Yara El Zakka. (November 6, 2020).

23 See Cinema Politica, "About Us: Cinema Politica," *Cinema Politica,* 2021, https://www .cinemapolitica.org/about-cinema-politica, Warren G Flowers Gallery, "Resistance and Resilience Artist Panel and Vernissage," *Facebook,* October 8, 2020, https://fb .me/e/R0ynJump and Oula Hajjar, "Le Liban: La Revolution Continue," *Facebook,*

January 6, 2020, https://www.facebook.com/photo?fbid=10162785048305181&set=a
.204883085180.

24　See Lebanese-Swiss Association, "Archive: Lebanese-Swiss Association," *Lebanese-Swiss Association*, 2021, https://lebanese-swiss-association.com/archiv/.

25　Skulte-Ouaiss and Tabar, "Strong in Their Weakness or Weak in Their Strength?" and Abdelhady, *The Lebanese Diaspora*.

26　Skulte-Ouaiss and Tabar, "Strong in Their Weakness or Weak in Their Strength?"

27　Impact Lebanon, *Impact Lebanon Fundraisers.* August 5, 2020, https://www
.impactlebanon.org/fundraisers.

28　See KAWA, *"Les valises pour Beyrouth,"* a Solidarity Initiative from Paris to Lebanon.
August 11, 2020, https://kawa-news.com/en/les-valises-pour-beyrouth-a-solidarity
-initiative-from-paris-to-lebanon/ and Meghterbin Mejtemiin Netherlands (@
lebanese.nl), "Project Lebanon," *Instagram,* October 12, 2020, https://www.instagram
.com/p/CGP_GDVpwBo/.

29　Employment in Lebanon has been strongly politicized in the sense that getting a job is hardly free from the interference of political leaders.

30　Toufiq, interview by Yara El Zakka. (November 13, 2020).

31　Chloe, interview by Yara El Zakka. (November 9, 2020).

32　See Lihaqqi (@LiHaqqi), "Lihaqqi: Political Organization," *Facebook,* October 6, 2017, https://www.facebook.com/LiHaqqi and Lihaqqi, *Lihaqqi,* 2021, http://lihaqqi.org/.

33　See Beirut Madinati (@beirutmadinati), *Beirut Madinati: Political Organization.*
February 4, 2016, https://www.facebook.com/BeirutMadinati/ and Beirut Madinati,
Beirut Madinati. 2021, https://beirutmadinati.com/.

34　Marie, interview by Yara El Zakka. (January 17, 2020). "Marie" is an active member at Beirut Madinati.

35　See The Lebanese Diaspora, "Webinars: The Lebanese Diaspora: United For Lebanon,"
The Lebanese Diaspora: United For Lebanon, 2021, https://thelebanesediaspora.net/
webinars/.

36　Dima, interview by Yara El Zakka. (November 4, 2020).

37　Meghterbin Mejtemiin's structure is headed by a council of elected city or country representatives, followed by an International Coordination Team and several committees.

38　Abdelhady, *The Lebanese Diaspora*.

39　Tabar, "Transnational Is Not Diasporic."

40　A solid diaspora is that which has satisfied these three conditions: voluntary or forced dispersal, cross-border relations strongly revolving around home of origin, and a strong maintenance of ethnic boundaries (Cohen 1996 in Tabar 2020).

41　Alan Gamlen, "The Emigration State and the Modern Geopolitical Imagination,"
Political Geography 27 (2008): 840–56 as cited in Tabar, "Transnational Is Not Diasporic."

42　Dima, interview by Yara El Zakka. (November 4, 2020).

43　Toufiq, interview by Yara El Zakka. (November 1, 2020).

Figure 1 Thousands of protestors gathered in front of the Lebanese Serail (seat of the prime minister) to demand the government's immediate resignation. October 18, 2019. The photo was taken by Jeffrey G. Karam.

Figure 2 The Grand Theater. "We will reclaim public property" is written on the banner at the top of the building. "We want a progressive tax on the rich" is written on the handheld poster. October 21, 2019. The photo was taken by Sana Tannoury-Karam.

Figure 3 Call for strike by the Independent University Professors Association in Lebanon. October 26, 2019. Source: https://www.facebook.com/IndependentProfessors (accessed November 2021).

لبنان ينتفض!

نحن تجمع مهنيات ومهنيين من قطاعات مختلفة.
نعلن أننا جزء فاعل من انتفاضة ١٧ تشرين الأول ٢٠١٩،
في وجه الطبقة الحاكمة منذ الطائف ونظامها السياسي
ونموذجها الاقتصادي، التي أثبتت عجزها عن إدارة الدولة
وأوصلتنا إلى الانهيار والافقار، رغم التحذيرات المتكررة.

ومع استمرار انتفاضتنا وتصاعدها، نعلن عدم ثقتنا بالسلطة
القائمة، ونرفض كل سياساتها الاجتماعية والاقتصادية والمالية
والنقدية والخدماتية. كما نرفض كل اشكال الاقصاء والتمييز التي
تمارسها هذه السلطة بحق النساء والفئات المهمّشة.

اننا نضم جهودنا إلى جهود شعبنا من أجل التغيير الديمقراطي وبناء
الدولة العلمانية على مبادئ العدالة الاجتماعية والمساواة.

انطلاقا من هذه المبادئ، ندعو جميع المهنيات والمهنيين للانخراط في
هذا التجمّع، والمشاركة الكثيفة في كل ميادين الانتفاضة لحثّ النقابات
والروابط على الانضمام إلى الانتفاضة من دون تردد.

تجمعات من مستقلات ومستقلين من المهن التالية:

● مهن صحية:
– طب
– طب اسنان
– صيدلة
● هندسة
● محاماة
● العمل الاجتماعي
● أساتذة جامعات
● صحافة
● اقتصاد
● سينما
● كتابة

٢٨ تشرين الأول ٢٠١٩

Figure 4 The first statement of the Lebanese Professionals' Association, released on October 28, 2019. Source: www.facebook.com/LebProAssociation/photos/a.101690577941 472/101894227921107/?type=3&theater (accessed December 2021).

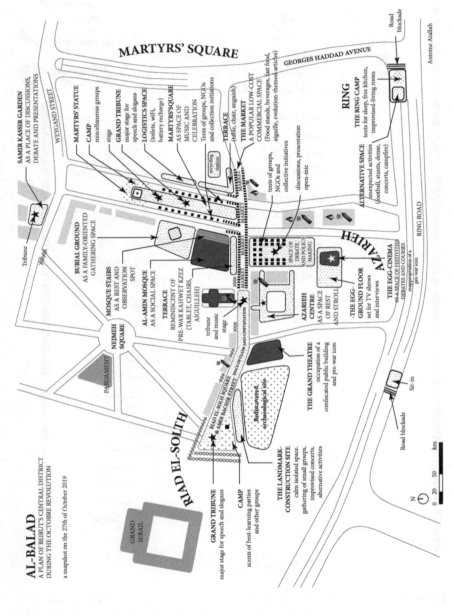

Figure 5 Map of Al-Balad (downtown Beirut) during the October Revolution in 2019.

Figure 6 "For your sake Nadine we will bring down the system." In tribute to the late activist Nadine Jouni. November 3, 2019. The photo was taken by Myriam Sfeir during the feminist march.

Figure 7 A wall in downtown Beirut sprayed with the phrase "political imagination is resistance." The photo was taken by Petra Halawi.

Figure 8 "The Revolution is Female." November 3, 2019. The photo was taken by Myriam Sfeir during the feminist march.

Figure 9 Protestors in Al Nour Square, Tripoli (North Lebanon). November 2, 2019. The photo was taken by Jeffrey G. Karam.

Figure 10 Protestor in Baalbek (North East Lebanon) producing street art in support of the revolution.

Figure 11 Graffiti in Downtown Beirut that reads: Lebanon Revolts; "All Means All"—Iraq Revolts; "Down to All, They Are All Thiefs." Photo taken by Rima Majed. March 30, 2020.

Figure 12 Protestors in support of refugees in Riad El Solh Square, Beirut. Banner Reads "The situation has long been bad, do not blame the refugees." Photo taken by Rima Majed. October 19, 2020.

Figure 13 Graffiti in Downtown Beirut that reads "The Unions are for the Revolutionaries." Photo taken by Rima Majed. March 30, 2020.

Figure 14 Graffiti in Downtown Beirut that reads "Down with Proposals." Photo taken by Rima Majed. March 30, 2020.

Figure 15 Graffiti in Hamra, Beirut post August 4, 2020. Port Explosion with the phrase "Justice to the Victims, Revenge from the Regime. We won't seek accountability, we will get our revenge."

Figure 16 Protester in Aley—Chouf Area (Mount Lebanon).

Khamenei.ir @khamenei_ir · Oct 30, 2019 · · ·
Who imagined the Zionist Regime - which couldn't be defeated by three
Arab countries in 6 days - would be forced to retreat by the devout
youth during the 33-day Lebanon War and the 22-day Gaza War?
Be sure that God surely fulfills His promises.

◯ 58   ⇄ 175   ♡ 843   ⬆

Khamenei.ir @khamenei_ir · Oct 30, 2019 · · ·
The people have justifiable demands, but they should know their
demands can only be fulfilled within the legal structure and framework
of their country. When the legal structure is disrupted in a country, no
action can be carried out.

◯ 97   ⇄ 244   ♡ 878   ⬆

Khamenei.ir @khamenei_ir · Oct 30, 2019 · · ·
I recommend those who care in #Iraq and #Lebanon remedy the
insecurity and turmoil created in their countries by the U.S., the Zionist
regime, some western countries, and the money of some reactionary
countries.

◯ 216   ⇄ 378   ♡ 1.1K   ⬆

Khamenei.ir @khamenei_ir · Oct 30, 2019 · · ·
The biggest damage enemies can inflict on a country is to deprive them
of security, as they are doing today in some countries in the region.

◯ 25   ⇄ 176   ♡ 909   ⬆

Khamenei.ir @khamenei_ir · Oct 30, 2019 · · ·
Coming in minutes: Statements from the graduation ceremony of cadets
in the Islamic Republic of Iran's Army concerning recent events in #Iraq
and #Lebanon

english.khamenei.ir/photo/7128

◯ 24   ⇄ 104   ♡ 798   ⬆

Figure 17 Some highlights from a speech by Khamenei, Open Source, October 30, 2019.

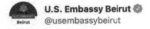

U.S. Embassy Beirut ✓
@usembassybeirut

···

الولايات المتحدة تقف الى جانب الجيش اللبناني تماما كما
تواصل الوقوف الى جانب الشعب اللبناني.
#InThisTogether

@LebarmyOfficial

Translate Tweet

IN MAY 2021 ONLY
في أيار 2021 فقط

1:37 | 10.8K views

11:23 AM · Jul 26, 2021 · Twitter Web App

Figure 18 Translation of the tweet by the US embassy in Lebanon: "The U.S. stands with (supports) the Lebanese Armed Forces just as it continues to stand with (support) the Lebanese people." Tweet by US embassy in Lebanon captures the duality of policy in Lebanon, Open Source, July 26, 2021.

Part Three

Experiencing the Revolution (*Thawra*)

Testimonies and Reflections from the Ground

19

The Cycle of Loss

Between Trial and Sabotage

Hani Adada

The weakness of the political opposition in Lebanon, mostly comprised of newly formed groups, cannot be entirely tied to objectively compulsory factors such as the health factor of the COVID-19 pandemic and the resulting lockdowns; or security[1] factors such as the oppression by security forces and militias, the waves of arrests, and the disastrous blast of the Beirut Port that destroyed vast parts of the city, killed hundreds and left thousands wounded, and the successive assassinations targeting security and political figures the last of which was writer and activist Lokman Slim; or socioeconomic and financial[2] factors such as the gradual devaluation of the Lebanese pound by nearly 90 percent,[3] the subsequent fall of more than half the population below the poverty line,[4] and the increase in unemployment to 39.5 percent in 2020,[5] which is likely to reach 41.4 percent in 2021 according to the International Labor Organization and the Lebanese Ministry of Labor.[6] Linking the reasons of this deterioration strictly to the objective factors, as frightening and dysfunctioning as they may be, is a way of running forward, of stickling and absolving oneself from the collective responsibility of the different groups and organized structures that have once again drowned in different forms of categorizing and fragmenting struggles and fanaticism, although most of the groups had lived and experienced 2015. What becomes of an opposition movement that calls for shaking the power structure and dynamics while committing those same mistakes or witnessing others make them only a few years back?

The successive crises that Lebanon has been going through have no doubt severely impacted the rising political opposition that has emerged with the October 17 uprising. However, this emergence remained temporary as the experience of the uprising itself by the different groups, most notably the youth groups that were experimenting and were the main generating force in demonstrations, fluctuated between the extremity of optimism by escalating toward full confrontation on the one hand and retreat and apathy on the other hand.

Two main approaches are to be considered here, which were prominent in the uprising to address a major aspect of the subjective factors contributing to the retreat of the opposition movement. The first is an experimental approach that manifests in widening the generational gap by blaming the older generations for today's disasters and that bases its rules for confrontation on the unfolding of daily events. The second is a disruptive approach that aims to limit the discourse within certain boundaries, to direct new opposition groups to the cycle of mere reaction, and to instill despair and frustration among people.

A Bare Minimum Agenda That Never Was

The so-called "Garbage Crisis Movement" of 2015 was a field for learning for everyone who would not learn from the experiences of others that preceded them around the world. It was in fact a lesson in the importance of building a nonstrategic front to work from (this does not go to say that such work was not part of the strategic vision of some), as long as it groups different political forces around common and tangible goals as part of a "bare minimum agenda" that is impossible to disagree or argue about achieving, as a step that is necessarily tactical or pragmatic in which no one needs to compromise internally or externally. However, that never took place, with the exception of a few experiences in some sectors such as student movements and professions. Nor will it happen easily, as the intricacy of social structure is manifesting in the failure to overcome individualistic tendencies and fragmented struggles on the one hand and the strong sentiments of tribal and clannish belonging to political or activist groups on the other hand.

The Crisis as Structural beyond Mismanagement

This shaky reality of the social structure reflects the crisis of the political structure as a whole, whether in positions of power or in the opposition. Needless to say, the culture of fast profit and the consumerist ideology dominant in Lebanese society played a major role in shaping the ways protests took place as well as the hasty and overestimated goals, and the ways that expectations were imagined—contradicting the subjective reality of the opposition groups on one hand. While on the other hand, this makes it easier for reformist groups to present themselves as revolutionaries each time the masses protest. How then do we explain the attachment of many to the myth of change through early elections? In such an electoral battle, equal chances for all participants would be impossible; it would be fought with the same sectarian electoral law and organized by committees and apparatuses with no credibility, in the worst economic and security conditions the country has seen and under a near full control of armed militias and aid boxes. Accompanied with the continuous, though conditional, support of the ever-disputing regional and international powers for the establishment. All for an imaginary small number of parliamentary seats in the midst of a complete economic and financial collapse, described by the World Bank as one of the three most severe crises since the mid-nineteenth century![7]

Uprising as a Field for Experimentation Rather Than an Experience

There is a thin line between the approach of experimenting and that of disrupting, with all their flaws. The October uprising saw a vast growth in experimental organizing behaviors not seen before in Lebanese society since the end of the civil war. That in turn made way for a wide horizon for youth groups in particular to enter political struggle and accumulate their own experiences in the face of the Lebanese system. Among dozens of new opposition groups that emerged in record time, with their different sizes and abilities to influence, many political currents emerged that differed and contradicted each other in terms of the structure and inclinations, along with other contradictions such as being hierarchical or horizontal, centralized or decentralized, leftist or rightwing or mixed, populist or elitist, principled or pragmatic. The majority only had their rejection of the old experiences of the political parties in common. The uprising was in fact a grooming ground for modern experiences of organizing despite the involvement of many traditional parties. But the chances of advancing these experiences were quite low, almost nonexistent, since the major defect of those groups was, in addition to their flawed class element and their presence limited to certain areas, their very same stronghold fueling and being fueled by spontaneous mobilizing for demonstrations, without even the least concern for the most important issue for all revolutionaries around the world: strategy and tactics.

An uprising is a tough test and a (near) open war and not merely a series of spontaneous popular demonstrations. Those organized politically in the uprising cannot go through it with the least possible amount of losses (since losses, and not defeat, are inevitable as opposed to gains) without moral perseverance and awareness of psychological reactions, and intellectual perseverance to produce tools and theoretical concepts that are clear, radical, and tied to the practical reality and its conditions for political change, and that leave no space for doubting the priorities of confrontation and its final aims, and to weaken the ruling-class propaganda that aims to break up their (groups') ranks or dilute their goals and mobilizations, or incite "public opinion" against them.

Rejection of Ideological Thought

The main reason for the conflict between strategy and tactics sometimes, and refusing to devise a plan other times, is the general sense of aversion of youth and student groups from ideology and ideological thought except for a marginal number of people with very little influence; even though these groups are the engine mobilizing all waves of uprising since 2011 in Arabic societies in general and in Lebanon in particular given the latter's extreme consumerism. This in turn adds an implicit ideological positioning, whether with predetermined knowledge or purely experimental, rejecting all that has to do with intellectual processes that lay the ground for political practice, from a delusional standpoint that considers all ideology is necessarily tied to archaic ideas detached from reality. This is a perfect example of an ideological stance on ideology itself that fails to differentiate between ideology and utopia on the one hand and on the other hand fails completely to revolutionize practical politics, which entails making politics accessible to the masses and stripping it from technocracy and representative democracy. What is worse is the fact that this "anti-ideological" ideology is the dominant one among youth groups organized in political and social movements, and that in turn it is the most appealing to the ideology of the dominant social class and its bourgeois discourse; it is even the ideal protector for this class.

Perhaps the most notable example of this dogmatic view of ideology has been the widespread endorsement of most groups for the slogan "All of them Means All of Them" (Kellon Yaani Kellon) to target and address prominent political figures of what is arbitrarily referred to as the "ruling political class." In the context of the dominant liberal discourse pointing at the flaws in the collective of ruling politicians as opposed to the system, and at the mismanagement as opposed to the structure, this slogan becomes limited and ambiguous, making room for figures of the establishment to maneuver their way for causing speculations and personalizing matters so as to defend individuals by distinguishing between good clean people and evil corrupt others. This slogan overshadowed others that would have emphasized the classist social reality and interests of the crowds protesting, and emphasized a clear understanding of what and who the enemy is. That would have led to accurately referring to the dominant social class as bourgeois and oligarchic, thus specifying the nature and magnitude of the battle and its actual scope.

Lack of a Unified Vision

The lack of a unified vision was evident among political groups across different stages of the uprising, with the exception of toppling Saad Hariri's government, which was the peak when protesters filled the streets and squares all around this small country in a breathtaking view and what constituted the biggest demonstrations since 2005.[8] That, along with disagreements on goals, was normal, before a new phase following the retreat of protests and the start of taking, or attempting to take, the struggle to an international level by religious and political figures from the heart of the system. That phase brought to light the fragility of many political groups that proved vulnerable to any disruption from whichever direction.

It is not a shame for one to admit that "they do not know," but it is fatal to hold on to the same pattern of mobilizing and thinking, ultimately drowning in an endless loop of reactivity without pausing for self-reflection. This applies to people who took on the experimental approach in political struggle and failed in rightful battles but cannot always assess the reasons for choosing and sticking to these battles in the first place and then assessing their impact. Examples of that include holding on to the "demand" of a transitional government with exceptional powers regardless of the general context and the events unfolding on the ground, as a "demand" endorsed and called for by small elitist groups working for fragmented causes; as opposed to a plan for a transitional council with wide popular support and representative power in political life (based on direct election and reversible delegation by electing popular committees, and not only vague support), regardless of the lack of support for this demand by protesters occupying the streets at the time. An uprising is also an open space to discuss and meet, where ideas and programs are put to test. Why then, after the battle, cling to what did not touch the masses?

The Traps of Politics and Ambush of Hezbollah's Arms

Perhaps the mistake that put opposition groups to rest was falling for two traps. The first was a race of political bidding, whereby the political and constitutional aspects (transitional government, early parliamentary elections, etc.) overshadowed mobilizing and community building. In addition, the lack of a sharp and serious approach to address Hezbaollah's arms, or considering this subject a taboo, was a further example of how the limits of politicization were set to serve the interests of the establishment, besides the fact that it was constrained within the rhetoric of the long gone March (14 and 8) confrontation. For years, the only outcome of this rhetoric was inciting fear and instigating regressive sentiments invested by Hezbollah and its opponents. The second was the trap of sheer economism, whereby demonstrating at the Central Bank was the utmost priority for some groups at all times regardless of the changing political circumstances, backed by a belief that the Central Bank's governor was the spearhead of the political system and everything else hence was a secondary and less significant battle that could wait! But those traps were mostly not "natural," and here we can speak of political disruption and how it was put into action on the ground. And if experimental groups refuse to learn from experiences other than their own and often interact with events outside of their historical contexts, then disruptive groups indeed follow the same failed methods over and over until they reach their goal.

Political Disruption

If we take the issue of political disruption by framing it in "disruptive binary" image, as an example, we find that there have been two groups tied to Hezbollah historically and politically (Al-Akhbar newspaper's team and editor in chief, presuming they are a "group" that actively produces daily political discourse) and the March 14 factions (such as "Ana Khat Ahmar" group, a collective of advertising executives linked to the Future Movement[9]). Both sides produce two rhetorics that may seem opposing on the outside and from seemingly revolutionary positions, from which they set their goals along with a pattern of protest behavior, which is why they would reach and influence many new groups active in the uprising. These sides share two common obsessions (as was the case for other groups as well): excluding Hezbollah from "All of them Means All of Them" (Kellon Yaani Kellon) and considering it part of the solution and not of the problem[10] and steering attention away from entities and individuals funded by the private sector in general by blaming "some" bank owners and executives and in turn considering the private sector a victim as opposed to part of the problem. In their "disruptive contradiction," the two sides would fuel and support protests at times, leading to counter results of this disruption. However, the danger lies in voiding the uprising of its radical social and political aspects in the long run. And that has already happened.

Ground Disruption

On the ground, there had been a clear pattern of disruptive behavior of the following examples.

Continuously blocking roads as per the orders of certain political parties in areas almost fully dominated by the Future Movement, the Progressive Socialist Movement, or the Lebanese Forces, among other bourgeois sectarian forces—some of which were areas with particular sectarian tensions despite the cease of roadblocks as announced during the uprising.

The demonization campaign against protesters by certain groups participating in the uprising. For example, on the infamous "banks night"[11] in Hamra, the group that called for a "week of anger" ("Ana Khat Ahmar") were the same people that waged a campaign against angry protesters who targeted banks, calling them "thugs"[12] and "party mercenaries."[13] It was also the same group that intentionally led to ending the general strike after having repeatedly called for it without a base of popular or syndical support—fully aware that they were contributing to the failure of one strike after the other. The same applies to their weekly calls for "protests of millions," also with the same awareness that this would create delusional expectations and obstacles that could cause frustration among protesters and reinforce the media's narratives in favor of the establishment. Lastly, they were also the same people who funded promotional advertisements on television and big billboards to relay messages that seem to be political without an added value but with a notable potential to instill doubts in the uprising among people.

There were also some who actively silenced dissidents that daringly criticized Hezbollah like any other party of the establishment, through playing the old card of "resistance" every once in a while, believing that this would protect Hezbollah from the accusations of being a partner in corruption and protecting the system. This was taking place all while the party was attacking and suppressing the uprising and viciously defending Hariri's government, tangibly proving the accuracy of accusations. And there were some "radicals" who believed that refusing to organize with other groups and stirring incitement against their political coordination and/or mobilization efforts would mean they were playing a "sacred" revolutionary role to preserve the purity of revolutionary struggle.

In addition to all of that, it was quite noteworthy that many were insistent on drawing the space for protesting on classist lines and deliberately distancing protests from popular neighborhoods, except for a few marches, with excessive focus on media at the expense of actual and direct communication with people. Spaces of protests and their class determined their influence on political reality.

Of course, we cannot reduce the issue of the subjective factors of opposition groups to mere disruption and experimentation alone, as the structures of most groups and the resulting tools and concepts—resulting spontaneously and automatically—must have a key role in their ability to reach the masses. At the present moment, they do not represent the fears and aspirations of the majority of people with nothing to lose anymore. And that is the majority of workers and unemployed people in addition to several other marginalized communities subjected to various forms of exploitation and abuse in Lebanon from migrant workers and refugees.[14] Instead, these groups represent the remains of a dying middle class struggling to preserve what it had accumulated over the past decades through loans and overconsumption. Thus most groups are characterized by a refusal to express ideology, especially from a social perspective, and calls for toppling the system on the very own conditions of this system, with utmost political aspirations being a call for early parliamentary elections and forming a transitional government with exceptional powers, or calling for a military coup, with disregard to the absolute collapse and its political and social aftermath. Those aspirations are all a reflection of a regressive view to politics, stemming from populist positions on the left as on the right and from a belief that past conditions can be retrieved. Or, ideally, a belief that the current situation can be changed and make way for a better alternative without undergoing a full destructive process that does not entail excluding the masses from the political process or organizing them in structures not clearly reflective of their interests.

Notes

1 Joseph Daher, "Counterrevolution and the Possibilities of Change in Lebanon."
2 Mohammad Zbeeb, "The Crisis of Lebanon's Economy: From Reconstruction to Explosion."
3 Anchal Vohra, "Nobody Knows What Lebanon's Currency Is Worth Anymore," *Foreign Policy*, April 5, 2021, https://foreignpolicy.com/2021/04/05/lebanon-currency -inflation-exchange-rates/.
4 "Lebanon Overview," *The World Bank*, Last Updated: April 12, 2021, https://www .worldbank.org/en/country/lebanon/overview.
5 Agence France Presse (AFP), "Lebanon's economic collapse in numbers," *The Daily Star* March 17, 2021, https://www.dailystar.com.lb/News/Lebanon-News/2021/Mar-17 /518513-lebanons-economic-collapse-in-numbers.ashx.
6 Mohamad Wehbe, "Unemployment to Reach More Than 37%," *Al-Akhbar*, April 26, 2021, https://al-akhbar.com/In_numbers/304851.
7 "Lebanon Economic Monitor, Spring 2021: Lebanon Sinking (to the Top 3)," *The World Bank*, May 31, 2021, https://www.worldbank.org/en/country/lebanon/ publication/lebanon-economic-monitor-spring-2021-lebanon-sinking-to-the-top-3.
8 "Lebanon Protests: Huge Crowds on Streets as Government Acts," *BBC News*, October 21, 2019, https://www.bbc.com/news/world-middle-east-50118300.
9 Rola Ibrahim, "Hariri Man Leading The 'Tax Revolution': Waddah Sadek Coopting the Uprising," *Al-Akhbar*, January 12, 2019, https://al-akhbar.com/Politics/280973.
10 "Ibrahim Al Amine: The Question Is Not Who To Designate for Prime Minister," *Al-Akhbar*, November 21, 2020, https://al-akhbar.com/Video/279808.

11 Mohammad Bzeih, "Night of the Banks." See Chapter 24 in this volume.
12 Khat Ahmar, "It Is Quite Easy To Differentiate Between A Revolutionary and A Rioter," *Facebook*, January 14, 2020, https://www.facebook.com/KhatAhmarlb/photos/149701923121090.
13 Khat Ahmar, "It Is Quite Easy To Differentiate Between A Revolution And An Attack By Parties," *Facebook*, January 14, 2020. https://www.facebook.com/KhatAhmarlb/photos/149701956454420.
14 Moné Makkawi, "Reworking the Revolution: Refugees, Migrants, and the Lebanese Uprising." See Chapter 17 in this volume.

20

"A Nation for All"

The Lebanon Uprising and Disability Rights in Lebanon

Grace Khawam

Introduction

The disability rights agenda in Lebanon has been fundamentally advanced by community-driven actions of disability activists, organizations, and other civil society actors, in the face of the persistent absence of state-protected disability rights and policies. The disability movement in Lebanon has withstood war, conflicts, multilayered crises across the years, and has a long-standing history of protests and collective political action.[1] Through interviews with self-advocates and disability activists (conducted between October 2020 and March 2021), I attempt to investigate the disability movement before, during, and after the October 2019 uprising. In this chapter, I portray this movement as a chain of activism, disruption, and eruption and situate the influence of the Lebanon uprising in this dynamic motion, while highlighting its reciprocal effects. I explore the interactivity of the uprising with mobilization, leadership, (un)equal representation, and hierarchy in the disability movement and discuss implications for the future of disability rights and cross-movement solidarity in Lebanon.

I began my fight for disability rights a couple of years ago, as an academic, a practitioner, and a mother. As I interview these fierce activists and pioneers in advancing rights for people with disabilities in Lebanon, I bow to their endeavors, admire their persistence, and am honored to learn from their experiences. If any advancement has been achieved for inclusion in various domains for people with disabilities across the past thirty years in Lebanon, it did not stem from state-protected measures but from these groups' actions and pressures. In this perspective, it is important to learn from the historical resilience of the disability movement in Lebanon across hardship and crises, and it is with a genuine concern to "carry on the torch" that the following analyses and reflections on the contribution of the Lebanon uprising to the disability movement are presented.

The Birth of Disability Resistance and Activism in Lebanon: A Historical Review

Conflicts and disasters in Lebanon have historically exacerbated the dire situation of persons with disabilities, with the destruction of rehabilitation institutions and the increase of war injuries and war-afflicted impairments.[2] The Lebanon Civil War (1975–90) prompted militia and social-religious groups to set up medical and rehabilitation centers to support the injured and the newly disabled.[3] These later became service provider institutions known as "care institutions," focused on segregated (and often residential) specialized care, which flourished in the 1990s with the outpouring of postwar funding.

In parallel, the Civil War coincided with the emergence of the global disability movement, which resulted from the collective "conscientization" of persons with disabilities.[4] The focus of this movement was on rejecting the medical model of disability and highlighting the societal barriers that exist and persist to "create disability" and exclude persons with disabilities. Inspired by this global movement, the disability community in Lebanon started to mobilize and self-organize. Disabled people's organizations (DPOs) were founded in the 1980s, such as the Lebanese Physically Handicapped Union (LPHU), the Youth Association of the Blind (YAB), and the National Association for the Rights of the Disabled (NARD). These DPOs dissociated themselves from the traditional charities or service-oriented institutions and militia groups, toward rights-based activism, hence forming a nascent disability movement.[5]

A Series of (Dis)unified Disruptions

With this onset of activism among persons with disabilities in Lebanon during the Civil War, DPOs took part in "disruptive" protests, which "seek to unsettle, derail, realign, or otherwise challenge the process of global governance."[6] Examples of disruptive protests include leading anti-war and anti-violence manifestations and organizing a four-day peace march in 1987.[7] These were defining moments in making persons with disabilities visible and heard, and as one activist stated in an interview with Kingston, P.: "We moved from being a marginalized group that has to be 'looked after' to a political force to be reckoned with."[8] The DPOs' association with the anti-war movement was strategic, showcasing persons with disabilities as a "vivid reminder of the war."[9]

As the movement continued with its actions in the postwar era, activist groups adopted more "coercive" types of protest,[10] such as members of the LPHU demolishing a newly built pavement in Beirut in the early 1990s because it was not designed in an accessible manner, as a move to pressure the government to adopt the newly drafted disability law proposal. One activist called this the "struggle from the pavement to the law." Others invested in more subtle community-level disruptions, advocating for inclusive education and community-based day care centers. These include parents' and self-advocacy groups such as the Lebanese Down Syndrome Association, the Lebanese Association for Self-Advocacy, Friends of the Disabled Association, and others.

However, it is crucial to state here that with this emergence of activism and historical initiatives from these DPOs, there was never "one" unified disability movement in Lebanon. In reality, the disability movement, as presented in this chapter, is the result of actions from several groups, powers, agglomerations of activities, and clusters of advocacy work, with often diverging paths and strategies, in what Kingston calls "the hidden world of disability governance."[11] Despite continuous initiatives to join efforts and raise united demands, the movement has typically witnessed power struggles and in-house quarreling over leadership and funding across the years. Internal disputes over authority and power often resulted in splits and factionalism within DPOs, ultimately leading to the parallel establishment of new separate advocacy groups, as illustrated through the interviews.[12] Also, a few of the humanitarian (and politically unaffiliated) service provision institutions joined the fight for disability advocacy, such as Arc En Ciel and Sesobel.[13]

From Disruption to Eruption and the Passing of Law 220

The end of the Civil War in 1990 was a unique opportunity for policy reform, and the disability movement started to invest in drafting a comprehensive disability law. In 2000, and after ten years of persistent campaigning, lobbying, and advocacy to influence public opinion and the political elite, Law 220 for the rights of persons with disabilities was finally passed. This was one of the first real victories of the disability movement in Lebanon, in what I present as a moment of "eruption," the apogee of disruptions, and advocacy work. However, ever since, barely any implementing decrees have been issued to enact the tenets of the law.[14] This failure is essentially due to the lack of political will to invest in rights-based discourses and disability policy reform.[15] Rights of persons with disabilities in Lebanon have been constantly pushed aside, deprioritized, and neglected through a persistent disablism from the state across the past decades.[16] "Now is not your time" is the response DPOs constantly receive from government officials, quoting one activist. Also, Lebanon has not yet ratified the United Nations Convention on the Rights of Persons with Disabilities.[17]

The Lebanon Uprising: A New Eruption in Disability Rights?

Access to quality education, fair employment opportunities, universal health care, and social protection are what people with disabilities have been continuously calling for. They fundamentally mirror the demands for basic human rights and dignified living of the millions of protesters roaming the *thawra* streets. The Lebanon uprising hence presented itself as a strategic opportunity to make the voices of persons with disabilities heard and advance their rights. However, was it the new eruption hoped for?

The attempt to answer this question would inherently involve taking a closer look at the intricate complex dynamics of the disability movement and how these undercurrents interacted with the Lebanon uprising.

Between Prospective Alliances and Lost Opportunities

Most members of the disability rights movement participated in the general protests of the 2019 *thawra* along with civil society members and fellow citizens.[18,19,20] Some also invested in organizing specific events or leading focused advocacy actions, such as the march organized on November 21, 2019, by the LPHU under the motto "Freedom and dignity for all, in a nation for all."[21] According to most of the activists interviewed, the Lebanon uprising created a unique opportunity to raise awareness on disability rights issues among civil society organizations and actors, to further expand a lobbying network by rallying allies and joining forces, and to build prospective alliances.

However, where the Lebanon uprising seems to have fallen short is in the operationalization of cross-movement solidarity. According to one well-known self-advocate, it was an unseized opportunity by civil society to model inclusion, by failing to rightfully illustrate how an inclusive "new Lebanon" should look like. "[Civil society groups] were calling for our rights, but when we went to Martyr Square, out of all the public toilets that were set up by these groups, not one toilet was accessible [for people with disabilities]"—stated the activist, criticizing the tokenistic underpinnings of the civil society leaders failing to enact inclusion.

Another shortcoming of the Lebanon uprising was the failure to achieve unity of demands within the disability rights movement. While political divergence may be normal and even healthy in all social movements, the historical (and present) fragmentation of the disability movement has been generally detrimental to its advancement of disability rights. "We didn't want to lower the threshold of demands" is the answer given by a prominent activist, when asked why they did not collaborate with other DPOs at a protest, showcasing this divergence. There is also an observed hierarchy within the disability movement, where persons with physical disabilities seem to be at the center of disability activism, while the cause of persons with other types of disability, such as intellectual disabilities, was relatively marginalized or even absent from the revolutionary political discourse.[22]

An emerging theme from the discussions with the various activists and self-advocates is the issue of leadership and representation during the Lebanon uprising and beyond. "It is time for us to step aside, [. . .] but we have failed to build a new generation of activists," said a prominent self-advocate, talking about the relative absence of "new and younger faces" of disability activists in the *thawra* (revolution) battlefields. All the activists interviewed mentioned a recent shift from collective representation to individualistic leadership, with emerging activists often working *solo* or establishing their personal/nominal organizations.

Clashing Identities and Conflicting Demands between DPOs and Care Institutions

As mentioned earlier, "care institutions" for persons with disabilities took power and hegemony in the postwar era due to the absence of universal state-managed service provision.[23] The polarity and chronic rivalry between DPOs and care institutions stems from the fundamental clash in core existential values with regards to disability and inclusion. DPOs essentially call for the removal of environmental and societal barriers impeding on full community participation and inclusion (social model of disability), while care institutions often perpetuate medical and/or charity-based models of segregated specialized settings of care and service. These institutions reinforce the charity discourse, perpetuating the image of persons with disabilities as passive service recipients, while paradoxically calling for inclusion. This was apparent in conflicting demands during the Lebanon uprising, with DPOs demanding the abolition of institutionalized and segregated care toward inclusion and independent living,[24] while care institutions demanded the government to pay its due subsidies for them to survive.[25]

Another significant cause for conflict is the hidden power of the sectarian politically affiliated care institutions. They rely financially and administratively on their political counterparts, through which political leaders have consistently used disability as a "political card" to showcase their "service to communities" and win electoral votes, reinforcing sectarian clientelism. These political ties were covertly reflected through the limited participation or absence of participation of these groups in the Lebanon uprising protests.

The Disability Movement in Lebanon after October 17: The Need for New Disability Politics?

The historical review of moments of disruption and eruption in the disability rights movement above shows that a judicious combination of several factors is necessary to contribute to change at the policy level: (1) a persistent mobilization across many years, (2) strategic and consistent disruptions enough to stimulate, ignite, or precipitate change, (3) a window of opportunity followed by an act of "seizing the moment," (4) a well-dosed political game play, (5) cross-movement solidarity, such as the anti-war movement, and finally, and most importantly, (6) an agreement on demands and pressures, beyond group-specific and individual divergences and interests. While the Lebanon uprising did indeed create a window of opportunity, a chance to seize a unique nationwide mobilization for change, with a consistent series of disruptions over an extended period (factors 1 to 4), it fell short in establishing deeply rooted cross-movement solidarity and convergence within the disability movement on targeted demands (factors 5 and 6). It also needs to be careful to not be falling into the trap of "elitist" activism and/or to inadvertently perpetuate the "Za'im" leader model of postwar Lebanese politics.

And, while the disability movement carries on in a hopeful form of political resistance across the various multifaceted crises the country has been going through,[26] persons with disabilities in Lebanon continue to be seen as individuals requiring clientelist medical and welfare interventions, instead of being recognized as productive citizens or as a collective political group. According to Shakespeare and Watson (2001), disability politics is first and foremost about establishing disability as a political issue, revolving around the identity of a minority group, disabled by society.[27] The (re) politicization of disability rights and mainstreaming into Lebanese civil rights battles are an imperative. It is only when disability rights are repositioned as a universal cause and not a separate one, when disability inclusion is integral to national political action away from sectarian clientelism, and when everyone fights for "a nation for all," that Lebanon would embark on a true revolutionary journey.

Acknowledgments

I would like to thank the activists interviewed and my doctoral research supervisory team: Prof. Cathrine Brun and Dr. Supriya Akerkar (Oxford Brookes University), Dr. Maha Shuayb (Lebanese American University), and Prof. Michele Asmar (Université Saint-Joseph).

Notes

1 P. W. Kingston, *Chapter 6. Chehabism from Below? Disability Advocacy and the Challenge of Sustaining Policy Reform, in Reproducing Sectarianism: Advocacy Networks and the Politics of Civil Society in Postwar Lebanon* (Suny Press, 2013).
2 Ibid.
3 N. Kabbara, *Non-Violent Resistance and Reform in Lebanon* (Positive Peace for Lebanon: Reconciliation, Reform and Resilience, 2012), 32–4.
4 Freire 1972 cited in T. Shakespeare and N. Watson, "Making the Difference: Disability, Politics, and Recognition," *Handbook of Disability Studies* (2001): 546–64.
5 Kabbara, *Non-Violent Resistance and Reform in Lebanon.*
6 Shakespeare, *Making the Difference,* 580.
7 Kabbara, *Non-Violent Resistance and Reform in Lebanon.*
8 Kingston, *Chehabism from Below?,* 199.
9 Kabbara, *Non-Violent Resistance and Reform in Lebanon,* 33.
10 C. Death, "Disrupting Global Governance: Protest at Environmental Conferences from 1972 to 2012," *Global Governance: A Review of Multilateralism and International Organizations* 21, no. 4 (2015): 579–98.
11 Kingston, *Chehabism from Below?,* 203.
12 Kingston, *Chehabism from Below?*
13 Ibid.
14 E. Combaz, *Situation of Persons with Disabilities in Lebanon,* K4D Report, 2018.
15 Kingston, *Chehabism from Below?.*
16 G. Khawam, "'What About Us?': The Unheard Voices of the Lebanese Revolution," *Kohl: A Journal for Body and Gender Research* 6, no. 2 (Fall 2020): 2.

17 Combaz, *Situation of Persons with Disabilities in Lebanon.*

18 M. Ajjan, *Lebanese with Special Needs Revolt*, in *Annahar*. 2019, https://www.annahar .com/english/article/1061058-lebanese-with-special-needs-revolt.

19 MaharatNews, *People with Disabilities Participate in the Revolution [translated from Arabic]*, in *Maharat News*. 2019, https://maharat-news.com/Disabilitiesinthere volution.

20 L. Ayoub, *The "Disability Movement" in a March in the Heart of the Capital: "Freedom and Dignity for All in a Nation for All"[translated from Arabic]*, in *The Legal Agenda*. 2019, https://legal-agenda.com/%d8%ad%d8%b1%d9%83%d8%a9-%d8%a7%d9%84 %d8%a5%d8%b9%d8%a7%d9%82%d8%a9-%d9%81%d9%8a-%d9%85%d8%b3%d9 %8a%d8%b1%d8%a9-%d9%81%d9%8a-%d9%82%d9%84%d8%a8-%d8%a7%d9%84 %d8%b9%d8%a7%d8%b5%d9%85%d8%a9-%d8%ad/.

21 Ibid.

22 Khawam, "'What About Us?'"

23 Kingston, *Chehabism from Below?*

24 Ayoub, *The "Disability Movement" in a March in the Heart of the Capital.*

25 G. Hamadi, *People with Special Needs Highlight 46th Day of the Revolution*, in *Annahar English* (Beirut: Annahar, 2019.

26 Khawam, "'What About Us?'"

27 Shakespeare, *Making the Difference.*

A Feminist Revolution Par Excellence

Myriam Sfeir

This chapter aims to underscore women's contributions to Lebanon's October 17, 2019, revolutionary uprising. The mass movements were unprecedented, erupting in various regions with the collective aim of bringing down the corrupt ruling elite, and where gender rights and the demands of marginalized groups[1] were upheld by the protesters.

Women were the thrust of the revolution, participating in the protests and calling for long overdue reforms and the importance of having a civil state where all citizens are treated equally and the government respects, protects, and fulfills its obligations to international treaties and women's rights. In this context, this chapter addresses the importance of feminist mobilizing during the revolution, sheds light on the shift in outlook from women's rights to gender rights, and showcases how an intersectional perspective generates more rights for marginalized groups.

The October 17 revolution was a watershed moment for what has historically been understood as the "women's rights movement."[2] Traditionally, the term "women's rights movement" has come to signify those organizations and individuals fighting for the legal rights of women and girls. In Lebanon, such legal activism for women's rights was recorded as early as the 1920s. However, against the backdrop of increasing NGOization[3] and international donor influence; infighting within the women's rights movement regarding "who" should be the focus of the movement and what "feminism" really means;[4] and the increasingly restrictive socio-legal landscape in Lebanon that has rendered women "second-class citizens,"[5] the traditional focus on the rights of Lebanese women and girls was overturned during the latest revolution. The depoliticization of feminist demands in favor of "singular issues" related specifically to Lebanese women—such as women's rights to confer their nationality, custody rights, imposing a quota system, and countering violence against women—was no longer viable. It is true that "smaller" grassroots feminist groups have long been intersectional in their approaches; however, thanks to the revolution they became more vocal and their work more visible. Such a shift, I argue, is indicative of a broader shift away from the umbrella concept of "women's rights"—which encompasses not only cisgender women's legal rights but also gender equality more broadly—toward gender justice, a much more inclusive term that is attuned to the ways that gender identity and sexuality are influenced by and equally influence other social inequalities along the lines of race, class, and citizenship status, to name a few.

"Women's Rights" and Women Mobilizing

Working on gender issues and women's rights has been my lifelong mission. I have always been in awe of our pioneering foremothers, such as Nazeera Zeineddine, Ibtihaj Kaddoura, Emily Fares Ibrahim, and Anissa Najjar[6] who took to the streets, against social norms, to advocate for the legal and socioeconomic rights of women since the nineteenth century.[7] Historically, political mobilization in Lebanon has been pivotal for women's rights activists, beginning with the formation of the Women's Union in Syria and Lebanon in 1924, which participated heavily in nationalist struggles, and the role of women's rights actors during *an-nahda al-'arabiya* (Arab Renaissance).

However, with the onset of a global discourse surrounding women's rights, most notably the United Nations Decade for Women,[8] the focus on a cohesive, singular women's rights movement—with a singular, universal call for the rights of cisgender women and girls—would overshadow the work of those leading other gender-based struggles and movements and those working independently from organizations. Further compounding this singular narrative of women's rights were the class and racial differences between those considered "women's rights activists" and those who remained outside of the feminist canon, or the dominant list of figures historically associated with the women's rights movement.[9] A few major examples are first, the work of women organizers in labor movements, specifically the tobacco strikes of the 1940s,[10] and second, the work of Lebanese mothers during the civil war who organized anti-war marches under banners of unity "no war, no violence, no sectarianism" or "la lil ta'ifiyya" (no to sectarianism).[11] These deeply intersectional movements and struggles, while absolutely critical of women's rights more broadly, remained marginalized in favor of a more cohesive, singular "women's rights" narrative that valued the work of elite Lebanese women who were able, as a result of their class privilege, to focus on single issues.

(Re)Politicizing "Women's Rights": The October 17 Revolution and the Shift toward Gender Equality

The October 17 revolution was a turning point in the history of gender justice and rightfully earned the status of a feminist revolution par excellence.[12] Women played multiple roles in the revolution: they became involved in political organizing, civic engagement, gender justice advocacy, de-escalation of violence, mediation, online mobilization, and media coverage. Along with the quest to bring down the corrupt ruling elite, many feminist groups were focused on toppling the prevalent patriarchal power structures that render women and marginalized groups second-class citizens.[13] The active participation of women in the revolution made us remember our feminist foremothers and their demands within the national struggle for liberation and independence.[14]

Women called for abolishing all personal status codes and adopting a unified civil law that is gender-equitable;[15] eliminating the *kafala*, or visa sponsorship system, that perpetuates an exploitative labor relation between women migrant domestic workers and their Lebanese employers; and amending the existing nationality law, which prevents Lebanese women married to non-Lebanese the right to pass citizenship onto their spouses and their children.

Hence, the revolution marked an important shift away from a singular "women's rights" movement toward a truly intersectional and inclusive call for gender equality *across* the hegemonic women's rights movement embodied by elite women actors and various internationally funded organizations. While the call for intersectionality has been present among actors and organizations of the hegemonic women's rights movement, intersectionality in practice has been inconsistent. But, in the moment of the revolution, the marginalized realities of those intersectional identities—specifically but not limited to migrant women workers, the LGBTQ population, and refugee women—were not simply "added" to an existing list of demands regarding women's rights but were organically at the core of the revolution's demands. Put differently, the broader discourse formerly considered to be a part of "women's rights" was forcibly expanded to include truly intersectional and consequently truly *feminist* demands for *gender equality*. Importantly, even the women's rights organizations that had historically disagreed on certain feminist demands, specifically the rights of nonheteronormative groups, had to later on put forward an intersectional approach for fear of being "left behind."[16] Further, women who fit the normative model of the "women's rights movement"—in other words, middle- and upper-class elite Lebanese women who work in the women's rights sector—marched for these demands.

I observed notable events during my participation in the revolution. First, the movement en masse of women from different socioeconomic and political groups—where they participated in open discussions (criticizing religious law in Nabatieh, a predominantly conservative Shiite area), organized with various groups, and slept in tents (in conservative areas such as Tripoli and the south)—marked a physical turning point toward an intersectional feminist reality. Further, many of the chants used across the protests openly called for sexual rights, countering harassment in all its forms, the importance of sexual pleasure, the rights of trans individuals, and freedom of sexual orientation and gender identity and expression. Such changes marked an important shift away from normative narratives about the "women's rights movement" toward a more inclusive call for gender equality.

Moreover, mothers played an active role, marching for peace and pledging never to allow conflicts to escalate to the level of civil war again.[17] This resulted in two landmark demonstrations: the first aimed at diffusing anger between two neighborhoods representing demarcation lines during the civil war and the second to prevent clashes between two areas where revolutionaries and anti-revolutionary groups live. In both demonstrations, women were armed with the Lebanese flag and white roses and marched chanting unity slogans and singing the national anthem.[18]

Unfortunately, the revolution lost momentum after Lebanon was plagued with compounded crises: the COVID-19 global pandemic and a debilitating economic/financial crisis that was exacerbated by the Beirut Port blast on August 4, 2020. The blast claimed the lives of more than 200 victims, injuring 6,000 others, and displacing 300,000. As such, people's hope for change was shattered.

The Beirut Blast: Mainstreaming Gender
and the Charter of Demands

The recovery plan following the Beirut blast failed to mainstream gender in the strategy put forth. As a result, feminist activists and women's rights organizations in Lebanon openly criticized this reform plan as gender-blind, stressing the importance of gender in recovery and calling for including gender specialists and experts in the decision-making bodies. Hence, in response to the oversight and thanks to the revolution that managed to put gender rights on the agenda, forty-six women's rights and feminist organizations came together and drafted the Charter of Demands by Feminist Activists and Women's Rights Organizations in Lebanon spearheaded by UN Women.[19] The charter called for putting feminist groups and women's groups at the heart of the response plan and demanded that aid be channeled to civil society organizations and delivered in an equitable and just manner. The charter called for recognizing and addressing existing gender inequalities and ensuring that the needs and priorities of all marginalized groups be taken into consideration. It also necessitated that the process follows clear accountability, due diligence, and transparency mechanisms. The Charter of Demands generated an informal Feminist Civil Society Platform—The Feminist Forum[20] that is expected to serve as a supervisory body for the advancement of gender rights. Several consultations and meetings took place with the signatories of the feminist charter that led to the unanimous agreement that such a national platform is needed and should expand its focus beyond the Beirut blast. The forum is envisaged to contribute to a stronger voice for women, women's rights groups, and marginalized groups through a combination of approaches, such as advocacy and lobbying; cooperation and coordination; research, assessment, and data; and monitoring and accountability. The mandate of this forum is to promote intersectional feminism and influence the women's rights and gender equality agenda in Lebanon. We hope that it will maintain momentum, influence policymaking for gender equality, and push forward the feminist intersectional movement.

Concluding Remarks

This chapter underscored the significant role that the revolution played in shifting away from "women's rights" toward adopting an intersectional approach to gender rights. Feminist activism during the revolution served as a reminder that gender rights are not secondary but pivotal to any political movement. Despite some backlash and pushback, a general societal acceptance of the leading role played by women and gender rights activists was evident. Women successfully broke the aura of censorship and silence surrounding "taboo subjects" and challenged the historical attachments to singular issues thus highlighting the importance of intersectionality.

Personally, it was very empowering for me and many activists to witness all these changes and the subsequent shift in narrative. For the first time, I am hopeful that gender rights will no longer be relegated to the margins.

Notes

1 Marginalized groups include women and girls, persons with disabilities, migrant and refugee women, women in conflict with the law, lesbian and bisexual women and transgender people, elderly women, sex workers/women in prostitution, and others.

2 For an in-depth discussion regarding the use of the term "movement," see Deema Kaedbay, "Building Theory Across Struggles: Queer Feminist Thought from Lebanon" [PhD Dissertation]. Ohio State University, Columbus, Ohio, 2014.

3 NGOization was coined by Islah Jad (2003) in the piece entitled "The 'NGOization' of the Arab Women's Movements," published in *Al-Raida*.

4 Such infighting is most clearly seen in regards to the issue of nonnormative sexualities and gender identities and whether or not the fight for the rights and dignity for these communities should be considered the purview of the "women's rights movement" more broadly.

5 S. El Masry and M. Zeaiter, *Breaking the Political Glass Ceiling: Enhancing Women's Political Participation in Lebanon* (Beirut: Lebanon Support, 2018), 6–7.

6 For an inclusive overview of the women's rights movement in Lebanon from its inception until the civil war of 1975, see the documentary film *Women in Time 2002*.

7 Ibid.

8 For more information, see "UN Decade for Women 1975–1985," published in *Al-Raida*, February 1985.

9 Kaedbay, "Building Theory Across Struggles."

10 M. Abi Saab, *Militant Women of a Fragile Nation* (New York: Syracuse UP, 2010).

11 See Mourad, S. in this volume.

12 I write that the October 17 revolution was a "feminist revolution par excellence" to reflect the broader consensus that the revolution had clear gender dimensions, with specific demands for gender equality and women's rights. This is most clearly demonstrated by the protest and chants of the revolution (see Issa in this volume); the graffiti of the revolution (see Rhayem, 2020); and, more broadly, the ways that the revolution was captured via the writing and reflections of various feminist activists. For more in-depth examples, see the 2020 special issue of *Al-Raida* entitled "Gender and Revolution" and the winter 2019 issue of *Kohl: A Journal for Body and Gender Research* entitled "Feminist Revolutionaries."

13 See El Masryand Zeaiter, *Breaking the Political Glass Ceiling*.

14 See *Women in Time 2002*.

15 There were a number of specific demands made during the October 17 revolution regarding the current personal status codes. Alongside their complete removal in favor of a unified civil code, protesters called for a law that criminalizes marital rape and sets a minimum age for marriage. They also demanded a civil code that legalizes civil marriage and one that ensures gender-equitable laws governing marriage, specifically on the issues of child custody and divorce. It is no surprise that some of these demands are directly related to the CEDAW articles to which Lebanon has made reservations, specifically Article 9 related to nationality and Article 16 related to family laws, and those reservations are often a point of contention between the CEDAW committee and the Lebanese government. For Lebanon's report to CEDAW and the criticism generated, see the UN Committee on the Status of Women's Concluding Observations on the combined Fourth and Fifth Periodic Reports of Lebanon, available here: https://digitallibrary.un.org/record/1655254.

16 One such example is the March 2018 demonstration that was organized on the occasion of International Women's Day. It called for feminist mobilization where the theme was "our causes differ but our anger is one." Due to infighting between actors within the traditional women's rights movement and newer feminist grassroots organizations on the issue of LGBTQ rights, some of the traditional activists decided to withdraw and the demonstration continued without them.

17 See https://lebanon.un.org/sites/default/files/2021-02/UN Women_Lebanon%27s 2019 Protests-042358-compressed.pdf.

18 Just like during the war years, where women played an active role in calling for peaceful coexistence, the first demonstration was led by a group of mothers from Ain el-Remmaneh and Chiyyah that sent a clear message of unity and aimed to diffuse the anger between the two neighborhoods where the Lebanese civil war began. Another women-led demonstration, which was organized between the Ring and Khandak el-Ghamik, made the same demands.

19 The full Charter of Demands by Feminist Activists and Women's Rights Organizations in Lebanon can be found here: https://lebanon.unwomen.org/en/digital-library/publications/2020/all-months/charter-of-demands.

20 The members of the Feminist Forum are nongovernmental organizations, grassroots organizations and community-based organizations, academic institutions, networks or coalitions of organizations, and gender and women rights activists, researchers, and academics.

22

Student Activism and the October Uprising

We Felt Once More That Everything Is Anew

Samir Skayni

It was the first student march we had organized in the street. It was not even meant to be a march. We were in Riad El Solh square, with our clear and loud voices: "University of Lebanon—Farajallah Honein."[1] We took the security forces by surprise, ran toward the Association of Banks, and managed to enter. That was the first time we felt as students that everything was anew. May 2018, during the fifty-day strike of the Lebanese University.

Going into the Association of Banks aimed to point at a fact ignored by many people at the beginning, before it turned out to be the right to do: the education sector was only marginalized for the sake of other sectors, as a way for the ruling class to reproduce itself. The same establishment that slashed the Lebanese University's budget engineered profits for the banks.[2] As the banks were thriving, the education sector was collapsing.

And just like that, education was being marginalized and, naturally, the students as well. Their basic rights were now commodified even before the issue of dollarizing tuition fees[3] in some private universities. The space they had as students was stripped from them, their democratic spirit was also killed by banning student elections[4] until their college years felt monotonous and all the same—until "October 17" happened.

The following parts break down the student spaces and movements in Lebanon just a few months before the uprising and the (economic) collapse and go on to a historical and analytic overview of the student movement, before going back to "October 17" and the positioning of students within it. The second part presents the crisis of the education sector, which led to where it stands today, before we conclude with a critique of the current experience for the sake of preparing ahead to position ourselves as students before the new upcoming wave.

Students Organizing Right Ahead of the Crisis

The fifty-day strike and the march to the Association of Banks both took place before "October 17." At the time, the Lebanese University was facing the first serious cut (36 billion LBP[5]) to its budget and to the salaries of its academic personnel. A number of students came together to join the strike alongside their professors, or rather ahead of them, to defend and preserve what was left of their university, and they created what was later named the "Lebanese University Students Union."

And here I wish to pause at the fact that a new crisis in the (Lebanese) University created an effective space for struggle and a "syndic" framework for students. That does not negate the many previous attempts that nonetheless did not necessarily succeed as planned and desired (such as the national student movement in 2018).

I use only a few examples of experiences that shortly preceded October 17. In the wider context, a climate of youth movement is still creating itself, aiming to crystallize enough to influence politics in the country. At times, the "youth upheaval" found an outlet in the sectors of some leftist parties, sometimes in independent university clubs, and at other times it remains inert due to the lack of such frameworks. We can also highlight the "demonstrations against the sectarian system" in 2011 as one moment that contributed to the rebirth of this movement.

The experience after the crisis of the Lebanese University's budget (2018) was by far the peak in terms of grassroots organizing and decentralized work outside Beirut; and that says something significant. I do not make use of this approach as a rule; a quick overview of the history of struggle shows us that the two directions of "movement-crisis" and "crisis-movement" are both valid and on the table. But it does seem that, in post-Taef Lebanon, we are stuck in the second direction in the wider emancipatory politics as in student politics. That is due to objective factors related to the country's politics and economic cycle and to the administrative approaches in universities. It is also linked to subjective factors that have to do with how well organized the opposition groups are, as well as the kind of the consciousness prevalent among students and how involved they are in public affairs.

Counterexamples: Students Who Organized before the Crisis and Mobilized the Streets

The first appearance of the student movement in the mid-last century in Lebanon is a good example. At the time, groups of people, from workers and youth and families, took to the streets until they founded the Lebanese University, joined by students and professors of private universities.[6] The student movement before the civil war[7] fits well into that context too; its dynamism and activity impacted those of the street and rather led and steered it, not the other way around. Among objective factors, the political struggle used to entice and engage social groups. While subjectively, opposition groups struggling for change had a significant role in this fight.

Another example, but on a wider scale (noting all the different objective and subjective conditions of both examples): France in Mai 68 (May 1968). The student movement sparked the uprising and created the "street," organized it, and involved the workers, without waiting for a preceding revolutionary push to commence their agenda. The preceding push was related to the students' ability to join everyone's struggles outside the campus as inside. They raised two slogans sparking a revolutionary wave that changed France as it was known at the time: (1) the issue of sexual liberation and (2) ending the war on Vietnam.[8] This cleverness that connected political and psychological struggles, the individual and the collective, the inside and the outside, is what enabled these forces to drive the change instead of being led by it.

Student Milestones from October 17

On October 17, the crisis moved the opposition forces and pushed them toward new frameworks and forms of organizing. The following are some of the most prominent moments and milestones, chronologically.

The first, titled "student march," took place on October 26, 2019. Its significance lies in how it positioned students on the map of the collapse and with the rest of the forces that tried to counter it. We raised clear slogans as to the causes of the crisis, and slogans that connected education to other state sectors, and others that offered solutions. It (the march) was also significant inside universities where it legitimized a new climate of student activism that political parties arrogantly monopolized. The parties' committees gradually started to decline in popularity until, at one point, they only included the members who were affiliated with the parties themselves (outside campuses).

After the student protests came heavy mobilization inside universities. The most eminent and memorable was the "Hadath Protest" in the Lebanese University on November 7, 2019. The protest had such significance in that it tore down the powerful status of the illegitimate student councils[9] that tried to intimidate students and pressure them not to take part—in addition to chanting the name of Farajallah Honein quite loud in the university's biggest campus. We even started saying "Farajallah Honein Campus" instead of the official name "Rafic Hariri Campus." And although changing the name of the campus had not gotten popular enough yet, I call on you, dear reader, to use the new name whenever you want to refer to this campus.

> The most beautiful scene in my memory was the Hadath campus. In front of the yard of Hassan Musharrafieh faculty stood the generation of Farajallah Honein, chanting for education and freedom and social justice, facing the thieves and capitalism. You are the pulse of the nation. (Wafaa Noun commenting on the Hadath Protest[10])

More than a thousand students gathered at the stairs, chanting their demands: free and democratic education, student elections, transportation and cafeteria and dorms, developed curriculums, and revived academic research.

Over time, marches going from one university to another became a ritual in the students' uprising. This helped in maintaining the momentum even in universities that did not have student groups involved directly in the uprising. This was preceded by a tent set up by Lebanese University students in Riad El Solh square. I remember that this tent did not remain intact during the attacks on October 25 and 29 when supporters of Hezbollah attacked the square[11]—as was the case for students of private universities who had tents there as well. "Student marches" were organized not only by university students but also by high school students.

With the growing momentum, slogans from students joined those in other marches and protests. I go back in time every once in a while and watch videos on my phone when thousands from all social classes and groups were chanting for "education, freedom, social justice." All (social) groups were supporting the Lebanese University and chanting for its budget: "the state's deficit will not be paid from the Lebanese University, go get the money from the pockets of thieves."

As for the Lebanese University's administration, it responded by circulating statements and issuing decisions[12] in an attempt to impose returning to classes. But the student movement was able to bypass the decision. And when it came to the administration's insistence on going back to classes, it was merely just a cover for a hidden aim to pull students from the streets and kill some aspects of the uprising. The circulated statement was brought down following a protest at the central administration, after some students closed their universities and classes with wooden chairs and others demonstrated inside their classrooms as a way to make use of this opportunity and try to convince hesitant students that in fact it was significantly in the interest of the Lebanese University for the strike to continue and for its people to be involved in the uprising.

The administrations of the private universities, however, were not better, as their presidents did not waste time and quickly went to meet the president of the republic during the uprising. If anything, that was in fact a step in support of the establishment, before they went on to oppress students and their uprising in many different ways.

Later, several milestones by students gave a stronger push to an uprising that was relapsing. By that, I am referring to student elections at the beginning of the academic year 2020–1 in private universities, particularly the exceptional results[13] achieved by certain student groups (mainly the Secular Clubs) and the following "Announcement of Students in Lebanon"[14] after that.

And here we add the recent student battles to the ones above:

1. The fight against dollarizing tuition fees,[15] noting that education had been commodified long before that. Many students organized against this decision by the administrations of the American University of Beirut and the Lebanese American University to force students to pay at the 3,900 LBP rate instead of the official 1,515.5 LBP rate.[16]
2. The fight to protect the Lebanese University and develop it, especially with the hardships imposed by the 2021 budget.

All of those milestones generally fall under a bigger framework of connecting political practice happening inside university campuses to that outside.

The Crisis of the Education Sector

Below is a quick overview of the crisis[17] starting from the top to the bottom, given that it manifests on many levels hierarchically and horizontally:

The Establishment's View of State Sectors

While the establishment's interests lie solely in rentier sectors, education is not considered a productive sector despite being at the core of the "production" process if we view, for example, students as a knowledge value able to develop itself and advance its society. A look at public budgets and distribution of resources of ministries and the budgets of universities[18] is enough, especially concerning the education sector.[19] In addition to the policy of prioritizing private education over public education and the marginalization of technical education with the establishment's efforts to promote it as a "failed" sector, even though it would constitute a solution to the education crisis in a situation like Lebanon's.

Cartel of Private Universities and Ascending the Lebanese University

The link is dialectical and goes both ways: the Lebanese University was only marginalized due to the extreme lengths that the cartel of private universities took, and the cartel of private universities only went to such far lengths only due to the deliberate paralysis of the Lebanese University inside out.

In Lebanon, by the way, the biggest 11 private universities created their own collective after the uprising and named it the "Group of Private Universities," which operates similarly to a lobby in order to pressure the state for what they want; much like the Association of Banks.

As for the power and influence of this group, they stem from the fact that these institutions are linked to:

1) Sect leaders and politicians, hence also to traditional political parties and the parliament;
2) Religious institutions that are bourgeois and authoritarian themselves, from the church to Islamic councils;
3) Big investors and donors who profit significantly from these universities, even if some are registered as "non-profits," which is of course a false premise.

Students: The Weakest but Strongest Link

The problem starts with dealing with students as commodities. Capital dehumanizes them as soon as set foot in schools up until they graduate from higher education. Contrary to popular belief, rentier economy is not limited to making money out of money but also out of "production": producing knowledge that is doomed to succumb to the dominant ideology and what it requires. You force students to accept being part of this dreadful cycle of the Lebanese economy that counts on remittances from expats abroad, among other things, most of whom are fresh graduates. This is what we call displacement, beyond emigration.[20]

This process has additional implications on the student movement in Lebanon that hurdle sustainable organizing and make it far more difficult to accumulate expertise among activist students to be shared smoothly from one generation to another.

Not to mention that those who stay are faced with social and economic burdens that prevent them from even thinking of issues beyond the curriculum, including taking down the system. A vast portion of the youth that are we imagine to be the most revolutionary, out of revolutionary nostalgia, do not have access to the tools necessary for the revolution due to their lived reality.

The collapse, on the other hand, had implications on students on many levels. Some who were already in dire conditions reached became worse off, some only saw their conditions get worse, some lost the privileges they once had, and for some others such *"privileges"* were services that they deserved after paying a high price. The point is, most students were marginalized in some way, even if not to the same degree, and they were the weakest link; except that they had an opportunity to create their own space of struggle where they could be the strongest link.

One of the implications of the crisis was the phenomenon of "student migration" on three levels, all leading to more burdens on public education in general and on the Lebanese University specifically. And here we mean the students that transferred to the Lebanese University after:

1. They had been continuing their education abroad which was no longer possible due to the arbitrary restriction by the banks on money transfers,
2. They moved from private to public education either because of the dollarized tuition or the devaluation of the Lebanese pound,
3. They graduated with a certificate of passing [without exams] for the academic year 2019-2020 then directly went into majors that did not require entry exams.

Add to all of the above the Lebanese University's students (around 80,000) and new students registering regularly, which creates an existential threat to the Lebanese University that will in turn implicate the quality of the education.

Then came the budget of the academic year 2021 and put the public sector to rest, including the Lebanese University as an institution on the one hand (through budget cuts) and its human resources as public sector employees on the other hand (slashing pensions, benefits, and Social Security).

This brief overview of the education crisis should be enough to understand its complexities and to realize that it is rather a structural crisis; and this is only when we speak of the education sector. However, the solution for this sector is related to solving a bigger crisis, which is the system as a whole.

Students to Be at the Core of the Next Revolutionary Wave

It seems evident to conclude and confirm through experience that student battles are not limited to students alone. It is crucial for different social groups to come together and ally against the intersecting crises, despite the fact that liberal thought promotes them as separate issues. It is necessary to amplify contradictions in all fields and to undergo the struggle without boasting or lagging for reasons that have to do with the different intensities of said struggle in different fields. It is beyond necessary for students, and the youth in general, to take steps forward and connect with other social groups including, and most importantly, workers in general, and in particular everyone who suffers layers of exploitation (migrant workers and migrant domestic workers, workers in rural areas and marginalized sectors, the feminist movement, etc.).

But all this could not have been achieved by the October 17 uprising. And here we get to wonder about the potential of revolutionizing an uprising versus carrying on with it without combining those elements, which are specifically where the most revolutionary powers of society lie. This way of connecting was a door that the uprising opened for us, except that we did not enter it, besides other doors.[21] And so it was a lacking uprising.

Although we admit that the "October 17 uprising" has ended, this does not deny the possibilities of new uprisings. This is not the end of struggle, nor is it the end of revolutionary waves that have and will hit our region, which were generally sparked in 2010 and echoed in Lebanon through the 2011 "demonstrations against the sectarian system," to the movement of 2015, and the uprising of October 17, 2019, until we reach the future revolutionary waves awaiting us.

Those are all key milestones and essential parts of a wider revolutionary process in which the youth had the biggest share in attempting to realize their dreams—as well as in its eventual demise.

And with each wave, we were clinging to a thread of hope among many layers of frustration and discouragement. With each upheaval, each protest, each chant, each "University of Lebanon—Farajallah Honein," we would live that "feeling greater than love."[22]

We felt once more that everything is anew, even if for a brief moment.

Notes

1 Farajallah Honein is considered the first martyr of the student movement in Lebanon. He was a law student at Saint Joseph University when he was killed in 1951 during a protest demanding to found the Lebanese University. He was also the first president of the student sector in the Lebanese Communist Party.

2 Remarkably, the budget of the Lebanese University is set by the government while the financial engineering is planned and executed by the Central Bank, which provides a clearer understanding of the kind of "establishment" in Lebanon: the establishment of the banks, political leaders, and big investors—or what is known as the "oligarchy."

3 On December 8, 2020, the American University of Beirut decided to set tuition fees at the exchange rate of 3,900 LBP, followed by the Lebanese American University a few days later.

4 Student elections in the Lebanese University have been banned since 2008.

5 Ministry of Finance, "Draft Law for the Public Budget and Expenditure Allocations for 2019" (Mashrou' Kanoun Al Muawazanat Al Aamma Wal Muwazanat Al Molhaka Lil Aam 2019), 440, the difference in expenses in the total of chapter 220.

6 Ibrahim Al Basha, "Lebanese Universities and Issues of its Development" (Al Jamiaa Al Loubnaniya Wa Kadaya Tatawouriha, 1981), 37, *Al Tarik*, February.

7 Fawwaz Traboulsi, "A History of Modern Lebanon," *Riad El-Rayyes Books*, 2018, fifth edition, 300, Students against the Community of Merchants (Al Tollab Dod Mojtamaa Al Tojjar).

8 Philippe Artières, Michelle Zancarini-Fournel, "68: A Collective History (1962–1981)," *Editions la découverte, Paris*, 2018, 407.

9 In general, the Shia Twin control the illegitimate student councils in the first branches of the Lebanese University, while Christian parties control the councils in the second branches. The councils are considered illegitimate seeing as student elections do not take place in the Lebanese University and given the resulting entailment among members of the dominant party.

10 A text by Wafaa Noun.

11 Read Joseph Daher's chapter in this book.

12 The administration of the Lebanese University issued a decision on October 26 for students to return to classes, which students did not abide by.

13 Samir Skayni, "The Win of Independents at the Lebanese American University: More than a Mere Breakthrough, Comrades" (Fawz Al Mostakellin Fil Jamiaa Al Loubnaniya Al Amerikiya: Innahu Akthar men Khark Ya Rifak, 2020), *Daraj Media*, October 11, https://daraj.com/57134/.

14 Saturday, December 12, 2020, student groups organized the "Announcement of Students in Lebanon" where they launched a document aiming to activate the role of students in political work and to advocate for their causes. The announcement followed the momentum of student elections in private universities.

15 Samir Skayni, "Private Universities Are Waging A War Against You; Fight Back" (Al Jamiaat Al Khassa Touhariboukom, Haribouha, 2020), *Megaphone*, December 18, https://megaphone.news/%d8%a7%d9%84%d8%ac%d8%a7%d9%85%d8%b9%d8%a7 %d8%aa-%d8%a7%d9%84%d8%ae%d8%a7%d8%b5%d8%a9-%d8%aa%d8%ad%d8 %a7%d8%b1%d8%a8%d9%83%d9%85-%d8%ad%d8%a7%d8%b1%d8%a8%d9%88 %d9%87%d8%a7/.

16 Preparation to dollarize tuition fees started months before the crisis; students tried to counter it early on: https://beirut-today.com/2019/09/02/university-student-activists -protesting-tuition-dollarization-lebanon/.

17 Samir Skayni, "A Vertical Reading of the Education Sector Crisis," *The Peace Building in Lebanon News Supplement,* December 9, 2020, https://www.peacebuildingsu pplement.org/articles/%d8%a7%d9%84%d8%aa%d8%b9%d9%84%d9%8a%d9%85 /517/undp-the-peace-building-news/en.

18 Samir Skayni, "The Lebanese University's Budget: Here is Where Commodification Starts" (Mizaniyata Al Jamiaa Al Loubnaniya: Houna Yabdaa Al Taslih, 2021), *Megaphone*, February 11, https://megaphone.news/%d9%85%d9%8a%d8%b2%d8%a7 %d9%86%d9%8a%d8%a9-%d8%a7%d9%84%d8%ac%d8%a7%d9%85%d8%b9%d8 %a9-%d8%a7%d9%84%d9%84%d8%a8%d9%86%d8%a7%d9%86%d9%8a%d8%a9/.

19   Samir Skayni, "Supporting Education in Lebanon and Excluding the University of the Poor" (Daam Al Taalim Fi Loubnan Wa Estethnaa Jamiaat Al Foukaraa, 2020), *Daraj Media*, September 21, https://daraj.com/55635/.

20   R. Majed, "Born to be exported"?: The Post-Civil War Lebanese youth (s) 1 and the Rupture between Education and Employment 2. In *Youth at the Margins* (Routledge, 2019), 83–103.

21   Samir Skayni, "On A Door Opened By The Uprising That We Did Not Enter" (An Bab Fatahthou Al Intifada Wa Lam Nadkholh, 2021), *Megaphone*, April 10, https://megaphone.news/%d8%b9%d9%86-%d8%a8%d8%a7%d8%a8-%d9%81%d8%aa%d8%ad%d8%aa%d9%87-%d8%a7%d9%84%d8%a7%d9%86%d8%aa%d9%81%d8%a7%d8%b6%d8%a9-%d9%88%d9%84%d9%85-%d9%86%d8%af%d8%ae%d9%84%d9%87/.

22   *A Feeling Greater Than Love* film (documentary—2017—93 min.), by Lebanese director Mary Jirnamnus Saba. Although the film is about the worker protests in the 1970s, it embodies a feeling experienced by everyone who joined the strike at the time. It seems as though this feeling is shared by workers and students and others, and by everyone who went through revolutionary struggle and witnessed the exception becoming a norm.

23

Roadblocking, Mass Strike, and the Qantari Collective

Rawane Nassif

I left Lebanon in the summer of 2006, a couple of weeks before the July war, and while my trip was supposed to be short, it turned into a fourteen-year travel. I experienced the war via distance, alone, powerless, looking at the collective from afar. And since then, my relationship to Beirut changed. I had missed a crucial part of the history of the country and it drifted us apart and it haunted me for years, the feeling of wanting to be back. Back in time, back in space. But I could never afford to. Migrating is one of the economic pillars and destiny of most Lebanese, and I became one of many lost in translation, forever looking for a home, forever longing, entertaining the perpetual curse of the fantasized return.

In 2019 my time had come, the clock ticked twice and my desire to settle became imminent. Allured by the insane interest rates that Lebanese banks were offering, I sent all of my savings to Lebanon, resigned from my job, booked a one-way ticket, boarded a plane, and looked from the window on top of the ever-stacked concrete blocks on the Lebanese mountain and wondered if I could squeeze in. It all looked simple from above. Small Lego blocks forming a country. But once in Lebanon, reality hit me. Our corrupt state that made me an immigrant stole my money and destroyed my home. Twice.

It is that anger that pulled me throughout the revolution to take my revenge, and my biggest vengeance was to actually enjoy it all, to love the city, to meet everybody whom I was longing to meet for years, to connect to as many groups as possible, to reclaim stolen spaces, to become part of the place, and to make up for the time that I wasn't there but wished that I was. And my biggest revenge was to help create the Qantari collective that blocked roads, targeted banks, connected with other groups, and self-organized in tools of public dissent.

On Self-organizing

In the first few days of the revolution, I was trying to understand and map as fast as possible all that was happening: groups forming in the downtown of Beirut, tents popping everywhere, food distributions, political gatherings, juice carts, dance parties, music trucks, meetings, debates, slogans, graffiti, and so forth. It was a huge bustle, but with the current plan of the city, the downtown was purposefully cut out from Beirut and pushed toward the sea and to restrict our activities, the authorities gated the so-called revolutionary area.[1] Therefore, it was necessary to not get trapped in it and to decentralize instead and be in various streets and in different traffic centers such as Qantari, which is the entrance of Hamra, a prominent street in Beirut, and a block before the Central Bank.

To keep the momentum and to keep the power balance in our favor, we needed to maintain the general strike, freeze the economy, and block all streets. Roadblocks became essential since companies and universities could only continue the general strike if the employees could not reach their work.[2] We needed to block the traffic to provide an excuse for people to not go to work and be able to join the protests and to keep the universities closed, so students, who are the largest mass, could remain in the streets.[3] Also to emphasize that we the people own the streets and our battle with the regime is a street battle.

I joined the next morning a roadblock. We gathered behind reversed burned garbage bins while I spotted two young men on mopeds standing on the side and asked them if they were with us. "Yes, we are the ones who brought the garbage bins, we blocked eight streets at 5 am today (October 25th)." They are a group of guys who camp at the ring and with their mopeds and a little gasoline, they block most city streets in half an hour. The problem is, they need people to stay around the garbage bins once the barricade is made, because at 6 a.m. the garbage trucks and firefighters go behind them and clean the streets. But if we manage to keep blocking the streets until 7 a.m. when the news channels and the traffic department state that the streets are closed, businesses and governmental institutions will announce that they are closed, and we win an extra day of general strike. "Do I need to have a moped?" I asked. "No, we can pick you up if you want, we have a WhatsApp group for blocking roads, pick the location that is closer to you, and we will be there."

And that was it. I chose the Qantari WhatsApp group and showed up at 5 a.m., on time to find garbage bins burning and no moped in sight. I then contacted people on the WhatsApp group.

Marwa

On October 26, I reached Qantari and Rawane met up with me. The energy I felt is indescribable. There was a restaurant on the corner that closed down to help us block the road and offered us breakfast. A flower shop offered us the use of their toilets and a lady offered her apartment and brought us biscuits and water. Another small shop offered us coffee.

One of the restaurant waiters got so excited when he knew that we wanted to block the road and asked us if we had a wheel and a flag. We said no. He jumped to his car and brought us exactly that. He went to work prepared, hoping to meet revolutionaries on the way. The restaurant closed and the full staff joined us including three Syrian workers and their mopeds.[4] By that time my American friend joined and two more Lebanese from the Qantari WhatsApp group. Then a Bangladeshi worker came from one of the nearby buildings asking if we needed anything. We needed a cardboard to write "the road is blocked" and another one with the names of the hospitals with an arrow. He got us two cardboards and a marker and stood with us. We formed two lines that rotated, one front line where we talked to cars and one back line with the flag. At some point there was at the front line three Syrians, one American, and one Bangladeshi and not a single Lebanese. I thought to myself, this is a revolution, when everybody living on this land had enough of the ruling mafia and felt empowered to speak up.

All other roadblocks had people on them and apparently ours stood the longest. At 2 p.m. we opened the road and walked to downtown Beirut. The euphoria that we all stood our ground, synchronized across the country, was unimaginable. Trusting each other and random guys on mopeds was so easy at the time. There were no thoughts of being infiltrated or watched. Qantari was one block below the house of Walid Jumblatt, leader of the Progressive Socialist Party, and his guard made sure to walk by us and show his gun and dog and took our car plate number. But we didn't care. We felt invincible.

On October 27, I went again to Qantari; there was another group of people, another car, another flag, many passersby, and many stories. There I met Fadwa. On that night, Fadwa and I took the contacts of the guys on mopeds and organized the first meeting for all road blockers of Beirut. Spontaneous meetings were easy since everybody was in downtown at all times. We met, exchanged strategies and names, divided into groups according to regions, decided on which roads we will block, drew a map of the city, made a WhatsApp coordination roadblocking group for all of Beirut, and wished each other luck.

That same night a friend and I spoke to all the people we knew and invited them to a meeting where Fadwa and I explained how we block the road, and we made a new Qantari WhatsApp group. The second day at 5 a.m. at the Qantari intersection, a bunch of misfits showed up with chairs, music instruments, cookies, banners, and flyers.

Jad

We put a sign with an indication to the hospitals and their names. The larger group was standing at the back playing music, singing and dancing. On the front line, we would approach the cars to give them directions and distribute cookies. We talked politely to everyone and refused to ask for any identity card. I even let an old man pass because he told me "God bless you, my son. I want to get to the hospital quickly." We are not bandits or thugs, we went to the streets for 12 days, but the government ignored us. We were forced to escalate, or else they would siege us. This is us, the ones fighting for our rights and yours, and they, the criminals.

We viewed ourselves as an extension of the revolution, but in the streets, a decentralization of the revolutionary squares. As if we extended downtown Beirut to Qantari and other roadblocking points, and on this front line, we could share our messages and an imaginary of how we wanted to live. Happy, creative, fearless, and free. We weren't fighting against a government only; we were also trying to collectively create a possibility. Or at least the image of it. The celebratory aspect of our oneness was essential, a reminder of our imminent victory, of taking back the streets. It wasn't a roadblock. It was a meeting space. A friendly neighborhood. A tent where we could discuss our views. Our revolutionary imaginary went to all parts of society, from farming to banks. While blocking roads we talked about what is next and then we self-organized as a collective with different tasks, an open access to join, subgroups of research and media and direct action, political and economic and artistic interventions, daily meetings, a manifesto, and a clear relationship to other groups in the revolution.

Sahar

> There were artists and students, people from Beirut, Hermel, Tripoli. Some were religiously conservative, others atheist. Some were anarchists, while others were interested in politics. Qantari was an attempt at organization that went beyond identity differences. Maybe it was love, maybe it was courage, I still find it difficult to grasp, but certainly humour and empathy made us last as long as we did.

There was so much love, so much laughter, so much hope. And a real understanding of why we were all present. An overreaching feeling of expansion, of a larger consciousness building.

Dangers of Roadblocking

Even though we took the name the Qantari collective, we had no ownership over the spot, and we had to negotiate with any other group that decided to close the same street. We negotiated to keep the hospital road open and to let ambulances and doctors and media pass. Very fast, one gets a sense of the power dynamic that builds up when we have the authority to open or close a road, so we needed to keep ourselves in check.

But the biggest specter that was haunting us was the image of the roadblocks of the civil war. Seeing us could trigger war memories for a certain generation, of barricades with ID controls and militia men deciding on who passes and who gets shot. So beside singing, we made sure to explain to drivers why we are blocking the road, and that emergency cases can pass, and we distributed a pamphlet that stated roughly:

> Because the road is blocked every time it rains, because the road is blocked each time a politician convoy passes, because the road is blocked by fraudulent street construction, because the road is blocked due to traffic mismanagement. Only this time, we are blocking the road, so we can together stop all other roadblocks.

Another danger was our portrayal in the media since most news agencies wanted to antagonize us against the public opinion.[5] "What does the street want" was the famous slogan that the media kept pushing to infantilize the revolution by asking repeatedly the same questions. In a famous example, a reporter asked a man who clearly was attacking the parliament, "what are you doing," to which he mockingly answered, "I am getting my pants hemmed." It was a nerve game. Drivers would come purposefully to pick a fight exactly when news stations were filming and then would repeat their show at other roadblocks. Twice we were run by a car from partisans of the regime. Once it carried two students on its roof and the driver stopped only when a guy jumped inside the car and pulled the hand brake. We literally became a street theatre where the ethics and morals of the revolutionary body were at play, and if we lost our cool in dealing with the drivers, we would be portrayed as thugs.

But while drawing the map of the city, while deciding on which roads to block and which cars to let by, we also accidentally decided on the means of transport that we wanted: motorbikes, bicycles, and pedestrians only. We reimagined a slower, smaller, friendlier, walkable city. One of my most precious feelings was when I was hopping from a motorbike to the other, gliding in a new world order that we planned, going from a roadblock to the other distributing refreshments and hugs. We truly were the queens of the streets. And I felt it. That exhilarating freedom of movement, of decision making, of walking in a potential dream scape of what we imagine our city to be, of reclaiming back our streets.

Jad

> During this period, while walking the streets of Beirut, I felt that those streets were mine. Not only the squares, but all the streets are mine, the city is mine, and wherever I set foot, it is mine.

I speak about Beirut a lot because this is where Qantari is, but in the decentralization of the movement, and with squares and tents and rallies throughout Lebanon, we had a space to visit in every city and a communal tent to enter without being invited. I felt a larger self in the whole country. We introduced ourselves as "revolutionaries" and that was enough to be welcomed in any tent, and to become part of the conversation. Because suddenly, we all had one conversation, the revolution.

Changing Tactics

In late October, we had already formed an extensive network of roadblocking and university groups and had daily meetings to discuss strategies. Communication between us was key, so was the trust that people would show up at 5 a.m., every single day. Students from a university would block the road of another university, and vice versa, so their administration would not see them. A weak point in the barricade map would make other points suffer, so our actions had to be synching on a national level daily.

But being on the front lines of the roadblocks, it was very easy to sense the pulse and the reactions of the street, and we knew that we couldn't hold the blockades any longer. A countrywide discussion and change of tactics had to happen, and we opted to change from blocking random roads to targeting specific locations such as the electricity building or the phone companies. It was a losing battle at the mercy of the public opinion.

Whatever we did, we were told to do something else. When we blocked roads, they said we should block centers of corruption. When we blocked specific institutions, they said we should go to the houses of politicians. When we went there with garbage bags, they said we were hooligans and that we should go to the presidential palace. When we went there, they said we should go to the banks. When we went to the banks, they said we should talk to the streets. When we made demonstrations across neighborhoods who actually welcomed us with rice, they said we should go to the justice palace. And the list goes on and on. We kept running around in circles wondering what to do next and loosing energy at deciding on a target, in the hopes that more people would join, while the public opinion remained very opinionated and inactive.

Looking Back

Oscillating between believing that our work is cumulative and understanding the complex nature of the beast ruling us and feeling the crippling weight of the economic meltdown was too much to bear and I lost hope. It is not only a corrupt government, a sectarian regime, a polluted landscape, an oppressive system, a lawless bunch of thieves, a racist population, and a hypocrisy that sieves into the air; but it is also a sleeping pill on top of it all. And time stops. The amount of time spent waiting for the electricity to come, the internet to load, the water to run, the traffic to move, the country to change. I could just sit and watch my hair grow.

Gaby

Be there hope or not we cannot stop trying. Owning this dissonant relationship between hope and hopelessness is powerful and in a country like Lebanon it is only dangerous when one takes over the other blindly.

"We truly were beautiful," said a friend while looking at videos of us. We had agency, we looked after each other, and we didn't look back. And that will remain with me.

Walid

There were people at work for their country, driven by no political agenda other than their own, in the most political moment in our current history, and their work was an event that will never go down in history. And that is what made it special.

Notes

1 See Harb and Tannoury-Karam in this volume.
2 See Hassan in this volume.
3 See Skayni in this volume.
4 See Choeb and Makkawi in this volume.
5 See Kozman in this volume.

24

Night of the Banks

Uprising against the Rule of Banks

Mohammad Bzeih

No one would have expected that Thursday, October 17, 2019, was going to be the beginning of new possibilities. On this evening, the popular uprising erupted, which was unprecedented in Lebanon's modern history for its wide geographical reach, mass participation, and duration in time. That was all concerning the form it took. As for it actually entailed, it was a popular uprising with vast participation by groups of society that had been affected severely by the "status quo" on many levels politically, economically, and socially. The uprising was like a stone thrown in the stagnant waters of all popular, social, and economic aspects of postwar Lebanon. The WhatsApp call tax, which was supposed to pass, represents the direction of austerity that the government was taking at the time and their intention to increase taxes on the poorest, in order to decrease its deficit and spending without considering poverty, unemployment, living conditions, the economic recession, and the deteriorating infrastructure. Those issues were at the core of the uprising's discourse, in addition to the disappointment in the power-sharing sectarian system, which (the discourse) went as far as demanding to topple it and take it down.

Nevertheless, one thing that was renewed in the popular uprising was the destruction of the myth of the "banking sector" at last. For years, the dominant narrative was that the banking sector was the backbone of the country, and the position of Riad Salame was so high up collecting one award after another until he eventually rang the bell of New York's stock market. But the facts and reality, even well before the popular uprising, had already started to weaken this aura. Banks were starting to impose restrictions on USD withdrawals in May 2019 at the latest.[1] The (initial) change in the exchange rate was first registered at least since August 1.[2] Fitch Credit Ratings Agency downgraded Lebanon to the position of "real possibility of default."[3] Then the popular uprising erupted and the Association of Banks (ABL) decided to close the banks. One must wonder about the conditions in which the decision was made as well as its implications.[4] The closure lasted two weeks while the image was becoming more clear; depositors would head to withdraw their money and come back disappointed. Where are the deposits? Depositors ask, and it turns out later that the deposits "vanished" and banks would have a hard time implementing the Central Bank's circular that stated that they can only keep 3 percent of foreign currency deposits at the correspondent banks![5]

This chapter will present some key events and points that drew the connection between the popular uprising and the banks and the banking sector in Lebanon, starting with the mobilization before the uprising on October 17, 2019, up until the night of January 14, 2020, now known as the "nights of banks."

October 17 versus Banks

Banks were the target of the popular uprising from the beginning, perhaps even before then. On October 11, 2019, the Youth and Student Sector of the Lebanese Communist Party broke into the headquarters of the General Labor Union where they called for a protest on October 13 at the headquarters of ABL through the government's Serail until reaching the Central Bank. The statement called on different groups to join from workers, farmers, students, and professionals as follows:

> Let us direct our struggle to the biggest cavern in our country, the den of the 1%, ABL where the people's wasted money is stacked in banks due to the triple alliance destroying this country: the troika of banks, the Central Bank and the political establishment.

With the uprising erupting on the evening of October 17, more actions took place and the Youth Sector along with other organized groups—some were old and others newly formed in the first few days of the uprising—such as "Taamim Al Masaref"(in Arabic: *Nationalizing Banks*), "Al-Haraka Al Shababiya Lil Taghyir" (in Arabic: *Youth Movement for Change*), Shabab Al Masref (in Arabic: *The Bank Youth*), Union of Lebanese Democratic Youth, and a number of individuals, all targeted the banks with their actions and efforts. That started by breaking into several branches of banks in Beirut and reading statements to show people the magnitude of the profits and interests that banks were making, and to call on making them pay the price for the collapse.

But the banking apparatus only became more stubborn and obstinate. While the banks were closing the doors and imposing arbitrary and selective Capital Controls, a group of powerful people were transferring their money abroad thus contributing significantly to the unprecedented deficit in the balance of payments by around 10 billion USD in 2020, in addition to banning dollars from a society that needs them for their most basic needs, from energy to medication and food.

January 14, 2020: "Night of the Banks"

In the context of escalation and growing subjugation of the people, actions at banks were increasing and spreading all around the country until Tuesday, January 14, 2020. That night, crowds were protesting at the Central Bank's headquarters in Hamra. Clashes started at the new "wall" of the Central Bank, which was made of wooden boards and metal. Protesters tried to bypass it, and the riot police responded harshly, using batons and throwing tear gas.

It was always remarkable how violent the riot police would be when defending banks, after the then minister of interior Raya El Hassan's instructions to spread security forces at banks to protect them from people's anger and after ABL had thanked her and the director of Internal Security Forces (ISF) Imad Othman in a press release for "responding fast and effectively to the Association's request."[6] That decision made clear the role of security forces as the "security apparatus of the oligarchy" who had been playing this role with utmost competency. Clashes started at the wall of the (Central) Bank. And once protesters were able to make a hole in the wall after removing a wooden board with their bare hands and going into the bank's yard, the riot police immediately attacked and beat them. They kept on trying to move protesters away from the bank toward Hamra street.

Clashes continued. Then the retreating crowds found a way to the branches of several banks. The first was the branch of Société Générale de Banque au Liban (SGBL) whose front glass was smashed. One of our comrades wished he had had some gasoline; unfortunately, we did not. This should give an idea as to whether or not the violence that night was predetermined (as were the accusations)!

And so the riot police were advancing, the protesters were retreating back and attacking the first bank they would see. The confrontation lasted hours, with ongoing hit-and-run and more tear gas. A crowd of retreating protesters at the branch of BankMed were met with three of four members of ISF, most likely coming from a nearby police station.

It was surreal. The three members stood at the front of the bank with its metal door, attempting to move and keep the protesters away. But they soon realized that this attempt was only a "blatant joke." Practically, they were surrounded by hundreds of unarmed protesters. The next day, photos and videos of them were leaked that were said to show the complicity of the ISF by not "dealing" with protesters as they should have. But in reality, an ISF member wearing a mask actually jumped in the street and fired in the air. But that did not get protesters to retreat and go back. Clashes were ongoing for hours, with constant hit-and-run until the crowds dispersed due to the heavy use of tear gas. The night ended with a vast wave of arrests of dozens of protesters,[7] which led to more confrontations and clashes the next day in Mar Elias street where they were detained in El Helou police station.

The Aftermath Following the Night of the Banks

A lot could be said about that "Night of the Banks." One remarkable thing was the "surgical-like" precision of the demonstrators' actions; despite all the violence against the banks, no one attacked any shops or people's properties. The Night of the Banks was quite significant in the context of politically sorting the general scenery especially within the uprising. The next day statements were released and denounced what had happened. The United Nations Special Coordinator for Lebanon Ján Kubiš tweeted:

Vandalism is never an appropriate way to manifest the legitimate anger and desperation of demonstrators. Beware of political manipulation, of infiltrators trying to hijack and compromise the legitimate protests, to provoke security forces that are also part of the Lebanese people.[8]

The following day, a newspaper titled its front page (in Arabic) "Hezbollah Hijacks the Revolution and Directs It against the Governor of the Central Bank."[9] Some people complained about the violence, and these opinions did represent the narratives we were facing since the beginning of the uprising: stigmatizing everyone who opposed the Central Bank's and the other (commercial) banks' policies as "Moumanaa" (i.e. pro-Hezbollah) on the one hand and diluting the struggle against the system on the other. This was ironic given that Hezbollah, despite the propaganda, did not conduct one single concrete measure against the social and economic role of the banking sector and the governor of the Central Bank Riad Salameh on the one hand, and the significant role of the banking sector in maintaining the political structure on the other. Those were traits of the neoliberal ideology manifesting in the uprising's discourse that throws the accusation of "economism" at everyone who demonstrates the mechanisms and institutions of exploitation and the dominance that the system relies on.

Is the violence against the bank fronts on par with the violence of the system that had been ongoing for decades? That night was also significant in that it made bank executives sense the seriousness of the streets, but that obsession later faded after we could not persist and commit with a methodology in that context. The Night of the Banks would have been a turning point in our fight against the system, but it never was. The reason was our inability to find a way yet for a political project endorsed by a front that would be the anchor for outreach efforts and in a context of democratic struggle—until now—on the roadmap to build a popular democratic state.

Between Economism and Pure Politicization: Banks Remain the Main Target

The "bank issue" was, and still is, a main determining factor upon which the contrast within the wings of the uprising is based. Despite all the accusations of "economism" that could have been, and were indeed, thrown at everyone that persisted in pushing the discourse on the banks to the political discussions, one cannot stickle and rise above the importance of the "bank issue." First, the collapse of the banking sector, including commercial banks and the Central Bank, might be unprecedented historically in terms of the massive hiatus and its impact on society and the economy. The collapse was just as vast as the cancerously expanding banking sector. The Central Bank today has a gap nearly three times the size of the gross domestic product, on top of the foreign currency deposits that evaporated whereby ABL attempted everything imaginable and unthinkable to evade the Central Bank's request to secure only 3 percent (of those deposits) to correspondent banks. ABL reached a point where it submitted a legal study aiming to use the spread of the coronavirus as an excuse for exceptionally extending the deadlines, in order to stall and not succumb to securing the minimal amount of deposited dollars after they (the banks) dissipated them.[10]

Second, we cannot simply ignore the fact that for a long time, the state's primary budget was making much surplus before it reached a deficit after paying the interest on the public debt. This means that the debt was accumulating to a large extent in order to pay the debt, which practically means that society has been working hard to service the interest of the debt, while being deprived of the most basic rights to education and other social services such as health care, energy, transportation, communication, employment, and development. All of that had been banned from society for the purpose of serving the banks' profits. Third, the bank capital was not taking a share of people's hard work exclusively through the mechanism of public debt but also through families' loans with their high interest rates. Even housing, the most basic human right, was turned by the banks into a mechanism to enslave families and youth to make high profits. Fourth, those who oppose talking about the banks and want to focus more on "politics" instead must define what is political in the first place! If people's freedom being restrained by the rule of the banks, among other restrictions, and their dignified living and prosperity and ownership of what they were producing with their own hands, and if living in a democratic society where they can participate in making their own fate as opposed to being destined for collateral damage or being used as fuel for the profits of a banker and the dominance of a ruler; if all this is not the essence of politics, then what is? Then they must prove how politicians and bankers do in fact consider themselves and their interests as inherently different and contradictory. It's not everyday, nor in every state, that we see the head of the Association of Banks attending government and presidential meetings and taking down an entire governmental plan. And here a very important story must be mentioned: anchoring the political system after the civil war was faced with a wide countercampaign by six banks that increased the exchange rate from around 700 LBP to around 3,000 LBP, which took down the government of Omar Karami and led to the formation of (Rafic) Hariri's first government.

Who Will Pay the Price?

The significance of targeting banks lies in being an act of society defending itself. Banks were, and still are, the most crucial part in answering the most important question in the times of collapse and that is "who will pay the price?" The accumulating losses need to be paid by someone. And contrary to the usual protocols that should have been followed to lay the responsibility on bank shareholders first and foremost then on debenture holders while leaving depositors to the end and protecting the smallest and medium ones, what is actually happening is the complete opposite. The oligarchy succeeded in flipping this logic, which is their own logic. And what has been going on for the past two years after the collapse of this (economic) model is forcing society to take the burden of the resulting losses and casualties made by the banks and the Central Bank, all in addition to the implications of the wealth made and owned by a small few. The oligarchy made one victory after another in its ideological war against society when it successfully convinced big portions of the population that the "corruption" of the state was the reason their money was gone and not that society was the prey of the mechanisms and gears of an economic system known as capitalism. This capitalism that was "shabby" in the Lebanese context did not advance its infrastructure and forces of production and political system. However, what many people missed, including ideological capitalists, was the fact that it was quite a competent capitalism within the logic of capital and its accumulation. The ideological war succeeded in convincing many people that the only way for salvation was to release prices and let the invisible hand balance the market and wreak havoc on society and the economy.

But the battle is not over yet. First because the battle of distributing losses is not finished. And second, because the war will not cease once that distribution is complete, since it is only one aspect of the process of restructuring society and moving to more misery and further exploitation if the oligarchy had the upper hand. It is the biggest portion of the population versus bankers and monopolizers with their sectarian regressive political and economic system. If there is a noble mission today, then it must be to ensure that what happened during the civil war will not repeat itself. Monopolizers and bankers entered the war and exited with more strength, more control, and more dominance. Our society is facing an existential necessity today to take the path for ending this social class and for reshaping the state that allows them to be and persist. And this was the rationale motivating the action against the banks during the October 2019 uprising, which must still mobilize and inspire further actions in the future as society defends itself against the ongoing aggression.

Notes

1 "No Withdrawals in USD from these Banks; Confusion in the Market" (La Soyhoubat Bil Dollar Men Hazih Al Masaref Wa Balbala Fil Aswak, 2019). *Almodon Online Newspaper.* https://www.almodon.com/economy/2019/9/22/%D9%84%D8%A7-%D8 %B3%D8%AD%D9%88%D8%A8%D8%A7%D8%AA-%D8%A8%D8%A7%D9%84 %D8%AF%D9%88%D9%84%D8%A7%D8%B1-%D9%85%D9%86-%D9%87%D8 %B0%D9%87-%D8%A7%D9%84%D9%85%D8%B5%D8%A7%D8%B1%D9%81- %D9%88%D8%A8%D9%84%D8%A8%D9%84%D8%A9-%D9%81%D9%8A-%D8 %A7%D9%84%D8%A3%D8%B3%D9%88%D8%A7%D9%82.
2 The exchange rate of the Lebanese pound to the dollar, https://lirarate.org/.
3 Fitch Downgrades Lebanon to "CCC," *FitchRatings.* 2019, https://www.fitchratings .com/research/sovereigns/fitch-downgrades-lebanon-to-ccc-23-08-2019.
4 "Lebanese Banks Reopen after Closing for Two Weeks amid a Relative Decline in Protests" (Al Masaref Al lpubnaniya Taftah Abwabaha Baad Eghlak Dam Ousbouayn Wist Trajoa Nesbi Fi Harakat Al Ehtijajat, 2019). *France 24,*https://www.france24.com /ar/20191101-%D8%A7%D9%84%D9%85%D8%B5%D8%A7%D8%B1%D9%81- %D8%A7%D9%84%D9%84%D8%A8%D9%86%D8%A7%D9%86%D9%8A%D8 %A9-%D8%AA%D9%81%D8%AA%D8%AD-%D8%A3%D8%A8%D9%88%D8%A7 %D8%A8%D9%87%D8%A7-%D8%A8%D8%B9%D8%AF-%D8%A5%D8%BA%D9 %84%D8%A7%D9%82-%D8%AF%D8%A7%D9%85-%D8%A3%D8%B3%D8%A8 %D9%88%D8%B9%D9%8A%D9%86-%D9%88%D8%B3%D8%B7-%D8%AA%D8 %B1%D8%A7%D8%AC%D8%B9-%D9%86%D8%B3%D8%A8%D9%8A-%D9%81

%D9%8A-%D8%AD%D8%B1%D9%83%D8%A9-%D8%A7%D9%84%D8%A7%D8
%AD%D8%AA%D8%AC%D8%A7%D8%AC%D8%A7%D8%AA.

5 Circular 154. *Central Bank*. Circulars and Decisions, https://www.bdl.gov.lb/circulars/
intermediary/5/37/0/2.

6 *Association of Banks in Lebanon*, 2019. Press release. https://www.abl.org.lb/arabic/
news/abl-news/press-release-19-11-2019.

7 Ilda Ghoussain, "The 'Battle for Liberating' Hostages in El Helou Police Station":
Violence of Security Forces. Under a Political and International Cover!" ("Maarakat
Tahrir" Rahaen Thakanat Al Helou: Ounf Al Kiwa Al Amniya. Bi Ghetaa Siyasi Wa
Douwali!, 2020), https://al-akhbar.com/Politics/282573.

8 https://twitter.com/UNJanKubis/status/1217426209644195842?s=20.

9 *Al Arab newspaper*. 2020. Cover page, https://i.alarab.co.uk/s3fs-public/2020-01/11588
.pdf?bKg5QE3EQfCvLMR4aaOP6kBwA7Gz10cW.

10 *Association of Banks in Lebanon*. 2021. Inclusion of laws suspending deadlines
awarded to banks as per the Central Bank's circulars, https://www.abl.org.lb/arabic/
publications-amp-resources/abl-miscellaneous-resources.

25

The Struggle for the Bisri Valley

Roland Nassour

Introduction

The Save the Bisri Valley Campaign (or *Save Bisri*) aimed to stop the World Bank-funded Bisri Dam, a US$617 million project[1] criticized for being inefficient, costly, and environmentally unsound.[2] Founded in 2017, Save Bisri was more than just an activism endeavor against a controversial project.[3] It was also a movement that challenged the paradigms in water and development policies, confronted the patronage system whereby sectarian leaders and former warlords control the government's resources for private gain, and hindered the World Bank's endless pursuit of large dams. The campaign engaged actively in the uprising of 2019, connecting issue-based activism to radical political action and placing the environment at the heart of the struggle for system change.[4] By adopting a series of strategies distinguished by their confrontational approach, multiscalar and diverse modalities, and by their abilities to build transversal solidarities, the campaign successfully halted the Bisri Dam project on September 5, 2020.[5] In this chapter, I offer a reflection on Save Bisri, its significance and outcomes in the context of the October 17 uprising, drawing on my role as a cofounder and the coordinator of the campaign.

A Product of the Patronage System

Originally conceived in the 1950s, the Bisri Dam is one of eighteen large dams envisioned in the government's water strategy of 2012.[6] This strategy is not founded on a comprehensive assessment of water demand and supply but instead stems from an outdated engineering-focused approach that seeks to build as many dams as possible, no matter the social and environmental risks. Dam proponents have long taken advantage of people's fear of water scarcity—a fear perpetuated by the seasonal water shortages resulting not from the need for additional projects per se but from the systemic mismanagement, corruption, and clientelism in the water sector in Lebanon: 50 percent of water supply is lost in the system before reaching the consumer due to leakages and illegal tapping.[7] 60,000 groundwater wells are unlicensed and unmonitored, leading to the depletion of the water table.[8] Ninety-six percent of Lebanon's sewage is left untreated[9] with most of the wastewater treatment plants currently nonoperational.[10] Moreover, the already built dams have failed to collect water because Lebanon's topography, dominated with highly permeable karstic rocks, is generally unfavorable for this type of infrastructure.[11]

Meanwhile, the dam-based water policies have primarily served the patronage system in which large-scale projects are negotiated among sectarian leaders and their affiliated contractors on a profit-sharing basis.[12] Using taxpayer money and international loans, the ruling parties distribute dams across sectarian geographies, entrenching territorial hegemony and maintaining the postwar clientelist arrangement. These maneuvers are often done within the confines of law and through state institutions designed for what we can call "legalized corruption." The most notable of these institutions is the Council for Development and Reconstruction (CDR), an extra-ministerial development agency controlled by a lobby of sectarian leaders who oversee the procurement processes.[13]

The Bisri Dam project, managed by CDR, is a remarkable model of this system, being the largest and most expensive dam in the government's water strategy.[14] The project is part of the one-billion-dollar "Greater Beirut Water Supply Project" (GBWSP) that aims to convey water from the South to the Greater Beirut Area.[15] Given the abundance of water sources in the direct vicinity of the capital, the GBWSP is arguably an inefficient and environmentally abusive scheme that reflects the greed of the ruling class. The Bisri Dam's significance to the government stems also from its location at the intersection of three sectarian territories:[16] Jezzine, dominated by the mostly Christian Free Patriotic Movement; Shouf, dominated by the majority Druze Progressive Socialist Party; and Iklim El Kharroub and Saida where mostly the Sunni Future Movement prevails. Additionally, Hezbollah and Amal, the largest Shia parties, were particularly interested in disseminating the project's narrative of providing water to the Shia community and others in Dahieh (the southern suburb of Beirut).[17] The dam garnered consensus from the entire ruling class, and the expropriation of land was voted unanimously by the coalition government in 2015.[18] Subsequently, the implementation contracts were allocated to politically connected companies based on clientelist sectarian calculations. The hiring of staff and workers followed the same logic.[19]

The Complicit Role of the World Bank

The World Bank was no less enthusiastic about the project than the Lebanese political class. In 2014, the Bank lobbied sectarian leaders to approve its proposed loan agreement for the implementation of the dam, claiming that the project can be a driver in reducing poverty and vulnerability.[20] Undoubtedly, the World Bank viewed the government's costly water strategy as an opportunity for scaling up their business in the Middle East. The reason why the Bank continues to promote large-scale dams everywhere in the world, despite the mounting evidence of their negative impacts, was explained in a World Bank strategy paper leaked in 2011.[21] The paper showed that the bank managers prefer to undertake large and centralized schemes because these are easier for preparation and supervision and therefore more profitable from an institutional self-interest perspective. With the approval of the loan, the Bisri Dam became the largest loan investment by the World Bank in Lebanon to date.[22] A World Bank-funded strategic environmental assessment (SEA) of the water sector strategy was completed later in 2015.[23] Paradoxically, the assessment recommended the revising of the strategy considering its social, economic, and environmental risks. It described the Bisri Dam as an example of land-greedy projects. Bank managers neglected those recommendations and continued with the project regardless.[24] Hence, the convergence of the World Bank's interests with the interests of the local patronage system would have a detrimental effect.

The Dam's Risks Outweighed Any Benefits

Left unchecked, the Bisri Dam project would have destroyed 600 hectares (ha) of land, affecting a wide variety of natural habitats, including pine and oak woodlands and a unique riparian ecosystem. The project would have also devastated 150 hectares of fertile agricultural land,[25] displacing hundreds of farmers. The reduced flow of the Awali River, because of the dam, would have severely impacted the availability of water for irrigation in villages downstream. Moreover, the project required the dismantling of fifty archaeological sites, including a one-of-a-kind Roman Temple, a Byzantine monastery, and the traces of the trading routes that historically connected the coastal Phoenician cities to the Bekaa.[26] Located on top of an active seismic fault, the project also posed risks of reservoir-triggered earthquakes, threatening the safety of many. Furthermore, despite the government's claims that the dam would provide 100 MCM/year of drinking water for Greater Beirut, recent measurements of the river flow revealed the inability of the dam to provide more than 45 MCM/year, which makes the project economically unfeasible.[27]

The Environmental Face of the Uprising

With the nearing of the project's implementation in 2017, we, a small group of activists, initiated the Save Bisri campaign to boost the valley's cause to the national level and make it a public opinion case.[28] The campaign worked on reappropriating the project's narrative using an extensive social media strategy. It also involved diverse tools of action ranging from recreational awareness activities to intense demonstrations and confrontation with security forces. These tools included petitions, lobbying, negotiations, expert studies, litigation, alliances, and more.

An important part of this campaign was to publicize the valley, previously unknown to most Lebanese citizens, as a symbol of the invaluable natural and cultural heritage of Lebanon—a representation of what is left of a country where hope has become a rare commodity. Save Bisri, among other activist-run campaigns, provided this much-needed hope. Through a deliberate use of imagery on various media platforms, particularly on Facebook, the campaign triggered a nationwide attachment to the Bisri

Valley, redefining the scale of the population impacted by the dam. The valley became an important political touristic attraction[29] as hiking events thrived in the area as a statement against the project.

We connected with the valley's community, emphasizing the value of local knowledge and culture and highlighting the human side of the dam's impact, especially the loss of livelihoods, the risks on people's safety, and the detachment from land.[30] Empowered by the growing national and international attention, many community members, originally submissive to the fate planned for the valley, mobilized in their turn against the project.[31] The interplay of advocacy efforts on both the local and national scales was crucial to the campaign's later success, and this serves as a clear indicator of the intersectionality in struggles across different cities and towns in Lebanon during the October uprising of 2019.

Save Bisri brought together experts across disciplines and developed a scientific critique of the government's claims.[32] The campaign's arguments were shared widely in an accessible language. Engaging actively in the discussions on the dam's efficiency and impacts, we went further to tackle broader issues of water, exposing problems of mismanagement and providing alternative solutions.[33] These alternatives ranged from direct technical interventions such as the rehabilitation of the Jeita-Dbayeh water canal to nationwide policy and management reforms such as restructuring water agencies, reforming of the groundwater sector, and improving monitoring and assessment, among others.[34] Save Bisri established itself as one of the key references on water management,[35] putting an end to the century-long dominance of the pro-dam policy discourse.[36]

Indeed, such paradigm shift could not be possible without a breaking of the structures of power upholding the dams' agenda. Unlike previous environmental campaigns in Lebanon, Save Bisri did not shy away from directly confronting the political elite. It exposed the corporate interests and sectarian drives of the project and capitalized on the growing dissent against the country's overarching injustices. In fact, the Bisri Dam represented everything the civil society has been fighting against since the 2015 protests, which were mainly about the trash crisis, another ecological disaster that blurred the lines between endemic corruption, narrow elite interests, and public health and safety concerns.[37] It is the epitome of bad governance that has exhausted the country's financial and natural resources alike. In addition to the wildfires that occurred days before the beginning of the October uprising in 2019, the campaign against the Bisri Dam served as another important trigger, especially during the economic crisis that emerged in July 2019 and culminated with the outbreak of the uprising. The involvement of all sectarian parties in the Bisri Dam backfired on the project: the dam became a representation of the uprising's slogan "kellon yaane killion" (all of them means all of them) denoting the collusion of all ruling parties in perpetuating corruption under the guise of religions. Thus, in many ways, the Save the Bisri Valley Campaign contributed to uniting protestors and opposition groups around a collective identity based on social and environmental equity. Save Bisri grew from a Facebook-based campaign in 2017 into a large network of actors with varied interests, all determined to stop the dam.

In addition to the active role of many warlords and sectarian leaders, the Save Bisri campaign considered the World Bank to be directly responsible for the project's risks. After a series of unfruitful discussions with the bank, we resorted to a more confrontational approach by filing complaints against their local management to the Inspection Panel in Washington, DC, exposing the World Bank's violation of its own policies and procedures.[38] We also launched an online petition addressed to the bank's board of directors, gathering around 140,000 signatures from around the world.[39] Demonstrations in front of the World Bank's headquarters in Beirut drew international attention to the campaign and increased the reputational risks of the project.[40] Save Bisri allied with regional and international organizations that tackle issues of dams or monitor the work of international financial institutions. The campaign held the World Bank's member countries accountable for the project, particularly targeting influential states represented in the board of directors, such as Germany, the United States, and the United Kingdom.[41] In collaboration with Lebanese expatriates, we organized protests abroad,[42] wrote letters to foreign officials,[43] and collaborated with international NGOs and political parties to influence their governments' role in the bank.

The Fall of the Dam

On the morning of November 9, 2019, at the height of the uprising, reporters left the city and headed to a remote area south of Beirut. This time, the large protest they wanted to cover was neither in a square nor on a street in a dense neighborhood; it was in a wide valley among orange orchards and pine woodlands—a very unusual scene. Thousands of people answered a call to action posted on Save Bisri's Facebook page:

> While the Lebanese people are revolting against corruption, power sharing, and sectarianism, the Council for Development and Reconstruction is continuing with the disastrous Bisri Dam deal. It is time that we all stand together against their deals which are overwhelming us with debt, destroying our environment, and endangering our health and that of our children. Join us on Saturday on the Bisri bridge. [44]

On that day, the large numbers of security forces, including the army, could not withstand the flow of angry protestors. We broke through the project's barriers erected by the government earlier that year. In fact, the collective action of hundreds of protestors stopped the works by force, installed sit-in tents, and declared the Bisri Valley's victory—the second notable achievement after Hariri's resignation in late October 2019. Meanwhile, two political parties, the Lebanese Forces[45] and the Progressive Socialist Party,[46] shifted position on the dam and called for the project's termination, which reflected the growing cracks in the political system.

On September 4, 2020, following years of resolute pressure, the World Bank announced its official withdrawal from the project.[47] The impact of this decision will be long-lasting. A recent assessment of investment risk in renewable energy in the Middle East conducted by RES4Africa and PwC showed that, following the Bisri Dam's cancellation, 50 percent of stakeholders in the private and public sectors consider social acceptance to be a serious source of risk for hydropower.[48] Such concerns were very unlikely only a few years ago.

Conclusion

The victory of the Save Bisri campaign is a multilayered achievement that stretches beyond the cancelation of the Bisri Dam. First, it marks the emergence of a new form of environmental activism that is more confrontational and highly politicized. This activism prioritizes tactics of language and symbols over organizational structures and uses remarkably diverse tools of action, operating on multiple venues for contestation. The synergy between issue-based activism and the struggle for structural change proved to foster collective identity and helped weaken the patronage system's networks of power and interests. Second, the victory marks a turning point in the history of water management and policies in Lebanon. On top of stopping the largest project in the government's water strategy, the campaign built a strong public opinion critical of large dams and aware of the impact of sectarianism and neoliberalism on water security. Finally, Save Bisri constituted a blow to the World Bank's support for large dams in the Global South. Today, the bank will likely think twice before embarking on similar projects. It is no surprise that, since the Bisri Dam's cancellation and the fact that the Lebanese government defaulted on its debts in March 2020, the bank has reassessed its relationship with Lebanon, tightening its requirements on the government and at least trying to engage further with the civil society.[49]

The October 17 uprising did not result in the direct overthrow of the sectarian regime, but it certainly exposed the weaknesses and fragilities of the system and demonstrated the power of people when unified and mobilized. The Bisri Valley, green and intact, will be a living testimony to this reality for many years to come.

Notes

1 The Bisri Dam's financing sources include a US$474 million loan from the World Bank, a US$128 million loan from the Islamic Development Bank, and an additional financing of US$15 million from the Government of Lebanon. For more information on the Bisri Dam project, see World Bank Group. 2014. "Lebanon Water Supply Augmentation Project." Project Appraisal Document, Washington, DC, http:// documents.worldbank.org/curated/en/265561468054261510/Lebanon-Water-Supply -Augmentation-Project.

2 Roland Riachi chapter.

3 Joey Ayoub and Christophe Maroun, "Stopping the Bisri Dam: From Local to National Contestation," *Arab Reform Initiative*, April 3, 2020, https://www.arab-reform .net/publication/stopping-the-bisri-dam-from-local-to-national-contestation/.

4 Save the Bisri Valley's campaign video explaining how corruption and sectarianism are at the root of the destructive Bisri Dam project: https://fb.watch/6mTABGQgbJ/.

5   See the World Bank Group's statement on the Cancellation of Water Supply
    Augmentation Project (Bisri Dam Project) on September 4, 2021, https://www
    .worldbank.org/en/news/statement/2020/09/04/cancellation-of-water-supply
    -augmentation-project-bisri-dam-project.
6   MoEW, "National Water Sector Strategy," 2012, 89, http://www.databank.com.lb/docs/
    National%20Water%20Sector%20Strategy%202010-2020.pdf.
7   Ibid., 9.
8   MoEW, and UNDP, "Assessment of Groundwater Resources of Lebanon," 2014,
    36, https://www.lb.undp.org/content/lebanon/en/home/library/environment_energy/
    assessment-of-groundwater-resources-of-lebanon.html.
9   MoEW, "National Water Sector Strategy," 40.
10 For more information on the failure of the wastewater treatment policies, see Farfour,
    Hadeel, "US$ 1.4 billion wasted on . . .," *Al-Akhbar Newspaper*, July 29, 2019, https://al
    -akhbar.com/Community/274237.
11 In his chapter, Riachi explains how the geology of Lebanon is unsuitable for large dams.
12 For more information on how public resource allocation in Lebanon benefits a
    narrow group of companies, see Sami Atallah, Ishac Diwan, Jamal Haidar, and
    Wassim Maktabi, *Public Resource Allocation in Lebanon: How Uncompetitive is CDR's
    Procurement Process?* LCPS, https://www.lcps-lebanon.org/publication.php?id=359.
13 "Much of the sectarian deal-making takes place at the Council for Development
    and Reconstruction, the opaque government agency that awards contracts for most
    of Lebanon's major infrastructure projects." Source: Vivian Yee and Hwaida Saad,
    "To Make Sense of Lebanon's Protests, Follow the Garbage," *The New York Times*,
    December 3, 2019, https://www.nytimes.com/2019/12/03/world/middleeast/lebanon
    -protests-corruption.html.
14 MoEW, "National Water Sector Strategy," 89.
15 For more information on the Greater Beirut Water Supply project, see https://projects
    .worldbank.org/en/projects-operations/project-detail/P103063.
16 Sectarian territories are understood here as the administrative areas dominated by
    a particular sectarian party that claims representation of the local community based
    on communitarian or religious grounds. This domination usually translates in the
    municipal and parliamentary elections.
17 Amal Khalil, "Hezbollah and Amal support Bisri against 'political manipulation,'"
    Al-Akhbar, July 30, 2020, https://al-akhbar.com/Politics/292164.
18 For more information on Decree 2066 that considers the private land in the Bisri
    Valley as "public benefit," see Bassam Kantar, "Bisri Dam: A 'public benefit' That
    Harms the 'public interest,'" *Al-Akhbar*, May 23, 2015, https://al-akhbar.com/
    Community/21327.
19 "Everyone down to the security guards who put up a barricade to prevent people from
    entering the valley was picked under the sectarian horse-trading formula." Source:
    Nabih Bulos and Marcus Yam, "Climate Change and Corruption Endanger an Ancient
    Valley in Lebanon," *Los Angeles Times*, February 21, 2021, https://www.latimes.com/
    world-nation/story/2021-02-21/bisri-valley-water.
20 World Bank, *US$474 Million World Bank Support to Address Water Shortages in
    Lebanon* (Washington, September 30, 2014), https://www.worldbank.org/en/news/
    press-release/2014/09/30/world-bank-support-address-water-shortages-lebanon.
21 World Bank Group, Committee on Development Effectiveness, "Energizing
    Sustainable Development: Energy Sector Strategy of the World Bank Group," Strategy
    Paper, 2011.

22 For more information on the Lebanese Government's loans from 1991 until 2019, see: https://ellira.org/loans-grants/overview.

23 Ecodit, "Strategic Environmental Assessment for the National Water Sector Strategy," 2015, 126, http://www.databank.com.lb/docs/Strategic%20environmental %20assessment%20report%20of%20the%20water%20strategy%20for%20Lebanon -Ministry%20of%20Environment%202015.pdf.

24 In their response to the Request for Inspection that Lebanon Eco Movement submitted to the World Bank's Inspection Panel in 2018, the Bank management claimed that the "concerns in the Strategic Environmental Assessment are addressed by the project [. . .]." For additional information see Inspection Panel, "Management Response to Request for Inspection on Bisri Dam," 2018, https://inspectionpanel.org/ panel-cases/water-supply-augmentation-project-p125184-greater-beirut-water-supply -project-p103063.

25 CDR, "Greater Beirut Water Supply Augmentation Project, Environmental and Social Impact Assessment," 2014, xiv of xciv, https://www.cdr.gov.lb/CDR/media/CDR/ StudiesandReports/Bisri/L12002-0100D-RPT-PM-02-REV-5-volume-1.pdf.

26 For more information on the cultural heritage of the Bisri Valley, see ICOMOS Lebanon, *Statement of Concern on the Destruction of Cultural Landscape Heritage.* September 4, 2020, https://www.icomos.org/en/178-english-categories/news/76406 -icomos-lebanon-statement-of-concern.

27 Saada Allaw, "Bisri Dam False Promises: No Water to Convey to Beirut," *Legal Agenda*, April 12, 2020, https://english.legal-agenda.com/bisri-dam-false-promises-no -water-to-convey-to-beirut/.

28 Save the Bisri Valley's Official Page: https://www.facebook.com/savebisri.

29 Photos of the first anti-dam hiking event organized in Bisri: https://www.facebook .com/media/set/?vanity=savebisri&set=a.906909959669286.

30 TV report of the first protest organized by Save Bisri and community members following the government's blocking access to the valley: https://www.facebook.com/ watch/?v=2206487626268611.

31 Video of a local woman expressing anger against the dam during a large protest in Bisri following the October 17 uprising: https://www.facebook.com/lucienbourjeily/ videos/433149714056327/.

32 "The campaign continues to have a strong presence both online and offline, monitoring the information being circulated around the project and steering the discussion by providing factual information supported by scientific evidence." Hadi Afif, "The Bisri Dam Project in Lebanon is a 'Ticking Atomic Bomb,'" *Beirut Today*, July 16, 2019, https://beirut-today.com/2019/07/16/bisri-dam/.

33 Riachi.

34 For more information about the campaign's proposed alternative solutions for water in Beirut, see Lebanon Eco Movement, *Request for Inspection on the Impacts of the Bisri Dam Project in Lebanon* (Inspection Panel, World Bank, 2019), https://www .inspectionpanel.org/sites/www.inspectionpanel.org/files/cases/documents/134 -Request%20for%20Inspection-24%20June%202019.pdf.

35 Following the emergence of the campaign, many journalists and reporters began to investigate the broader issues of water in Lebanon, inviting the Bisri Valley's activists for interviews (e.g., Sky News Arabic's documentary on failed dams). Also, several academic and research institutions invited Save Bisri's activists and experts to speak in their conferences on water (e.g., Conference on Media Coverage of Lebanon's Water Crisis).

36 In her thesis in 2013, Neemat Abou Cham noted that dam projects retained "an almost idealized place" in Lebanon's water policy, and that dam projects have not been subjected to public debates. See Neemat Badaoui Abou Cham, *Building Dams as a Policy Instrument Within Lebanon's National Water Strategy: n Overview* (Beirut: American University of Beirut, 2013).

37 Riachi.

38 To know more about the process of Save Bisri's two complaints to the Inspection Panel in the World Bank, see Request for Inspection, 2018, https://www.inspectionpanel .org/panel-cases/water-supply-augmentation-project-p125184-greater-beirut -water-supply-project-p103063 and Request for Inspection, 2019, https://www .inspectionpanel.org/panel-cases/water-supply-augmentation-project-p125184 -greater-beirut-water-supply-project-p103063-0.

39 Save the Bisri Valley Online Petition: http://chng.it/dJ8RNfDhFg.

40 The Bank Information Center (BIC), an international organization advocating for the transparency and accountability in the World Bank, published concerns about the Bisri Dam project. See https://bankinformationcenter.org/en-us/project/bisri-dam -project/.

41 Timour Azhari, "German MPs ask Government to Reject Bisri Dam Project," *Beirut Today*, February 9, 2020, https://beirut-today.com/2020/02/09/german-mps-reject -bisri-dam/.

42 Protest in front of the World Bank headquarters in London, UK, July 25, 2020, https:// www.facebook.com/savebisri/photos/a.423801177980169/1184250761935203/.

43 Roland Nassour, "An Open Letter to the World Bank's Board of Directors: Stop the Bisri Dam in Lebanon," *Jadaliyya*, December 4, 2018, https://www.jadaliyya.com/ Details/38210.

44 The call to Protest in on Save Bisri Facebook page: https://www.facebook.com/ savebisri/photos/968796046814010/.

45 "We will not allow a dam in Bisri," Georges Adwan, VP of the Lebanese Forces Party, July 19, 2020. https://www.lbcgroup.tv/news/d/lebanon/535173/سد-في-ما-بسري-من-عدوان ar./يعني-ما-في-سد.

46 "Our position on the Bisri Dam has changed as a result of the objection of the people and the environmental activists," Rami El Rayes, Adviser of PSP president Walid Joublat, July 23, 2020. https://www.elnashra.com/news/show/1432322/-:النشرة-لالريس-رامي التجا-نتيجة-تبدّل-بسري-موقفنا.

47 Cancellation of Water Supply Augmentation Project (Bisri Dam Project), World Bank, September 5, 2021. Link: https://www.worldbank.org/en/news/statement/2020/09/04/ cancellation-of-water-supply-augmentation-project-bisri-dam-project.

48 RES4Africa; PwC, "Assessing investment risk in renewable energy in SEMC," 2021, https://www.pwc.com/it/it/industries/energy-utilities/assets/docs/assessing -investment-rick-in-renewable-energy.pdf.

49 Since 2020, the World Bank has been more responsive to the civil society's concerns over the government's handling of multiple issues, such as the COVID-19 pandemic and the post-blast recovery efforts. For example, the World Bank threatened to suspend financing for coronavirus vaccines in Lebanon following activists' outrage over MPs' jumping of the vaccine queues. See: https://apnews.com/article/world -news-financial-markets-lebanon-coronavirus-pandemic-31e2b62e118b81d6a5725f2 2b240ef4b.

26

Reconstructing the Uprising in Tripoli

The Revolution that Never Left the Square

Tamim Abdo

Introduction

During the height of the October 2019 uprising, the media and many activists described Tripoli as "the bride of the revolution."[1] This was due to many factors, notably the thrill to see the poorest city in Lebanon joining the movement to topple the post-civil war regime and the vibrant party-like scene in its Abdul-Hamid Karameh square—informally known as the Nour Square[2] that has been the scene of Islamist mobilizations for a long time. Despite this nationwide praise, the scene and real-life events in the square were far from the romanticization propagated by activists and the media.

In this chapter, I will reflect on my experience in the revolution square in Tripoli where I participated mainly as someone deciding to put his professional chef skills to engage with people by establishing a food stand to distribute the food I cook to people in the square. Through this activity I was able to talk to people, especially those coming from the poorest parts of the city. Their stories, and later my involvement in organizing efforts, made me realize that the square has become a microcosm of Tripoli. Suddenly, an entire city crammed itself into one square. This has not only translated into reenacting the same class power dynamics but also amplified the shortfalls of prevailing activism and its propensity to transform a significant politicization and organizing space into events unable to understand and connect with those who face daily oppression.

In the following passages, I will explain how the revolution in Tripoli, and my trajectory within it, shifted over time. I will start by explaining how the euphoria of the beginning gave us a strong feeling of wanting to stay in the squares, then I will discuss how the square became dominated by a middle-class dynamic of activism that excluded the more popular/marginalized section of society, before finally ending with a reflection on how I moved with time to perceive the square as an alienating place that can no longer sustain the uprising or push it further.

Revolutionary Tripoli: A Place to Remain

As the protests broke out in Beirut on October 17, I thought that it would be another version of previous mobilizations in the country: demonstrators gathering in downtown Beirut trying to enter the Nejmeh Square (where parliament is located) and people from other cities, like Tripoli, going to Beirut to join them. This has been the ritual of alternative political mobilizations in Lebanon, at least since 2011. There was no reason to believe that something different will happen this time. I had little expectations. However, as soon as people in Tripoli started gathering at Nour Square, I rushed to see what was happening, out of curiosity. As I arrived, I was overwhelmed by the sheer number of people; there was an unprecedented energy among the crowd, as if at this very moment everyone was ready to channel their decades-long frustration, anger, and despair into a great movement where we all felt that we shared this city, where Nour Square would become a space for harnessing collective power and for experimenting a new sense of community. At that moment, I felt that the giant sculpture that reads "Allah" (or "God" in English) put by the Islamic Tawhid Party decades ago became irrelevant; it became a footnote somehow amid everything that was happening around it.

From this moment, things progressed quickly. I reconnected with some friends. They informed me that they just started organizing through WhatsApp, to set up roadblocks as it was the case all over the country. I was eager to join them to contribute to the movement. At first, I set up roadblocks with them and I helped in providing sandwiches and water to ensure the sustainability of our action. However, with time, I felt that roadblocks were beginning to backfire at us. Rumors started circulating that essential supplies like wheat couldn't be delivered to Tripoli, not to mention that political parties in power started sending their men to block roads pretending to be part of the popular movement. Back then, not many shared my views, so I decided to go back to the square where I thought I could contribute more to the movement, specifically through the skills that I have: cooking. I had returned from my training as a professional chef in Italy just two months before the revolution. When the uprising broke out, I was still looking for work. Thus, with the help of a few friends, we set up a tent to distribute food and interact with people. I saw this as a political act and not a charitable endeavor. Not only it was an entry point to engage with people, especially the most marginalized, but also to create a sense of solidarity. People shared their stories with me, and we created bonds with street vendors surrounding the tent, such as the men selling coffee or *kaek*[3] who would regularly invite me for coffee and food as well. The tent became part of the square's fabric, a meeting place for people from all walks of life.

The "island of tents" surrounding the square started to grow organically. The first ones to set up tents were Lebanese University students, the Lebanese Communist Party, a group of army retirees, and the families of Islamist prisoners in Roumieh. At first, these tents were just to occupy parts of the square without having any noticeable activity other than calling on people to participate in the protests. A week into the protests, a group called "the guardians of the city"[4] quickly set up on the rooftop of one of the main buildings in the square a platform with speakers.

Two weeks into the revolution, some of the people camping in Nour Square organized a bonfire night, where people would gather around a big fire to chant, talk, and eat. I was there; there was a sense of collective power, grief, and hope that I have rarely seen in Tripoli. For me the city has always been a place that I had to leave. Not that night though. Some of the people who knew me from the tent asked me to chant a slogan that I had written a couple of days before: *Maalmi, Maalmi* (roughly translated into "My Master, My Master"). When I started chanting, the slogan spread quickly, not only among those present but also beyond as it was being filmed.[5] Soon after, some friends from my village at the outskirts of Tripoli rushed to the square to take me out as they feared for my safety. That night, I felt that the city has changed, and its people too. The chant explicitly named Tripoli's powerful and rich men.

Prior to the revolution, it was almost inconceivable for many to shout the names of these powerful men in the streets in disdain. I felt, amid the euphoria of people chanting with me and the fear of what might happen next, that Tripoli had become a place where I must remain. The next day, this chant spread like fire, and for a moment I thought now they fear us, and we are not holding back. I did not have any expectations of what we might achieve; I only had to be in this moment of time, among Tripolitans openly rejecting and rising against those who were considered as untouchables. It was a feeling of liberation that I rarely saw among the people in the city.

Romanticizing the Square, Invisiblizing the Misery

The scene at the square was exceptional in many ways. The sheer joy and excitement of people dancing at the sound of music and chants seemed like experiencing collective exorcism after years of infighting in the city and the rising specter of Islamism that had become almost the only thing depicted in the media about Tripoli. Surrounding this revolutionary festival, the "island of tents" grew bigger by the day as more tents were set up. The square became everything in the city. Beyond the political discussions where people were eager to hear and give their opinions, a strong sense of solidarity was created in the square. We lent hands to each other, helped each other set up tents, installed a heating system, distributed food and clothes, and even attempted to plant some vegetables. This system of mutual support extended to include the provision of medicines that were either unaffordable or that couldn't be found. There were attempts to turn this space to a sort of a commune where all people can take refuge.

The food I was sharing with people was also a portal to speak to them, especially those who came from the most marginalized and exploited parts of the city. The usual charities that are politically connected were no longer operating, as they were not welcomed in the square. The most marginalized came to us for food, told us their stories, and found a space where they can just sit and be. They came back every day, and some never left. Talking to them led me to a painful realization: our aspiration for a better reality is a lot harder to achieve. The hype and excitement around the square clouded this fact and the harshness of Tripoli's reality and the arduous aim for genuine change. This made me see clearly what was going wrong in the square and the activity around it. Its geographical openness and the services that some of us were delivering drew many poor who are usually locked in the deprived areas of the city.

Deprivation is mostly felt in the old city of Tripoli, specifically east of the Tripoli Boulevard that cuts longitudinally through the city. Its west side is prosperous and hosts middle- and high-income residents and commercial activities, and the cite of major real estate development activities since the late 1980s, whereas its east side hosts impoverished communities wrecked by security turbulences.[6] Nevertheless, the existing and nascent organizing and activism in the square still excluded them. Somehow, without realizing, the usual landscape and dynamics that we have always decried in Beirut have now been reproduced in Tripoli.

Many elements contributed to this reality. First, protests in Tripoli remained limited to the middle- and upper-class parts of the city. Most marches took a path starting from Nour Square, passing through Tell Square, then the entrance of the old Souks (without going further), followed by returning to Azmi Street, Maarad Street, and then back to the starting point. Popular and poor neighborhoods were completely excluded from the trajectory, even though chants were directed against the local businessmen-turned-politicians in Tripoli who impoverished the city and incited armed clashes. Indeed, most of the organizers were middle-class activists, and many of them worked in NGOs in Tripoli. Therefore, the demonstration trajectory probably seemed the safest for them as they marched through streets they knew. On the other hand, beyond the organizers, protestors were more diverse, ranging from the poorer classes to higher-middle income groups; it reflected the composition of people in the square itself. However, the dominance of middle-class activists' discourse on the scene in Tripoli also played a role in marginalizing people from exploited neighborhoods. Indeed, the complicated history of the city with Islamic movements, the Tebbeneh-Jabal Mohsen war, and the media sensational portrayal of Tripoli as a place of poverty, war, and extremism[7] has made the middle-class Tripolitans somewhat obsessed with proving to outsiders that Tripoli is "civilized." Thus, there was an immediate rejection of any sort of violence, especially that involving the poorest. Suddenly, and as the economic crisis started to clearly unfold around the end of 2019 and beginning of 2020, Tripoli soon became a center for displays of charity by philanthropists and in some instances activists and political groups from both Tripoli and Beirut. I remember an instance where a philanthropist sent a pickup full of aid boxes into the middle of the square to distribute them. At the moment the truck arrived, people flocked toward it, and they started pushing each other to be able to get a box. This kind of scenes were usually the exclusive doings of Tripoli's powerful men. Quickly, the poor in Tripoli, once seen as the forefront of the revolution, returned to be at the receiving end of charity.

The Revolution Will Not Be in the Square

As the events unfolded in the country, the counterrevolutionary forces made their way into the square in Tripoli. Slowly, the building that hosted the platform mentioned earlier became controlled by the army that also controlled access to the building, thus to the platform. In addition, new cameras were installed in the square that did not exist before the revolution. Furthermore, after the prime minister, Saad Hariri, resigned on October 29, 2019, the Future Movement has lost some of its shackles and many of its active members joined the people in the square, especially to demand toppling the president and speaker of the parliament. The resignation of Hariri gave them breathing space and they were not staunchly rejected as in other places in Lebanon. Also, suddenly some people organized with a group of followers who led some sporadic sit-ins and roadblocks with explicit coordination with the army. Many of those people were known in the city to have allegiances to some of the city's powerful men. It became very clear that the square became a sort of container to the revolution and later on a playground for counterrevolutionary forces.[8]

We tried to change course of events as we saw things unfold, especially as the uprising prolonged and became more sustained. We tried to form a coalition joining alternative groups in Tripoli to organize marches in the poor and popular neighborhoods of the city. We organized two marches from Nour Square walking through the Tebbaneh area; it spanned many of Tripoli's most deprived neighborhoods. It was not an easy task. When the idea was proposed during meetings, it was not unconditionally welcomed. Some groups said that we need to coordinate with the residents of Tebbaneh, despite that there was a revolutionary momentum. Others warned it wasn't safe and many people there are drug addicts, therefore more caution was needed. At the end, we organized the march, however we were only a couple of hundreds, a fraction of the people who walk in the regular demonstrations in well-off areas in Tripoli. Moreover, most of the groups we talked with never officially and openly called for the protests. Although I was not surprised, I was angry and sad at the same time. Even some leftist groups and parties did not support our calls. On these days, it became clear to me that the revolution will not be at the square.

Beyond the joy and excitement, the square became a microsome of the city. Despite the huge number of people present there, there was a separation and disconnect between the new middle-class city and the old poor and working-class city, people standing next to each other in the square but rarely organizing together. The square also presented a missed political opportunity for mobilization and organizing. However, the square also was filled with intelligence officers, informants, cameras watching over those who thought a different future was not only possible but also imminent.

Conclusion

In this chapter, I attempted to provide an analysis of the revolutionary events in Tripoli and their developments through my personal experience. Like many, I had not anticipated that October 17, 2019, would turn into an unprecedent uprising in the country, and I did not imagine that the Karameh Square in Tripoli would turn into one of the main squares of the revolution forming a commune-like space that would inspire many. The revolutionary fervor quickly invaded the city and myself along with it.

The first weeks of the revolution in Tripoli saw the city reinvigorated after decades of frustrations, wars, and exploitation; there were a lot of possibilities. The revolution square became a mixture of Hyde park and commune, a space of solidarity where people not only discussed politics but also found food, shelter, clothing, a support system, and more. Nevertheless, beyond the euphoria of what was happening, the square had also reproduced the dynamics that existed within the city. It failed to create connections and solidarities between the people of the different parts of Tripoli. Middle-class activists dominated in terms of mobilization, discourse, and trajectory of the marches, and people from poor and marginalized areas of Tripoli stayed at the fringes of mobilization. The limits of the square became the limits of the revolution.

As time passed, the economic and COVID-19 crisis unfolded, the square returned empty, and the window of opportunity to establish a basis for organizing and mobilizing beyond the uprising failed to materialize. Nevertheless, the brief revolutionary moment in the city constituted for many Tripolitans a material evidence that different realities are possible, and this in itself was a seed planted, a blueprint for a different future.

Notes

1 F. Anderson, "In Pictures: Inside Lebanon's Tripoli – The 'bride of the revolution,'" *Middle East Eye*, November 16, 2019, https://www.middleeasteye.net/news/pictures -inside-lebanons-tripolithe-bride-revolution.
2 It was renamed by the extremist Islamic Tawhid party when it briefly ruled this city during the civil war; see A. Mahoudeau, Tripoli (Lebanon), a historic field of dissidence. 2016, https://tcatf.hypotheses.org/211.
3 *Kaek* is a type of bread with sesame, part of our popular culinary culture in Lebanon.
4 The Guardians of the city were set up in 2015 to "protect Tripoli" from garbage being transported to the city from Beirut during the waste management crisis. In 2019, they played a role in managing the square and coordinating with the ISF "to protect protestors." For more information, please check: https://www.almodon.com/society /2019/10/28/%D9%85%D9%86-%D9%87%D9%85-%D8%AD%D8%B1%D8%A7%D8 %B3-%D8%A7%D9%84%D9%85%D8%AF%D9%8A%D9%86%D8%A9-%D9%88 %D8%B3%D8%A7%D8%AD%D8%A7%D8%AA-%D8%A7%D9%84%D8%AB%D9 %88%D8%B1%D8%A9-%D9%81%D9%8A-%D8%B7%D8%B1%D8%A7%D8%A8 %D9%84%D8%B3.
5 For a video from these chants in the square, please watch: https://www.facebook.com/ tamim.abdo.3/videos/3180898232037964/.
6 For more on poverty in Tripoli check: Oumaima Jadah, *Poverty in the City of Tripoli: National and Local Interventions (in Arabic)* (ESCWA, 2014); and Adib Nehme, *Urban Deprivation Guide: Methodology and Results of the Field Study in Tripoli (in Arabic)* (ESCWA, 2014).
7 Check this article that shows how the view of the city shifted during the revolution: https://theconversation.com/tripoli-the-lebanese-city-of-contrasts-thats-now-the -bride-of-an-ongoing-uprising-126223 / For more information on Islamic movements in Tripoli: https://library.fes.de/pdf-files/bueros/beirut/06882.pdf.
8 For a more elaborate discussion on the counterrevolution, check Joseph Daher and Jeffrey Karam's chapters in this book.

27

The Mobilization in Baalbeck-Hermel

On the Incomplete Uprising of the First Days and the Dissidents That Carried on Despite Everything

Lamia Sahili

"The morning of October 12, I felt the revolution was over"; these were the words that young Ali used to summarize, without much attention, the bulk of what happened in the Baalbeck-Hermel district. "Why the rush? We just got here."

On the first three days of the October 17 revolution, like everywhere else in the country, diverse crowds of people took to the streets in the towns of Baalbeck-Hermel, including many who would often be referred to as the support base of the Shiite duo, that is, the supporters of Hezbollah and the Amal movement. It was not long before those crowds left the streets shortly after the infamous speech of Hezbollah's secretary general Hassan Nasrallah on the evening of October 19.[1] But their retreat in the towns dominated by the *Duo*, such as Baalbeck-Hermel, was harsh and divisive as a vast number of protesters left the streets. A few people remained in the streets including historically opposing figures to the sectarian political class in addition to independent groups of youth and students or people coming from dissident and leftists families.

This chapter poses the anxiety that was caused by the October 17 uprising in its first few days onto the factions of the political class in Baalbeck-Hermel, specifically the Shia Duo after they successfully got a vast portion of supporters to go down to the streets, making use of a general state of dissatisfaction of the performance of their members of parliament (MPs) and municipalities—in addition to making use of rising voices of opposition among the ranks of their support base. This anxiety was reflected in the initiative taken by Nasrallah himself, with what he represents from the high regard he enjoys among this popular base to the speeches aiming to get them to understand that he does not support the uprising, as a way to make them leave the streets. The chapters also highlights the impact of the withdrawal of this segment of the population on those who stayed, on their ways of protesting and confronting the factions of the ruling class, as well as on the trajectory of their movement—while insisting that the mere fact of their perseverance in the streets was an accomplishment in the local context.

Section 1[2]

The First Three Days: The Incomplete Uprising

The act of taking to the streets by the support base of the Shia Duo constituted an expansion of a common state of dissatisfaction starting with the performance of the Duo's MPs in Baalbeck-Hermel—a dissatisfaction resulting in an actual electoral battle[3] that the area had not seen in quite some time. That act was also an extension of a popular state of disapproval of the performance of the municipalities, commonly expressed on Facebook pages such as "Haki al Baladi"[4] (Municipal Talk) founded by a few young people, among others, from within the groups dominated by and supportive of Hezbollah. That state of disapproval was further expressed through complete electoral lists running against Hezbollah and the Amal movement in the last municipal elections whereby the opposition lists were a threat that crystallized in a total state of alert among the Duo's electoral machine, and in a game of political cards in elections that are, supposedly, mainly about development—of course, in addition to playing the card of accusation of treachery.[5] For all that, Nasrallah had to take action and contain those among his supporters that participated in the popular protests, in a speech he gave on October 19 when he considered the uprising as a hostage manipulated and exploited by parties of the ruling class and as merely an arena for settling political scores.[6]

Reasons for Participation

Huda, a teacher, frames her participation in the first days in the context of spontaneous action resulting from the accumulating disappointments in the ruling class. She adds local reasons related to the widespread disappointment in MPs that "do nothing for the area," before she goes on to draw a distinction between MPs of Hezbollah and those of the Amal movement: "Amal's MPs rob and wreak havoc in state institutions while Hezbollah, their close ally, just stands still and watches." Mohamad Ali, who belongs to this "ideological line" as he prescribes himself, agrees and adds that "this act (of watching Amal) drags Hezbollah to political games and makes the party vulnerable to blackmail by its supposed political ally."

These stances highlight a widespread state of disapproval that Mohamad Ali confirms "existed before the revolution, in all aspects of development where there are clear shortcomings" that pushed many, including Huda, to boycott the last parliamentary elections.

Hence, the spontaneity of the uprising comprised an opportunity for dissidents to express these stances and positions publicly, which was a brief moment of rebellion in which they contributed to the wider state of opposition that was October 17.

Reasons for Retreating

After the revolution brought that state of opposition to light in the environment of the Shia Duo, it was crucial to bury it quickly out of fear that it might spread further within that environment given the several factors allowing for that. This burial then does not mean the state of opposition was over, but that it was no longer public.

Huda linked her retreat from the streets to "things that started to uncover, entities that *co-opted* the uprising and jumped the wagon to take advantage of the crowds," criticizing the slogans against Hezbollah's arms: "it was clear that there were agendas besides revolting against the political system, so it was better to step back and avoid being accused of treason and called an agent." She further emphasized the factors that repelled people: "swearwords, alcohol and dancing."

Mohamad Ali explains that "Hezbollah's support base retreated from the streets either because they believed that logically change is nearly impossible in Baalbeck-Hermel, or out of faith in the credibility of the secretary general's vision given that most people trust in every word he says." He added more reasons such as "repelling protesters through many acts"—similar to what Huda had to say. However, to him, the biggest factor was "directing denouncement at the resistance arms and the position of Hezbollah's as a partner in corruption, along with the Sayed's wishes, with due respect to the revolution and rightful demands."

The reasons for retreating confirm two things. First, the uprising is no longer that spontaneous moment for the support base of the Shia Duo, with the "unveiling agendas" as propagated by the ruling class and with slogans different than those they believe to be rightful for the causes they believe in (which also means they did not find their place in the revolution; or in other words, that they did not feel they found a place in an environment that respects the particularity of their positions and does not repel them by attacking what is scared to them such as Nasrallah's status or Hezbollah's arms).[7] Second, the trinity of *resistance, politics, and religious party* protected the latter, that is, Hezbollah, from the potential of its bases' participation in the beginning of the uprising becoming a wider-spread phenomenon.

In conclusion then, the participation of Hezbollah's audience on October 17 might be the true uprising that was killed while still in its cradle. As described by an activist in Hermel's movement, "it is like a balloon that was inflated then went back to its natural size as if nothing happened, we were happy in the first few days when we saw many new faces and a diverse crowd but it was soon forced back out [of the streets]."

Section 2[8]

Post-October 20: A "Sophisticated" Movement That Did Not Want to Poke the Bear

The activists that stayed in the streets after Nasrallah's speech, including leftists and independents and youth groups, comprehended the retreat of the Duo's supporters and that they were now on their own as they had always been, and that the cover that could have protected them from the "beast" that is the Duo's "thugs" was unveiled as soon as that base left the squares. As a result, they avoided provocative slogans, which in turn did not hold any political essence aimed directly at either of the Duo but rather held "the sectarian political system responsible for the crises" and demanded to "fight corruption" and to "take down the capitalist and banking class." They did not block roads either, except in the first days and only when there would be enough people for the roads to be blocked[9] automatically.

"We took the movement from the context of blocking roads and chaos to introduce political content beyond populist discourse," says one protester. Another protester from the "Baalbeck Revolutionary Group" says that "blocking roads would have negatively affected us. So, we took aim at the governor's violations, rising security concerns, unregulated arms, lack of development, and shortcomings of municipalities."

There was a consensus among activists that steering away from swearwords and confrontation could get their message across to as many people and as clearly as possible without conflicts potentially caused by slogans that would provoke the Duo's supporters. This, according to lawyer and activist Firas, is what "protected the movement" from being pulled into altercations in the streets with components of the ruling class.

The Particularities of the Movements

Baalbeck: A Wider Margin for Protest

At the beginning of the uprising, people took to the streets spontaneously in Baalbeck and surrounding towns and automatically gathered at the "Jabali" meeting point, an open area at the western entrance of Baalbeck. Later, with less and less people and more disagreements on approaching the issue of (general) amnesty, those that remained in the streets chose to gather in poet Khalil Motran square for what it represents of cultural and historical value among the town's residents. Indeed, the square's value and significance were reflected in the different ways of expression that activists chose, who clearly wanted a cultural aspect[10] to their movement. They set up a tent (which later became two tents due to the differing opinions about excluding Saad Hariri from the common slogan "Kellon Yaani Kellon" [All of Them means All of Them]), according to interviews with activists from Baalbeck. The tent was a platform for awareness talks, cultural meetings, and for outreach,[11] where specialists were hosted to give talks at the historical Palmyra hotel.[12] To attract people to the squares, Baalbeck's activists resorted to concerts hosting Marcel Khalife and Ahmad Qaabour, both of whom are historically known for supporting revolting against the system.[13]

Baalbeck's activists had a bigger margin to protest than other towns. First because they were bigger in number, since Baalbeck is a bigger city and because the square gathered protesters from surrounding towns and villages. And second, because the religious and sectarian diversity of the crowds offered a kind of protection from accusation of stirring (sectarian) sentiments or tensions.[14] And so, the city saw several continuous marches, often with a big turnout. And given the centrality of Baalbeck in the governorate, and hence the several state institutions there, the city had steered movements and actions—most importantly closing the Central Bank's branch for a week, breaking into Electricity of Lebanon after power was out for fourteen days in Baalbeck and forcing employees to return it, closing the administration of the finance ministry for eleven days noting that it is affiliated with the Amal movement, and confronting Ogero's branch manager after activists spoke with employees about the waste of massive amounts of money in comparison with their low salaries. That day, the manager intervened and was confronted with the activists.[15]

Hermel: Low Number and Significant Perseverance

The evening of October 17 held moments that would go down in Baalbeck's history as it saw the first march since the beginning of the Shia Duo's domination of every aspect of life in the area, which made dissidence in the streets impossible. The march included supporters of Hezbollah and the Amal movement, especially young people, for the reasons cited in the first section, among nearly 200 people. It started from the city's square to the entrance near the Assi bridge. Protesters from Hermel's movement say that many faces affiliated with the two parties joined the gathering near the bridge, and in a moment of popular zenith, many young men climbed the electricity poles and burned their flags. This led to a clash that ended in dispersing the crowd and moving one group of around thirty protesters inside the city, in front of the Serail of public administrations, which they later made their permanent headquarters for their movements starting that day.

Hermel did not have public administrations like in Baalbeck. Protesters took to the squares every day to chant, sing, wave flags, and hold banners.[16] Despite that and their small number, they saw pivotal instances in the local context such as "the meeting of residents" or "the meeting of open microphone" that took place in the square and gave space for people to express their concerns, as well as going into the branch of Electricity of Lebanon and two bank branches where activists read statements out loud. And to pour life into their actions, they invited rapper Jaafar Touffar[17] to the square and organized many talks.[18]

Fakiha, the Fruit That Fell Far from the Duo's Map: Sanctuary for Fugitives

The town of Fakiha was a particular case, first because the Duo's influence was weak there where the Future Movement was the most dominant besides a number of leftist movements, which is why it was a sanctuary for activists from the towns dominated by the Duo like Al Ain, Labweh, Al Nabi Othman, and Al Jammaliya where they were unable to organize due to their small number. These towns were also the center for major events bringing people together, most notably "Baalbeck-Hermel's Sunday" on November 10, which hosted Ahmad Qaabour[19] and saw a huge crowd from all towns of the area.[20]

Omar, a prominent activist in Fakiha's movement, states that protesters came from all different kinds of political and social backgrounds and ages, and that the big crowd allowed activists to set up a tent they borrowed from an organization.

In Fakiha, activists' main strategy entailed organizing activities so that parents, especially mothers, could participate without having to worry about their children.

That strategy worked in getting many women to join and keeping the momentum[21] at the tent for longer than in neighboring towns.[22]

"Students' Uprising"[23]

Activists in the three areas are proud of the participation of students in actions and protests and count on it for the sake of accumulating momentum in the future. Schools in the town, like in other parts of the country, joined the strike and hundreds of students joined marches in Baalbeck and protested at the municipality and headquarters of the governorate.[24]

In Fakiha, students would join the strikes every day during school strikes and "would start a protest from their schools to the protest tent, and what helped at the time was the support of the teachers and principals for the revolution," says Omar.

In Hermel, students' participation in streets was not complete, as we are told by students and female activists about a famous incident in one school whose students left the classrooms and were about to march toward the Serail in the square, right before a man and his wife from Hezbollah's "education sector" came and forced the students affiliated with the Duo back into the school.[25] That happened in the context of a wider campaign to pressure parents and principals to prevent students from joining protests, which eventually worked.

Pressure and Indefinite Retreat

Despite all attempts by protesters to avoid conflict and provocation, they were still subjected to the pressure that came with the demonization of the uprising by people who endorsed the conspiracy theory mostly known in the infamous expression "something bigger than me and you, is cooking."[26]

With the gradual retreat of more people in Baalbeck and division of the square into two tents, the square was subjected to three attacks by supporters of the Duo.[27] The Fakiha's movement was attacked three times before the tent was eventually burned[28] on December 17, 2019, and the Facebook pages of opposition groups were hacked. As for Hermel, female activists talk about pressure on many people and threats against their source of income and job security. Unidentified individuals also burned the "revolution fist" installed near the Serail by activists.[29]

In addition to activists' inability to attract people affiliated with political parties, this led to a significant decrease in the number of protesters over time in the squares of Baalbeck-Hermel, as was the case in other squares, and it added to the demotivation of those who remained in the streets.

But when we ask activists about the accomplishments of the revolution in Baalbeck-Hermel, Mohamad answers that "to face the domination of the Duo and what it represents in the area is an achievement in and of itself." Firas adds that "it was the first time [since the start of the duo's grip over the area] that an opposition movement took place in the street outside the religious party context dominant in Baalbeck-Hermel."

Consequently, these few people were able to bring to light, with the little support that they had and the little coverage by traditional media, the existence of people in faraway places with one dominant color who reject the sectarian political and banking class like their fellow comrades in other squares. They were also able to save face through significant actions that were important in the local context as a precedent in the area not seen in quite a long time and insisted on remaining part of the ongoing revolution in other parts of the country.

"There were moments where I was so sure we would succeed," says Amani from the movement in Hermel, "then when we started being less and less people, I started to realize that the change we wanted was very big. But at the same time, we stayed because we had a sense of responsibility; to say that we are here."

Notes

1 Full (Arabic) text of the speech can be found in this link: https://almanar.com.lb /5851100.
2 All quotes in this section were taken from phone interviews conducted last March and April 2021 with people from the Duo's environment who were in the streets during the first few days of the revolution.
3 "Baalbeck-Hermel Achieved Historical Election Results . . . Habchi and Al Hojeiri Broke The Monopoly" (Baalbeck-Hermel Hakkakat Nesab Ektiraa Tarikhiya . . . Habchi Wal Hojeiri Kasara Al Ouhadiyya), Wissam Ismail, *Annahar*, May 8, 2018.
4 "Hermel: Zero Vision, Zero Ideas, Zero Projects!" (Al Hermel: Sefer Roaya, Sefer Afkar, Sefer Mashari'!), *Al-Akhbar*, June 28, 2017.
5 "Hezbollah Wins Referendum In Baalbeck-Hermel" (Hezbollah Yafouz Bi Istiftaa Baalbeck-Hermel), Sobhi Amhaz, *Almodon*, May 9, 2016.
6 Nasrallah addressing protesters in his speech: "If Hezbollah took to the street the movement would have gone somewhere else, it would have turned into a political struggle, a battle of axes (. . .) today you must be careful with your movement while certain political parties in the establishment endorse it (. . .), this means that your movement will shift from social demands to political demands, (. . .) the popular movement is now being exploited in a political battle, in a race to settle political scores." Full speech can be found in this link: https://almanar.com.lb/5851100.
7 Read Mortada Al-Amine's chapter in this book titled "The Lebanese Uprising through the Eyes of Loyalists."
8 All quotes and information in this section on the mobilization and events in the area were taken from interviews conducted last March and April 2021 with activists either over phone calls, on Zoom, or in person.
9 Read Nizar Hassan's chapter in this book titled "The Power and Limits of Blocking Roads: How the October Uprising Disrupted Lebanon."
10 The decision to introduce a cultural aspect to the movement was made generally by activists in the area first because they had decided to avoid conflict and second because they wanted to start building on a certain awareness among the active youth. Interview with a prominent activist in Baalbeck's movement conducted on March 13, 2021.
11 "A Tent in Baalbeck to Discuss Matters of the 'Revolution'" (Khayma Fi Baalbeck Li Mounakashat Kadaya Al "Thawra"), Youssef Mansour, *Nida Al Watan*, December 9, 2019.

12 Live stream of the social-economic talk on an activist's Facebook profile, by journalist Mohammad Zbeeb at the hotel on December 22, 2019.

13 Snippets of Ahmad Kaabour's concert in Baalbeck on December 1, 2019, can be seen through this link: https://bit.ly/3gjDShn.

14 Several activists stated in separate interviews that the reasons why the square in Baalbeck was not attacked by the Duo's supporters, as opposed to the squares in Tyre and Kfar Roumman, at least in the first few days are due to the sectarian diversity of the crowds protesting as there were fears of any attacks potentially leading to sectarian tensions and clashes.

15 Some of these actions were not documented by traditional media, and the coverage by alternative media was insufficient. Photos of the instance of breaking into Electricity of Lebanon can be found in this link: https://bit.ly/2T9WRmy. A photo of the demonstration at the branch of the Central Bank in Baalbeck can be found in this link: https://www.facebook.com/sawtelghadlb/posts /3573844942656255.

16 The Facebook page of the "Popular Movement in Hermel" was active, although it could not attract enough people outside the area in order to act as an alternative media platform in the absence of traditional media. Videos documenting actions of the movement can be found in this link: https://bit.ly/2RBMS94.

17 Video of rapper Jaafar Touffar in Hermel from MTV's YouTube channel where he was singing one of his famous songs, which had significant implications in the local context: "I want a revolution that protects the people and erases Israel."

18 The movement in Hermel hosted many prominent faces of the uprising including journalist Mohammad Zbeeb and activist and lawyer Wassef El Harakeh.
   Snippets of Zbeeb's talk can be seen through this link: https://www.facebook.com/ watch/?v=2579727778913122.
   Snippets of El Harakeh's talk can be seen through this link: https://www.facebook .com/watch/live/?v=2674327035984238&ref=watch_permalink.

19 Interview with a prominent activist in the movement in Fakiha conducted on March 20, 2021.

20 Activists from all squares in Northern Bekaa took part in this event that can be watched through this link: https://www.facebook.com/watch/?v=430037557913524.

21 Invitation to a musical event organized by the movement in Fakiha, accessible through this link: https://www.facebook.com/fakehaday3tna/posts /428167571184828.

22 "Shia and Sunnis against sectarianism" chants in a joint march organized by activists in movements of neighboring towns and Hermel in particular: https://www.facebook .com/watch/?v=2263196503971370.

23 Read Samir Skayni's chapter in this book.

24 This video shows a crowded student march in the streets of Baalbeck on November 9, 2019: https://www.facebook.com/amirs.shalha/videos/948088485570653/.

25 This incident indicates Hezbollah's keenness on preventing the younger generations from going to the streets due to the potential influence on them given their young age.

26 This expression became widespread after Nasrallah's speech at the beginning of the revolution as a reference to its supporters' theory that there was a conspiracy behind the revolution. Check the puzzle of the Lebanese uprising: ?

27 The link includes videos documenting the attack on Khalil Motran square on November 26, 2019, by the Duo's supporters: https://bit.ly/2TguNOx.

28 Burning The Uprising Tent In The Town Of Fakiha (Ehrak Khaymat Al Intifada Fi
    Baldat Al Fakiha) (video), *Annahar newspaper*, December 17, 2019.
29 The demonstration by activists in Hermel's movement denouncing the demolition
    of the "revolution fist" can be viewed through this link: https://www.facebook.com/
    permalink.php?story_fbid=145736120215757&id=108298880626148.

28

Experiencing the Uprising in the Chouf and Aley Region

Alaa Al Sayegh

The days of October took me through ecstatic feelings I had never thought I could possibly experience. Some days I would be lucky to get three hours of sleep. I would sleep in my village, Sharoun, wake up early, circulate between mountain tents and protest points, and by noon I would be in the protest squares in Beirut. Day in and day out. Drive. Arrive. Mobilize. Repeat. Every single day had a purpose and held a plan. I've never felt more determined in my life.

Introduction

For nearly a decade, there has been a steady buildup being cultivated to oppose the ruling government among the youth from the Chouf-Aley area. Chouf and Aley are two adjacent districts located in Mount Lebanon, southeast of the capital, Beirut; they are also the most religiously diverse districts in Lebanon.[1] The relative proximity of the region to Beirut (in comparison to Tripoli or Tyre for example) made it possible for many to earn an income by working in the capital. Inhabitants of the Chouf-Aley region are mostly of a middle-class income. Additionally, people from the region are members of the larger Lebanese diaspora community, living and working abroad. Consequently, these citizens are more likely to oppose their own regions' societal views because their livelihood is independent from the reigning system and its clientelistic networks. They do not depend on the ruling oligarchy of party/parties in the region to meet their very basic human rights, such as food, clean water, housing, and health care. However, challenging this inherent system puts one at high risk, as will be discussed in this chapter. The three main reasons that drove the communities of Chouf-Aley to oppose the status quo and actively participate in change are: (1) socioeconomic, (2) environmental, and (3) political. As I will outline in this chapter, the uprising of 2019 had been in the making since 2011, as part of the dynamics unleashed in the region with the first wave of Arab uprisings, and proceeded to escalate until we found ourselves in the midst of a full-blown revolution.

The Making of 2019

Against the backdrop of the Arab Spring in 2011, Lebanese protesters mobilized in Lebanon demanding a change to the sectarian regime.[2] In contrast to the big rallies of mainstream political parties, the number of demonstrators in the 2011 wave of protests against the sectarian regime was limited.[3] Nonetheless, it triggered the conversation around potential alternatives to the regime and possible options for opposition mobilization. Activists taking part in the *isqat an-nizam at-ta'ifi* ("downfall of the sectarian system") movement[4] did not have a ready alternative, but their goals were clearly about beginning a discourse surrounding state secularism. At that time, the youth in Chouf-Aley were mobilizing and installing tents in Aley, Chouf, and Beirut, to start the conversation around the anti-sectarian narrative:

> These narratives go beyond merely criticizing and fighting sectarianism. Rather, they include a critique of the confessional system, sectarian affiliations, and religious extremism, in addition to the repudiation of corruption, ineffective governance, and social injustice, and demands for public spaces, accountability, transparency, gender equity, and so on.[5]

That collective of people and activists inspired mobilization and built trust relationships among the activists of Chouf-Aley at later stages, particularly to protest environmental, socioeconomic, and political issues outside of their region.

Thus, in 2015, community members of the Chouf and Aley areas were actively participating in the "You Stink" movement that sparked because of the waste management crisis.[6] This subsequently led to the decentralization of coordinated efforts for protesting. Many grassroots emerged including the Mount Lebanon activist group "The Community Campaign to close the Naameh landfill" and others that were against the landfill.[7] Initially, the crisis was solely viewed as an environmental hazard.[8] Upon discovering that certain political parties had struck certain deals[9]—traded the health and livelihoods of people for personal financial profit—the demonstrations transcended into a political mobilization against political leaders. Politicians who were implicated feared the loss of their political power and, more importantly, monetary gain. The year 2015 proved to be significant for activism/opposition in the Chouf-Aley region, specifically. The fact that the Naameh landfill is situated geographically in the area facilitated the decentralization of the campaign and motivated the mobilization of the inhabitants of the region.

During the parliamentary electoral campaigning period of 2017–18 (the first elections after the 2015 turning point) many grassroots initiatives were formed around the elections in the Chouf-Aley area, leading to the formation of a solid and progressive political narrative manifested through the electoral campaign of the *Kulluna Watani Alliance* ("We are all our Nation"). The alliance included *Sabaa* (a nationwide secular political party), *Libaladi: "For My Country"* (Beirut 1 district), and *Lihaqqi: "For My Right"* (Mount Lebanon 4 district).[10] The *Kulluna Watani Alliance* was a major anti-sectarian movement (among others[11]), characterized by a unified democratic body providing an alternative to the corrupt sectarian rhetoric in many areas of Lebanon, including Chouf-Aley.

The years 2011, 2015, and 2018 were part of a process that prepared for 2019 in the Chouf-Aley region. This timeline of events shaped the opposition in the region and contributed to creating cracks in the political hegemony of traditional parties/leaderships in the area.

The Regional Waves of Change of October 2019: The Revolution from a Grassroots Lens

Wildfires and Taxes: Igniting the Uprisings

The boiling point for Chouf-Aley citizens was the rampaging wildfires in October 2019, which heavily affected the Chouf region. The accumulation of issues caused by the ruling government had overwhelmed the area and its people. While the wildfires were rapidly trailblazing through the Chouf, a few days prior to the eruption of the uprising on October 17, 2019, there was a salient absence of any official entity to assist in fighting the fire and protecting the inhabitants of the affected areas. The state did not even have the equipment to interfere to stop the fires, although later, it was revealed that three helicopters had been donated to Lebanon in 2009, yet had become obsolete for lack of maintenance—due to sheer negligence.[12]

Political figures from the regime were resorting to hate speech and instigating sectarian tensions instead of diffusing the tension. For instance, a prominent political figure, Mario Aoun, blatantly suggested that the fires seemed to be blazing in Christian areas alone, and as such, it was a conspiracy against Christians.[13] Subsequently, a volunteer of civic defense, Salim Abou Moujahed, died as a result of overexertion and smoke inhalation while fighting the fires.[14] This incident pulled on peoples' heartstrings, triggering a sense of fury and rage toward the incompetent regime and enabling a sense of solidarity among the people.

Simultaneously, the Saad Hariri government issued a six dollar per month WhatsApp tax—on October 17, 2019—among many other taxes, which led to a huge wave of resentment and rage among the people. WhatsApp is a free internet-based service, and the tax was not only unjust but also illegal. Moreover, it is key to highlight the anger behind this unjustified tax that was attributed to the fact that WhatsApp is a core communication tool for those who are members of deprived communities and, more generally, a highly used tool in light of the ridiculously expensive costs of communication bundles imposed by telecom companies. The WhatsApp tax ignited the uprising.[15]

Instantly, the media committee at Lihaqqi issued a public petition against the WhatsApp tax, and thousands of signatures were attained, highlighting a unified sense of fury. Instinctively, people sensed a need to rush to the streets and, on that same day—October 17—a protest was formally called for, by Lihaqqi:

> Hours after the government announced the tax, it reversed the decision. But it was
> too late. The grassroots progressive political organization Li Haqqi had already

sent out a message via—what else?—WhatsApp calling on people to block roads in protest. "Let us take action against the unfair taxes! To Riad al-Solh Square today (17 October) at 6 p.m., to foil the government's efforts to pass unfair taxes on telecom, gas, and others," it read. That night, protesters burned tires in the streets and clashed with police.[16]

A handful of people gathered in front of the Lebanese parliament building in Beirut, including activists from Chouf-Aley, on that fateful night.

Dynamics on the Ground: Conflicts and Confrontation

Coincidentally, it was then and there (the evening of October 17) that Akram Chehayeb's (former minister of higher education) convoy was passing. It is important to note here that Chehayeb is from the Chouf-Aley area and he is a member of the Progressive Socialist Party (PSP), led by Walid Jumblatt since 1977, that is in control of the region/ religious community in Chouf-Aley. As his convoy was passing, the protesters clashed with his bodyguards, and one of them fired his assault rifle into the air in an attempt to make way for his leader's car to pass. It was at this moment where we witnessed a female protester, Malak Alaywe, deliver the famous kick to an armed bodyguard's groin.[17] This image instantly became the icon of the October Revolution[18]—symbolizing an undeniable uprising and resistance to the regime, oligarchy, and outdated patriarchal political system.

The first official protest in Mount Lebanon took place in Bhamdoun, on the evening of October 17, and from that very first night, the Lebanese army attempted to forcefully and violently remove the protesters from the street. This aggressive and excessive force began to happen in the areas outside of Beirut long before we began to witness such violence within the capital due to more media coverage, which would have exposed the ruling regime's tactics.

During the first two weeks of the revolution, the PSP (dominant party in the region) attempted to hijack the revolution in Chouf-Aley by entering the tents and raising their flags. Immediately, the activists turned to the media, releasing a statement saying those PSP hijackers do not represent "us," the protesters, and this is a progressive, peaceful protest. Afterward, the PSP tried to shame the protesters (namely those with former affiliation to the party) and prevent people in the region from protesting. They did this by blackmailing the protesters in Chouf-Aley, and this failed, so they turned to violent tactics. The PSP went as far as creating and distributing a "blacklist" of names, via social media, of activists they wanted to attack. The approach of the dominant party/parties of the ruling regime in the area of Chouf-Aley was explicitly threatening, oppressive, and violent—the same approach witnessed in previous years, yet increased post-October 17. For example, we witnessed the attacking of the Aley tent[19] and burning of the Sawfar tent,[20] destruction of the Baakline tent, and blackmailing of protesters by the PSP keyboard warriors. Members of the PSP explicitly attacked protesters in Baqaata-Chouf,[21,22] Saraya Aley,[23] and Qabrshmoon-Aley[24] (in the same week)—clearly, the Lebanese army could not protect the activists—and as a result, activism and protests slowly declined to a halt in Chouf-Aley. Thus, proving the deep-rooted and integral power of the ruling regime—a regime of violence, oppression, and, ultimately, erasure.

Tents in Chouf-Aley: Progressive Politics and a Sense of Solidarity

Despite the aforementioned attempts to infiltrate and demolish the revolution, each region was successful in constructing a tent—Aley, Abadieh, Baalechmay, Chouf, Sawfar, and others—and every tent had its own spirit and dynamic. There were two general categories: (1) protesters/protest groups who maintain a political stance against the ruling government and leaders, in general, but do not have a clear political identity or program and (2) those who maintain a progressive political stance, in search of an alternative to the traditional sectarian regime (in line with grassroots organizations).

The tents and the people who occupied them conferred a decentralized aspect to the movement, yet a localized one at the same time. Unlike past protests in Lebanon, people were not fooled by traditional tactics such as co-optation, because locals were active in their respective region's tent, making it easy to identify any infiltrator. These tents were a safe space to engage in reformist conversations, new social ties, and discourse around alternative options to replace the existing political model.

A high sense of solidarity and a striking positive energy were palpable. We witnessed numerous social events including Christmas parties, yoga classes, marriage proposals, and birthday parties in the tents. Bakeries were making *manakish* (Lebanese street food) and distributing them to the people in the tents. Teachers in Aley even held their classes on the ground, allowing their students to participate in the progressive debates and discussions held in the *thawra* (revolution) tents.[25]

As such, we were finally witnessing progressive, anti-sectarian values being pushed to the forefront (i.e., rising against all leaders despite religion, refusal of religious/sectarian speeches, reception to secular values in the tents) in the context of Lebanon. The tents brought forward discussions around alternative syndicates (a way to regain power to the people), progressive politics and decision-making processes (horizontal and democratic), and a political agenda for each day of the revolution. The geographical location of the tents is significant because the people of each region were able to confront their respective "leader(s)." Hence, all political/sectarian groups were being challenged—dismantling the politico-sectarian divides. People were no longer fearful of their regions' powerful leaders, and all protesters, as different as they may be, were united under the slogan "*kellon yaani kellon*" ("all of them means all of them"), with respect to the incompetent and corrupt politicians.

Conclusion: Lebanon Post-2019 and Future Implications

The decentralization of the revolution and its grassroots approach was a solid ground for people from all over the country to participate in coordinated actions and challenge the existing system. The narrative that emerged as a result of the uprising was one that called for replacing the corrupt system of the ruling parties with one that is just, fair, democratic, and secular.

This momentum has proven to be sustainable and has continued to spread in Lebanon, as we have seen during the COVID-19 pandemic[26] and during and post the August 4 Beirut Port explosion.[27] The pandemic caused the people to withdraw from the streets, resulting in empty tents that were eventually removed by the security forces, from Beirut to Baalbek.[28] However, the sense of solidarity that transpired during the October Revolution reappeared in August, after the devastating Beirut blast. Yet again, the youth of Chouf-Aley gathered and mobilized in the streets of Beirut to assist in the massive city cleanup. Once more, the government and political figures were nowhere to be found in assisting the people of Lebanon.

As I hope has been made evident in the chapter, Lebanon is in dire need of change to the regime. On several occasions—in the environmental,[29] economic,[30] and the political realm—the leaders of this country have proven themselves inept. Thus, it is no surprise that the October 2019 moment emerged the way it did—a moment years in the making. It was a point of intersection of several factors that have been building throughout the years: political tendencies aspiring for change (which the Chouf-Aley area is rich in), local grassroots activist groups that have been striving for years against the corruption related to environmental hazards, and the continuous social and economic deterioration.

Notes

1 https://en.wikipedia.org/wiki/Chouf_District.

2 M. N. AbiYaghi, M. Catusse, and M. Younes, "From *isqat an-nizam at-ta'ifi* to the Garbage Crisis Movement: Political Identities and Anti Sectarian Movements," in *Lebanon Facing The Arab Uprisings*, ed. R. Di Peri and D. Meier (London: Palgrave Pivot, 2017), 73–91, doi: 1057/978-1-352-00005-4_5.

3 J. Wood, "In Lebanon, a More Patient Protest," *The New York Times*, April 13, 2011, https://www.nytimes.com/2011/04/14/world/middleeast/14iht-m14-anti-sectarianism.html (accessed May 21, 2021).

4 AbiYaghi et al., "From *isqat an-nizam at-ta'ifi* to the Garbage Crisis Movement."

5 Ibid., 79.

6 For more information on the 2015 waste crisis in Lebanon, see N. Hilal, R. Fadlallah, D. Jamal, F* El-Jardali, *K2P Evidence Summary: Approaching the Waste Crisis in Lebanon: Consequences and Insights into Solutions*. Knowledge to Policy (K2P) Center (Beirut, Lebanon; December 2015), Online: https://bit.ly/3wabwMp.

7 An-Nahar, "Hirak al jabal Picketing to Preserve Public Safety," *An-Nahar Online*, September 15, 2015, https://www.annahar.com/arabic/article/284494 (accessed May 1, 2021).

8 S. A. S. Daou, "The Closure of Naameh Landfill, What's Next?", *Green Area*, July 17, 2015, https://bit.ly/3fZ2USC (accessed April 30, 2021).

9 H. Naylor and S. Haidamous, "Trash Crisis Sparks Clashes over Corruption, Dysfunction in Lebanon," *The Washington Post*, August 23, 2015, https://www.washingtonpost.com/world/middle_east/lebanon-rattled-by-protests-over-trash

-crisis-corruption/2015/08/23/9d309ef8-2c2f-447b-9fff-3c5c62543da9_story.html (accessed May 20, 2021).

10 N. El Kak, "A Path for Political Change in Lebanon? Lessons and Narratives from the 2018 Elections," *Arab Reform Initiative*, July 25, 2019, https://bit.ly/3yKbT2N (accessed May 25, 2021).

11 For a comprehensive list of parliamentary electoral alliances and nominations in the 2018 parliamentary elections in Lebanon, see: https://bit.ly/368AUro.

12 A. Sewell, "Why Are Lebanon's Firefighting Helicopters Grounded?", *The Daily Star*, October 15, 2019, https://www.dailystar.com.lb/News/Lebanon-News/2019/Oct-15 /493585-why-are-lebanons-firefighting-helicopters-grounded.ashx (accessed May 15, 2021).

13 Fires that Lebanon has not witnessed before . . . ignite the fire of "sectarianism" again: https://bit.ly/3qRPUU9.

14 T. Azhari, "Lebanon's Year of Fire," *Al Jazeera*, October 16, 2020, https://www.aljazeera .com/features/2020/10/16/lebanons-year-of-fire (accessed April 30, 2021).

15 "Lebanon Scraps WhatsApp Tax as Protests Rage," *BBC News*, October 18, 2019, https://www.bbc.com/news/world-middle-east-50095448 (accessed May 21, 2021).

16 H. Sullivan, "The Making of Lebanon's October Revolution," *The New Yorker*, October 29, 2019, https://www.newyorker.com/news/dispatch/the-making-of-lebanons -october-revolution (accessed May 1, 2021).

17 See Part II, Chapter 11: Appearing as Women: Gender, Publics, and Revolution by Sara Mourad, in this book, to read more about Malak Alaywe and gender roles in this revolution.

18 M. Chahine, "The Icon of the Lebanese Revolution," *L'Orient Today*, October 26, 2019, https://today.lorientlejour.com/article/1192726/the-icon-of-the-lebanese-revolution .html (accessed May 26, 2021).

19 https://www.aljadeed.tv/arabic/news/local/2212201974.

20 M. Ghazaleh, *Tents Persevere in Baakleen, Aley and Sofar: Drawing up the Uprising in the Chouf and Aley Districts through the Activities of its Squares.* 2020, https://bit.ly /3jIIWiG.

21 Video evidence of Socialist Party supporters attacking demonstrators in Baqaata https://bit.ly/3dGPn1X.

22 https://twitter.com/salmanonline/status/1279433177472385026.

23 Aley tensions during the revolution: https://bit.ly/3Atr01t.

24 Video: Socialist supporters attack protesters in Qabrshmoon https://bit.ly/3xtvbIo.

25 See Aley Tantafid and Shouf Tantafid Facebook pages for photos, videos, and posts regarding the *Thawra* tents and the various activities and displays of solidarity mentioned throughout the chapter.

26 N. El Kak, "Capitalizing on the Pandemic: Party Responses and the need for Grassroots Organizing in Lebanon," *Jadaliyya Online*, July 9, 2020, https://www .jadaliyya.com/Details/41404 (accessed May 18, 2021).

27 H. Mirshad, "Grassroots Groups Hold Beirut Together, yet Big NGOs Suck up the Cash," *The Guardian*, August 27, 2020, https://bit.ly/3i5XzeU (accessed May 20, 2021).

28 El Kak, "Capitalizing on the Pandemic."

29 See Part I, Chapter 7: A Political Ecology of Disasters in Lebanon by Roland Riachi in this book to read more about environmental crises in Lebanon.

30 See Zbeeb's chapter in this book.

29

Reflections from Two Revolutions

From the Ignition of the Tunisian Revolt to the Lebanon Uprising

Olfa Saadaoui

Revolutionary Recipes

"Prepare the tomato sauce, pour it on the sliced bread, put it in a huge oven pan, arrange it so you make sure you fill all the space, pour beaten eggs on them and, if available, add shredded cheese on top, keep in the oven for 20-30 minutes. Then, it's ready to go to the guys around the street corner!"[1]

My sister nostalgically recalled to me over a phone call I had with her from Beirut, she being in Gabes, my hometown in south of Tunisia. We are at the end of May 2021. I had started thinking about writing on how I have experienced the Lebanon uprising, my second uprising within a decade. And the most compelling starting point to recall the Tunisian one could have only been the midnight meals that my sister and neighbors alternated preparing for the men of the neighborhood who took shifts in protecting the area.

Early on, the protests in northwestern and southern cities, especially in Sidi Bouzid, Kasserine, Kairouan of Tunisia, involved heightened confrontations with the police.[2] Days succeeding those outbreaks, sit-ins and peaceful protests in the capital Tunis were organized in condemnation of police exaggerated use of force.[3] A general state of instability reigned over Tunisian cities and instances of break-ins, looting, and vandalism increased in frequency.[4] And it was then up to the citizens to take matters of their safety and security in their hands. Neighborhood groups called "Revolution Committees" were quickly formed across governorates.[5]

Those late nights where my brother would come home, pick the pan of improvised pasta my sister invented, and then head back to the rest of the group were one of my very few recollections of the revolution's early unfolding. I was thirteen and growing up in an apolitical family made it hard for me to fathom what the country was going through. I have witnessed the Tunisian uprising through my sister's recipes, my father's rather reluctant opinions, and my newly adopted social media curiosity. Naturally, and like everyone around me, we observed the unfolding of the Tunisian revolution along with the subsequent ones in Libya, Syria, Egypt, Bahrain, and Yemen, among others.

I struggle to define my positionality when it comes to the two revolutions. Writing about those uprisings one and a half year into a pandemic is for me an exercise of existing in a parallel space and time. It is an exercise of reexisting in the streets of a city I left behind—Beirut, during the time of a revolution whose potentialities are challenged by an ongoing collapse and a global sense of insecurity. In this chapter, I attempt to walk through the journey of my political consciousness formation from the early days and weeks of the Tunisian revolt in December 2010 to the Lebanese October 2019 uprising.

The chapter is also a space to present a processual reflection of revolutions and to contest their perception as punctual historical events conditioned by tangible outcomes. That is for two main reasons: the first being my considering of revolutions to be a process, whereby a regime fall would only be a start of a "broader teleological endeavor."[6] This is the case of the Tunisian revolution where the fall of the regime did not slow down revolutionary aspirations for dignity and social emancipation that come after.[7] The second reason is, even with a failure to dismantle a regime, revolutions still create remarkable social shifts; and individual and collective revolutionary experiences shape societies in irreversible ways,[8] which is the case of how I lived the Lebanon uprising.

Ten Years

"*Dēmos – kratos*," Greek for "people rule," was my earliest introduction to the term in our history class in middle school. Notions like democracy, freedom of speech and expression, individual rights, and liberties used to all be merely notions we encounter in civic education classes. They are definitions we learn at school, commit to memory for the examination at the end of each trimester, then give away the notebook pages to the neighborhood kiosk to roll sunflower seeds in them and sell them back to us.[9] Those notions did not mature yet when Ben Ali fled—or when a constitutional assembly was formed and elections were announced on January 13, 2011.[10] However, the absence of these possibilities for the Syrian, Libyan, or Yemeni peoples the subsequent years opened my eyes to how vital it is to have a voice in shaping your very existence within the borders of the country you inhabit and beyond.

Those ideals gradually became integral to my political consciousness—to the point where I have a deep belief in the inevitability of revolutionary struggles. This belief is not a naïve optimism of regimes falling and peoples' will reigning like in the books and in political utopias. But for people having endured protracted years of dictatorships, colonization, settler colonization, or any other forms of oppressive regimes, an uprising becomes imminent. For revolutionary counterstrategies toward those long-seated oppressive regimes are essential liberatory and even existential processes. Again, regardless of the outcome.

Rewinding back to December 2010–January 2011, the echoes of Bouazizi's self-immolation in Sidi Bouzid, a city in the center of Tunisia, caused great popular distress in solidarity with the Bouazizi case and as a first ignition of the Revolution of Freedom and Dignity[11] or what was more romantically coined "The Jasmine Revolution."[12] I spent days of school closure glued to the TV screen listening to the ex-president Zine El Abidine Ben Ali's speeches that started with blatant threats[13] to the protestors and progressed to promises of reform, addressing the people for the first time in the local dialect.[14]

All of that was new to me. I haven't grown up in a leftist family and my grandfather did not fight the French colonizer with the Fellagha[15] and left us with a revolutionary legacy. My inelaborate political imagination was hence intrigued by the December 2010 events and the journey began.

The Lebanon Uprising of 2019

I was a university student when massive street mobilizations erupted on October 17, 2019. One e-mail sent by a professor to his students at my university immediately brought me back to my thirteen-year-old reaction to leaving school for the streets: "The streets are the classroom!" I still remember when I cried in confusion the day N., a one-year older friend, was shaking my shoulders in the yard of my school back in 2011. "Can't you see," he told me, "the streets are bulging, and all students are out protesting. You cannot be in the classroom." But I stood my grounds, and at that time, the thirteen-year-old still conventional girl that I was believed we belonged to classrooms. "Education was our form of revolution, and it is not to be compromised by interruptions and strikes, or any other form of political protests." That's what I thought then and what I said to him, while he obviously stood unconvinced. Little did that girl know that almost a decade later she would be the one encouraging her university classmates to join the protests.

Those ten years have morphed my sense of mobilization and politicization from fearing for my education to an awakened anger against existing structures and a more conscious contestation thereof. Being in Lebanon, in the streets of the revolution, I can now finally materially experience and verbally communicate my growing understanding of mobilization that I have been cultivating throughout a decade of compelling political observations. It seemed as if I just got a second chance at revolution—I deem myself lucky for this.

Generation Revolution: Revolutionary Depression, Revolutionary Euphoria

I spent hours sitting at "The House of the People," sharing late-night snacks and eating tear gas-flavored corn. The streets of Lebanon in the first few weeks since October 17, 2019, by far resembled this generation the most. Our generation grew up with street chants and awakened politically by echoes and local expressions of "Ash-sha'b yurīd isqāṭ an-niẓām" ("The people want to dismantle the system"). This eruption felt like the most natural thing to have happened. It seemed as if our collective imagination, or at least how mine and that of the peers around me came to be shaped, is programmed in a way to leave a space for the possibility of a revolution. For a generation that grew up into those realizations and who so naturalized the clarity, the potentialities that being in the street can offer, and who normalized a daring outlook of life and politics beyond perpetual state power, meaning was found in the streets. And even beyond this generation, meaning was found through the power of togetherness. For

> only where (wo)men live so close together that the potentialities of action are always present can power remain with them. [. . .] And even "after the fleeting moment of action [the revolution] has passed," power is kept alive through remaining together. And whoever, for whatever reasons, isolates him(her)self and does not partake in such being together, forfeits power and becomes impotent, no matter how great his(her) strength and how valid his(her) reasons.[16]

And for me, meaning was also found in the streets. Those familiar streets were a space to exist and belong. It seemed as though this was the perfect time to bond with the city I had lived in for more than three years, and not once did it feel so inviting. All kinds of people I could befriend. All types of conversations I could have. And all the persons I could become. The people I met during the revolution have become a significant part of my life and growth. In that sense, the personal and social, being in the streets has been transformative. I sometimes fail to remember how my life looked before the revolution, the friends I made and the places I went to. It seemed as if the revolution shaped my relation to the city and its people in a few months more than what I could build in three years before.

Revolutions are incomparable times (and spaces) for personal growth. I think back to the many times I would resist singing certain chants, because I felt unentitled. Let the people who have endured it, speak about it. I'd observe. I'd absorb. I'd assimilate later. To think how all that changed, and to think that now my relationship to Beirut occupies such a huge part of my identity, the Lebanon revolution for sure succeeded on some level: The personal. For that reason, maybe, it seemed as if I needed a second chance at a revolution. The togetherness of the revolution is then not just an experience and a generation of political power but also of personal empowerment. It is an experience of community, of friendship, of love, and of belonging and growth. It is an experience of depression, frustration, awkwardness, and anxiety.[17] All in being together and in existing in reclaimed spaces, a "Space of Appearance."[18]

Conclusion

Reflecting back now, I know I was in the streets for individual motives. Unintentionally so. Or at least for the impractical ones. I was not in the streets because I believed my existence will help my "Lebanese friends" get rid of yet another infamous Arab regime, nor because I believed that one extra voice in the squares of the capital, Beirut, and elsewhere in the country will bring down the failed state and its famously incompetent political elite. Through different protests, and my daily roaming of the streets of downtown Beirut, I have listened to fables of corruptions and endless lousy ways the country's warlords-turned-leaders are robbing the country of its resources.[19] With every interaction in the streets from leaflets or sit-ins to bar chats and WhatsApp conversations, I further realized the difficulty of the task of dismantling the regime. I clearly am a product of those ten years of repeated revolutionary setbacks, and I have internalized some hints of nihilism when it comes to the extent to which we can take the corrupt rulers down, at least in the foreseeable future. However, If the Arab uprisings and their revolutionary cycles have taught anything, it would be that no matter how rigid and egregious the regime, the only dignified role to play is to revolt, in whichever shape or form. To be on the streets. To write. To perform. To contest in public or in private spaces. To continuously condemn corruption and avoid normalizing oppression and exploitation. Peacefully and violently so.

Notes

1 This took place in Chmati, a neighborhood in the southeastern Tunisian city of Gabes.
2 Multiple events following the Bouazizi's self-immolation involved heightened confrontations with the police forces, most of them leading to injuries and deaths. Some milestones to be found here: https://www.bbc.com/arabic/middleeast-46865244.
3 Ibid.
4 "*Neighborhood Committees Help Restore the Citizen's Sense of Security as Life Gets Back to Normal,*" Deutcshe Welle retrieved from: https://bit.ly/2UVn4WG.
5 Ibid.
6 Abrams, The End of Revolution, and its Means. Processual and Programmatic Approaches to Revolution in the Epoch of Revolution debate, retrieved from https://discovery.ucl.ac.uk/id/eprint/10069308/7/Abrams_The%20end%20of%20revolution%2C%20and%20its%20means.%20Processual%20and%20programmatic%20approaches%20to%20revolution%20in%20the%20epoch%20of%20revolution%20debate_AAM.pdf.
7 Ibid.
8 Leyla Dakhli, *L'Esprit de la révolte, 2020.*
9 In Tunisia, neighborhood kiosks called حمّاص exist abundantly in neighborhood that use old notebooks to wrap the nuts in them and sell them in 100 gram batches. It is a childhood ritual to give away our old school books to those neighborhood kiosks.
10 Ben Ali has announced he will no longer run for the presidential elections of 2014. Early parliamentary elections were also announced on January 13, 2011, in Ben Ali's desperate attempts to calm the public sentiments. Retrieved from: https://www.bbc.com/arabic/middleeast-46865244.
11 Revolution of Freedom and Dignity is how Tunisians in the street chose to refer to the events unfolding between 2010 and 2011. It is a revolution of freedom because it is a break from 23-year-old state of oppression and censorship. It is a revolution for the freedom of media, expression, assembly, political action, etc. It is a revolution for employment, social equality, access, and dignity. The term "Revolution of Freedom and Dignity" is most representative of how Tunisians in the street experienced this period.
12 The term is more widely used in Western media more so than in Tunisia itself. It was first coined by an American journalist (https://www.npr.org/sections/thetwo-way/2011/01/13/132888992/tunisia-protests-social-media). The term is problematic for

it undermines the levels of violence protestors endured in the streets and undertones their anger and frustrations. It is also the term Ben Ali used to describe his own takeover on November 7, 1987 (https://arabist.net/blog/2011/1/17/why-you-shouldnt -call-it-the-jasmine-revolution.html).

13 First speech of ex-president Ben Ali delivered on January 10, 2011, retrieved from: https://www.youtube.com/watch?v=zFc9T4X4atk and commentary on retrieved from https://www.france24.com/ar/20110111-ben-ali-tunisia-speech-deception-protestets -youth-tunis-sidi-bouzid-bouazizi-.

14 Ex-president Ben Ali's speech delivered on January 13, 2011. Retrieved from AR: https://www.youtube.com/watch?v=IzgNrbCsyx4&t=4s translated to English EN: https://www.youtube.com/watch?v=kpG6Pt6J0o0

15 Fellagha is an Arabic word literally meaning "Bandits." It refers to groups of armed militants affiliated with anti-colonial movements in French North Africa. Here referring to Tunisian anti-colonialists who adopted violent means to push the French out of Tunisia, usually in mountainous regions in the South and Northwest.

16 Hannah Arendt, *The Human Condition*.

17 "Anxiety of/from Politics," a dossier on experiencing mental health, fighting anxiety, and getting it in the streets of the revolution. Essays published in the dossier pertinently reflect how the personal is being hugely intertwined with the political.

18 Concept of Appearance was expansively analyzed in Sara Mourad, "Appearing as Women," in *The Lebanon Uprising of 2019: Voices from the Revolution*, ed. Jeffrey G. Karam and Rima Majed (London: I.B. Tauris and Bloomsbury, 2022), 17.

19 Public talks were held in the protest squares in Downtown Beirut where civil society organizations, nascent parties, and activist groups have organized round tables and open discussions to create a space for exchange and learning. Those not only informed many uninformed, but it also helped give a voice to the residents of the country, their concerns, grievances, and socioeconomic and political aspirations out of the uprising.

30

From Syria to Lebanon

We Felt Again That Everything Is New

Saad Choeb

I never understood what does "again" add or take from the meaning of the new. Can we repeat the new?

I asked Zey[1] what first comes to her mind when I say revolution; she immediately replied, "Revolution reminds me how much of a coward I am."

It feels very strange to reflect on two still intact pasts that I both called revolutions—the experience of Syria in 2011 and that of Lebanon in 2019. If we are to adopt the understanding of revolution as a process, then we are reflecting from within a very confusing stage in that process. The disruptive beginnings of the revolutions were followed by counterrevolutions. This was followed by the 2020 pandemic, which warned from the danger of the social, after it was cheerfully applauded and redefined in the streets. This influx of new/old variables, that came all at once, has entertained surrealism as a goofy attitude and a defense mechanism against the dreadful present of people living on this spot of the world. Moreover, the political systems that we are dealing with criminalized hope, after our countries turned into no-agency zones with nauseating geopolitical considerations. This made the prompt of "better-future" to sound like a talk of superstition, or an old campaign for Hariri, or a slogan for the American University of Beirut. If these few pages represent anything at all, it is the disruptive pattern in our memories when we are forced to remember.

While watching the demonstrations in Egypt on TV, a few weeks before the Syrian revolt in 2011, both my dad and my uncle were sure that "Syria is different." They told us that "there is no way to infiltrate the Syrian regime because of its specificity," with the 1982 Hama massacre[2] in mind. My friend Yehia[3] says that whenever his mother tells him God bless you, he genuinely thinks that she was referring to Hafez al Assad. When Hafez al Assad died in 2000, an immigrant son called his mother in Syria to fact-check the news of his death; the mother immediately hung up the phone. Hafez al Assad does not die, and you cannot say that over the phone.

This is only a portion of the tradition that we used to derive answers from to our political curiosity. It was only in March 2011 that our imagination extended beyond the internalized fear of the consequences of rejection. In 2014 in Damascus, the Syrian official flag was painted over all the ancient wooden doors of Souk al Hamidieh. This was complementary to the chain of flags in the sky of the city that became like borders. The culminated domination of the visual field soon started to feel like squeezing a stone inside our stomachs (a feeling that I believe made pissing on the statue of Hafez al Assad to be more liberating). We do not want to see your signifiers. Destroying the visual symbols of the regime was a lived fantasy that facilitated new ways of seeing.

Nevertheless, the specificity my dad and my uncle were talking about turned out to be true. Death proved to be the eternal "again." After the beginning of the revolt, the 1982 massacre established itself again in the form of counterrevolution. The first demonstrations in March 2011 looked like the proper funeral for Hafez al Assad where people were jumping in circles and singing "May your soul rot in hell, Hafez." The celebration was always followed by funerals of many, which very soon became the pretext to gather and preserve the durability of the new social reality that emerged out of solidarity. Death in Syria is specific to our imagination in a defining way. It did not only define the gruesome tradition of the past, but it also defined our perception of the Syrian revolution.

The irreversibility of death as an act of sacrifice defined the Syrian revolution. Salah[4] told me that he used to say goodbye to his mother each time he went to protest in Daraa. My father had gathered us once, me, my brother, and my mother, around a table to impose a decision that the four of us must respect. "Listen," my dad said hours after the regime had assassinated two activists in Damascus, "No one of us is going to participate in their funeral tomorrow. One of the good guys in the branch of political security had informed me that they have orders to shoot on the march after the funeral. We are not ready to sacrifice our life for anything." We all silently agreed. I was very relieved that I did not have to worry about my family's safety because I was going to protest regardless of my dad's speech. "Death over humiliation," we were chanting the second day. My brother was with us! "Saad! what are you doing here?" Rami is yelling/chanting at me. I continued enjoying my political activity and ignored him, but it was very hard to ignore my father who we saw joining the march with a big delegation of the teacher's union. Although he definitely ignored us, I am very suspicious that he was able to also ignore the Zalghouta of my mother who entered the protest among the feminist group in a theatrical scene, as if she was screaming for all of us, the personal is political!

The act of sacrificing life during revolution is paradoxical. On one hand, we express through our chants and slogans that we protest in order to have a better life. On the other hand, we die while protesting, negating our initial expressions that call for life, or rather for a decent one. Hannah Arendt articulated this problem when she said,

> If we think of politics by its very nature . . . then the linkage of [political action] and life results in an inner contradiction that cancels and destroys what is specifically political about politics. This contradiction finds its most obvious expression in the fact that it has always been the prerogative of politics to demand of those engaged in it that under certain circumstances they must sacrifice their lives.[5]

Death as an ultimate expression of freedom exemplifies the tension that is brought forth in the moment of revolution for Arendt, as both a moment of beginning and an ending. In as much as the fact of death confirms an eternal cyclicality of life, the act of sacrificing life interrupts this cyclicality in the sense of beginning. While life is defined by the continuity of time with a certain faith that the past can be temporarily extended into the future, beginnings disrupt this line of temporality. Temporal dysfunction in revolution, when life can get sacrificed, is a radical feeling of confusion that is coupled with euphoria during the celebration of the present.

But what does it really mean to break the cyclicality in "again"?

It meant freedom for us, and it was fun. We did not want to allow the past to look like the future anymore. Why now? Nobody can tell or foretell. But we knew that life got boring, the answer to the previous question can be banalized to the level of boredom. We found happiness in playing and identified with newness. We were free to make noise and impose a game that plays with our boring existence that had been always enslaved by biological survival and the burden of frustration. We owned our dark humor and we liked being political subjects. "We used to do many fun things," Salah laughed and said, "like when we decided to go shout in the streets in Dara'a Allah Akbar to provoke the army when the electricity goes off, leaving them shooting left and right while we run."

After breaking fear of the dark when lights are off, you can start to entertain the new possibilities that darkness can suggest, as a different visual experience, as if you are in another world. In this sense, the electricity went off in Syria in March 2011. Imagine what would happen after the confusion of not seeing in the dark disappears? I guess you will start seeing differently and maybe act differently. You start to recognize new shapes that suggest other shapes until a new image becomes clearer. You might also need to howl, stretch your hand in blind move to meet your surroundings, and finally liberate your middle finger and celebrate the dark.

An ex-Hezbollah fighter was blocking the road with us in Beirut during the revolt of October 2019. "I apologize," he said, referring to his past. On October 19, I was covering my face when I was holding a banner in Arabic to test the waters amid the crowd in Riad El Soleh. The banner says, "Syria and Lebanon: one revolution against tyranny." Many different interactions, I first thought that one of them was invasive when an old man stopped me. He first took a picture of the banner, to then push it down from my hands to hug me roughly. He whispered in my ears: "We apologize." This story made me hesitate to criticize romanticizing revolutions again. Although I am not sure how a Syrian mother with a child killed by Hezbollah would feel about romance in the Lebanese revolution or what would another Syrian family say after witnessing the forced removal of the corpse of their four-year-old child because that cemetery is only for Lebanese. However, we know that October 2019 contained the possibility of an opening, or of beginnings for fast-forwarded reconciliation.

There was a sensible collapse of order and time in the spaces of the revolution. In between two major massacres in Dara'a, the security forces withdrew completely from the city for more than two weeks. People started seeing differently; they organized local councils and a relief network with youth as traffic police. Omar Aziz who died under torture in Assad prisons reported that "the efforts one must undertake in order to independently detach his or her social formations under authority and separate 'the period of power [or authority] and the period of revolution' is the extent in which the revolution will successfully create an atmosphere of victory."[6] This victory of independence from the time of the regime was sensed in many of the spaces. But how can we sustain the independence of revolutionary time? A question that the regime, rescued by its allies, made sure to answer in terms of total annihilation of space; the monuments of Putin, Nasrallah, and Khamenei were far away from us to piss on, and that was frustrating.

During a group conversation in Syria in 2013, we were asked to imagine what would you save from your home if you were bombed? I closed my eyes, opened them on August 4, and saved nothing. The borders between Syria and Lebanon are now open. Welcome to the counterrevolution where Hafez al Assad is alive, again.

"This is not a civil war! Christians and Muslims are brothers!," a man in his sixties hysterically shouts in the streets of Beirut on August 4. Minutes after the blast, the narrative of the civil war was automatically recycled. His bloody hands were crossed to each other to emphasize irrelevant fraternity in an apocalyptic scene where closed spaces became wide open after the blast. According to Salma, my twenty-year-old Libyan neighbor, August 4 marks the third time she gets bombed in her life: Libyan government, NATO, and then anonymously bombed in Beirut. She felt, again, that everything is repeated. Counterrevolution reimposes the faith that was abolished during revolution: the past will look like the future in a cyclical manner. Kids now will learn; see how your finger will get chopped if you try to stop a spinning fan?

Lights were on, again.

Total annihilation of space is the totalitarian interpretation of "all means all." In as much as the beginning of the revolution implants a sense of political subjectivity in humans, counterrevolution strips off what was political in us. It strips off our action. Biological survival is what determines our existence now, just like animals. People are no longer in control of the tsunami that they created in 2011 or 2019, and this is scary. The political action by subjects is what created the conditions that reduced people to creatures that cannot be political. Revolution force turned against itself. The end is expansion, a capitalist one in nature, expanding over our subjectivity to execute it and destroying the world over our heads to then rebuild it.

I asked Zey what first comes to her mind when I say revolution; she immediately replied, "Revolution reminds me how much of a coward I am." She continued, "My parents made the decision on my behalf, and I ended up not participating. This removed the guilt feeling in the sense that the decision not to participate was imposed on me."

Leitmotif.

What would you save from your home if you were bombed? I closed my eyes, opened them on August 4, and saved only a poster from my destroyed apartment. "We felt again that everything is new" printed in blue on the brown paper. I never understood what does "again" add or take from the meaning of the new. Can we repeat the new?

First, we felt that everything is new.

Then, we felt, again, that everything is new until we were conscious about the repetition.

It is now 4 in the morning, of August 12, 2021, one year after the August 4 explosion, two years since the Lebanese revolution, and the Syrian revolution happened ten years ago.

It is now 4 in the morning, of August 12, 2021. "Christians and Muslims are Brothers." Doors are locked. There is a new war outside; amazement from people's resilience. And Syria is almost cleansed from all the conditions for beginnings.

Can we repeat the new? Wouldn't it become old? We are feeling, again, that everything is old.

Notes

1   Zey is from Swaida, and she was fourteen years old when the revolution started in Syria.
2   The 1981 Hama massacre was an incident in which thousands of the residents of Hama, Syria, were killed by government security forces after sensing an attempt of insurgency by a group of Muslim Brotherhood.
3   Yehia is from a city in northeast Aleppo that was very involved in the revolution before ISIS took over in 2013 when he moved to Lebanon. He identifies as a Syrian refugee.
4   Salah was in his senior high school in Dara'a when the revolution started. He continued studying fine arts in Damscus, and he came from a family of photographers.
5   Hannah Arendt, *The Promise of Politics* (New York: Schocken Books, 2007), 19.
6   Omar Aziz, *A Discussion Paper on Local Councils in Syria* (Theanarchistlibrary, 2013).

Afterword

How to Speak Up about a Revolution: A Case Study

Leyla Dakhli

Il s'est produit ceci d'inouï. Nous nous sommes mis à parler. [This extraordinary thing happened. We started speaking.]
—Michel de Certeau, *La Prise de parole [The Capture of Speech]*[1]

This book is not just another testimony. It is not simply an aggregation of militant and scholarly voices. It is proof of what the revolutions underway in the Arab world are producing: a community of meaning, of dreams and imagination. A community that moves forward, from experiment to experiment, from uprisings and enthusiasm, from failures and violence to disasters. A community that builds through struggle but also through knowledge, a community that learns and gives lessons for itself and for the world.

For the Arab revolutions, which began with the impetus of "enough is enough," with the desire to see the walls that stood in front of the people fall, have for more than ten years produced spaces for a more dignified future. One of the aspects of this dignity that has been recovered and is to be reclaimed involves words and concepts. It is not only expressed in programs and manifestos; it is expressed in a certain way of looking at the world and of telling it. I will describe it here.

First, it stems from an asserted desire not to separate the "militant" and the "scientific." This statement, which may seem simple, is not. It goes back to a very deep habitus of the academic world. The demand for neutrality, the belief that one understands things better from a distance, the shortcomings of self-involvement, while they have often been discussed and distorted, remain complex subjects at a time where science is being called into question, and where it has become difficult to say the word "truth." What this attempt asserts is that there is a value in starting from a committed experience in order to identify the truth of an experience. And to value experience as a legitimate place of knowledge. It also affirms that the question of intellectuality can be reexamined within a renewed framework, which is critical of the professionalized and standardized position of academics to explore other ways of producing (and transmitting) knowledge. It also takes note of an intellectual heritage that was largely built outside of universities subject to state or economic powers. Finally, it proposes that intellectuals no longer consider themselves as representatives, spokespersons, or witnesses but as fragments of a world, among the world.

A second characteristic complements the first. It involves not separating the languages and intimately mixing formal and in-depth explorations. If this book is relatively classical in its form, it considers multiple approaches and languages to express the revolt. It makes room for multiple languages by anchoring the word in the territory, in the Arabic language, and in the other languages that populate it: those of the arts, of the bodies, of the living beings that inhabit it. Thus, it defends a position that promotes a living and connected indigenous thought.

The third requirement that I see consists in establishing a new and powerful link between the individual and the collective, between singular voices, to revisit another prerequisite of the social sciences, that of "representativity." In the unique moment of the revolutionary experience, isn't it the most unique that is the most representative? This book seems to tell us. And this question should not be taken as an attempt to escape, because it puts the finger on one of the difficulties we encounter in dealing with the history of these moments, which are beyond the reach of the sociology and other fields adapted to more "sedate" times. When everything is on the move, it is difficult to adjust the instruments social scientists are used to deal with. One has to adapt to the changing realities, to stay aware, be prepared for the changes, and still careful with what remains. The everyday practices in the production of knowledge are then also experiencing the transformations affecting society as a whole: space, time, language, bodies, everything is on the move. Here, the singularity of voices supports a political demand, one that challenges the order of social differentiation by confession or by wealth through clientelism, to bring the recognition of the freedom to do things differently, the guarantee of being able to be outside the framework into a new civil framework. Specifically, looking at a people on the move, the authors gathered in the volume experience other ways of naming their society, by freeing them from old labels. The new civil framework they build have comprehensive and common historical roots, a shared geography, a reservoir of multisituated and interacting voices, and a space for political debate and struggle.

Thus, this third requirement is naturally linked to a fourth. The contributions in this book show how the Lebanese revolution was able to combine societal causes with an approach that recognizes power and class relations. Again, this might seem obvious from an intersectional perspective. However, the tension between these two fields of claim is real and acute in the Arab space. The massive presence of NGOs in the space of what was thereafter called civil society, the work of international institutions, the weakness of a certain number of social intermediaries such as trade unions could have led people to think at the beginning of the 2000s that the frameworks to describe society had definitively put aside class and power relations. Of course, social movements had continued in the meantime, but the Thawra succeeded in associating and connecting them to other demands linked to minority rights, feminism, and the question of civil status. It showed, through its many interventions, how these two sides of the movement were intertwined, in the struggles for the rights of domestic workers for example.

The fifth requirement, which could actually be the first because it lies at the very foundation of the book, is to leave traces, to be aware of what is being played out in terms of visibility, communication, competing voices, even when one appears to have "lost." The Syrians, Egyptians, and Yemenis have shown us over the months and years what it means to think about defeat in a revolution. It means reflecting on the event, but perhaps not (only), as one might think, to identify mistakes and learn from them, but to keep its revolutionary charge in the past. It seems to me that the authors gathered here want to capture the magic. They want to fight against the retrospective effects of disenchantment, the way it comes down on what has been experienced to take away the magic. This gesture, magnificently embodied by the most personal texts of the book, but also by lucid and precise retrospective studies, is very close to the act of archiving. It is also what made me think of the famous text of De Certeau. For he puts it well: writing comes when the traces fade away, when, as he says, "the after restarts the before." Then, one writes to understand and relive the before, in a form of battling nostalgia.

Finally, all these requirements seem to me to be part of a conscious desire to account for the singularity of a collective experience, affirmed as indigenous and radically specific, while linking it to an equally strong feeling of belonging to a common world that goes beyond the national framework. For there is no trace here of chauvinistic discourse on the most beautiful, the most radical, or the most revolutionary of revolutions. We find the affirmation of a position in a history that is also constructed beyond borders. Here, Lebanon's belonging to the movement that shakes the Arab world as a whole is expressed, starting from its specificity, but with its empathy for the other Arab peoples.

Throughout the texts, we feel the link with the struggles of previous years, and the place given to two Arab subjectivities in Lebanon marks this link. Being Palestinian in Lebanon seemed to be an identity that had been fixed for decades. As a "brother" welcomed with varying degrees of courtesy, as a companion of misfortune, as a third-class citizen, the Palestinian had no real right to a place in the city, even though he constituted one of the essential components of the country's culture, aspirations, and projections.

During the Thawra, Palestine as a cause does not come to speak for the Palestinians of Lebanon, who come to tell their Lebanon, the one they share daily. On a different note, the Tunisian migrant sees the revolution deploying very familiar notes in front of her eyes, echoing her experience of the 2011 Tunisian revolt. She shares here her experience. Unlike the Arab revolutionary circulations of the 1960s and 1970s, which were built on political and ideological affiliations, today's solidarities are built on the living, on common experience, on shared experience, on the recognition of a sister-brotherhood, on site. Beyond sympathy and solidarity, these pages contain a series of deviations from the imposed frameworks of thought and a reworking of the question of emancipation on a regional scale and beyond, which sounds to me like an invitation to continue writing the history of the Arab revolutions.

As some chapters mention, the Lebanese political structure was not, at the time of the Thawra, in any way comparable with those of the countries of the 2011 revolutions. It seemed that at the heart of the revolutionary act was a pattern, very much staged in 2011: the lasting embodiment of power by a single man. The revolutions wanted to bring down the regime, and this regime had a face. Some came to believe that this face was the regime.

However, it is clear that it is not enough to topple the tyrant, even if it is necessary to do so in order to topple the system he heads. The ten years of revolutions have shown us many configurations: places where the head resisted, with more or less repression and violence (in Syria of course, but also in Morocco, or in Jordan); others where the head was replaced by a clone (in Egypt); those where violence rushed into the vacuum left by the fall of the authoritarian power (Yemen, Libya); and finally, those where it was discovered that the system was much more complicated than we thought and that it would take time to proclaim democracy (Tunisia and Sudan). These ways of describing the situations are obviously schematic, but they allow us to show why, when Lebanon, and before it Iraq, embarked on a revolution, they were able to be recognized as sisters by those that preceded them. Of course, there was not just a single head (but all heads, as the protesters said), but there was a system that held it all together. The contributions gathered in this book provide many keys to understanding and naming this system in the Lebanese context, and I will not go over them in detail here.

It is more its kinship with other situations in the Arab world (and beyond, perhaps) that I would like to highlight. For in reality, if we are willing to ask the question of uprisings in the right sense (i.e., not why did people rise up but why don't they do so more often), the elements to justify the revolt do not simply boil down to autocracy, or the denial of democracy in the most procedural sense of the term.

The Thawra is not just another demand (that's how I understand the slogan of the streets of Beirut, *Thawritna mich Hirak*, our revolution is not just another struggle or another movement). It has not become a fashionable denomination simply by mimicry. However, it should not be denied that this dimension exists. Like a refrain or a catchphrase that is repeated, the revolution circulates between spaces, each one seeking to give it a new interpretation. The same tune, with different arrangements, greater and greater challenges, a bit of emulation and even envy, a bit of chauvinism about the most beautiful, the strongest, the first, the new revolution. This is an obvious dimension of what has emerged in the streets of the Arab world today. Never mind, or better still, let's take it into the revolutionary bag. The revolutionary waves have these vogue effects, why despise or criticize it, why deduce that it's all a sham?

Because revolution is performance, it is part of an experience; it improves, borrows, adjusts, and adapts. The Lebanese Thawra was off to a flying start, it had already made Lebanon a certain avant-garde through all the movements that had agitated it in recent years, it was also the receptacle of the violence of what was being played out on the other side of the border in Syria, it was still home to so many survivors of the Palestinian wars and guardians of its own revolution for national emancipation. Lebanon is the terrain of these experiments; it has made a revolution that, in many aspects, contains others.

Despite all the misfortunes the country had experienced, its revolts had a festive air, an engaging soundtrack, a smooth face. However, it was a revolt of misery that we were witnessing, which was getting worse by the day. Collapse rarely accompanies a revolution to this extent. It precedes or follows it. Here, it came before the mobilizations, then accompanied them, then ended them. A series of crises, which led the country to bankruptcy, pushed a large part of the population into misery and poverty.

The social crisis has again transformed the protest landscape as it has transformed the Lebanese landscape as a whole: forced exile and migration have given new forms and new borders to political protest. The mobilization takes transnational contours, reactivating the diasporic structure of the Lebanese population and creating new centralities and new solidarities arising from the exile. This is the case in a city like Berlin, where the Lebanese of this new exile join the Syrian, Egyptian, Iraqi, Palestinian, and Afghan exiles. In these refuges, solidarity of experiences and exchanges are built again. The social crisis has numerous consequences, leading to a global transformation of the spaces of power and the spaces of contention.

What faces, what landscapes emerged then? A massive explosion on August 4, 2020, people's bank deposits and lifesavings under siege, barricades to cut off access, power cuts, giant blackouts, fires, unemployed people, and empty fridges. In the face of this, the revolution invented other ways of dealing with it, while replaying the revolution as a declaration of war. First of all, because it was triggered by a refusal to pay, a refusal to pay taxes, which is the first form of protest. The national community, founded on solidarity, breaks down on injustice, its apparent disloyalty is the affirmation of another community, that of anger.

This warlike comparison is not insignificant, but it must also be understood as arising from the last years experienced in the Arab world, and in Lebanon in particular. For this country is living through the time of hopes, uncertainties, and fights that the whole region has been experiencing at least since 2011. This period has been transformed into a kind of war of attrition in which both powers and peoples readjust their assaults and strategies, in which the most brutal methods of repression are deployed as indignation wanes, and in which the methods of resistance and urban guerrilla warfare are refined. But Lebanon is also living in a postwar period that is dragging on, a post-civil war period that keeps on reminding of the ruptures, the wounds that emerged and still occupy spaces, hearts, and souls.

Revolutionary speech is born out of the political and media noise, but it is also grafted onto silences and omissions, and this is what makes it so overwhelming. It is in the way of occupying space that the exploration of wounds is most strongly visible. The revolutionaries have taken over the space, the space marked by borders, trenches, ditches, and impossibilities inherited from the war and rebuilt with the "reconstruction" that has made the roads overrun with vehicles, that has increasingly ravaged the infrastructures reduced to rubble by the war. In this country, closing off the street paradoxically means circulating, making straits in the city where one is forced to cross paths, to meet.

Taking to the street means linking a territory that was previously simply crossed, occupied by cars, crossed by flows. Like the *Piqueteros* in Argentina in 2001, who used to block the highways to stop the economic flows and to represent the place of impediments that the people of the shantytowns could reclaim, the new Lebanese *piqueteros* made their presence visible by means of barricades, by trying to reinterpret the blockade over and above the traumatic memories of a fifteen-year war in which one could no longer pass. The revolution then becomes an experiment, in the scientific sense of the term. The revolutionaries spread out and test, try out new gestures and rituals.

The developments of the revolutionary moment as well as the gestures accomplished in this book are steps to write the common history of the first revolutions of this century. They are also stones on the path of other ways of writing the desire for emancipation. They constitute an experience that we already know is, as Michel de Certeau wrote, "unassailable" (*imprenable*), simply because it took place.

Note

1   Michel de Certeau, *La Prise de parole (et autres écrits politiques)* (Paris: Seuil, 1994), 41. These texts were originally written between June and September 1968.

Contributors

Tamim Abdo is a cook specializing in Italian cuisine who currently runs an Italian restaurant in the family's backyard. He has been previously a member of the Socialist Forum in Lebanon.

Hani Adada is currently a research assistant and archivist at the Department of Sociology, Anthropology, and Media Studies at the American University of Beirut (AUB). He holds a BA degree in economics from the Arab Open University (AOU). He is currently a member of the Revolutionary Communist Group in Lebanon (RCG) and previously a member of the Union of Lebanese Democratic Youth (ULDY) and the dissolved Socialist Forum (SF) and Lihaqqi organization.

Mortada Al-Amine holds an MA degree in general psychology from the American University of Beirut. His academic research focuses on the social-psychological study of intergroup relations and collective action. Mortada took on a research fellowship at Synaps, where his research dealt with the narratives of political party loyalists and the impact of the state's mismanagement of the water sector. Currently, he is pursuing a PhD in social psychology at the University of Groningen.

Alaa Al Sayegh is a social innovator and a political organizer. He is also an innovation consultant in socioeconomic solutions and a founding member of Daleel Tadamon (an organization that supports, organizes, and develops solidarity structures and institutions of a Democratic Economy). Alaa has more than ten years of experience in conceptualizing and implementing innovative tools to solve socioeconomic problems and uses lessons from grassroots organizations, the digital world, and lean methodologies to drive change. He holds a BA in business administration from the Lebanese International University and entrepreneurial studies from Stanford University. Alaa Sayegh is currently the director of innovation and growth at Daleel Tadamon, board member at SMEX, and political activist at Lihaqqi.

Lara Bitar is an independent media worker who works in Beirut, Lebanon, and the founding editor of *The Public Source*, a leftist publication she launched in January 2020 with a series of "Dispatches from the October Revolution." She also contributes reports on social movements and civil unrest to grassroots media projects in the United States and Lebanon.

Mohammad Bzeih is an activist and an MA candidate in applied economics at the Lebanese American University (LAU).

Saad Choeb is a visual artist from Syria. He is currently an artist-in-residence in Ashkal Alwan, Beirut. His practice is primarily concerned with the optics of rupture, using images, sculpture, and life observation as visual resources. He studied Fine Arts at Damascus University and holds a BA in political studies from the American University of Beirut.

Joseph Daher is a visiting professor at Lausanne University, Switzerland, and is a part-time affiliate professor at the European University Institute, Florence (Italy). He notably participates in the "Wartime and Post-Conflict in Syria Project" at the European University Institute, Florence (Italy). He is the author of *Hezbollah: The Political Economy of Lebanon's Party of God* (2016) and *Syria after the Uprisings: The Political Economy of State Resilience* (2019). He is the founder of the blog Syria Freedom Forever.

Leyla Dakhli is a full-time historian in the French Center for National Research (CNRS), presently settled in the Marc Bloch Center in Berlin. Her work deals with the study of Arab intellectuals and the social history of the South Mediterranean region, with a particular focus on the history of women and the question of exiled intellectuals and activists. She is the principal investigator of the ERC-founded program DREAM (Drafting and Enacting the revolution in the Arab Mediterranean). She is a member of the editorial committee of the International Review of Social History (Amsterdam) and Le Mouvement social (Paris), and of the Scientific Committee of the MuCem (Musée des Civilisations de l'Europe et de la Méditerranée, Marseilles). Her last publications include Histoire du Proche-Orient contemporain, Paris, La Découverte, 2015; Le Moyen-Orient (fin XIXe-XXe siècle), Éditions du Seuil "Points Histoire," Nov. 2016; L'Esprit de la révolte. Archives et actualité des révolutions arabes, Éditions du Seuil, Oct. 2020. With Amin Allal, Layla Baamara, Giula Fabbiano, Cheminements révolutionnaires. Un an de mobilisations en Algérie (2019–20), Paris, CNRS éditions, 2021.

Nadim El Kak is a Beirut-based researcher, freelance writer, and graduate student. He works at The Policy Initiative (TPI)—a new local think tank—where he leads research projects on Lebanon's growing landscape of anti-establishment actors. He holds a double BA in Political Science and Middle Eastern Studies from Amherst College and is completing his MA in Sociology at the American University of Beirut (AUB). His current academic research examines the interplay between neoliberal rationality, counterrevolutions, and radical imaginaries in Lebanon's uprising. He was previously based at the Lebanese Center for Policy Studies (LCPS), where he studied sectarian politics, Lebanon's 2018 parliamentary elections, collective actions, and alternative political groups. He also helped found the Alternative Frequencies podcast, which he cohosted and produced. Since 2019, Nadim's work has been published in the *New Middle Eastern Studies Journal* and by *Jadaliyya*, *openDemocracy*, *The Public Source*, *Arab Reform Initiative*, *FES-Lebanon*, *Asfari Institute*, *L'Orient Le Jour*, *Al Arabiya English*, and *An-Nahar English*, among others.

Nay el Rahi is a feminist researcher, writer, and activist. She has a BA in journalism from the Lebanese University and an MA in global media and postnational communication from the School of Oriental and African Studies (SOAS), University of London. Since 2008, she has been working at the intersection of advocacy for gender justice and the production of critical knowledge around relevant themes. Nay has published in many platforms, including *Assafir, Al Modon, Sawt Al Niswa,* and *The Guardian.* She has also worked with Oxfam in Lebanon and Tunisia, Hivos International, Raising Voices (Uganda), and Kafa, among others. She teaches gender and communication and public speaking at the Lebanese American University (LAU). Nay is the cofounder of HarassTracker, an initiative to fight the normalization of sexual harassment in Lebanon. She also serves on the board of the Lebanese Association for Democratic Elections (LADE) and in the leadership of the Beirut Grassroot of the political collective LiHaqqi.

Yara El Zakka is currently an LAU graduate student in migration studies (MA). Yara's current research examines the interrelationship between youth development and spatial configurations, taking Palestinian refugee camps in Lebanon as a case study. Yara's main interest revolves around understanding space from a sociological perspective and analyzing the different socio-spatial layers of built environments.

Samer Frangie is currently an associate professor at the Department of Political Studies and Public Administration at the American University of Beirut. He specializes in political theory, intellectual history of the Arab world, and Middle Eastern politics. His research has been published in edited books and academic journals, such as *Modern Intellectual History, International Journal of Middle East Studies,* and the *European Journal of Social Theory,* among others. He is currently working on a number of international research projects, including Other Universals: Theorizing from Postcolonial Locations on Politics and Aesthetics, housed at the Centre for Humanities Research at the University of the Western Cape, and Drafting and Enacting the Revolutions in the Arab Mediterranean (1950–2013) with the European Research Council. In addition to his academic work, Frangie has published a number of editorials and essays, which appeared in the *Journal of Palestinian Studies, e-flux,* and *al-Jumhuriya.* Currently, he is a senior editor at the independent media platform, Megaphone News.

Mona Harb is Professor of Urban Studies and Politics at the American University of Beirut where she is also cofounder and research lead at the Beirut Urban Lab. Her ongoing research investigates governance in contexts of limited statehood and crises, configurations of collective life, and intersections of urban activism and oppositional politics. She is the author of *Le Hezbollah à Beirut: de la banlieue à la ville,* coauthor of *Leisurely Islam: Negotiating Geography and Morality in Shi'i South Beirut* (with Lara Deeb), coeditor of *Local Governments and Public Goods: Assessing Decentralization in the Arab World* (with Sami Atallah), and coeditor of *Refugees as City-Makers* (with Mona Fawaz et al.). She serves on the editorial boards of *MELG, IJMES, EPC,* and *CSSAME.*

Nizar Hassan is a Beirut-based researcher and political organizer who writes on politics and social change in Lebanon and cohosts The Lebanese Politics Podcast. Nizar holds a BA in politics and a diploma in media from the American University of Beirut and an MSc in "labour, social movements, and development" from SOAS, University of London. His master's research attempted to analyze the 2015 protest movement in Lebanon from a class perspective. Nizar has also worked as a researcher and trainer with nongovernmental entities in Lebanon including the Lebanese Center for Policy Studies (LCPS) and the Arab NGO Network for Development (ANND). He has written among others for *The New Arab*, *The Daily Star*, *L'Orient Le Jour*, and *ROAR Magazine* on economic policy, politics, and social movements in Lebanon.

Jeffrey G. Karam is Assistant Professor of Political Science at the Lebanese American University (LAU) and a Research Associate at Harvard University's *Middle East Initiative*. Karam is currently a visiting research fellow with the Global Scholarly Dialogue Programme of the Rosa Luxemburg Stiftung, a EUME (Europe in the Middle East-The Middle East in Europe) fellow at the Forum Transregionale Studien, and a research affiliate at the Center for Middle Eastern and North African Politics and the Otto-Suhr Institute of Political Sciences at the Freie Universität in Berlin. He is the editor of *The Middle East in 1958: Reimagining A Revolutionary Year* (2020). As an interdisciplinary and multilingual scholar, his research focuses on the politics of US intelligence and foreign policy in the Middle East during revolutionary times and political change. His work has been published in both academic and public outlets, including *Intelligence and National Security*, the *Arab Studies Journal*, *The Washington Post*, *H-Diplo and ISSF*, the *Daily Star Lebanon*, *Megaphone*, *Jadaliyya*, *openDemocracy*, and other venues. He was previously a Visiting Assistant Professor of International Relations and Middle East Politics at Harvard University's Division of Continuing Education, a Postdoctoral Research Fellow in the International Security Program at Harvard University's Belfer Center, and a Visiting Assistant Professor of International Relations at Boston University's Pardee School of Global Studies.

Lama Karamé is a doctoral candidate at the Centre for Socio-Legal Studies at the Faculty of Law, University of Oxford. Her thesis investigates the socio-legal construction of the child in Lebanon, and her research broadly examines the intersection of law and society. Lama is a lawyer and president of The Legal Agenda where she previously directed the Strategic Litigation Department. She holds an LLB in public law from the Saint Joseph University of Beirut and a bachelor's degree in sociology from the Lebanese University. In 2015, she graduated with an LLM in law, culture, and society from SOAS, University of London. Lama was previously a visiting scholar at the Columbia Law School; her research focused on the role of legal professions in promoting social justice.

Grace Khawam is a doctoral researcher, public health professional, and disability activist, currently undergoing PhD studies in disability and development studies at Oxford Brookes University (UK). Grace holds an associate fellowship in higher education teaching and is a lecturer at the Masters in Public Health program at Saint Joseph University (Lebanon). She holds a doctorate in pharmacy, a master's degree in public health from the American University of Beirut, and a certificate in global mental health from Harvard University, with a focus on refugee trauma. Grace has worked for more than twelve years in the development and humanitarian fields in Lebanon and has been involved in disability rights activism as a Steering Committee member of the Disability Hub and a board member of the Lebanese Down Syndrome Association. She is currently based in London working as a research fellow in disability research with the University of Edinburgh.

Claudia Kozman (PhD, Indiana University) is an assistant professor of multimedia journalism and the research director at the Institute of Media Research and Training at the Lebanese American University. Her research primarily focuses on news content, with particular attention to news values, sourcing, and framing in Arab media. She is interested in media coverage of conflict in the Middle East as well as public opinion and perceptions during political turmoil.

Rima Majed is an assistant professor of sociology at the Sociology, Anthropology, and Media Studies Department at the American University of Beirut (AUB). Her work focuses on the fields of social inequality, social movements, social identities, sectarianism, conflict, and violence. Dr. Majed has completed her PhD at the University of Oxford where she conducted her research on the relationship between structural changes, social mobilization, and sectarianism in Lebanon. Prior to that, she has worked as a program assistant and a senior researcher at the United Nations Development Program—Arab States Bureau. She was a visiting fellow at the Mamdouha S. Bobst Center for Peace and Justice at Princeton University in 2018/19. Dr. Majed is the author of numerous articles and op-eds. Her work has appeared in *Social Forces, Mobilization, Global Change, Peace & Security, Routledge Handbook on the Politics of the Middle East, Middle East Law and Governance, Oxford Handbook of the Sociology of the Middle East, Global Dialogue, Idafat: The Arab Journal of Sociology, Al Jumhuriya, openDemocracy, Jacobin, Middle East Eye,* and *Al Jazeera English.*

Moné Makkawi is a PhD candidate at New York University. Her research focuses on the intersections between refugeehood, migration, space, culture, and political economy in southern Lebanon. She is currently working on her dissertation, which examines how refugees and migrant workers shape urbanism in Tyre, Lebanon, through agricultural labor and ideas of environmentalism.

Sara Mourad is a writer interested in the relation between desire, deviance, and dissidence and the fictions/frictions of private and public life. She has published on these subjects in English and Arabic and her writings have appeared in the *International Journal of Communication, Critical Studies in Media Communication, Jadaliyya, Al Jumhuriya, Rusted Radishes,* and *Megaphone,* among others. She received her PhD in communication from the University of Pennsylvania. Since 2016, she is an Assistant Professor of Media Studies and founder and codirector of the Women & Gender Studies program at the American University of Beirut. She is currently working on her first monograph on women's auto/biographical practices and the making of female subjectivity in contemporary Lebanon. In 2018, she was a Global Visiting Scholar at NYU's Center for the Study of Gender and Sexuality. In 2021/22, she is a EUME fellow at the Forum for Transregional Studies in Berlin.

Rawane Nassif is a Lebanese filmmaker and anthropologist. She directed several documentaries and wrote a book on the politics of memory in Lebanon, worked with immigrants in Canada, researched nomadic traditions in Kyrgyzstan, taught anthropology in Tajikistan, wrote children's books based on oral histories in Honduras, and worked as a researcher on art films in Qatar.

Roland Nassour is an urban researcher, planner, and activist. He is the cofounder and coordinator of the Save the Bisri Valley Campaign, which stopped the World Bank-funded Bisri Dam project. Roland was among the initiators of the anti-dam movement in Lebanon, challenging the sectarian power-sharing system that controls the water and land. He also worked on projects related to public space, urban pollution, and housing rights, advocating for more equitable and inclusive cities. Following the Beirut blast, Roland contributed to the planning and implementation of various projects for the recovery of the affected neighborhoods. He holds a master's degree in urban planning and policy from the American University of Beirut and a master's degree in architecture from the Lebanese University. Furthermore, he pursued studies in urban management and climate change at Erasmus University in the Netherlands as well as in sustainable urban design at Lund University in Sweden.

Roland Riachi is an associate researcher at the Department of Political Studies and Public Administration at the American University of Beirut (AUB). Based in France, he teaches critical geography and development studies at the University of Paris 8. He previously worked as a visiting assistant professor, lecturer, and postdoctoral fellow at AUB. He also served on several occasions as an economist in different United Nations agencies, namely ESCWA and ILO. Roland's research is at the intersection of political economy and ecology, with an emphasis on environmental, water, food, and development studies in the Middle East and North Africa. His ongoing research is investigating the political ecology of food regimes and metabolic rifts in the Arab world, exploring *longue durée* links between property, technology, capitalism, and power.

Olfa Saadaoui is a politically engaged strategy consultant, with hints of a writer. Olfa was born in Gabes, Tunisia, and lived in Beirut where she pursued a degree in business administration with a minor in international law at the American University. Olfa was also politically active during her student life and is still engaged through writing and side projects, alongside her profession. Her writing areas of interest include relations to space, exile, and the intricacies of our experience of cities as material and living environments.

Lamia Sahili is a journalist, translator, and editor. She is currently a member of the editorial team at Legal Agenda and a journalist and senior editor in the journalism department at Legal Agenda. She worked in several media outlets, where she gained experience in creating content in both traditional and digital contexts. Before joining Legal Agenda, she was freelancing for leading media organizations both in Lebanon and the Arab region as a translator and writer in fields ranging from politics and education to technology and entrepreneurship. She also led the website editorial team at *Al Hayat* newspaper and worked as a translator in the "Capital" supplement in *Al-Akhbar* newspaper and with several media institutions.

Myriam Sfeir is the director of the Arab Institute for Women (AiW) at the Lebanese American University. Previously she served as senior managing editor of *Al-Raida*, a journal published by AiW. She has over twenty-five years of experience working in the area of women's rights and gender equality and ample experience doing research, expert analysis, training, and teaching. She has worked extensively on projects related to gender rights and justice, oral history, movement building, and marginalized groups.. She earned her BA in philosophy from the American University of Beirut and her MA in interdisciplinary women's studies from the University of Warwick, UK.

Samir Skayni is a writer, architect, and holds an MA degree in philosophy from the Lebanese University. He is also a political activist and a member of the Youth Sector of the Lebanese Communist Party. Samir has several publications in local newspapers and media commenting on political, social, and student-related questions. He is also the author of two novels in Arabic, covering the subject of civil war, history, and the memory of the place. Currently, he works as a digital journalist at the independent media platform Megaphone News.

Paul Tabar was the director of the Institute for Migration Studies and a Professor in Sociology/Anthropology at the Lebanese American University, Beirut campus, between 2004 and 2021. Recently, he published *Migration and the Formation of Political Elite in Lebanon* (2021). He is the primary author of *On Being Lebanese in Australia: Identity, Racism and the Ethnic Field* (2010) and a coauthor of *Bin Laden in the Suburbs: Criminalizing the Arab Other* (2004) and *Kebabs, Kids, Cops and Crime: Youth, Ethnicity and Crime* (2000). He is currently working on two projects: one on migrant habitus focusing on second-generation Lebanese Australians as a case study, and the other on social inequalities in Lebanon using a Bourdieusian perspective. Dr. Tabar has published many articles on Lebanese and Arab migrants in international journals and is currently an adjunct professor at WSU, Institute for Culture and Society.

Sana Tannoury-Karam is a historian of the modern Middle East, writing on the intellectual history of the Arab Left. She is currently a EUME fellow (2020/22) at the Forum Transregionale Studien in Berlin and a research affiliate at the Center for Global History, Freie University. She was most recently a Visiting Fellow at the Center for Lebanese Studies at the University of Cambridge, an Early Career Fellow at the Arab Council for Social Sciences (2019–2020), and a Post-Doctoral Fellow in History at Rice University (2018–2019). Her work has appeared in a range of publications including the *Journal of World History*, *Jadaliyya*, *Megaphone*, and *Trafo Blog*. Her most recent publication is a coedited volume *The League against Imperialism: Lives and Afterlives* that came out with Leiden University Press in September 2020.

Mohammad Zbeeb is an economic journalist based in Beirut, Lebanon.

Index